Anglo-German Foundation for the Study of Industrial Society

The Anglo-German Foundation for the Study of Industrial Society was established by an agreement between the British and German governments after a state visit to Britain by the late President Heinemann, and incorporated by Royal Charter in 1973. Funds were initially provided by the German government; since 1979 both governments have been contributing.

The Foundation aims to contribute to the knowledge and understanding of industrial society in the two countries and to promote contacts between them. It funds selected research projects and conferences in the industrial, economic and social policy areas designed to be of practical use to policy-makers.

Titles include:

Bernhard Blanke and Randall Smith (*editors*)
CITIES IN TRANSITION
New Challenges, New Responsibilities

John Bynner and Rainer K. Silbereisen (*editors*)
ADVERSITY AND CHALLENGE IN LIFE IN THE NEW GERMANY AND IN ENGLAND

Maurie J. Cohen (*editor*)
RISK IN THE MODERN AGE
Social Theory, Science and Environmental Decision-Making

Dagmar Ebster-Grosz and Derek Pugh (*editors*)
ANGLO-GERMAN BUSINESS COLLABORATION
Pitfalls and Potentials

Rainer Emig (*editor*)
STEREOTYPES IN CONTEMPORARY ANGLO-GERMAN RELATIONS

Karen Evans, Martina Behrens and Jens Kaluza
LEARNING AND WORK IN THE RISK SOCIETY
Lessons for the Labour Markets of Europe from Eastern Germany

Stephen F. Frowen and Jens Hölscher (*editors*)
THE GERMAN CURRENCY UNION OF 1990
A Critical Assessment

Eva Kolinsky (*editor*)
SOCIAL TRANSFORMATION AND THE FAMILY IN POST-COMMUNIST GERMANY

Mairi Maclean and Jean-Marc Trouille (*editors*)
FRANCE, GERMANY AND BRITAIN
Partners in a Changing World

Howard Williams, Colin Wight and Norbert Kapferer (*editors*)
POLITICAL THOUGHT AND GERMAN REUNIFICATION
The New German Ideology?

Anglo-German Foundation
Series Standing Order ISBN 0–333–71459–8
(*outside North America only*)

You can receive future titles in this series as they are published by placing a standing order. Please contact your bookseller or, in case of difficulty, write to us at the address below with your name and address, the title of the series and the ISBN quoted above.

Customer Services Department, Macmillan Distribution Ltd, Houndmills, Basingstoke, Hampshire RG21 6XS, England

Financial Competition, Risk and Accountability

British and German Experiences

Edited by

Stephen F. Frowen
Fellow Commoner
St Edmund's College
Cambridge, and
Honorary Professor
Institute for German Studies
The University of Birmingham

and

Francis P. McHugh
Emeritus Fellow
St Edmund's College
Cambridge

palgrave

in association with
Anglo-German Foundation
for the Study of Industrial
Society

First published 2001 by
PALGRAVE
Houndmills, Basingstoke, Hampshire RG21 6XS and
175 Fifth Avenue, New York, N. Y. 10010
Companies and representatives throughout the world

PALGRAVE is the new global academic imprint of St. Martin's Press LLC Scholarly and Reference Division and Palgrave Publishers Ltd (formerly Macmillan Press Ltd).

Outside North America
ISBN 0–333–73590–0

In North America
ISBN 0–312–23466–X

This book is printed on paper suitable for recycling and made from fully managed and sustained forest sources.

A catalogue record for this book is available from the British Library.

Library of Congress Cataloging-in-Publication Data
Financial competition, risk and accountability : British and German experiences / edited by Stephen F. Frowen and Francis P. McHugh ; in association with Anglo-German Foundation for the Study of Industrial Society.
p. cm.
Includes bibliographical references and index.
ISBN 0–312–23466–X
1. Financial institutions—Great Britain. 2. Financial institutions—Germany. 3. Competition—Great Britain. 4. Competition—Germany. 5. Risk. I. Frowen, Stephen F. II. McHugh, Francis P. III. Anglo-German Foundation for the Study of Industrial Society.

HG186.G7 F545 2000
332.1'0941—dc21

00–027828

10 9 8 7 6 5 4 3 2 1
10 09 08 07 06 05 04 03 02 01

Printed in Great Britain by Antony Rowe Ltd, Chippenham, Wiltshire

Contents

List of Tables and Figures

Tables

Figures

Notes on the Contributors

Forrest H. Capie is Professor of Economic History at City University Business School, London. After a doctorate at the London School of Economics in the 1970s and a teaching fellowship there, he taught at the University of Warwick and the University of Leeds. He has published widely in the fields of money, banking and international trade – around 100 articles and almost 20 books. He has been a British Academy Overseas Fellow at the National Bureau, New York, and for the past seven years has been editor of the *Economic History Review*.

Martin Donnelly is a UK Treasury civil servant, at present Deputy Head of the European Secretariat of the Cabinet Office. He studied at Oxford University, the College of Europe, Bruges and the École National d'Administration in Paris. He spent four years on secondment to the European Commission in Brussels, in the Cabinet of Sir Leon Brittan, and has also worked in the French Tresor.

John G. Ellis joined the Bank of England in 1978 and worked on a wide variety of subjects, including international debt, the Euromarkets, UK money markets and finance for industry. He was later responsible for the supervision of all North American banks operating in the UK until in 1998, he was appointed to the new Financial Services Authority as Head of the Japan, Australasia, North America and Europe Department. He also serves as the FSA's Business Ethics Adviser. An Elder of the United Reformed Church, he is a director of three companies with community and charitable objectives.

Stephen F. Frowen is a Fellow of St Edmund's College, Cambridge, Senior Research Associate of the Von Hügel Institute, Honorary Professor at the Institute for German Studies, University of Birmingham, and Honorary Research Fellow in the Department of Economies, University College London. He was formerly Bundesbank Professor of Monetary Economics in the Free University of Berlin. Prior to this appointment he was Visiting Professor at the Universities of Würzburg and Frankfurt, and for many years held senior teaching posts at the Universities of Greenwich and Surrey, following appointments as Research Officer at the National Institute of Economic and Social

Research, London, as Economic Adviser to the Industrial and Commercial Finance Corpration (now 3i) and as Chief Editor of *The Bankers' Magazine* (now *Financial World*). In 1980–1 he served as Special Adviser to UNIDO, Vienna. He has published widely in monetary and macroeconomics and in banking. He is the editor of many collective works and a Contributing Editor of *Centre Banking*. In 1993 he received the Grand Cross of the Order of Merit of the Federal Republic of Germany, and in 1996 was honoured with a Papal Knighthood of the Pontifical Order of St Gregory the Great.

Stephan Herten is a PhD candidate at the Institute for German Studies at the University of Birmingham, concentrating on monetary policy within different financial systems. He previously held a temporary lectureship at the University of Leeds Business School. He studied at the universities of Heidelberg, Bonn and Berlin (Freie Universitat), where he subsequently took up an appointment as research fellow. He has published in the areas of transition economics, input–output analysis and federalism.

Glenn Hoggarth graduated in economics at Warwick University and gained a MA degree at Cambridge University, He joined the Economics Division of the Bank of England in 1989, advising mainly on UK monetary policy, after seven years as a private sector economist. Between 1994–6 he was Adviser on Monetary Policy at the Bank's Centre for Central Banking Studies and an IMF external adviser on monetary operations and policy in Eastern and Central Europe and Asia. Since 1997 he has been working in the Bank's Financial Stability area — first as Senior Economist in the Financial Intermediaries Division and currently in the Regulatory Policy Division.

Jens Hölscher is Senior Lecturer at the University of Brighton. Previously he served as Senior Fellow at the University of Birmingham and as Lecturer at the University of Wales, Swansea, and at the Free University of Berlin. He held Visiting Professorships at the Halle Institute for Economic Research, Chemnitz University and the Kazakhstan Institute for Management, Economics and Strategic Research. Publications concentrate on monetary and transition economics.

Barry Howcroft is Professor of Retail Banking and Director of Loughborough University Banking Centre. He was previously employed by

National Westminster Bank and has experience of corporate banking in both domestic and international banking. He is an Associate of the Chartered Institute of Bankers and an assessor for the Quality Assurance Agency for Higher Education. He has lectured extensively throughout the UK, Europe and the Middle East and is a management consultant for several major banks and building societies. His main research interests are in the area of strategies in retail banking, and within this field he has published extensively on delivery channels, quality of service, customer retention and branch efficiency. He has written a large number of articles and is the author of, and contributor to, 20 books on banking. In 1992 he received the Literati Club award for excellence for the most outstanding paper, and in 1997 he received the most outstanding paper award.

Elias Karakitsos is Professor of Economics and Head of the Economics Section at the Management School, Imperial College, London, where he has pioneered research on the design of economic policy and has been a principal investigator in the programme of research into Optimal Policy Evaluation run by Imperial College since the early 1980s. Since 1987 his research interests have shifted from economic policy to financial markets. He is currently Chief Economic Adviser to the Strategy Committee of Citibank/Citicorp, Europe and USA, an Adviser to Abbey National, Kredietbank, Belgium, Oppenheimer International Capital Markets, New York, and Chief Economic Adviser to the European Commission. Previously he worked as an economic consultant responsible for analysing the German economy through large-scale econometric models. He has published widely in the area of economic policy and asset price volatibilty and determination. His book on *Macrosystems: The Dynamics of Economic Policy* was published in 1992.

Norbert Kloten was President of the Land Central Bank in Baden-Württemberg and an *ex officio* member of the German policy-making Central Bank Council from 1976 to 1992. Since 1967 he has been a member of the Economic Advisory Council at the Federal Ministry of Economics (Chairman from 1992 to 1996). Other activities include membership of the Board of Academic and Non-Academic Associations and the Trilateral Commission. His Professorship at the University of Tübingen (1960–76) was combined with membership of the German Council of Economic Experts (Sachverständigenrat) from 1969 to 1976, being its Chairman from 1970–6. He has published extensively on the principles of economic policy and in the area of monetary and international monetary economics, on the theory and policy of transition and development, and on the methodology of economics. He holds two honorary doctorates from the University of Karlruhe (1980) and the University of Stuttgart (1993) respectively, and is the bearer of the Commander's Cross with Badge and Star of the Order of Merit of the Federal Republic of Germany.

Benedikt Koehler, General Manager of the London Branch of the Norddeutsche Landesbank, attended Yale University and took his doctorate at the University of Tübingen. He is the author of a biography of Ludwig Bamberger (1999).

Jan Kregel is Professor of Economics at the University of Bologna (Italy). He is the author of several books and numerous articles in the field of economics.

Francis P. McHugh, a Catholic priest and political economist, is Director of the Von Hügel Institute of St Edmund's College, Cambridge, where he is resident Emeritus Fellow. He read PPE at Oxford and the Diploma in Political Economy. He was awarded his PhD by the University of Cambridge. His recent publications include *A Keyguide to Resources in Business Ethics* (1988); *Things Old and New: Catholic Social Teaching Revisited* (edited jointly with Sam Natale) (1993); and *Financial Decision-Making and Moral Responsibility* (edited jointly with Stephen F. Frowen (1997). He is also a member of the editorial board of *International Journal of Value-based Management*, *La Societa* and *Ethical Perspectives* (University of Leuven).

Alistair Milne holds an MA in economics from the University of Cambridge and a PhD from the London School of Economics. He is currently Senior Lecturer in Banking and Finance at City University Business School. His research interests include banking competition and performance, bank regulation, and links between financial markets and the macro economy. In the past he has been an economic adviser at the Bank of England, a lecturer at the University of Surrey, a research fellow at London Business School, an economic assistant at HM Treasury, and has worked for the government of Malawi.

Mathias Moersch is currently Senior Economist with Dg Bank, Deutsche Genossenschaftsbank AG in Frankfurt/Main. He holds a PhD in economics from the University of North Carolina at Chapel Hill, and is the co-editor of *Competition and Convergence in Financial Markets.*

Eric Owen Smith is Senior Lecturer in Economics at Loughborough University, a Visiting Professor at the University of Trier and a Visiting Fellow of the Institute for German Studies at The University of Birmingham. His research interests are in German economic performance and comparative studies of collective bargaining in Germany and Britain. As well as numerous publications in these fields, he has written the definitive English study on *The German Economy* (1994). He is also an independent chair of the Appeals Committee of the Open University, an ACAS arbitrator and a member of Industrial Tribunals.

Juliane Pfau is a Senior Research Officer at the Institute for Financial Services (IFF e.v.) in Hamburg and since 1999 has been at the University of Colorado with a research grant from the Friedrich Ebert Foundation.

Udo Reifner is Director of the independent Institute for Financial Services (IFF e.v.) and has been Professor of Commercial Law at the University of Hamburg since 1981. He was a Guest Professor of Commercial Law at McGill University, Montreal (1976), the Universite de Louvain-la-Neuve in Belgium (1990), De Paul University in Chicago (1994), Birmingham University (1997) and New York University (2000). He has published extensively in the fields of banking law, sociology of law, history of law, legal theory, financial services, consumer protection and social economy. Recent books include *Credit and New Entrepreneurs* (1998); *Community Reinvestment* (1998); and *Social Responsibility of Banks in the European Community* (1998).

Leo Schuster is Professor of Banking and Finance at the Catholic University of Eichstatt in Ingolstadt (Germany). He was previously Professor of Banking and Director of the Banking Institute at the University of St Gallen in Switzerland and Visiting Professor at the University of Lausanne. In 1998 he held a Visiting Fellowship at the Von Hügel Institute, St Edmund's College, Cambridge. His extensive publications in the area of banking include strategic planning, marketing, intercultural management, banking systems and organisation. He is a member of the board of directors of a Zürich-based international bank and a major insurance company in Germany and an adviser to several financial institutions. Professor Schuster is also the Chairman of the German Compliance Association in Frankfurt and co-editor of banking journals in Germany, Switzerland and Belgium institutions.

Jan Toporowski has worked in fund management, international banking and economic consultancy, and is currently Reader in Economics at South Bank University. He is the author of *The Economics of Financial Markets and the 1987 Crash* (Edward Elgar, 1993) and *The End of Finance: The Theory of Capital Market Inflation, Financial Derivatives and Pension Fund Capitalism* (Routledge, 2000).

Andrew Tylecote is Professor of Economics and Management of Technological Change at the University of Sheffield. He was educated at Sussex and Oxford in philosophy, economics, politics and sociology. His most recent book was *The Long Wave in the World Economy: The Present Crisis in Historical Perspective* (Routledge). From 1992–8 he was Treasurer of the European Association for Evolutionary Political Economy. He is currently coordinating a six-country EC-funded project on Corporate Governance, Performance and Product Innovation.

Andreas Wagner worked with Bayerische Hypo- und Vereinsbank from 1987–9 and then read business administration from 1989 to 1994. From 1994–9 he was a research assistant and lecturer in the Department of Business Administration of the Catholic University of Eichstatt in Ingolstadt, where he also took his PhD on Business Ethics for Banks. Since 1999 he has been working for the Bäyerische Landesbank, Munich, where he is a strategy specialist in the corporate development department. His main research interests are located in the fields of accounting and financial management of banks and in financial ethics.

Norbert Walter is Chief Economist of the Deutsche Bank Group and Managing Director of Deutsche Bank Research in Frankfurt/Main.

Justin Welby was born in 1956 and educated at Trinity College, Cambridge. He worked for eleven years in the oil industry, with Elf Aquitaine in France and then as Group Treasurer of Enterprise Oil, the third largest UK oil company. In 1989 he went to Durham University, reading theology, to train for ordination in the Church of England. He is presently Rector of Southam, in Warwickshire, England. He is also a non-executive director and Chair of the Audit Committee of a local general hospital and Personal and Ethical Adviser to the UK Association of Corporate Treasurers.

Geoffrey E. Wood is currently Professor of Economics at City University London. He has also taught at the University of Warwick, and has been with the research staff of both the Bank of England and the Federal Reserve Bank of St Louis. He is the co-author or co-editor of ten books which deal with, among other subjects, finance of international trade, monetary policy and bank regulation. Among his professional papers are studies of exchange rate behaviour, interest rate determination, monetary unions, tariff policy and bank regulation. He has also acted as an adviser to the New Zealand Treasury. He is a managing trustee of the Institute of Economic Affairs and of the Wincott Foundation.

Bernd Zugenbühler is a Director of the Dresdner Bank AG in Frankfurt/Main.

This book is dedicated to
Hans Tietmeyer

Introduction

The index to a book is often a better key to a writer's or writers' purposes than the table of contents. A discerning reader or a reviewer looking for a controlling idea will find in the index to this book under the term 'ethics in banking' that there are twenty-four entries relating to matters of moral concerns in the world of money and finance; and there is a further search point in the index, perhaps a more unexpected one, 'companies as moral agents'. Most tantalizing of all, there is an entry for twelve pages on 'ethics of Economic and Monetary Union', written by a senior official from the UK Treasury. Maybe there is a modern struggle for the soul of the financial sector.

Over a period of eight years, the Von Hügel Institute, St. Edmund's College Cambridge, has been hosting regular seminars and occasional conferences on finance ethics. These have been organized on the principle that a credible morality of money is more likely to come from within the financial sector than from an isolated ethics constituency, whose growing literature on morals and money tends to be out of touch with the realities or is so jargonised as to turn off the hard-pressed banker, financiers or government departments. The approach in the seminars and conferences has been interdisciplinary, but more than they, the lead has been taken by the practitioners and economic theorists, whose thought patterns, concepts and language is scrutinized for an ethical agenda. The ethic is to be read out of the experience of the practitioners with informed ethicists acting as the midwife to the generation of a rigorous and vigorous finance ethic. This is not to downgrade the importance of ethics or to suggest a reduction of ethics to financial statements, but, rather, to articulate ethics in connection with the complexities and subtleties of modern markets and global operations. A model of the procedure can be found in Chapter 7 of this collection, which explores the role of ethics in derivatives markets.

The specific attention to ethics varies from one contribution to another. Some writers deal at length with financial structures, competition, risk management and accountability, paying little attention to formal ethical considerations. But the ethical dimension of ideas like risk, financial stability and banking supervision is at least identified and other contributors draw out the nature and place of ethics in the debate. Some chapters thus contribute to the challenge with which ethicists must deal. British and German experiences are in the forefront of the issues under discussion.

In his keynote speech (Chapter 1) Norbert Walter points out that globalization means rapid expansion of world trade and foreign direct investment, but that it also means new opportunities for travel and unlimited exchange of information and knowledge. We have quantum leaps in data processing and telecommunication allowing us to produce more quickly and cheaply in a global configuration. He identifies 'the signs of the times' as competition, innovation and new strategies. Strangely enough, contemporary Catholic moral thinking has appropriated the term 'signs of the times' as central to the exercise of interpreting the ethical dilemma of modern life. The sharing of the term opens up important avenues for ethics in the banking sector explored by Norbert Walter. Mergers between banks, strategic acquisitions in new fields, specialization in niche markets and the whole process of rationalization cannot be removed from moral interpretation.

The perceptive comparison of the UK and German banking systems presented in Chapter 2 by Glenn Hoggarth, Alistair Milne and Geoffrey Wood not only highlights differences in banking performance but raises questions about the relationship of structures and the level and volatility of bank profits. In so far as systemic factors such as loose monetary policy and unsustainable increases in property prices are part of this analysis, ethicists must face them. Ethics is corporate as well as personal.

In Chapter 3 Jan Toporowski carries this discussion forward by looking at the issue of different institutions, conventions and histories causing problems in making systematic comparisons of financial systems in various countries. However, sectoral balance sheets can be made and compared to reveal institutional differences, economic changes and the fragility of financial structures. Its extensive foreign liabilities make the UK's financial system more fragile than that of Germany. This suggests that the European Monetary Union may be more stable without UK membership. But government debt gives assured liquidity to financial portfolios. The fiscal provisions of Maastricht therefore limit the security of the emerging European financial system.

Commenting on the Toporowski paper, Andrew Tylecote points out that the debt of trustworthy governments, arising from past deficits, helps stabilise financial systems, but present or expected future deficits are unhelpful. Currently in many countries the 'pension overhang' leads to expectations of future deficits. There is, in the world as a whole, a shortage of sage would-be borrowers. How can this be allayed? According to Tylecote by

1. Government borrowing for high return investments with positive externalities – particularly primary and secondary education.
2. State backing for long-term borrowing by individuals for tertiary education. The ethical issue of poor countries and poor people being helped to become 'good risks' is an important question of finance ethics.

In the 1992 Von Hügel Lecture at the University of Cambridge Hans Tietmeyer, the former President of the Deutsche Bundesbank, raised the whole matter of monetary stability as an ethical issue in central banking.[1] In this spirit Forrest Capie and Geoffrey Wood explore in Chapter 4 of this collection the crucial question of the relationship of stability to industry in the comparative conditions of British and German banking. Different forms of behaviour in banking crises are identified as important and the weakness of lender-of-last-resort activity in the German system is viewed as a defect. A moral response to mitigate the effects of crises on citizens would need to look to structural adjustments as the beginning of appropriate policy.

Jan Kregel analyses the role of trust banks in Chapter 5. Starting with a discussion of the central issues of self-interest in market competition and the need for trust and confidence in financial markets, he gives an interesting historical account of legislation governing trust deeds and the development of trust banks in, for example, the UK, USA, Germany and Italy with their different types of regulation to produce trust relationships. In view of the trust banks' contribution to financial stability, the author quite rightly regrets the trend for trust banks being transformed into equity owned profit-maximizing banks and stresses the positive benefits being derived from a symbiotic coexistence of trust-based and profit-based banking organizations.

Chapter 6 by Barry Howcroft examines the traditional function of commercial banks as financial intermediaries between deficit and surplus sectors. Fundamental to this function has been the assumption

---

[1] Tietmeyer, Hans (1993) 'The Value of Monetary Stability in the World Today', in P. Arestis (ed.) *Money and Banking: Issues for the Twenty-First Century. Essays in Honour of Stephen F. Frowen*. Foreword by Helmut Schlesinger (London: Macmillan; New York: St Martin's Press), pp. 25–40.

that banks can intermediate at lower costs than those prevailing with direct financing arrangements, but developments in corporate wholesale financing over the past twenty years or so have significantly undermined this 'cost imperative' for large national and international companies. This has resulted in significant disintermediation of commercial banks by large companies and introduced a large degree of product innovation in wholesale corporate finance. These innovations have meant that commercial barks have become more investment bank oriented. Traditional on-balance sheet services for large companies have, therefore, been largely replaced by the off-balance sheet activities of providing investment advice, making replacements, the provision of standby facilities, etc. These fundamental changes in business activity have had a marked effect on the commercial banks' principal sources of income and the risks inherent in their business. Just as important, however, is the fact that innovations in corporate wholesale banking have far-reaching implications which go well beyond the corporate wholesale market and have fundamentally changed the commercial banks' 'business philosophy' and methods of management.

In Chapter 7 Justin Welby seeks to defend the use and development of derivative financial products, albeit with some caution. It concentrates on the concept of risk management, as a necessary duty of business managers. Derivatives are seen not as means of avoiding but rather as means of managing and allocating risk. If used to do this properly they are of great potential benefit. The paper looks at the ethical issues raised from a consequentialist, a rule-based and a virtue-based approach, finding the last to be the most useful in moving towards an ethical basis in finance.

Chapter 8 by Andreas Wagner draws attention to the fact that the banking industry is facing broad public unease because of a wide range of scandals such as insider trading, money laundering or misuse of funds. In this climate ethical questions have become more relevant for banks, especially because there is awareness that only the tip of the iceberg has been exposed. Regarding these developments, banks seem to need some good advice on how to cope with their ethical problems, in order to regain public acceptance and reputation. One main argument in this chapter is that the increase of disastrous incidents in banking is no evidence for the decay of morals in banking. It is much more likely that the structural incentives are wrongly placed in the sense that immoral behaviour pays out and moral considerations are being punished. The installation of an ethics management therefore seems to be gaining in significance.

Chapter 9 by Stephen F. Frowen and Elias Karakitsos presents an extended challenge to ethical thinking on the subject of savings-ratio behaviour in globalised money and capital markets. In a chapter that has independent value in finance theory, the need for ethicists to deal with complex realities is raised, even if no detailed ethical solutions are proposed. The question of short-term Keynesian stability policy and 'convinced' monetarist policy, with their different influences on inflation and on the behaviour of different classes of citizens is clearly an important ethical issue which has been tackled by careful attention to the realities identified by the comparison of UK and German policies drawn by the two authors.

After briefly surveying and comparing the performance of monetary policy in the UK and Germany, the authors introduce a model analysing the adjustment of consumption in the business cycle, investigate the savings ratio in UK business cycles and the effects of financial deregulation and liberalisation on the UK and other economies. While in the traditional view, the savings ratio varies pro-cyclically because households are involved in consumption smoothing, this chapter points to the empirical evidence in the 1980s and 1990s which shows that in some countries the savings ratio varies counter-cyclically. This chapter identifies that such behaviour can be explained by an adjustment of the savings ratio not only in response to fluctuations of current to permanent income but also because of deviations of wealth from its target level. These fluctuations in wealth are the product of financial deregulation, liberalisation and globalisation and are triggered by changes in monetary policy. The more leveraged an economy is the greater the volatility of wealth and hence the more apparent the counter-cyclical adjustment of the savings ratio. The behaviour of the highly leveraged Anglo-Saxon countries and the less leveraged Continental Europe is compared and the role of monetary policy is analysed.

Eric Owen Smith's Chapter 10 is in part a thoughtful response to Chapter 9 by Frowen and Karakitsos. He focuses on the phrase 'conduct and ethical underpinnings of monetary policy'. This is a model for finance ethics in the complex setting of modern money markets, facing head-on perceptions of right and wrong and the moral obligations of monetary policy-makers. His quotation from Paprotzki that 'money is a fascinating subject of study because it is so full of mystery and paradox' might stand as a rubric for finance ethics. The author draws out the ethical implications of Friedman and Keynesian paradigms and illustrates the importance of these ethical considerations to the analysis presented by Frowen and Karakitsos. Thus, it can justly be claimed that Chapters 9 and 10 constitute a paradigm for finance ethics.

In Chapter 11 Norbert Kloten investigates the behaviour of leading central banks vis-á-vis increasingly complex financial markets in a globalised world. The Bundesbank incessantly strived for stable money guided by internal monetary targets. Volatile exchange markets, the spreading of financial tremors and international responsibilities are likewise only secondary elements of the European Central Bank's decision-making. And the Fed – driving force (in cooperation with the US-Treasury and the IMF) behind any major international monetary agreement – acts as an autonomous, on-home-affairs concentrating central bank. Even the Bank of Japan, showing more or less voluntary solidarity with initiatives of both the IMF and the Fed, finally tries to serve national objectives. Paul Volcker, Chairman of the 'Bretton-Woods-Commission', stated in 1994 that Germany, the USA and Japan are not prepared 'to move toward a more formal system of exchange rate construction over time'. Time has not yet come for a Bretton Woods II. However, the Asian crisis, shedding a rather unfavourable light on both the Fed and the World Bank, has made obvious that internationally coordinated measures are imperative to consolidate the international financial system in order to safeguard a proper relationship between private commercial operations and an effective surveillance by national and international authorities, to agree on a reasonable set of sanctions in case regulations are disregarded, and finally to strengthen governance by the Fed. However, some of what needs to be done, is beginning to take shape.

As the United Kingdom has started to build its new Financial Services Authority, John Ellis explores in Chapter 12 some of the ethical dimensions of the key policy debates. The new Authority has responsibility for the whole financial sector. The globalisation of financial activity and the disappearance of old boundaries between different types of financial institutions present new challenges to regulators. They need to reassess whom it is they are seeking to protect, where responsibility lies for decisions in international institutions and what penalties are appropriate. The relationship of ethics and regulation is the underlying theme. Ethics stimulates regulation and continues the moral debate beyond the limits of what regulation can achieve.

Chapter 13 by Martin Donnelly presents a clear case of the finance practitioner as an ethicist by debating the question of whether Economic and Monetary Union is an ethical issue. In setting the question, initially, in terms of winners and losers the writer immerses himself in the debate about the relationship of facts and values in ethics. The analysis is sustained throughout by the definition of *economic* union, compulsion, freedom, sovereignty and the operation of these through exchange rates and international financial structures. The thorny question of ethics and the art of the possible runs through every paragraph of this chapter.

In Chapter 14 Stephan Herten and Jens Hölscher analyse arguments in favour of either a credit-based or capital-based financial system for transition economies. The first part describes corporate governance theory and empirical research relating to financial development. On this basis they then describe some macroeconomic features of both systems and look for elements for a development strategy. This is contrasted in the subsequent sections with real-world attempts of transition economies. Finally, they argue that the way of solving the bad debt problem and hence the restructuring of the banking sector influences the type of financial system, which ultimately emerges. They come out in favour of a strategy of semi-liberalisation.

Chapter 15 by Udo Reifner and Juliane Pfau covers the need for and availability of social banking and affordable housing in Germany as an example of an inclusive bank product. The authors develop and evaluate ideas on how banks could be helpful in upgrading the social situation in metropolitan areas without relinquishing profits. They see a decisive role for banks to play in this field and conclude that the 'bank's name is needed for trust and reputation, its credit facility is necessary to give adequate and cash-flow-adjusted credit to the residents at affordable rates, its knowledge in marketing financial products could help to raise own-capital, and its tax advisers and lawyers may settle the necessary disputes with the internal revenue services'. Of course, there are fundamental differences in the way housing markets are financed in Germany and the UK, but some lessons could possibly be learned in the UK from the German experience and vice versa.

In the final Chapter 16 Leo Schuster deals with the role of compliance in Germany's banking culture. Every period of time has its favourite topics and even fashionable catchwords, the propagandists of which are primarily the media. This is also true for business, one of whose latest terms in banking is 'compliance', which in Germany is connected especially with insider trading. Compliance clearly has to have a double function: it should be, at once, a protection of customers' interests (namely shareholders, investors and issuers) and of employee and manager positions.

This book does not provide – and is not meant to provide – a theory of finance ethics. It allows its authors, looking mainly at German and British experiences, to set out parameters for the debate, guidelines for ethical considerations (both of a corporate and personal nature) and some finance-based examples to ethicists intent on developing finance ethics.

STEPHEN F. FROWEN
FRANCIS P. MCHUGH

Acknowledgements

I should like to acknowledge particularly the generous financial help provided by the Fritz Thyssen Stiftung, Cologne, which enabled us at the Von Hügel Institute, St Edmund's Colledge, University of Cambridge, to organise the conference on which the papers contained in the present volume are based. I am also most appreciative of the ready response of the Anglo–German Foundation for the Study of Industrial Society, London, to collaborate with us and support us in every possible way. Its support contributed greatly to an occasion, which was intellectually as well as socially memorable.

My warmest personal gratitude is offered also to Tim Farmiloe, the now retired publishing director of Macmillan who originally accepted these conference proceedings for publication and who has for many years rendered me such inestimable help in a relationship which has developed into a much treasured friendship.

I further wish to record the great debt I owe to Keith Povey for the endless patience and care he has lavished on yet one more manuscript of mine, in copy-editing and supervision of detail, in a manner quite beyond praise.

Frank McHugh, my co-editor and much esteemed colleague, and I also wish to take this opportunity of expressing the feelings of appreciation and gratitude to Brian Heap, Master of St Edmund's College, for his imcomparably kind support and encouragement.

This book is dedicated to Hans Tietmeyer, the former President of the Deutsche Bundesbank, who, amongst the leaders of the financial world, has been in the forefront of setting new and essential ethical standards.

Cambridge STEPHEN F. FROWEN

1
Competition Forces and Institutional Structure in the UK and Germany

Norbert Walter

Introduction

The term 'globalisation', which has been the subject of much public debate for some time now, triggers a mixed reaction in many people. They associate it on the one hand with worldwide trade in goods, new opportunities for travel and an unrestricted exchange of information. But globalisation also means the disappearance of old orders. National policies reach their limits earlier and more often when there is transnational freedom for people, capital and management. This is often a source of fear and resistance.

The forces behind global economic integration

A major characteristic of our time is the rapid expansion of world trade, whose volume is currently almost one hundred times that of 1950. The relative importance of the goods traded has also changed. The focus has shifted from raw materials to consumer products and highly specialised industrial goods; cars and computers have overtaken crude oil and iron ore in their importance for world trade.

Moreover, the international distribution of labour is undergoing a fundamental change. The newly industrialising countries of Asia, which had previously specialised in simple mass-produced goods, are gaining ground with more complex products such as cars and machine tools; the Latin American countries, which lost a decade following the debt crisis, are striving for greater integration into the world economy; and since the fall of the iron curtain, the reforming countries of

Central Europe have emerged with low-cost, qualified labour forces right on our doorstep.

The increasing global diversification of business activity is adding another dimension to the world economy. This is visible in the dynamic growth of direct investment. In 1995 alone, companies invested US$315 billion worldwide in subsidiaries, production facilities and, increasingly, research facilities outside their home countries. The lion's share of cross-border investment continues to be made between the highly developed western industrial countries, but a growing proportion flows from industrial countries into newly industrialising and developing countries, particularly in Southeast Asia.

The stimulating effect of FDI on growth is clear. Many of today's newly industrialising countries recognised this early on and have encouraged the inflow of capital and know-how with market reforms and a very open attitude towards foreign investors. Countries such as, for example, the Asian tigers offer not only low wage costs but also a low level of regulation and favourable tax rates. Another attraction, though a potential problem in the long term, is relatively low environmental and safety standards. The advantageous conditions offered by these new competitors in the fight for investment cannot be ignored by economic policy-makers in the industrial countries, especially not in Germany.

Globalisation – just a short-term phenomenon?

Despite the obvious changes, many in Germany think globalisation is just a fashionable word for the familiar trend towards a greater international division of labour. They remind us that world trade growth rates have been high in previous decades and cite the strong flow of direct investment, particularly across the Atlantic, back in the 1960s. They say that Germany, with its traditionally high ratio of exports to GDP – 40 years ago it was already just over 20 per cent, not much below today's 23 per cent – has always had to face international competition. And since it has so far managed to hold its own among the exporting nations, there is no cause to worry or even turn away from the supposedly proven German economic model with its omnipresent, interventionist, redistributionist state.

This point of view contains many distortions. Of course trade and change are not new phenomena, but it is abundantly clear that the trend towards 'one world' has progressed in leaps and bounds in the past few years and that global integration has attained a new quality.

The triumphal march of the market economy since the mid-1980s has produced a more lasting change in the world economy than is apparent from the bare figures, that is a doubling of global trade, which had already happened in the preceding decade. The new start in Eastern Europe is not the only manifestation of the new era of globalisation. The market reforms in the second and third worlds, as well as the change of tack in industrial countries such as New Zealand and the Netherlands towards market forces – often ignored in Germany – contradict the idea that this is a steady development.

In addition, there have been quantum leaps in technology. New developments, especially in data processing and telecommunications, allow business to be done globally in new time dimensions. The international distribution of labour used to mean high transaction costs, particularly in the form of time loss. Now, in our world of data highways, distances can be covered with ease in fractions of a second. These new possibilities have revolutionised the financial markets and unleashed a wave of changes in other sectors, especially services. A global use and efficient combination of resources in order to produce goods and services quickly and cheaply within a global organisation and thus meet the needs of the customers in the best way possible, will become essential to the survival of a growing number of companies, including medium-sized enterprises. Where new jobs are created in this environment will depend more than ever on the framework of conditions set by the makers of economic policy.

In the mid-to-late 1990s, companies have a wide choice when planning an investment abroad. The up-and-coming countries of Asia, Latin America and the newcomers among the reforming countries of Central and Eastern Europe are not the only ones offering favourable conditions. Many industrial countries also have considerably lower taxes, levies and labour costs than Germany. This applies in particular to the UK and the USA, both of which are, from a German point of view, low-wage countries with labour costs around 40 per cent lower than at home. In neighbouring France, too, labour is more than a third cheaper.

The right way for Germany

If we want to keep our prosperity and the opportunity it offers to provide social security, which cannot exist without the right economic basis, and if we plan to remain a reliable trade partner not only for the large industrial countries but also the reforming states of Central

Europe, we must face up to the challenges of globalisation. As it is neither possible nor – from the consumer's point of view – desirable to make global megatrends follow continental European rules, as called for by many, then we must be the ones to adjust if we are to get Germany into shape to compete internationally. It is time to correct the mistakes caused by disregarding Ludwig Erhard's concept of the social market economy and embracing the welfare state.

Since 1970, government spending has risen from around 38 per cent of GDP to over 50 per cent. This alone shows that the public sector has in the past 30 years taken on too many tasks that should belong to the private sector – which could do them better and more cheaply. This is a key area for change; the state must be trimmed back to a normal size. 'Lean administration' must become more than a fashionable expression.

A root-and-branch reform is most urgently needed in the social services. Experience shows that cost-cutting programmes alone – as about to be prescribed yet again for the pension system – cannot halt the rising trend in social insurance contributions. If the vicious circle of increasing contributions and growing demands on the state are to be broken and the upward trend of non-wage labour costs reversed, then we must turn the wheel in the direction of more private healthcare and pensions.

Not only the need to curb burgeoning non-wage labour costs but also demographic developments call for rapid action. The state is as little prepared for the surge in costs facing not only the state pension system but also the healthcare insurance system and state nursing care insurance as it is for the millions of civil service pensions falling due after the turn of the millennium. To hold on to the current collective pension system in its outsize form would mean shifting an enormous burden into the future, which would harbour many risks and would constitute cheating the younger generation. The tottering edifice of the state pension system must be supported by pillars of private provision. Occupational, but particularly also private, pensions must be established as an essential basis for a sustainable system which will not collapse under the strain of demographic distortions.

To finance the tasks which are indisputably the domain of the state, we need a modern tax system which is more conducive to investment and achievement. The on-going tax reform, which began in 1999, fortunately gives clear economic incentives to individuals and businesses, especially foreign companies. It must say that achievement in one's official job and willingness to take risks and invest in Germany will start to pay off again. It must offer the prospect of a top income tax rate below 40 per cent. Tax privileges must be consistently reduced in order to finance lower rates for high performers and those with low incomes.

A return to the social market economy also means cutting back on regulation and broadening the individual's scope for action. Above all, the labour market must be freed from rigidities if our economy is to become more flexible and competitive. The current rules forcing companies to provide a social plan for employees adversely affected by business changes and the dismissal protection regulations discourage employers from taking on new staff. These rules must be reviewed. Even more important is a reform of the wage negotiating process. We must move away from wage cartels and collective obligations, and give more influence to market forces and negotiations between individuals. It is time to loosen the straightjacket of industry-wide wage agreements and allow companies greater freedom in setting pay and working conditions. Opt-out clauses or restrictions on the principle which fixes the collectively agreed wage as the minimum wage would at least be a first step towards a strategy to lead Germany out of its employment dilemma.

It is often said there is little reason to hope at present. One reason for this is possibly the shortcomings of the federal system in Germany. Important decisions can only be taken with the agreement of the state governments in the Bundesrat. If this upper house of parliament is controlled by a different political camp from that which reigns in the lower house, or Bundestag – which often happens – then there is constant pressure to compromise and water down reforms. The result is extreme inertia, at a time when rapid adjustment is called for. Other countries, such as the UK where the system of constitutional checks and balances does not go as far as in Germany, seem to find it easier to make the necessary changes.

For some decades now politicians have talked about cutting subsidies. According to the Kiel Institute of World Economics, all grants, tax breaks and other measures amounted to DM 187.3 billion in 1995. The federal and state governments heavily subsidized transportation (24%), housing (18.2%), agriculture (16.3% for structural measures) and mining (6%). The overall level of subsidies is simply too high; they are rarely extended on a regressive and limited basis, and often the policies are hardly effective at all. Governments still have to live up to their commitment to wind down obsolete programmes, to focus payments on real bottlenecks such as East Germany's infrastructure, and to generally extend subsidies only for a limited time and on a regressive basis.

Stronger ties are essential in Europe

While Germany must put its own house in order, this will not be enough to secure the competitiveness of its economy. To make the leap from a national to global economy, we need further economic and political integration in Europe. Europe must establish institutions which give companies greater freedom to act and create certainty and security for citizens. The introduction of the single currency is of crucial importance for this.

The single currency is the logical complement to the single market. Only when the euro has been introduced will the four basic freedoms of the single market in place since 1992 come into full effect. The advantages are obvious: currency-related transaction and hedging costs as well as currency risks will disappear, as exchange-rate turbulence within Europe will become a thing of the past. This means cost savings and planning security for investors. More important than these economic arguments, however, is that the euro will make a crucial contribution towards strengthening political union within Europe. Stronger ties in Europe are important for Germany if only because 57 per cent of our exports still go to EU countries.

Let us now turn from this overview of the problems facing Germany in general to the financial sector. Surprisingly, this industry has not succumbed to the virus of inertia.

Banks and financial markets – in a state of flux

For some years the German financial sector has been subject to rapid change caused by many different trends. Changes in the banking system and in the strategies of leading banks, growth in the stockmarket, orientation towards shareholder value, the increased significance of corporate governance, new laws reforming the financial market and EMU-induced innovations are the salient features of this process.

Let us first look at the banking industry itself. For some years the banks have been aware that small steps are not enough to meet big challenges. So what is changing? Customer behaviour is altering, new banking technology is being developed and electronic banking is on the rise. As in America, customers of German banks are demanding that standard services be made available quickly, simply and by telephone, and the use of new technology is increasing. Branch banking is bearing the brunt of the changes; Germany is overbanked and will have to cut down. At the same time, direct banking is expanding. While individual services which require intensive consulting will remain, the trend is towards standardisation.

Second, the fields of business where banks must be present are changing. Investment banking and asset management are becoming more important, and trading and commission business in the securities markets are making an increasing contribution to operating profits. Classical lending continues, of course, but is becoming less and less profitable. Competition to attract big customers – but also small and medium-sized enterprises – is extremely tough. Long-standing relationships between banks and their customers are little protection against competition in either case.

Squeezed margins, the need to invest in technology and in building up areas of business with high earnings potential, growing competition from non-banks such as credit card companies and financial subsidiaries of industrial companies, and soon from the internet – all this points in one direction: economies of scale are becoming more important. Mergers between banks, strategic acquisitions in new fields, specialisation in lucrative niche markets and rationalisation of branch networks are all part of the picture. The structural consolidation of the European banking industry is well under way. The merger of BV and Hypo-Bank and the acquisition of SMH by UBS are only two moves played in a long game to decide the new order in Europe.

Third, the securities markets, particularly the equities market and direct financing, are experiencing an upturn which is far more than a rise in prices. The way German industry is financed will likely undergo a permanent structural change. Companies will issue more bonds to raise funds, for example. New market segments for risk capital, the plans to permit the creation of Anglo-Saxon-type pension funds, the growth of investment funds in general, the diversification of international investors into European and German equities, the debate over the significance of shareholder value as a maxim of corporate governance: these developments have not yet created as strong an equity culture as seen in the Anglo-Saxon countries, but the era of corporate financing through bank lending alone is over. Germany's stockmarket capitalisation, still at a very low level, has the potential to reach great heights.

The corporate rationalisation programmes necessitated by the cost situation, by good economic conditions (interest-rate level, dollar, growth upturn) and the focus of management in many companies on key earnings figures have driven stock prices higher in the second half of the 1990s. Banks have taken the opportunity to boost their securities business, smaller firms are daring to become 'AGs', that is public limited companies – IPOs are 'in' – and the federal government is pushing ahead with its privatisation policy. Only the federal states seem not yet to have succumbed to the charms of the markets. They still have a broad range of stakes in industrial companies, regional savings banks, tourism companies, energy utilities, spa resorts, ports and airports which would be better sold off to the private sector, whether via the stock exchange or through a private placement.

Closely related to this development is the debate over corporate governance in Germany. After discussing at length the power wielded by the banking sector, parliament produced a moderate bill whose main contribution was new rules on the representation of banks on company supervisory boards. But this problem is illusory. The institutional structures of the German system – management board and supervisory board, employees' rights to co-determination – have proven their worth, but they are coming up hard against their limits. Only the market can offer a genuine test of efficiency – measured by key earnings figures. Takeovers, including hostile bids, must become a test of management as well as an intensive exchange between strategic investors and companies. Foreign investors, but also German insurers and investment companies, are already spearheading the beginnings of change.

Fourth, lawmakers realised back in the 1980s that the German financial markets no longer complied with international practices, and many reforms are already signed and sealed. Germany now has a securities watchdog, rules on insider trading and other elements of a modern capital market. The third law to promote the financial markets, scheduled to go into effect in 1998, continued the reform process. Among other things, it lifted certain investment restrictions for funds, allowing the creation of special pension funds, stock index and closed-end equity funds, making it easier for companies to obtain a stockmarket listing, reducing creditor protection to a normal level (prospectus liability and statute of limitations in investment consulting) and amending many other rules.

The 'financial centre Germany' still has its work cut out, however, particularly regarding taxation in the pension system, the abolition of minimum reserve requirements, deregulation in the labour market and the services sector, as well as in the finance industry and in the tax system in general. In particular, a critical mass has not yet been achieved in terms of financial market research and training. But the signs of change are unmistakable.

Fifth, the advent of monetary union in Europe will turn the financial markets and bank lending on their heads. The rules of the game will change not only because of the size, liquidity and growth of the European financial markets, but also through the increase in competition across the old currency borders. To mention some of the consequences: the focus of asset allocation in fund management will shift from country analysis to a Europe-wide sectoral approach; the integration of the equity markets will obtain a substantial boost from the disappearance of currency restrictions and also through the rise of electronic trading; competition on the money markets will intensify; and the bond market in the participating countries will become extremely deep. Competition has already flared up between Germany and France for the role of benchmark issuer. Products will disappear from the futures markets: euro fixed-income futures and a few currency-hedging instruments will dominate. Banks, stock exchanges and financial service providers will have to adjust to new products, strategies and competitors. London will remain no. 1 for forex trading, equities and international financing; but Frankfurt's money market will have greater potential, and Frankfurt will presumably take first place in bond trading in EMU. The futures exchanges, DTB, MATIF and LIFFE, are already involved in skirmishes.

The institutional structures will have to adjust to the changed environment, although their foundations are unlikely to be shattered. The continental European model of corporate governance will be complemented by the market rather than replaced by it. Employee co-determination is not in danger; and banks, insurers and funds will continue to behave as strategic investors rather than short-term hunters for the biggest return on investment.

But the dynamics of the financial markets are already bringing many changes to strategy, product mix and the competitive environment. Financial services providers will have their work cut out to react successfully to all these simultaneous processes; they, too, are under pressure to perform. The traditional image of the German bank whose *raison d'être* is lending to small and medium-sized companies is not consistent with a picture of banks in a state of change, on the road to lending and securities business in the global capital market, facing a harsh wind but with a strong backbone. The results of this inevitable new start will not be possible to judge until many years have passed. But the signs of the times in the financial sector are competition, innovation and new strategies. The years when Germany could attract investment with the minimum of effort are over: its banks, especially, must face up to this new challenge.

2

Alternative Routes to Banking Stability: A Comparison of UK and German Banking Systems*

Glenn Hoggarth, Alistair Milne and Geoffrey E. Wood

The banking systems of Britain and Germany are among the most stable in the world. In both countries bank failures are exceedingly rare, and even periods of difficulty among more than a few banks very uncommon. Yet the two systems are very different. They differ both in structure and in how banks in the two countries behave. In this chapter we compare the two systems, so as to bring out the key features which have contributed to their stability and to see if anything can be said about the prospects for their continuing stability in the future. We start, though, by looking at recent periods of major instability – not in Britain and Germany, where there have been no such episodes for many years but in other countries, so as to highlight the kind of events which can bring serious disturbances to a country's financial system. Then we turn to describing the systems of Britain and Germany, showing how both have experienced substantial liberalisation in recent years. This leads to a comparison of banking profitability in the two economies, and to an appraisal of the factors which may have contributed to the radically different experience of the two countries in this regard. This enables us to offer some suggestions as to the impact of liberalisation and of inflation on banking sector stability.

Over the past two decades, banks in a number of countries have experienced severe problems. In some cases the institutions would have failed without taxpayer support, and in others whole sectors of the financial system would have failed without a period of low interest rates in which they could restore profits and rebuild capital.

* We are indebted to Clive Briault, Professor Otmar Issing, Professor Harold James and Dr Anna J. Schwartz for comments on an earlier draft.

Such episodes appear to require a double trigger – financial deregulation along with a period of macroeconomic instability. The effects of these seem to be transmitted through rapid growth in bank credit and asset prices.

There are various explanations for this linkage. One is quite simply that deregulation allows banks and other institutions to enter new areas of business, where they have no experience. Some maintain that problems have been exacerbated by an increase in the variability of asset prices, while others (eg Hellwig, 1996) suggest that economies have become more volatile.[1] It has also been claimed that deregulation affects stability not simply by promoting bank expansion, but by changing institutional and ownership structures. This affects attitudes to risk, and the consequent changes may well be not only frequently unpredicted but actually unpredictable.

How does the evidence bear on these explanations of why the combination of liberalisation and macroeconomic instability may lead to a period of financial instability? Recent unpublished work by the Bank of England has made cross-country comparisons, drawing on the experience of developed countries. Table 2.1 sets out an overview (derived from that study) of financial problems and associated economic conditions. Certain features stand out from this table. Most important, financial liberalisation was a necessary although not a sufficient precondition for banking problems. A downturn in the economy, usually accompanied by a severe downturn in asset prices across a range of markets, also seems to be required. This is consistent with two wide-ranging studies of developing economics and of smaller industrial ones. Lindgren *et al.* (1996) analysed eight countries which faced systemic banking problems in the 1980s – six developing ones (Argentina, Chile, Ghana, Philippines, Uruguay and Venezuela) and two developed ones (Norway and Finland). In every case, an economic downturn accompanied the crisis and liberalisation preceded it.[2] Kaminsky *et al.* (1998) sought to provide leading indicators to warn of an approaching crisis on the basis of a study of previous crises in 25 larger emerging and industrial countries over the years 1970–95.[3] They found the best indicators to be a rise in broad money relative to monetary base (a proxy for financial liberalisation), a rise in real interest rates, and declines in the growth of output and in equity prices.[4]

This certainly does not, however, imply that financial liberalisation produces instability. A number of economies which were liberalised for some time before an economic downturn – including Germany – did not experience banking problems when an economic downturn came.

Table 2.1 Recent banking problems in major economies

(1) Systemic

		Pre-crisis			*During crisis*	
Country	*Year*	*Macroeconomic*	*Type of financial liberalisation*	*Asset price bubble?*	*Macro-economic downturn*	*Induced by higher interest rates?*
Finland	1991–94	Boom; loosening in monetary policy	Credit quantities; foreign banks	Equities, residential and commercial property	Yes	Yes
Norway	1987–93	Boom; loosening in monetary policy	Credit quantities; interest rates	Equities, residential and commercial property	Yes	No – oil price fall
Sweden	1990–93	Boom; loosening in monetary policy	Credit quantities; interest rates	Equities, residential and commercial property	Yes	Yes
Japan	1992–present	Boom; loosening in monetary policy	Credit quantities; interest rates	Equities, residential and commercial property	Yes	Yes

(2) Bank loan losses

		Pre-losses			*During losses*	
Australia	early 1990s	Boom; loosening in monetary policy	Credit quantities; interest rates	Equities and commercial property	Yes	Yes
United Kingdom	early 1990s	Boom; loosening in monetary policy	Credit quantities; interest rates	Commercial and residential property	Yes	Partially
United States	early 1990s	Boom; loosening in monetary policy	Bank licensing made easier (intense competition)	Commercial property	Yes	Partially

Table 2.1 Recent banking problems in major economies – *continued*

3) No real problems (late 1980s/early 1990s)

	Lessons from past		*Late 1980s/ early 1990s*		*During late 1980s/ early 1990s*	
Canada	Yes, 1985	Boom	No recent changes; foreign banks faced capital controls	Commercial property	Yes	Partially
Netherlands	Yes, late 1970s/early 1980s	Boom; loosening in monetary policy	No recent changes	No	Modest	Yes
Germany		Boom*	No recent changes; limited new entrants	Commercial property	Yes*	Yes*

* Following German unification.

Most, indeed, appear to have banking systems with well-developed methods of containing risks. The picture rather seems to be that there is vulnerability *during the process* of liberalisation, a process in the course of which new entrants, both domestic and foreign, fare worse than established institutions.

Another feature of Table 2.1 is the key role property prices appear to play in triggering financial problems. This was highlighted again in the recent financial crises in east Asia.[5]

Credit and asset prices in the UK and Germany

Table 2.2 shows that the growth of bank credit relative to GDP has been more volatile in the UK than in Germany over the past 25 years, as has aggregate asset price inflation. Disaggregation shows that property price inflation has been consistently more volatile in the UK. Table 2.3 shows correlations between the annual growth in real asset prices and total credit/GDP in the UK and Germany, split into two periods – 1971–82 and 1983–97. The earlier period broadly coincides with the period prior to the lifting of credit controls in the UK.

The whole period correlations suggest there is a strong positive relationship between growth in the credit/GDP ratio and residential property prices in the UK since the early 1970s. The sub-period correlations suggest that in the UK the interaction has been stronger since the early 1980s.

But in the UK and Germany the combination of financial liberalisation and the interaction between credit and asset prices is not sufficient to explain the difference in banking sector experiences that is summarised in Table 2.1. Financial liberalisation had already gone a substantial way in both countries. (See annex 2.1.) It therefore remains to be explained why both the interaction between asset prices and credit, and the impact of these variables on bank performance, were more pronounced in the UK than in Germany. We explore answers to these questions and draw out some implications in the remainder of the paper.

Liberalisation, structure and performance

Although both countries experienced considerable financial liberalisation, the impact of this on their financial sectors has not been the same. There are considerable differences in the institutional structure

Table 2.2 Standard deviation of annual growth in real asset prices and credit/GDP 1971–97

	Credit/GDP	*Real total asset prices (1980 = 100)*	*Real house prices (1980 = 100)*	*Real equity prices (1980 = 100)*	*Real commercial property prices (1980 = 100)*
1971–97					
UK	7.92	9.42	9.83	26.57	–
Germany	2.18	–	8.67*	22.82	–
1971–82					
UK	10.38	11.60	12.07	38.50	–
Germany	1.90	–	10.73+	13.13	–
1983–97					
UK	5.62	7.52	8.04	11.56	18.72
Germany	2.44	5.14	6.82	27.24	15.60

* 1972–97.
+ 1972–82.
Data source: Bank for International Settlements, Jones Lang Wootton.

Table 2.3 Correlations of annual growth in credit/GDP and real asset prices

	Total credit/ GDP	*Total asset prices*	*House prices*	*Equity prices*	*Commercial property prices*
1971–97	UK	0.30	0.66	–0.27	–
	Germany	–	0.29*	0.30	–
1971–82	UK	0.18	0.65	–0.40	–
	Germany	–	0.59+	–0.26	–
1983–97	UK	0.57	0.68	0.28	0.14
	Germany	0.01	–0.11	0.35	–0.36

* 1972–97.
+ 1972–82.

of the German and UK banking systems. This is reflected in the shares of assets held by different types of institution in the two countries (Table 2.4).

While there are few legal or regulatory barriers which impede the choice of business activities by German banks, there is in fact a clear demarcation into a number of different categories. The UK banking system, on the other hand, is dominated by a few large commercial banks all engaged in a wide range of business. In 1994 the largest five banks accounted for 57 per cent of banking business in the UK compared with 17 per cent (1995) in Germany.[6] Annex 2.1 shows the main episodes of financial deregulation and liberalisation in the UK and Germany. Interest rates have been market-determined in both countries for many years – in Germany since 1967 and in the UK since 1971. While the volume of lending has also been left to the market in Germany, the UK introduced controls (the 'corset') which restricted the volume of bank credit during much of the period 1973–80. Deregulation of bank activities was thus only completed in the UK by 1980. In neither country were there restrictions separating commercial and investment banking activity.

Table 2.4 Shares of assets – December 1997

*Germany banking system**	*% of total bank assets*
'Big Banks' (Deutsche, Dresdner, Commerzbank)	10
Regional banks	13
Landesbanken	18
Savings banks	19
Co-operative banks	14
Mortgage banks	15
Specialised credit institutions	9
Branches of foreign banks	2
Private banks	*1*
*UK banking system***	*% of sterling assets booked in UK*
UK banks	67
Foreign banks	23
Building societies	10

* *Source*: Deutsche Bundesbank, *Bankenstatistik*, May 1998.
** Bank of England Monetary and Financial Statistics, May 1998.

Another key feature of the UK banking system is the presence of a large number of branches and subsidiaries of foreign banks in London. International and investment banking is a major industry in the UK, but because of its international nature this business is not directly relevant to the question of what triggers losses in the domestic banking system. For this reason the figures in Table 2.4 are restricted to UK sterling assets, the best available measure of domestic banking business. This shows that foreign banks have a significant share of total sterling business in the UK, although this is largely in wholesale lending to large corporates and to local authorities.

Innovation in retail banking products and payments services has proceeded more rapidly in the UK than in Germany. This is especially true in the mortgage and credit card markets, but corporate debt markets, in both short-term commercial paper and long-term bonds, have also developed much further in the UK than Germany.

According to published accounting data, the principal difference in the performance of the aggregate banking sectors of the two countries is that profitability has been higher but more variable in the UK. Over the past 25 years the pre-tax annual profits of UK retail banks averaged about 1.2 per cent of total assets, and ranged from a minimum of 0.4 per cent to a maximum of 1.6 per cent. The annual profits of the German banking system, by contrast, were less than 0.6 per cent of total assets on average over the past 25 years and, according to the published data, varied much less than in the UK, from a minimum of 0.4 per cent of total assets in 1990 to a maximum of 0.75 per cent in 1983. The lower variability might at first glance simply imply better risk control, but something more must be involved, because even in the worst year the return on assets of UK commercial banks was only very slightly below those of German banks. In all but four years out of the last 25 the return on assets of the banking system in the UK was higher than in Germany.[7]

Unlike British banks, German banks still maintain hidden reserves. It is important to consider how and to what extent this practice distorts the published picture. Rather as British banks did before the Second World War, German banks use these reserves to smooth fluctuations in profits. It is said by those aware of the true picture that although these reserves may affect profits for several years in a row at an individual bank they do not influence the trend level of operating profits for the banking system as a whole. Also that they are not sufficiently large to smooth volatility of the size shown in Britain, to the level reported in Germany.[8]

Table 2.5 Profit and loss accounts

% of total assets (except costs/income)	*Germany*		*UK*
	All banks 1992–97	*Excluding Landesbanken and mortgage banks 1992–97*	*Major banks and building societies 1992–97*
Net Interest Income	1.8	2.3	2.2
Non-Interest Income	0.4	0.5	1.4
Staff costs	0.8	1.1	0.8
Other costs	0.6	0.8	1.3
Costs/total income	65	67	60
Operating profits	0.8	0.9	1.4
Provisions and exceptionals	0.3	0.3	0.4
Pre-tax profits	0.5	0.6	1.0

Source: British Bankers Association, Annual Abstract of Banking Statistics and Deutsche Bundesbank, *Monthly Reports*.

Table 2.5 summarises the sources of bank income in the two countries. Using Bundesbank data we obtain the figures for all German banks shown in the first column of the table. However, it is probably not appropriate to compare these figures with statistics for the UK banking system, because they include the costs and income of the Landesbanken and mortgage banks which, for special reasons, operate with extremely low interest margins and costs in relation to assets.[9] We therefore compare, in the final two columns of this table, UK banks with German banks excluding the Landesbanken and mortgage banks.

The comparison of UK major banks and building societies with German banks (excluding the Landesbanken and mortgage banks) suggests that German and UK banks have similar levels of interest income, as a proportion of total assets, but that there is a substantial difference in both non-interest income and costs.

Staff costs are higher in Germany, reflecting in part higher social security costs and the much higher number of branches per head of population. In 1994 there were 5,272 people for every bank branch in the UK compared with only 1,832 per branch in Germany.[10] More of a puzzle is the fact that both non-interest income and non-staff costs are higher in the UK than in Germany. Much of the non-interest income of UK banks is fees and commissions on their purely domestic banking activities. One possible explanation of these differences is that UK banks have gone a great deal further than German banks in introducing new products and information-based banking services (eg telephone banking); and that they also sell more non-bank products to their customer base. In Germany, the supply of retail banking services is dominated by state-supported and mutual institutions – the savings banks and credit co-operatives – which have relatively little incentive to substitute electronic forms of delivery for branches. Supplying a greater range of services and products involves higher non-staff costs but may produce more than proportionately higher non-interest income, thus raising profits in relation to assets.

During the 1990s, provisions and exceptional items have been very similar shares of banking assets in the two countries. The higher level of non-interest income and the lower staff costs (which more than compensate for higher non-staff costs) are the main explanation of why UK banks produce a higher average level of profits than German banks.

Determinants of bank performance

Output fluctuations

What explains the greater variability of banking sector profits in Britain than in Germany? The behaviour of real GDP cannot explain the greater variability in the UK; for over the past 40 years fluctuations in real GDP were very similar in the two countries.

A comparison of the annual growth of output in the two countries from 1961 onwards shows that the average growth rate in Germany has exceeded that of the UK, but fluctuations in growth rates, and the depth and duration of recessionary episodes, have been similar. Nor indeed are the fluctuations in growth rates closely associated with bank performance. One of the most severe recessions in both countries was between 1980 and 1982, but this was far from the period of weakest bank performance. We conclude that in neither country were the fluctuations in real aggregate output sufficient on their own to trigger substantial financial difficulties.[11]

Inflation

Nominal macroeconomic instability appears to be more relevant for banking performance. A major difference between the economic performance of the two countries, at least until recently, has been the higher and more variable rate of inflation in the UK. Using the consumer expenditure deflator measure, inflation in the Federal Republic of Germany has never exceeded 8 per cent per annum in the post war years and has averaged less than 4 per cent per annum since the beginning of the 1960s. UK inflation reached 25 per cent in 1974 and 20 per cent in 1980, and was well over 10 per cent per annum, on average, in the 1970s and over 5 per cent in the 1980s. Only since 1992 has the UK inflation rate fallen back to levels close to those witnessed in Germany.

High and variable inflation has a major impact on bank earnings. Unexpected increases in inflation and consequently in interest rates cause cash flow difficulties for borrowers. These can lead to premature termination of loan arrangements and thus precipitate loan losses. Further, it appears that high and variable inflation encourages bank-financed investment in property markets, an investment strategy which can be profitable as long as control over inflation remains weak but can lead to substantial losses if monetary policy is tightened and the inflation rate falls, for property is often used as loan collateral.

Asset prices and new entry

Regarding German and UK property prices in money terms, commercial property prices in both countries experienced big falls since the early 1970s – UK prices fell by 50 per cent between 1988 and 1992 while German prices fell by around 30 per cent between 1991 and 1994. The impacts on the two banking systems were, however, rather different. In the UK the price collapse contributed to the sharp deterioration in banking sector performance in the early 1990s, but in Germany there seems to have been no significant impact.

This may in part reflect the more cautious lending policy and lower loan to value ratios of German banks. But more relevant to bank performance may have been a tendency for pfandbrief mortgage lending arrangements to discourage high loan to value ratios. This can help explain the stability of German bank earnings in the 1970s and 1980s. This is not, however, an entirely satisfactory explanation. Why have German banks not made greater use of non-pfandbrief sources of finance to increase loan to value ratios and loan to income ratios? In the 1990s there has been increasing competition for mortgage business in Germany, but this has not yet led to a rapid build up of personal debt/income on a scale such as occurred in the UK in the late 1980s. The different arrangements for financing property-related lending do not appear to be a fundamental explanation of the greater variability of UK bank performance. Rather our interpretation is that the much greater aggressiveness of UK banks in property-related lending was a conscious strategy; and that German banks had the freedom to be similarly aggressive in lending to property markets, but chose not to be so.

New entry and increased competition in these markets has played a greater role in the UK than in Germany. One source of increased competition is entry by foreign banks into domestic banking markets. Table 2.4 highlights the much greater relative importance of foreign banks in the UK than in Germany. The large number of foreign banks in London came originally to undertake investment and international banking. Having incurred the costs of establishing a presence, a natural step was to branch out into corporate and local authority lending. Foreign banks (including German banks) have also conducted a significant share of commercial property lending in the UK in the past decade.

Competition has also increased amongst UK institutions with, for example, building societies exploiting the new powers offered to them by the 1986 Building Society Act and engaging in lending secured on commercial property, and banks entering residential mortgage markets from the beginning of the 1980s.[12]

The greater impact of property price fluctuations in the UK may have been produced by the combination of a recession in which income fell, leading to inability to maintain loan repayments, together with a fall in nominal property prices. The latter meant that when banks took possession of and sold properties with the aim of recouping their loans, the proceeds from property sales did not cover the original sums lent.[13]

In both countries the nominal price of residential property shows relatively small declines of around 10 per cent in value (this happened in the UK in the early 1990s and in Germany in the mid-1980s). Losses on residential mortgage lending did not contribute very substantially to UK bank loan loss provisions. Nonetheless, declines in residential property prices did have an impact on bank loan performance in the UK, because of the practice of securing small business loans on residential property. A large proportion of UK bank loan losses in 1992–4 were on small business related lending.[14] The extent of these losses was greatly increased by the sharp decline in residential house prices in the south-east of the country.[15]

This mechanism – the experience of high and uncertain inflation and the resulting instability of residential and commercial property prices – thus seems central in explaining the level of bank losses experienced in the UK during the early 1990s. An implication is that now that control over UK inflation has been much more firmly established than in the past and has been made the explicit target of the Bank of England, property prices and UK bank earnings are likely to be more stable than in recent years.[16]

Risk taking

High and variable rates of inflation, and new entry, seem to go a long way towards explaining the greater variability of UK banking profits, but several other factors may have had an impact. One further possible cause of poor bank performance is a major failure of risk management, especially in relation to a relatively new area of business. This was most notably the case in relation to UK bank losses on LDC lending, which was originally extended during the 1970s.

Repayment difficulties on these loans emerged in 1982, and provisions for loan losses were eventually made in 1987 and 1989. A major cause of these losses was a failure adequately to assess the risks on this lending. Subsequently UK banks have been much more cautious about lending to emerging markets.

In the past, competition of business generally, not just in the property sector, may have been lower in Germany than in the UK. State-owned and cooperative institutions are much more important in the German banking market. The savings banks, the Landesbanken and a large proportion of specialised lending institutions are state-owned. They account for over 40 per cent of German banking assets, and since the German cooperative sector accounts for a further 14 per cent of banking assets (see Table 2.4), less than half of bank assets are held by private institutions (the commercial, regional, and mortgage banks).

Private sector firms are likely to be reluctant to enter a market dominated by state-owned enterprises, which may have access to capital raised by exploiting a sovereign risk rating, and certainly an owner with a wider range of sources of funds than do private sector firms.

Summary and conclusions

In this paper we have compared the UK and German banking systems with a view to understanding why banking performance has differed between the two countries. In particular we have sought to investigate those features that have reduced the level and volatility of bank profits in Germany relative to those of the UK.

Cross-country comparisons indicate that most episodes of large scale, or systemic, banking sector problems have been associated with preceding periods of financial liberalisation, loose monetary policy, and unsustainable rises in property prices.

The contrast between the UK and Germany is illuminating because at lease one of these pre-conditions, a full liberalisation of interest rates setting and removal of most institutional barriers restricting competition between different banking markets, has been present in both countries. However, there have been substantial differences between the two countries both in the structure of their banking systems and, at least until recently, in the conduct of their monetary policy.

Although the two banking systems are very different, the risk of bank losses leading to a wider financial crisis has been low in both the UK and Germany. UK banks have had sufficient profits to absorb even their worst experience of loan losses in the early 1990s, and there seems (even after making allowance for the practice of maintaining hidden reserves) to have been less variability of profits in Germany than the UK.

We observed a strong correlation between credit and asset prices, especially in the UK and particularly since the early 1980s. The level and growth rates of both the credit/GDP ratio and real asset prices have been more volatile in the UK than in Germany, with the UK exhibiting particularly marked falls in property prices. Property prices, especially commercial property prices, played a major role in triggering the bank losses that were experienced in the UK in the early 1970s and again in the early 1990s.

Why did these differences in rates of growth of bank credit and in the volatility of commercial property prices occur?

First and most importantly has been the tight control over inflation exerted by Germany monetary policy. Higher and much more variable past rates of inflation seem to have been the main reason for past fluctuations in UK property markets and the more variable growth of total bank credit.

Also important have been structural differences between UK and German banking markets, especially the fact that state-owned and cooperative banks (which pursued very conservative policies throughout most of the period covered by this paper) account for over half of German banking assets, and that a substantial part of property lending is, in effect, off balance-sheet in Germany.

What lessons can be drawn for the future? In the UK an important lesson has been learned and acted on. In the 1990s there was a shift to a more disciplined monetary policy stance than in the previous two decades. Monetary discipline and the credibility of monetary policy have been further reinforced by the operational independence given to the Bank of England.

The UK has now succeeded in establishing a relatively low and stable rate of inflation. Our analysis suggests that if this performance is maintained, the risks of bank losses are considerably less than in the past. In any event, the UK banking sector continues to earn high levels of profits which would serve as a substantial cushion against any future loan losses.

There is some evidence in recent years that competition is increasing in the German domestic banking sector, while German banks have become more aggressive in lending abroad. Lending by German banks to emerging markets has grown much faster than that by UK (or Japanese and US) banks since the early 1990s. This increase in risk taking has involved an increase in bad loans, particularly those arising from the recent east Asian and Russian crises.

With further increases in competition likely, the question that the German banking system faces is whether a higher average level of profits will adequately compensate for an expected increase in profit variability.

But all that said, it is clear that price stability – the avoidance of inflation and deflation – is the foundation of a stable banking system. The continuation of such a benign climate in Britain and in Germany should be a major safeguard against banking sector problems in both countries.

Annex 2.1: summary of financial liberalisation and deregulation

United Kingdom

1971	Competition and credit control: abolition of direct credit controls applying to banks. The interest rate cartel of London clearing banks and Scottish banks dismantled at official request (Recommended Interest Rate System of building societies continued). However, lending guidance continued to be practised through the 1970s and into the early 1980s, and was not formally withdrawn until January 1987.
1973–80	Restrictions on interest-bearing eligible liabilities of banks working as indirect restrictions on credit expansion ('corset'): first introduced in December 1973, suspended in February 1975, reintroduced in November 1976, suspended in August 1977, reintroduced in June 1978 and finally abolished in June 1980.
1976–87	The Trustee Savings Bank Act starts the reorganisation of the trustee savings banks movement (which culminates in the 1987 privatisation of the Trustee Savings Bank in 1987 and thus in the institution's full integration with the banking sector).
1979	Abolition of exchange controls in October 1979.
Early 1980s	Cash management services introduced. TAM sharing arrangements among groups of banks. Interest-bearing current accounts introduced (often as part of financial services packages).
1982	Acquisition by a large clearing bank of a nation-wide chain of estate agents.
1983	Nationwide announcement that the clearing banks intend to develop a national system for Electronic Fund Transfer at the Point of Sale.
1983–4	As part of moves towards dual capacity on the Stock Exchange (ie securities firms being allowed to act as

	both brokers and jobbers), large banks form shareholding links with Stock Exchange firms.
1984	Recommended Interest Rate System of building societies discontinued.
1986	Stock exchange 'Big Bang' abolishes fixed minimum commissions and single capacity trading.
Jan 1987	The 1986 Building Society Act came into effect, widening the scope for commercial lending, allowing societies to provide other services relating to house purchase and finance, and allowing societies (from 1988) to operate in the EEC. The Act also made provision for societies to convert from mutual to corporate status (also from 1988), and created the Building Societies Commission to supervise the societies.
1989	Abbey National Building Society converts into a bank.
1995	Cheltenham and Gloucester acquired by Lloyds; Lloyds and TSB merge.
1996	National and Provincial Building Society acquired by Abbey National.
1997	Halifax, Woolwich, Alliance & Leicester and Northern Rock Building Societies convert into banks; Bristol and West acquired by the Bank of Ireland.

Germany

March 1965	Official agreement on bank lending and deposit rates replaced by Interest Rate Decree ('Zinsabkommen') deregulating interest rates on long-term bank loans (maturities of four years and over) and longer-term deposits (maturities of two years and over).
April 1967	Abolition of Interest Rate Decree, ie full deregulation of bank lending and deposit rates.
Since early 1970s	Introduction of 'Eurocheque' (guaranteed cheque). Strong expansion of lending to the government sector (Federal Government, Federal Railways, Federal Post Office Authorities, Länder) against promissory notes ('Schuldscheindarlehen'). Strong expansion of mortgage lending. Fixed-interest medium-term lending to enterprises. Diversification of savings instruments (saving with premium, savings

plans, savings accounts with bond-market related interest rates etc).

Strong promotion of sale of investment fund certificates and related fund management. Introduction of common credit card (Eurocard) (1977).

Since early 1980s gradual introduction of automated payment facilities (ATMs, EFT methods).

Further development of introduction of the following activities/instruments:

- leasing, factoring, venture capital, cash management programmes, management consultancy business;
- issue of new types of DM bonds for domestic and foreign issuers (zero-coupon bonds, floating rate notes, dual currency bonds, and bonds linked to interest rate and foreign currency swaps on own or customer account (authorised in 1985);
- the outstanding volume of negotiable DM certificates of deposit, though authorised since May 1986, is practically nil due to the incidence of the securities turnover tax.

1989 Amendment to Stock Exchange Act: authorisation of listing of securities in foreign currencies and in electronic stock exchange dealings. Foreign branches permitted as lead manager of DM bond issues.

1993 Creation of Deutsche Börse

1994 Money market funds authorised

Remaining restrictions on commercial bank activities:

- insurance underwriting business (insurance brokerage business is allowed);
- own issues of mortgage bonds and communal bonds (subject to special law);
- building society ('Bausparkassen') business (subject to special law);
- issues of foreign-currency bonds on own account (restrictive authorisation practice of the Bundesbank); however, there are no restrictions for those foreign-currency issues which are offered by a syndicate composed of non-resident banks only.

Annex 2.2: The German Pfandbrief market

German banks conduct much of their property-related lending through the issue of Pfandbrief bonds, matching the maturity and interest rate structure of these assets and liabilities and effectively taking risks off balance sheet.[17] Pfandbrief accounted for some 37 per cent of total bond issue in Germany in December 1996.[18] Of these around one third financed mortgage loans (for owner occupation, residential letting and commercial property) and the remainder public sector loans.

The issue of Pfandbrief is strictly regulated, under legislation originally passed in 1900 (for mortgage bonds of Hypothekenpfandbrief) and in 1927 (for public sector bonds or öffentliche Pfandbrief). Mortgage bond issue is only possible for the 24 mortgage banks restricted to mortgage business alone and to the three mixed mortgage banks (classified as regional commercial banks in the Bundesbank statistics) permitted to engage in universal banking activities. Hypothekenpfandbrief are used extensively to finance commercial as well as residential property (mortgage and regional banks hold about two-fifths of German commercial property loans). While mortgage bonds may be issued only up to 60 per cent of property value, successive legislative amendments since 1968 have given lenders freedom to engage in additional non-Pfandbrief mortgage lending. Total financing packages now typically embody loan to value ratios well in excess of 60 per cent.

Public sector bonds are issued by the publicly-owned Landesbanken, other public law financial institutions such as municipal enterprises, and also by the mortgage banks and mixed mortgage banks. The legal framework allows the use of Pfandbrief to finance the acquisition of EU public sector debt. In practice they are primarily used for the purchase of the debt of the Länder and the communes. For both types of bond, collateralisation is aggregated, ie all the Pfandbrief mortgage assets of a bank act as collateral for its entire mortgage bond issue and all the Pfandbrief public sector assets act as collateral for its entire public sector bond issue. A system of registration is used to monitor this collateral. This collateralisation and the legislative framework provides strong protection to Pfandbrief holders, in the event of an insolvency, and allows the Pfandbrief to be given credit ratings which are often stronger than those of the issuing institutions.

Notes

1. M. Hellwig (1996) 'Financial Innovations and the Incidence of Risk in the Financial System', in F. Bruni, D. E. Fair and R. O'Brien (eds), *Risk Management in Volatile Financial Markets*.

2. C. J. Lindgren, G. Garcia and M. I. Saul (1996) 'Bank Soundness and Macroeconomic Policy', International Monetary Fund.
3. G. Kaminsky, S. Lizondo and C. Reinhart (1998) 'Leading Indicators of Currency Crises', *IMF Staff Papers*, vol. 45, March.
4. In addition, they found two external factors important – an appreciation of the real exchange relative to trend and a decline in the growth of export volumes.
5. These crises have also directed attention to banking supervision, particularly as a means of preventing systemic crises. Because this paper examines only crises that happened, rather than ones which might have but did not, we do not attempt to assess the effectiveness of supervision as a stabiliser.
6. See A. Prati and G. J. Schinasi (1997) 'European Monetary Union and International Capital Markets: Structural Implications and Risks', *IMF Working Paper 97/62.*
7. The higher rate of inflation, and therefore, nominal interest rates in the UK than Germany during the 1970s and 1980s partly explain the difference in income in the two banking systems during this period. The contribution to income and profits of non-interest bearing liabilities increases with the general level of nominal interest rates (the endowment effect).
8. It is also worth noting that there is a substantial tax disincentive to the use of one category of hidden reserves for smoothing reported profits. Some assets are booked at cost of acquisition rather than their current valuation, thus implying a substantial reserve cushion. But those 'undervalued' assets cannot be realised without triggering a capital gains tax liability, at a tax rate of 60 per cent.
9. The Landesbanken obtain most of their finance from savings banks and thus avoid the costs of collecting retail deposits. Their interest margins are narrow because their assets consist mostly of low risk public sector loans, and because the Landesbanken are themselves guaranteed by the Länder. The German mortgage banks operate with low costs, since they raise much of their finance through the issue of Pfandbrief bonds, again avoiding the need to collect retail deposits, and with narrow spreads, since the rules of the Pfandbrief market require high levels of collateral on mortgage lending and transfer remaining risk onto bond holders. The Pfandbrief market is described in Annex 2.2.
10. See A. Prati and G. J. Schinasi (1997), *op. cit.*
11. It is worth noting that interest rate spreads in Germany appear to be counter-cyclical, and that banks' cost of funding declines as the economy slows.
12. Prior to 1986, building societies could lend only on residential property; after 1986 they could hold a proportion of assets secured against commercial property.
13. The lower loan to value and loan to income ratios prevalent in Germany would have made that system less susceptible to this kind of problem had such a cycle occurred there.
14. Barclays Bank acknowledged losses on small business lending of more than £1 million per week during the worst part of the recession in the early 1990s.
15. Residential property prices in the south-east of the UK fell by nearly 40 per cent between 1989 and 1993.

16. The use of Pfandbrief bonds has allowed German mortgage banks to avoid any mismatching of interest rates, such as triggered the US savings and loans crisis in the 1980s. But interest rate risk does not explain the greater variability of UK bank profits. In the UK, mortgage lending is typically conducted at short-term variable rates of interest, so UK mortgage lenders are also protected from any flattening of the yield curve. UK commercial property lending is also either conducted at floating rates of interest or with some other financing arrangement that hedges the lending institution against interest rate risk. Neither system of finance has the exposure to interest rate risk which generated problems on the scale which arose amongst the US Savings and Loans.
17. For a description of the Pfandbrief market we have relied on a briefing paper: 'Banks Ratings Criteria: Criteria for Rating German Pfandbrief', Standard and Poor's Bank Rating Service NY, July 1997.
18. A further 33 per cent of total bond issue were government bonds with the remainder issued by bank and private sector institutions.

3

European Destiny and Macroeconomic Responsibility in the Financial Systems of Germany and the UK: A Balance-Sheet Approach

*Jan Toporowski**

Introduction

European economic integration and the advent of a common European currency raise fundamental questions about the operations of the financial systems that are supposed to support these changes. Prominent among these questions is how banks and financial institutions operating in different ways and with different histories and traditions will deal with increasingly common European business as financial systems merge into one. The conventional wisdom is that competition between financial firms will ensure that those with competitive advantages (for example, British merchant banks with greater capital market expertise) will survive, while those firms which have fewer competitive advantages (for example, perhaps Germany's small co-operative banks) will fail. In other words, that some common marketplace for financial services will sort out the less efficient from the more efficient, and ensure that the former are driven out of busi-

* I wish to acknowledge the financial assistance of the European Institute of South Bank University which enabled me to employ Mr. Aleksander Janiszewski to extract and process data on the financial systems of Italy, Germany and the UK. I am very grateful to him for his efficient and scrupulous research and statistical analysis. I also wish to thank Victoria Chick and Stephen Frowen for helpful information and useful insights at various stages of this research, and Iain Begg for comments on an earlier draft.

ness or are forced to become more competitive (see Chick 2000 for a perceptive discussion of these issues). Implicit in this view is the notion that systemic factors, that is the way in which a financial system supports the intermediary firms in it and is vulnerable to changes in aggregate financial flows, do not influence the business of particular financial firms.

This chapter puts forward a different approach starting with the view that financial systems have to be looked at as a whole. An epistemological reason for such an approach is that such a comprehensive view is the only basis for systematic statistical comparison between different financial systems and between the firms operating as intermediaries in them. It has also been argued recently that the scope and efficiency, or what one recent author has described as the 'functionality' (Studart, 1995), of a financial system and the intermediary firms in it depend on the nature of the claims and liabilities represented in its balance sheet. An earlier study of the effects of financial system evolution and reform on the efficiency of that system was confined to one country (Chick and Toporowski, 1995). The statistical analysis in that study allowed historical comparisons of different stages in the evolution of a particular economy's financial system. But, for the reasons given below, it is unsuitable for comparisons of financial systems in different countries. In order to make such comparisons, it is necessary to overcome fundamental statistical and methodological problems.

This chapter discusses these problems and their consequences, and suggests a way of overcoming them. It then applies the proposed methodology in a study of the recent evolution of the German and British financial systems, the two largest financial systems in the European Union. It concludes by arguing that the integration of those systems in pan-European and global financial arrangements has affected these systems in different ways. The study suggests that monetary union and the resulting common financial system would be stronger for having a smaller share of funds supplied by the foreign sector and a larger share of government finance in it.

The burden of history undoes the clarity of statistics ...

The most general methodological problem in making statistical, or indeed any systematic comparisons between financial systems in diverse countries arises out of the different ways in which the banking and capital markets in these countries have evolved. As is well-known, in the UK commercial banks engage in short-term lending and management of the payments system, and separate investment or merchant banks and brokerage houses organise the capital market; in Germany, a different, universal banking tradition prevails, in which the major banks also organise the capital market, so that the capital market function is subsumed within a more general banking function (for a more historical view of these differences see Hu, 1975; Kindleberger, 1993, chapters 5 and 6; and Toporowski, 1994). Because of these historical differences, broadly similar activities such as the management of deposits and loans and the issue and trading of securities are carried out by *functionally different* institutions in the two countries, albeit with some recent convergence as UK banks have set up capital market operations and German banks have bought into London merchant banks.

Any statistical comparison between the two countries, and arguably any systematic comparison between countries which have different financial traditions and conventions, therefore meets two problems. First of all, the categories into which firms and institutions may be divided for the sake of aggregation will not be exactly the same in the two countries. For example, for statistical purposes, the main agency for gathering financial statistics in the UK, the Bank of England, defines the banking system as essentially the commercial banks which it regulates. This excludes the investment banking and brokerage firms which operate the stockmarket in London, as well as the mutual building societies which are the British equivalent of savings banks. Apart from the Scottish and Northern Irish Clearing Banks, there is no regional banking, or any system of state-owned regional banks.

By contrast, because of Germany's universal banking tradition and the system of regulation by a nominally independent agency alongside the German central bank the Bundesbank, statistics for the German banking system cover a much wider span of financial activity, which is divided up into different sub-categories that include regional banks and savings banks. It may be possible, by adding and subtracting sub-categories, to get a category of data covering, say, banks, which might be broadly comparable between the two countries. However, this would be a false comparability as long as the firms and institutions within the category were engaged to a significant extent in different activities: Because firms call themselves banks does not mean that they perform the same banking functions.

The taxonomic problems of banking statistics are relatively obvious and familiar to researchers who have attempted cross-border comparisons. Less obvious, but no less important, are the problems of comparing financial *parameters* between different countries. Because of the increase in international financial flows since the 1970s, tables of, say, interest rates or exchange rates for different currencies are now staple elements of financial analysis. Yet it follows that if particular markets have different functions in different countries, as argued above, then the prices in those markets are not statistically comparable.

For example, in the UK the inter-bank market plays a central role in this country's financial system and, in the market for US dollars, the London Inter-bank Offered Rate, and to a much lesser extent, the London Inter-bank Bid Rate, act as benchmarks for international loan agreements. The interest rates in this market are therefore hardly comparable with the rates in the German inter-bank market, which plays a relatively peripheral role in the German financial system. These differences may not matter when these interest rates operate within one market, for example the market for cross-border deposits known as the Euro-currency market. But when these parameters belong to markets which are relatively distinct from each other, such as domestic banking and capital markets, international comparisons risk an implicit presumption of perfect capital or financial markets, thereby assuming away precisely those differences which are being investigated.

There has therefore been a tendency to avoid such comparisons, concentrating on thematic comparisons (for example Gardener and Molyneux, 1990), or functional comparisons of, for example, regulation of particular functions (for example Goodhart, 1988; Kregel 1992). The classic 'comparative' study of European banking avoided any comparison at all (Sayers, 1962). However, many reports, even by international agencies which ought (given the subject of their expertise) to know better, merely ignore these problems of institutional comparability (for example, International Monetary Fund, 1996).

...but clarity of conceptualization can overcome historical peculiarities

On an aggregate scale these difficulties can be substantially overcome if the financial system is viewed as a process of financial intermediation in the course of which claims (assets) and liabilities are created. This is in line with the approach taken by Minsky at its most general (Minsky, 1976, 1978 and 1986). According to Minsky, the financial system at any one time consists of the claims (financial assets) and liabilities of economic units. Over time such claims and liabilities are created and realized as economic units experiencing a financial deficit issue future payment liabilities, or realize claims on other units, while economic units whose income exceeds their expenditure (surplus units) advance claims for future payment (that is, liabilities) to deficit units. In a modern market economy, such transactions are conducted through financial intermediaries, so that the claims and liabilities of *all* economic units correspond to the liabilities and claims respectively of *all* the financial intermediaries. While the classification of those financial intermediaries may vary according to national tradition and convention, the classification of economic units into economic sectors has for some time been standard in flow-of-funds accounts for the advanced market economies published by the Organization for Economic Cooperation and Development in Paris (OECD).

The book value of the financial system's balance sheet, at point of time *t*, may be defined as:

$$ {}_0f^tL \equiv {}_{0.}f^tA \qquad (3.1)$$

where *L* are the net liabilities of the financial system issued to the non-financial sectors (that is, non-financial economic units' surpluses placed with the financial system minus those units' withdrawals); and *A* are the assets or net advances of the financial system (that is, funds advanced to non-financial units, minus repayments).

Supposing that records of advances and liabilities issued commenced at point of time *m*, an unknown *initial* balance sheet can be defined as:

$$ {}_0f^mL \equiv {}_{0.}f^mA \qquad (3.2)$$

such that

$$ {}_0f^mL + {}_mf^tL \equiv \int {}_0f^mA + {}_mf^tA $$

That is, the unknown initial balance sheet plus the sum of recorded net liabilities and net assets issued by the financial system is identically equal to the balance sheet defined in (3.1) above.

The epistemological problem is now reduced to determining the degree to which the *known* balance sheet,

$$ {}_mf^tL \equiv \int {}_mf^tA \qquad (3.3),$$

approximates to the actual balance sheet defined in (3.1) above; in other words, how small is the initial balance sheet relative to the actual balance sheet.

An obvious factor in this is the relative duration of recorded financial intermediation in the total history of financial intermediation. As t approaches infinity, the initial balance sheet will approach zero, and the respective sums of recorded net financial advances and liabilities issued (3.3) will approach the actual balance sheet of the financial system. While waiting until the end of time to sum up all the financial flows recorded by then will give the closest approximation to the balance sheet of the financial system, it is, in the meantime, also useful to know that summing longer consistent time series of financial flows will give closer likely approximations than summing shorter consistent time series. There remains a tendency to underestimate the actual balance sheet by the amount of the initial balance sheet, but this underestimation may be reduced by other factors as will be discussed later.

Therefore, if we are solely concerned with obtaining the most reliable estimate of the balance sheet of the financial system, we can simply add the longest consistent series of financial flows. However, this is not very satisfactory if we wish to obtain a time series of balance sheets, to see how this evolves over time, to verify credit cycles, the effects of deregulation and so on. It could be argued that, if summing the longest consistent time series of financial flows gives the most reliable estimator of the balance sheet, then deducting from that the most recent period's financial flows will give the most reliable indicator of the balance sheet at the end of the previous period; deducting from that the next previous period's financial flows will give the most reliable indicator of the balance sheet at the end of the next previous period, and so on back to m, the point of time when records began.

There are two problems with this reasoning. The conceptual problem is that as we approach m, the share of the unknown initial balance sheet in the actual balance sheet of the financial system gets larger, so that our estimates (from sums of recorded financial flows) for earlier years become increasingly biased downwards. A more practical problem affects the more recent financial flows that are deducted from the sums of all recorded financial flows to get estimates of the balance sheet in recent periods. Flow-of-funds accounts are drawn up from data supplied by a number of different financial sources, and are adjusted to ensure consistency with the national income accounts and the capital account of the balance of payments. Since national income and balance of payments statistics themselves are frequently revised, sometimes up to ten years after initial publication in the case of the balance of payments data, the most recent financial flow estimates are also the least reliable.

The second problem cannot be overcome. Perhaps the only way of overcoming it, by excluding the more recent years, is a less than full-information solution. In the case of the unknown initial balance sheet that looms as earlier years are estimated by summing fewer recorded financial flows, another economic trend comes to our assistance. General price inflation depreciates the value of financial assets and liabilities issued in the past relative to more recently issued claims and liabilities. The higher is the rate of general price inflation, the greater will be the share of recently issued financial contracts in the balance sheet of the financial system.

Innovation and inflation in the financial system

To this must be added two important considerations. First of all, it is unlikely that any individual financial firm will have a balance sheet whose structure approximates, on a smaller scale, to the balance sheet of the financial system as a whole. The balance sheets of particular financial institutions are likely to reflect regional and business peculiarities and traditions. In a universal banking system it is possible that particular institutions will have an approximately average structure to their balance sheets because the range of their business is broadly similar. However, the balance sheets of particular institutions will vary in structure more and more as specialization proceeds.

Specialization is nowadays associated with financial innovation, especially since central banks and other financial authorities have tended to require institutions undertaking new financial activities to do so in separately capitalized subsidiaries, so that unanticipated losses do not affect more mainstream business. In principle it should be possible to classify the balance sheets of financial firms according to the novelty of the claims and liabilities in them. In a growing economy, and especially with financial inflation, one may expect innovative activities to increase more rapidly than more traditional activities. If the more-innovative firms take proportionately more business as financial inflation proceeds, one would expect less-innovative firms to be left with older claims and liabilities depreciating more rapidly.

A second consideration affecting the representative nature of the balance sheet of the financial system as a whole concerns the distribution of the maturity of particular claims and liabilities. Again, in a truly universal banking system in which the assets and liabilities in individual institutions' balance sheets have a maturity that is more or less average for that class of financial instrument, one would expect those balance sheets to be more or less similar in structure and composition to the balance sheet of the financial system as a whole. However, once financial institutions specialize in activities of different maturity, as in the UK's capital market system, particular institutions will be affected differently by general financial inflation. In a process of financial inflation one would expect banks engaged in short-term lending and borrowing to renew their balance sheets as existing claims and liabilities mature, higher money value deposits are taken in and the nominal value of new loans increases with the general inflation. However, the rate at which pension funds and insurance companies, which engage in more long-term capital activities, may renew their balance sheets depends on the rate at which existing claims and liabilities are replaced by new assets and liabilities with a higher nominal value. In a perfect capital market (which means, among other things, no capital market transaction costs) firms may well issue additional capital stock as prices rise. With significant capital market transaction costs, rising product prices would encourage firms to greater reliance on internal finance, allowing their capital market liabilities to depreciate with inflation. In these circumstances, banks would end up with a disproportionately higher share of new claims and liabilities, and longer-term capital market institutions would have a disproportionate share of old and depreciating claims and liabilities.

It is important to bear in mind this differential effect of inflation upon banking and capital market institutions in comparing the financial systems of Germany and the United Kingdom. There are two reasons for this. First of all, the two economies have different histories of inflation. Germany was, until 1990, a low-inflation economy; whilst, with the exception of the mid-1980s and the mid-1990s, the UK has experienced considerably more inflation. Secondly, the financial institutions of the two countries have different degrees of specialization in financial instruments of different maturity. The UK has the most advanced institutional distinction between long-term capital markets, and short-term banking activities. Germany still has its stockmarkets operating for industrial and commercial companies through the mediation of its larger banks, with government stock constituting the bulk of the assets of German pension and insurance funds.

Therefore, a tentative conclusion is that the balance sheet of the financial system as a whole is unlikely to be very representative of individual financial institutions, except perhaps in Germany with its low degree of specialization, relatively slow rate of financial innovation and, until recently, low rates of inflation. This then leads to a fundamental methodological issue of what really is the economic significance of balance-sheet data for a country's financial system as a whole. Exactly the same question was raised by Hayek about monetary theory, citing the same objection to aggregate data as that put above, namely that if financial and economic trends affect particular markets and firms in different ways, then our aggregates are unrepresentative and cannot reveal the economic processes that may be under way (Hayek, 1935, pp. 3–5).

It is not possible to answer this question conclusively without dealing with many more questions about institutions, the ways in which they operate, and the ways in which they evolve. One factor is the fungibility of funds between institutions and markets. This lies at the heart of the intermediation function in a financial system. Hence, the access of financial firms to credit and liquidity in the economy, either directly or through an intermediary, may be said to make them functionally dependent on the aggregate flows of funds. It can also be observed, alongside Minsky, that in using such access to credit and liquidity particular financial institutions and agents enter into contractual obligations which constitute claims on their future incomes and credit. The functioning of the financial system depends on an ordered realization and renewal of these claims and liabilities (Minsky, 1978). The remainder of this chapter is devoted to an examination of how such obligations have been issued in Germany, and the UK.

Recent financial histories compared

The table below shows the credit raised and the funds supplied in Germany and the United Kingdom by the five economic sectors, respectively the government, non-financial enterprises, households, the overseas sector and financial institutions. In respect of funds supplied, the financial sector is subdivided into monetary institutions (that is, banks) and other financial institutions (essentially non-bank financial institutions). The figures given for each sector are percentages of the total funds raised or supplied in the economy. This allows a comparison of financial flows in different currencies in the two countries.

The flows are summed over five years showing, for example, in the case of the columns under 1970–74, the portfolio of assets of the financial systems in the two countries that were acquired during those five years, represented by the credit funds raised during this period against the liabilities of the two financial systems issued during the five-year period, represented by net funds supplied.

Table 3.1 Summary table of flows, Germany and UK (by sector, %)

	1970–74		*1975–79*		*1980–84*		*1985–89*		*1990–94*	
	Germany	*UK*	*Germany*	*UK*	*Germany*	*UK*	*Germany*	*UK*	*Germany*	*UK*
I *Credit funds raised by*:										
General government	11.7	15.8	21.4	25.6	20.5	13.1	14.6	2.9	14.3	10.6
Non-financial enterprises	50.4	23.1	21.2	19.2	23.2	14.9	26.3	22.5	25.7	16.2
Households	7.5	15.5	24.6	18.4	22.1	22.6	13.7	21.5	14.5	13.7
Rest of the world	6.6	37.0	12.7	22.8	10.7	40.4	30.4	32.1	19.9	31.9
Financial institutions	23.8	8.6	20.1	14.1	23.5	9.1	15.1	21.1	25.5	27.7
II *Net funds supplied directly by*:										
General government	4.2	11.2	2.6	9.1	2.6	8.4	2.5	0.5	2.4	–3.0
Non-financial enterprises	4.6	5.4	7.8	8.8	9.9	8.6	9.2	9.9	14.4	3.8
Households	14.1	–4.0	7.4	–3.7	9.2	–1.0	11.8	–4.5	8.7	–0.9
Rest of the world	6.0	7.7	3.6	15.5	12.3	2.8	14.3	16.7	14.5	28.6
Monetary institutions	61.5	58.3	72.0	33.2	57.1	60.5	54.6	59.3	55.0	41.7
Other financial institutions	9.6	21.4	6.6	37.1	9.0	20.6	7.6	18.0	4.9	29.7
III *All sectors*	100.0	100.0	100.0	100.0	100.0	100.0	100.0	100.0	100.0	100.0
(DM bn£m)	(708.71)	(10450)	(1090.96)	(169926)	(1489.91)	(384723)	(1526.83)	(964804)	(3951.12)	(980355)
Growth in nominal GDP	45.8	62.8	35.7	84.7	19.7	39.7	22.6	44.4	36.9	21.3

Source: Author's calculations from Organisation for Economic Co-operation and Development, *Financial Accounts of OECD Countries*, various issues.

The table shows the percentage distribution among economic sectors of these assets and liabilities, thereby avoiding the problems of comparisons being affected by different currencies and different rates of inflation in the two countries. The total of the funds supplied and raised in the two countries in their respective currencies is shown at the bottom of each country's table, followed by the percentage nominal growth of GDP during the five years. The original data were taken from OECD flow-of-funds statistics and hence use a standard classification of sectors.

Five-year periods were chosen in order to average-out relatively unstable annual flows of funds, which in this analysis constitute marginal changes to the actual balance sheet of a financial system, while revealing changes occurring over the long period since 1970. Volatile annual flows of funds suggest that the results of the study may be overly sensitive to the particular five-year period chosen as representative of a half-decade. For example, a series of observations for 1969–73, 1974–78, 1979–83, 1984–89, 1990–93 may differ significantly from the observations shown for 1970–74, 1975–79, 1980–84, 1985–89 and 1990–94. However, a parallel study taking different five-year periods gave similar results (Toporowski, 1997).

During the first five-year period, 1970–74, West Germany stands out for the very high proportion, over 50 per cent, of funds advanced being issued to non-financial enterprises. In the UK, the sector with the highest share of funds raised was the overseas sector (the 'rest of the world'), with 37 per cent of funds raised. In both countries, more than half of the funds supplied were through the banking system: in Germany its share of funds supplied was 61.5 per cent; in the UK it was 58.3 per cent. In Germany, households were the next largest suppliers of funds, advancing 16.4 per cent of the total. In the UK, 'other financial institutions', that is non-bank financial intermediaries, were the next largest suppliers of funds, advancing 21.4 per cent of funds.

The next five-year period, 1975–79, was notable for the effect of oil price rises on trade balances and the fiscal position of governments in the two countries. In both of them, the share of funds raised by the government rose, to a quarter (25.6 per cent) of all funds raised in the UK, and 21.4 per cent in Germany. The share of funds raised by non-financial enterprises fell significantly in this period in Germany, from 50.4 per cent in the preceding five-year period, to 21.2 per cent in 1975–79. In the UK the share of credit funds raised by the overseas sector fell during this period to 22.8 per cent.

In Germany, the funds supplied by the banking system rose to nearly three-quarters (72.0 per cent) of all funds supplied. In contrast to this, the share of funds supplied by the banking system fell from 58.3 per cent between 1970 and 1974 to just under a third (33.2 per cent) between 1975–79 in the UK, which experienced at this time its secondary banking crisis. As a result, the share of funds supplied by non-bank financial institutions rose from 21.4 per cent in 1970–74, to 37.1 per cent in 1975–79. The increasing role of the London markets in the intermediation of the oil exporting countries' trade surpluses is reflected in the doubling of the share of funds supplied by the overseas sector, from 7.7 per cent in 1970–74, to 15.5 per cent in 1974–78. The UK also recorded a high increase in nominal GDP, which rose by 84.7 per cent over the period. Funds supplied largely by banks, non-bank financial institutions and the overseas sector were used to finance government, corporate and overseas-sector deficits.

In 1980–84, the foreign sector emerges as the main raiser of funds in the UK, taking 40.4 per cent of funds raised. In Germany, the government and non-financial enterprises took much larger shares of funds raised than did their counterparts in the UK. However, in both countries just over 22 per cent of funds were raised by the household sector. Again monetary institutions supplied most of the funds, but Germany overtook Britain in the share of funds supplied by the foreign sector. This rose to 12.3 per cent in Germany and fell in the UK to 2.3 per cent.

In the five-year period that followed, 1985–89, Germany with its strong foreign trade performance established an even stronger presence in international financial markets. The foreign sector took 30.4 per cent of funds raised in Germany during this period. However, Britain was even more orientated towards supplying funds overseas, with 32.1 per cent of funds raised in the UK financing the overseas sector. The role of the foreign sector as a source of finance increased in both countries. In Germany this sector supplied 14.3 per cent of funds in this period, and in Britain, it supplied 16.7 per cent of funds. The growth of nominal GDP rose during this five-year period almost twice as much in the UK as it did in Germany.

The most recent five-year period under examination, 1990–94, was marked by a reversal of fortunes in the two countries. Nominal GDP rose by only 21.3 per cent in the UK while Germany in its post-unification boom had a rise in its nominal GDP of 36.9 per cent. The German financial system also reverted to more domestic business as the foreign trade balance moved into deficit, with the share of the rest of the world in funds raised falling to 19.9 per cent. In the UK this share remained over three-fifths at 31.9 per cent. Monetary institutions advanced more than half of their funds in Germany. In Britain, for the first time since the secondary bank crisis of the 1970s, the share of banks in funds advanced fell to less than half, or 41.7 per cent during the five years.

Certain long-term trends emerge from this data. The essential difference between the German universal banking tradition and the British capital market tradition is apparent in the low share of net funds supplied by other (that is, non-bank) financial institutions in Germany, compared to the UK. Although there has been some development of the capital market in Germany since the 1970s, it has evidently been largely through the banking system, because the share of net funds supplied by other financial institutions in that country virtually halved between the first five-year period and the last, declining from 9.6 per cent in 1970–74 to 4.9 per cent in 1990–94. Another trend is the apparently stubborn refusal by British households as a whole to become rentiers: the net amount of funds supplied by the household sector in the UK has been negative in most years since 1969. Evidently, the British inclination to invest in their own homes has been greater than the apparent success of privatisation share issues. A more important trend has been the emergence of the intermediation in foreign funds as a significant activity in the financial system in Germany. In the final period, almost a fifth of all funds supplied in Germany were for its foreign sector. However, this international financial activity was still less in Germany than it was in the UK, both in terms of funds raised and funds supplied.

Domestic and foreign exchange risks in financial systems

The accommodation of the financial deficits of particular sectors represents the acquisition of assets by the financial system. The risks associated with those assets are largely specific to the sector issuing those assets as liabilities of the economic units in the sector. Funds advanced to non-financial enterprises may be imperilled by adverse business conditions affecting the ability of industrial and commercial companies to service their liabilities to the financial system. Money borrowed by households may be put at risk by a fall in collateral values (for example the collapse of the housing market in the UK during the 1990s). Funds advanced to the foreign sector may be somewhat more secure because only larger companies and governments can raise funds abroad. But such advances may also be put at risk by changes in conditions of trade and, since 1969, fluctuations in exchange rates.

Whereas the servicing and repayment of funds supplied to other (non-financial) sectors is dependent on the income, credit and liquidity of the economic unit raising the funds, advances to governments are not so constrained. Governments themselves decide what constitutes legal tender and can issue it, while in countries with modern financial systems, governments can always honour claims against them with the issue of new claims. Funds advanced to other financial intermediaries are also claims on their assets. If those assets are insufficiently liquid then those advances to financial intermediaries would also have to be honoured by realizing claims against the government. In general, the liquidity of a financial intermediary, and the security of the financial system as a whole, depends on having claims against the government that are sufficient to service their liabilities when payments on assets in other non-financial sectors are insufficient. Lender of last resort facilities operating through the banking system offer the financial system an important way of securing liquidity by realizing claims against the government.

However, as the 1980s sovereign debt crisis revealed, this advantage may only be useful if the new claims can be used to service the liabilities of the intermediaries. In the case of foreign intermediaries, whose liabilities have to be serviced in foreign currency, the ability of new claims issued by the government to service those liabilities depends on the availability of foreign currency and its rate of conversion into the legal tender issued by the government.

With this in mind, Table 3.1 can be re-examined to see how the assets and liabilities of the financial systems in Germany and the United Kingdom have become less secure since the end of the 1960s. In Germany, the government's share of assets of the financial system has risen from 11.7 per cent of assets issued between 1970–74, to 14.3 per cent of assets issued between 1990–94. However, there has also been a rise in the net funds supplied by the overseas sector, from 6.6 per cent of funds supplied between 1969–73, to 14.5 per cent in 1990–1994. This rise in the liabilities to the foreign sector is balanced by a rise in the foreign assets of the German financial system, whose acquisition peaked in the 1985–89 five-year period at 30.4 per cent of total financial assets acquired in Germany. While the German currency remains convertible at a good rate against the US dollar (the predominant currency in international financial markets), the financial system's liabilities to the foreign sector should be easily serviced with the financial system's claims against the German government.

In the UK, by contrast, there has been a decline in the financial system's acquisition of claims against the government, from 15.8 per cent of financial assets acquired in 1970–74, and 25.6 per cent of assets acquired in 1975–79, to 13.1 per cent of financial assets acquired in 1980–84, 2.9 per cent in 1985–89, and 10.6 per cent of assets acquired in 1990–94. Financial assets held abroad have fluctuated at around a third of total assets acquired without any distinct trend in this proportion. However, there seems to be a distinctly upward trend in the liabilities of the UK's financial system to the foreign sector. These rose from only 7.7 per cent of financial liabilities acquired in 1970–74, 15.6 per cent of 1975–79 liabilities, and 2.8 per cent of 1980–84 liabilities, to 16.7 per cent of financial liabilities acquired in 1985–89, and 28.6 per cent of 1990–94 liabilities. This increase in foreign liabilities combined with a decrease in the share of claims against government in the overall balance sheet of the financial system represents an increased possibility that the government assets of the financial system may be insufficient to balance lower than expected returns on non-government assets.

Conclusion: currency risk and monetary union

The greater share of internationally mediated funds in the funds supplied in both countries represents significant additional risks for their respective financial systems. This is because the ability of claims against the government of each country to satisfy the liquidity requirements of foreign suppliers of funds depends on those suppliers' evaluation of the currency risk associated with foreign assets. In this respect, the widely perceived strength of the German currency and the relatively small proportion of its funds supplied from abroad makes its financial system still the stronger of the two. In Britain, where the currency's exchange value has been more volatile, the financial system is somewhat weaker. These weaknesses are exacerbated by the declining share of claims against the government among the total assets of the financial system.

With greater and lesser enthusiasm, both countries are now in the forefront of preparations for a common European currency. When this is instituted, a large proportion of the foreign funds supplied to their respective financial systems will turn out to come from within the same currency area, although this proportion is likely to be smaller in the more global financial markets of London. The currency risk associated with claims against the government will no longer be a factor affecting the evaluation of suppliers of funds from within the currency area.

However, the ability of governments to issue obligations is severely circumscribed under the common currency regulations, in accordance with the principles underlying the Maastricht conditions for monetary union. This may affect the ability of the enlarged financial system of the whole area to obtain safe, that is government-backed, assets. Moreover, given the currency risks associated with foreign sector funding, the exclusion of the UK, the main market for international funds in Europe, may paradoxically strengthen the financial system of the European currency area.

References

Becker, J. (1998) 'Banking Supervision: Who is Doing What?', in S. F. Frowen and R. Pringle (eds), *Inside the Bundesbank* (London: Macmillan; New York: St Martin's Press), pp. 5–57)

Chick, V. and Toporowski, J. (1995) 'Evolution and Sudden Transition in Banking: The Polish Case Considered', *Research Papers in International Business,* no. 29, Summer.

Chick, V. (2000) 'Big Banks, small Business and the Regions in Bankers' Europe', in J. Toporowski (ed.), *Political Economy and The New Capitalism: Essays in honour of Sam Aaronovitch* (London: Routledge).

Frowen, S. F. (ed.) (1997) *Hayek: Economist and Social Philsopher: A Critical Retrospect* (London: Macmillan; New York: St Martin's Press).

Frowen, S. F. and Karakitsos, E. (1997) 'An Evaluation of Inflation Targeting in Germany and the UK', *Kredit und Kapital,* vol. 30,no. 4, pp. 501–32.

Gardener, E. P. M and Molyneux, P. (1990) *Changes in Western European Banking* (London: Unwin Hyman).

Goodhart, C. (1988) *The Evolution of Central Bank* (Cambridge, Mass.: MIT Press).

Hayek, F. A. von (1935) *Prices and Production.* (New York: Augustus M. Kelly).

Hu, Yao-Su (1975) *National Attitudes and the Financing of Industry* (London: Political and Economic Planning), vol. XLI, broadsheet no. 559, December.

International Monetary Fund (1996) 'Banking Systems and Loan Markets', in *International Capital Market* (Washington D.C.: IMF).

Kindleberger, C. P. (1993) *A Financial History of Western Europe.* (Oxford: Oxford University Press).

Klausinger, H. (1997) 'From Neutral Money to Competing Currencies: Hayek on Monetary Policy', in S. F. Frowen (ed.), *Hayek: Economist and Social Philosopher: A Critical Retrospect* (London: Macmillan; New York: St Martin's Press), pp. 195–214.

Kregel, J. A. (1992) 'Universal Banking, US Banking Reform and Financial Competition in the EEC', *Banca Nazionale del Lavoro Quarterly Review,* no. 182, September.

Minsky, H. P. (1976) *John Maynard Keynes* (London: Macmillan).

Minsky, H. P. (1978) 'The Financial Instability Hypothesis: A Re-statement', *Thames Papers in Political Economy* (London: University of Greenwich), Autumn.

Minsky, H. P. (1986) *Stabilizing an Unstable Economy* (New Haven: Yale University Press).

Organization for Economic Co-operation and Development, *Financial Accounts of OECD Countries*, various issues (Paris: OECD).

Sayers, R. S. (1962) *Banking in Western Europe* (Oxford: Clarendon Press).

Studart, R. (1995) *Investment Finance and Economic Development* London: Routledge.

Toporowski, J. (1993) *The Economics of Financial Markets and the 1987 Crash* (Aldershot: Edward Elgar).

Toporowski, J. (1994) 'Banking and Financial Institutions', in P. Arestis and M.C. Sawyer (eds), *The Elgar Companion to Radical Political Economy* (Aldershot: Edward Elgar).

Toporowski, J. (1997) 'Comparing Financial Systems in Italy, Germany and the UK: A New Approach', typescript (available from author).

Comments on 'European Destiny and Macroeconomic Responsibility in the Financial Systems of Germany and the UK: A Balance Sheet Approach', by Jan Toporowski

Andrew Tylecote

Is there a cause for concern over the stability of the UK financial system?

I see in Toporowski's paper a contemporary application of an insight of Minsky's: that it is highly beneficial for a financial system to be, so to speak, anchored by large quantities of government debt, mainly because this is, at least in a stable western state, the very safest kind. In the 1920s and 1930s this helped to stabilise the British financial system by comparison with that of the USA; in the 1950s and 1960s it stabilised both. From this arises something of a paradox: financial stability demands large amounts of government *debt*. However it is generally accepted that the general stability of the economy is not at all enhanced by a large government *deficit*. Yet it is only through deficits that we create debt. So long as the deficits are in the past, and the debt is in the present, perhaps we need not worry: whether due to war, or to Reaganite cold war, or for whatever other reason the debts have been accumulated. Surely they are large enough to serve as our financial systems' anchor for many years ahead?

In fact I accept Toporowski's conclusion that there is reason for concern, and I think the concern may be broadened from the British case. It seems to me that the root of the problem is in the old joke that banks only want to lend to those who don't need to borrow. To put it another way, there are three categories of agent in any financial system, those who do not wish to increase their liabilities, those who do and can safely be allowed to do so, and those who do but cannot safely be allowed to do so. The joke refers to banks' difficulty in finding enough in the second category to provide them with safe and profitable business, and in identifying and avoiding those in the third category. There are always two dangers: that agents in the second category will migrate to the first (because their cash flow becomes positive) or that they will migrate to the third (because their debts become excessive or their investments too risky). In the Japanese 'bubble period' of the middle to late 1980s, the first danger materialised first: large Japanese manufacturing firms, traditionally the mainstay of the system as borrowers, found their cash flow positive and steadily ran down their bank borrowing (and total debts). This helped to make loans too easily available to borrowers who were already in the third category, or who were encouraged by the situation to migrate into it. In Britain over the same period large manufacturing firms were under pressure from shareholders to increase their dividends faster than their profits, and for that and for tax reasons found it convenient to *increase* their debts. Though this may have had undesirable effects on the 'real' economy, it presumably helped to stabilise the financial system, since most of these firms belonged firmly in the second category.

During most of the 1990s, banks and other suppliers of capital throughout the West have been frustrated by the low demand for capital, and low returns, at home, and have accordingly gone looking for customers in 'emerging markets'. As the crises of Mexico in 1994 and East Asia and elsewhere in 1997 have made clear, they looked rather too hard and have ended up with a large fraction of their 'emerging' loans and investments in the third category. From Toporowski's figures it looks as though the UK exposure to 'emerging' debt is likely to be considerably greater than that of Germany. (It is thus the greater fraction of overseas *assets* in the UK financial system which is the more worrying than the greater fraction of overseas *liabilities*.) However, we are seeing a new justification for the old financier's willingness, remarked on by Keynes, to do stupid things as long as everyone else was doing them. Too much (it is judged) is at stake in the 'emerging markets' for the greedy western lenders to be allowed to learn from their mistakes. The Japanese economy and financial system, for example, is too fragile to be exposed to the full force of the Korean competition which would be unleashed if matters were allowed to take their course and the won to find its own level. The IMF must make unprecedented loans in order to avoid that, even if the result is to nurture moral hazard among lenders in future.

The role of government debt and deficits

Let us now return to the question of government debt and deficits. No western government, as a borrower, can be assigned to the third, 'undesirable' category – let alone the UK government, which has not defaulted in 300 years. Thus Minsky's point. And yet financiers are not simply grateful when the state plays a major role in the second category. They worry – whether they should or not, they do – about the consequences of large deficits and increasing debt. They are afraid that the consequences, whether willed or not, are that the government will lighten its burden by causing inflation. Accordingly, they reduce their demand for long-term debt, its price therefore falls, and *ipso facto* long-term interest rates go up. We have seen the reverse process, of increasing confidence and falling interest rates, over the last two years in Italy – as the government attacked the budget deficit – and in Britain, as it handed over monetary policy to the central bank.

Unfortunately, at least in continental Europe, we have reason to fear an uncomfortable conjunction: financiers concerned about excessive government debt in future, while in the present, public sector deficits fall or remain low. This arises from the 'pensions overhang': the governments of France, Germany and Italy, and most other continental European countries, are committed to generous retirement pensions, and these commitments are within the context of pay-as-you-go (PAYG) schemes, within which no assets are accumulated but pensions are paid out of the contributions of those now at work. Given the demographic position, there will be a great increase in the numbers of pensioners over the next 20 years, and a fall in the number of contributors. This represents, for the governments concerned, an invisible debt roughly equivalent in size to their existing, visible, debts. Clearly, little as they like the prospect they will have to take far-reaching actions to reduce this liability, and one of those actions will be to oblige those currently in work to make extra payments – on top of PAYG contributions – to accumulate assets out of which at least some part of their future pensions can be paid. However, this extra saving will represent an extra inflow into financial markets, looking for assets to accumulate – looking for would-be debtors in our 'desirable' second category.

What, then, can be done to expand the supply of desirable liabilities?

First, we cannot simply accept as given the current general aversion to public sector deficits. The financial markets must be educated to understand that there are deficits and deficits: for the public sector as for the private sector, borrowing to invest is one thing, borrowing to consume is another. Equally, however, it is not enough that the public borrowing should be for *any* investment purpose: it must be for one which will yield a reasonable return. Here we may distinguish between private and social return. A public sector issue of securities to build a new harbour, airport or railway line might perhaps be expected to yield a private return – a stream of net revenue from users – equal to the interest cost. In that case financial markets could have no justification for treating the issue any differently from one by a trustworthy private firm. Specifically, they should not mark up long-term interest rates because public sector borrowing for such purposes had risen.

It might be, however, that a large part of the total return to the economy – the social return – took the form of positive externalities, gained by firms and households from whom it was not possible to appropriate them directly. This would be the case for most roads, for example, under current arrangements which do not allow them to be charged for directly according to use. It might also be the case for railway lines to the extent that governments feel obliged to subsidise them for environmental reasons – to attract traffic away from roads.

It may still be justified for governments to borrow money in order to spend it on projects which will yield a social return equal to or above the cost of capital, even when their private return from it is low or zero. They, unlike private borrowers, are in a position to take back, from the private sector, in taxes, what they have given up to it in the form of positive externalities. However, for those marginal projects for which the social return is expected to be only *equal* to the cost of capital, there is a disadvantage: the increased tax take must be equal to the increase in national income. That means that the tax take as a percentage of national income must rise, which for good economic as well as political reasons is to be avoided as far as possible. As far as possible, then, means should be found to make the return a private one to government, by charging directly for use. I have argued (Tylecote, 1997) that this will in future be entirely possible and highly desirable for roads, through electronic road pricing. This will not only improve the environmental and fiscal effects of roads and the traffic on them, but it will remove the need for any subsidy on competing modes of transport. Given the negative externalities arising from all forms of motorised transport (noise, accident and pollution), governments in future will be able to make transport a 'cash cow' rather than a highly subsidised activity requiring finance out of some form of taxation.

There are other investments, currently now a charge on government, for which the private beneficiaries could be charged, and some of them could be charged in the present rather than the future. The most important case in point is higher education. In general, the private return to higher education is substantial, since the degree-holder is thereby at an advantage in competing for the better-paid occupations in the economy. It is arguable, indeed, that the private return exceeds the total social return, because part of the gain to the degree-holder is at the cost of others who will not now get well-paid jobs that they could have performed perfectly well. Throughout Europe, fees charged to students in higher education are zero or very small in proportion to the cost of providing the education – and thus, again, the burden must fall on the taxpayer, at the time or later. This makes a case for charging full-cost fees, and providing no subsidy towards living expenses. However, high as the expected return to their education may be, few students have assets sufficient to pay the expense of it at the time. The private market might in principle provide finance, but not efficiently given the lack of collateral for most borrowers, the length of term involved and the proportion of borrowers who would be genuinely unable to repay. The solution is a state-administered loan scheme such as is now being planned in the UK, whereby the state takes responsibility for extracting payments through the personal taxation system as and when the ex-student is in a position to pay, and the state pays the cost of the proportion who will never repay. Whether or not the money is technically borrowed by students from the public sector or from a private company, the certainty of repayment means that the cost of capital need be no higher than the interest on state debt.

A third category of investment is spending on the nursery, primary and secondary school system. For a number of reasons this must be treated quite differently from higher education. First, the beneficiaries are not adults, and thus cannot be expected to borrow for their own future benefit; if the state is not to pay, then their parents must, and we come up against the question of willingness and ability to make intergenerational transfers. Second, there is stronger evidence that the social return exceeds the cost of capital, particularly for the younger age groups. Third, since children in all classes benefit – and since children of richer families may attend private schools – there is little danger of state spending being skewed towards the children of the rich, as it clearly is in higher education. Here, then, we have a category of state spending which must remain a charge on the state and which must be paid for, at the time or later, out of general taxation. It should, however, no longer be treated as current, but as capital spending, and should be presented to the financial markets accordingly, without apology.

Indeed the beauty of such spending is that it raises the profitability of other investments which need not be so funded. The more children are well-educated through to (say) the age of 18, the more can, and will, profitably undertake tertiary education for which they will borrow and pay. The better the quality of the education of the labour force, the higher the rate of private business investment. Quite apart from the gain in terms of *future* national income arising from these three parallel streams of investment, there is (following Keynesian reasoning in an economy below full employment) an immediate gain in the level of aggregate demand and income – and therefore an increase in tax revenue at given tax rates. The future tax burden on the state arising from education spending is thus very much reduced.

Equality, inequality and the conditions for safe lending

The essence of any financial system is of course that it transfers resources from those who presently have a positive cash flow, and plan to have a negative one in future, to those who presently have a negative cash flow, and plan to have a positive one. Likewise the essential problem of all financial systems is the possibility that this future positive cash flow may not materialise. What is required, to give the financial system real scope to work, is a sort of balanced inequality: among businesses, for example, there should on the one side be some which are making profits but have poor opportunities to invest them, and on the other side should be businesses which have excellent opportunities for profitable investment but currently few or no profits to invest in them. (Conglomerates which match 'cash cows' with capital-hungry businesses tend to do the financial system out of a job.) Likewise, for a vigorous and stable world financial system there should be poor countries (or at least countries short of capital) with excellent opportunities for growth, matched by rich countries with much inferior opportunities.

Before the First World War the USA, Canada and Argentina on the one side, and the UK and the Netherlands on the other, played these matching roles perfectly. Since then, there has never been such a good match of countries again: at least twice (in the early 1930s and the early 1980s) we found that countries which needed the money – poor countries, mostly – were ones to whom in retrospect no sensible banker should have wanted to lend. (The great exception to this mismatch was a match largely missed by private capital: in the 1950s continental Western Europe and Japan showed themself very well able to find profitable investments for other countries' funds, but for the most part the funds were provided by Marshall Aid.) In the flood of private capital into 'emerging markets' in the 1990s – bank capital, portfolio capital and foreign direct investment – we may well be witnessing a third case in which there are many mismatches. The problem in essence is that within the international economy there is a fundamental polarisation which leaves many or most of the poorer countries needing more than loans to develop successfully (Tylecote, 1992, ch. 7).

Likewise among individuals within one economy and society there may or may not be good matches for the financial system to make. The cohesive traditional middle-class family is akin to the conglomerate in matching 'cash cows' (parents or grandparents) with children and young adults, and thus 'doing the financial system out of a job'. The state may do likewise, if it taxes the parents and grandparents heavily and subsidises the children's education. If the family becomes less cohesive and the state, in this respect, less redistributive, the financial system gets its chance to lend to the young – as proposed above. But we are increasingly seeing our societies polarised between rich old and poor young who are not even related. This arises first because better and better provision is made for the old, and because it is the richer members of society who tend to live longer; second, because it is the poor (including immigrants) who have more children – exacerbated by the fact that having more children tends to make one poor! The danger, then, is that although the young poor have good reason for borrowing, indirectly from the rich old – for their education, and for their housing, for example – they may not be seen, or see themselves as, or be, 'good risks'. It is a challenge that must be addressed first by the state, and by states, and second by the financial system, to help poor countries, and poor young people, to become 'good risks'.

References

Tylecote, A. (1992), *The long wave in the world economy* (London and New York: Routledge).

Tylecote, A. (1997), *The economic principles of making green policies election winners,* PERC Policy Paper, no. 3.

4

What Kind of Stability Helps Industry? Contrasting Experiences with British and German Banking

*Forrest H. Capie and Geoffrey E. Wood**

Introduction

The banking industries of Britain and Germany have for many years maintained distinct traditions with regard to lending to industry. British banks have viewed firms as customers, lending to them on a short-term basis. German banks, by contrast, have viewed firms as partners, lending to them for long periods of years, building up associations, often having representatives on the firms' boards. This has, in turn, encouraged banks to take a long-term view of 'industry's' long-term plans, to the mutual benefit of both banking and manufacturing. So, at least, the story goes.

Bank lending in the UK

In this chapter we re-examine that story. First we review the nature of bank lending in Britain. Was it really as short-term as the conventional wisdom suggests? Or is there perhaps in that conventional view some confusion of form with substance? That re-examination comprises the first section. We then consider the difference for the stability of the two banking systems that could result from the contrast in the forms of lending that each practised. This discussion is first analytical, and then illuminated by points from nineteenth-century banking history in Britain. That comprises the second part of the chapter. In the third part we show how these different lending practices had different consequences for their respective economies in a particular episode when

* We are indebted to Dr Benedikt Koehler for his most useful comments on an earlier version of this paper.

(unlike the nineteenth century) both Britain and Germany had fully-developed central banks so that there would be no possibility that the problems we discuss resulted from the lack or embryonic nature of a central bank. The fourth, and final, part of the chapter then proposes an answer to the question which comprises the chapter's title, and on the basis of the answer suggests a regulatory implication.

The question we address first is the following: has British banking been short-termist? The City of London has often been accused of short-termism; a literature has developed that defines that problem in different ways and comes to a variety of conclusions. When the complaint is made against banking in particular it is usually couched or explained in the following sort of terms. Banks are claimed to have lent short-term only (constrained by the liability side of the balance sheet) and to have spurned long-term relationships with, in particular, industrial customers. This is said to have been the case from the second half of the nineteenth century onwards, and supposedly proved a major handicap to British industry and was a big part of the explanation for Britain's relative economic decline.

There are three main points we would make here. The first is that the whole capital market should be considered. The second is that looking at structure alone is not conclusive. And the third is that the actual practice of the two systems needs close scrutiny.

We take these in order. Any criticism of British commercial bank practices has to be set in the context of the whole capital market. If we accept that British banks stuck to short-term lending it may be that other parts of the capital market were providing other forms of finance. We know this was likely to have been the case, with merchant banks arranging new issues and a long-established stockmarket. In the late nineteenth century family firms financed themselves or got working capital from banks, and large firms went to the stockmarket. An example demonstrates this. Watson (1996) examined the issue of banks failing industry with specific reference to brewing (then one of the largest industries). Banks never provided brewers with long-term funds. (So they cannot be accused of another supposed failure, deserting customers in times of distress.) But the brewers in any case preferred to exploit the new issue market. Brewers did use banks for transitional funds and their demands for these were generally satisfied. Watson concludes that the absence of long-term loans in brewers' portfolios is not indicative of bank failure. The difference between Britain and Germany in how long-term finance for industry was provided arose from the different times of origin of the two banking systems. In

Britain many aspects of finance and investment were in the domain of well-established merchant bank groupings. Commercial banks had long been the providers of short-term finance. In Germany, by contrast, it was only after 1871 that commercial banks and multinational industrial firms developed. The two types of firm developed side by side, the first meeting the others' demands for finance.[1]

Our second point is on company structure. In discussion of corporate governance a great deal has been made of the differences in structure between Anglo-Saxon/American companies and the German/European model. The claim is that with interlocking directorates in the latter, flows of information were greatly improved, incentives more clearly defined, and monitoring facilitated. There is no doubt that German banks had close knowledge of their customers' business, and they were well-placed to advise on a range of matters and on flotations if necessary. With bankers sitting on boards of companies and industrialists on bank boards better opportunities were seen and taken, investment was higher and German growth faster, goes the story.

However, a long list of criticisms have been made of this account. Big business was favoured, and smaller firms (comprising almost invariably the more dynamic part of the economy) were neglected to the detriment of German growth (Neuberger and Stokes, 1974). More recently it has been shown that there were no interlocking directorates of any significance before the turn of the twentieth century, a point *after which* German growth had experienced its spurt. Furthermore, in another recent criticism it has been shown that the relationship between banks and industrial firms applied only to industrial *joint stock* companies and that the vast majority of the industrial capital stock in Germany before 1914 was accounted for by firms that were not joint-stock companies (Edwards and Ogilvie 1996)

Even if we were to accept that German structures looked superior it would still remain an empirical matter whether or not behaviour was significantly different. In fact the debt/equity ratios of German and British companies are remarkably similar. Further, from quite early times English provincial banks used the overdraft (a Scottish invention) in a flexible way. Certainly by the late nineteenth century British commercial banks were in effect lending long-term by means of the overdraft. Overdrafts were rolled over and over for as much as twenty years or more (see Capie and Collins, 1996). Lending may have been short-term in form, but it was long-term in substance.

Did British banks become more conservative in their lending practices as is sometimes suggested? Market data can provide a means of assessing banks from the perspective of contemporaries and allows such a judgement to be made. Monthly share prices were used to examine the changing riskiness of individual banks and of the banking sector as a whole (see Capie and Mills, 1995). This evidence provides no support for the view that British banks became more conservative from the mid-1890s onwards. We do not, however, rule out the possibility that the generally flat trend in relative volatility may have been produced by off-setting factors. For example, there may have been factors operating to increase the exposure of banks that compensated precisely for their assumed increasing conservatism. One possibility is the rising interest rates that date from the mid-1890s and the accompanying falling prices on fixed interest securities. Although banks had always held fairly substantial amounts of such assets in their portfolios, this seems unlikely to be a long-term factor that could provide the explanation required.

The interwar years

The behaviour of the commercial banks was slightly different after the First World War. Their balance sheets show that over the 1920s and 1930s there was a trend to greater liquidity; wereas in the late 1920s the proportion of assets in advances to industry was 52 per cent, that fell in the 1930s to 41.2 per cent in 1936–38. This took place while the domestic economy was growing quite rapidly. Part of the explanation lies in the effects of the authorities' debt management. There was a sharp increase in the public debt in the First World War, and the clearing banks had been obliged to be large purchasers. In the 1920s the banks managed to divert some of their resources towards the private sector, but the authorities took advantage of the low interest rates in the 1930s to shift the composition of the national debt from short-term to long-term. (The proportion of the debt with a maturity of more than 25 years rose from 32 per cent to 40 per cent between 1930/31 and 1938/39.) If long-term government securities and private advances were reasonably close substitutes, then government funding may have crowded out private finance.

But there were nevertheless factors operating to bring banks and industrial customers closer together. The commercial banks were certainly drawn more deeply into industrial finance. For example, where non-repayment of loans was threatened it was often sensible for banks to extend repayment periods and even to lend further to ensure the survival of firms and hence the eventual repayment of the original loan. Added to this was pressure from the Bank of England. For example, Holmes and Green (1986) illustrate how the Midland Bank behaved, supporting its own industrial customers. One striking case was the Royal Mail Group, a major rescue operation that required the deep involvement of the Midland in the 1930s. The Royal Mail Group accounted for 15 per cent of the country's merchant fleet and was also in shipbuilding and steel. A Midland affiliate, the Belfast Bank, was heavily extended to the group (outstanding loans of £3.5 million) and this resulted in close involvement by the Midland in the Group's affairs for several years.

The banks may not have supplied venture capital, but they certainly did become closely involved with industrial customers, probably on a scale never seen before. Duncan Ross (1992) has recently provided more evidence on this, and shows that the actions taken by the banks actually conflicted with the positions they adopted before the Macmillan Committee.

Stability

British banks have taken a great deal of (ill-founded) criticism for alleged deficiencies, but it has been impossible to deny that they provided stability. There was no banking panic and no financial crisis in Britain after 1866, and from 1890 to 1940 (and beyond) there was a period of remarkable stability. There were, however, sharp fluctuations in the economy – in 1921; then (less deep but more prolonged), in 1929–32; and there was a relatively mild and brief recession in 1937–38. This is reflected in the behaviour of the banks and the public as captured in the cash and reserve/deposit ratios. It is important to remember, though, that while these recessions reflected some of the problems in the rest of the world economy, Britain's experience was for most of the time much milder than in other countries. For example, in the great depression of 1929–32 which affected many economies, output in Britain fell in total by 6 per cent compared with falls elsewhere of over 30 per cent. Partly as a result of this, and in contradistinction to the USA and much of Europe, British banks did not get into the same kind of difficulties as were experienced in Europe and the USA.

But the causality was not one-way. British banks were stable because of the comparative modesty of the recession; but the recession was comparatively modest because of the stability of British banking. We now turn to discussion of one important factor behind this banking stability.

Form vs substance: does it matter?

So far we have argued that both before and during the interwar years the supposedly different relationship that German and British banks had with their respective groups of customers was in fact usually different only in form. German banks entered into long-term lending agreements; indeed they sometimes held equity in their customers. British banks lent on a short-term basis. That was the form. But the substance was that in general British banks established long-lasting relationships with their customers, rolled over loans, often for many years, and were expected to do so by their customers so long as mutually, and usually explicitly, agreed conditions were met. So the banking systems actually behaved in a very similar way in practice.

Nevertheless, there was a crucial difference, one which in extremely unusual circumstances – such as a time of financial panic – could become very important. We first briefly describe the classic response to such a panic, then we show how the different lending practices of the British and German banking systems could interact in quite different ways with that classic response. We then turn to an episode when these differences were of the very greatest importance.

Reaction to a crisis

How should a central bank react to a financial crisis so as to stop it turning into a crisis for the real economy?[2] It should act as 'lender of last resort'. Walter Bagehot is often credited with urging this action on the Bank of England, and by extension on central banks generally, but in fact the Bank well-understood the nature and importance of lender-of-last-resort operations before Bagehot wrote. What Bagehot did in *Lombard Street* (1873) was to urge the Bank to commit itself, publicly and in advance, to act in this way; for, he argued, that very commitment would make crises less likely.

A 'classic' banking crisis occurs when a bank fails and depositors lose their cash. This failure gives rise to fears that other banks will fail, so depositors 'run' to withdraw their funds. Since no bank holds cash equal to deposits, the scramble for cash can cause bank after bank to fail. Such a wave of failures has serious consequences. These consequences can be for two quite distinct reasons, and are discussed below.

To prevent these consequences, and prevent the wave of bank failures which produces them, the central bank has to act as lender of last resort. That is to say, it injects cash into the system *in return for securi-*

ties discounted with it. The fact that the cash is injected on the basis of discounting securities is what distinguishes a lender-of-last-resort operation from a bail-out. The market is helped, not individual institutions, because cash is provided to whomever brings in the security. And since cash is given only on security, if an institution runs out of discountable securities before it has paid off its liabilities, and is therefore insolvent, it can no longer obtain help.

There are, of course, problems in practice over what securities to accept and the rate at which they should be discounted. But these were perfectly capable of solution in practice. The rate was above prior market rates, both to prevent too frequent recourse to the central bank and to reflect the fact that, in time of crisis, securities of lower quality than usual were accepted. The attitude over what to discount is made clear in Jeremiah Harman's famous description of such an operation in 1825 by the Bank of England:

> We lent it [gold] ... by every possible means and in modes we had never adopted before: we took in stock on security, we purchased exchequer bills, we made advances on exchequer bills, we not only discounted outright, but we made advances on the deposit of bills of exchange to an immense amount, in short, by every possible means consistent with the safety of the Bank and we were not on some occasions over nice. (Quoted in Bagehot, 1873)

The kind of behaviour that Harman described was well-understood by the Bank of England, and came to be understood by other central banks as they emerged or were created through the nineteenth and into the twentieth centuries. For example, when the Federal Reserve was established in the United States one of its roles was to provide an 'elastic currency' – a term which can be seen in the Fed's actions from time to time, even the inadequate ones in the Great Depression, embraced lender-of-last-resort actions.

British and German lending

Now it becomes clear when British and German bank lending practices could matter. In 'normal' times they may not – because in both countries the practice was the same. But in a crisis the difference mattered very much – because in Germany there was not the abundant supply of discountable paper that there was in Britain. Hence, should a banking crisis occur, classic lender-of-last-resort operations could not be carried out, on any but a trivial scale, by the Reichsbank. Even when there were securities which were in principle discountable – and often there were not – they were long-term bonds, or even equities. The Reichsbank would, to prevent a banking crisis, have had to take a direct equity stake in German industry. It had neither the authority nor the inclination to do so, and, perhaps more important, nor did it have the capital.[3]

Accordingly, then, the Reichsbank was not in a position to stop an individual bank failure turning into a general banking crisis.

Why it matters

Banking crises do great harm to an economy. One route by which they do so is unanimously accepted; the other is somewhat contentious.

The well-accepted one is that a wave of bank failures, by wiping out bank deposits, destroys a part of the money stock. A sharp monetary contraction causes a recession – especially as a contraction produced by such a means is unusually unanticipated. The best-known example of this, and also the most dramatic, is the Great Depression in the United States (see Friedman and Schwartz, 1963, ch. 7, for a vivid description).

The second mechanism was described by Bernanke (1983). This involves the failure of banks destroying channels of credit – partly because the institutions which gather up deposits and then on-lend have gone out of business, and partly because the information the banks possessed about the creditworthiness of prospective borrowers is, while not destroyed, certainly temporarily unavailable. Benston (1991), for example, has objected to this, arguing that new banks rapidly take over where old ones have failed, often employing much of the same staff as the failed institution, therefore reinstating both the channel of credit and the information necessary for credit to flow through the channel. But, be that as it may, what is at issue is not whether banking crises cause harm, but only by how many channels they do so.

To summarise so far, then, the different forms of behaviour of the British and German banking systems generally were differences of form rather than substance. But, as we have argued above, those different forms would actually matter in a financial crisis; for the German form of behaviour did not allow lender-of-last-resort action on a large scale, while the British form did.

As was remarked earlier, the difference could not matter before the twentieth century, simply because there was then no central bank in Germany. But in the twentieth century it could; and, in a very dramatic fashion, it did.

Banking stability between the wars

As has already been remarked, Britain's interwar recessionary experience was very mild compared with that of most of the rest of the world. That comparison certainly includes Germany, which between 1929 and 1932 experienced a severe recession. Did the banking systems matter in any way in producing these different outcomes?

They did. British banking was stable: no bank of any significance failed, and even their profits remained both positive and reasonably stable from year to year. This latter was true, it should be pointed out, only for published profits (which were 'window-dressed'). So far as can be seen, the true underlying profits remained positive but fluctuated. (An account of the profitability of British banking in this period, devoting considerable effort to disentangling underlying profits and providing a full description of the methods used to do so, is provided in Capie, 1988.)

By contrast, in Germany banking collapsed. It may be said that the contrast is unfair, that German banking faced problems on a scale so different from those of the British system that comparison is inappropriate. But that is to some extent the point. The British banking system both because of its structure and because there was a lender of last resort, did not by failure exacerbate the recession; and because the recession was not severe, the British banking system experienced little strain.

In Germany the collapse of the banking system contributed to monetary disorder and the drying up of channels of credit; which in turn made the recession deeper and the strain on the banking system still greater. Recent discussion of the problems for banking stability, not just in Germany but throughout the whole of Central Europe in this period caused by the lack of discountable collateral can be found in Schubert (1991).

Accordingly, while the differences in the form of bank lending to industry did not matter in normal times, they did matter very much in times of stress, and the differences then favoured Britain and the British system of lending.[4]

Summary and conclusions

In this chapter we have first reviewed the practices, with regard to lending to industry, of the British and German banking systems. The latter is often contrasted favourably with the former, on the grounds that it engages in long-term lending, and that practice is supposedly desirable. We have shown that although British banks did not enter into formal long-term loans, they did in practice lend long term – and that they would do so was well-understood by their customers. But this different approach did mean that the British banks could, in a time of crisis, offer discountable securities to the central bank, while German banks could not. The British system was thus better placed to withstand shocks, which mattered a great deal in the interwar years.

Accordingly, the supposed contrast between the two systems is not so simple as often claimed. British banks did not make long-term loans; but they did lend long-term. Did this difference of form but not substance matter to their customers? Whether it did in normal times we have not examined in this paper, although evidence we have cited suggests it did not. But it certainly mattered in time of crisis. The kind of stability provided by the British system of bank lending was more beneficial than that provided by the German system; for it is a stability which did not turn out to be illusory when put under pressure.

This does not mean that bank regulators should insist that every country's banks should henceforth adopt the British banking system's methods of industrial finance. For, as we stressed earlier, while it is possible to appraise the banking system's contribution to economic stability by looking at the banking system alone, when considering wider aspects of economic performance it is necessary to consider how well not just banks but the whole of the capital market works so as to facilitate the efficient allocation of capital. Nevertheless, a regulatory implication does follow from our analysis.

It is currently fashionable for commercial banks to try to transform loans on their own books into securitised debt, as this both reduces the capital required by regulation and may allow the sale of the debt itself should that become advantageous. Regulators should be concerned about this, for while such behaviour reduces the exposure of any one bank to a shock which absorbs capital, it does not do so for the banking system as a whole. The regulatory treatment of securities, in so far as it affects capital adequacy, may require reconsideration. But securitisation also has another aspect. While not protecting against shocks to the solvency of the system, if the debt is discountable at the central bank then it *does* provide protection against shocks to liquidity. Central banks should resolve what sorts of debt created by securitisation they would discount, and then make public that information. They would thereby take advantage of the conclusion on the kind of stability that helps industry to which the comparative study of British and German bank-lending practices has led.

Notes

1. It is worth observing that even today a flourishing venture capital industry has yet to develop in Germany.
2. This discussion describes Bank of England practice from early in the nineteenth century, but it applies to the Reichsbank only from around 1910, by which time it had become a 'proper' central bank by clearly accepting that it had responsibilities extending far beyond its shareholders to the economy as a whole, and by recognising that it was complementary to, rather than competitive with, other banks in Germany.
3. The important and often neglected role of a central bank's capital was demonstrated very clearly in a letter by Roger Alford in the *Financial Times* of 9 March 1995. Commercial banks can of course fail through shortage of capital as well as through shortage of liquidity. Here the structure of British commercial banking, widely diversified both geographically and by type of customer, provided some protection in Britain, while the 'universal' nature of German banks' activities provides some protection in Germany.
4. It is worth remarking that the protection against crisis which the British system provided does not seem to have been at any cost to performance, at any rate by large firms. Cassis (1997) examines the performance of big firms in Britain, France and Germany across a long time period, and concludes that by a variety of measures, including both profitability and survival, performance by big firms in Britain was superior to that by big German firms.

References

Bagehot, W. (1873) *Lombard Street.*

Benston, G. J. (1991) ' Does Bank Regulation Produce Stability: Lessons from the US', in F. H. Capie and G. E. Wood (eds), *Unregulated Banking* (London: Macmillan).

Bernanke, B. S. (1983) 'Non-monetary Effects of the Financial Crisis in the Propagation of the Great Depression', *American Economic Review*, vol. 73, pp. 257–76.

Capie, F. H. (1988) 'Structure and Performances in British Banking 1870–1930', in P. L. Cottrell and D. E. Moggridge (eds), *Money and Power* (London: Macmillan).

Capie, F. H. and Collins, M. (1996) 'Industrial Lending by English Commercial Banks, 1860s-1914', *Business History*, vol. 38, no. 1

Capie, F. H. and Mills, T. C. (1995) 'British Bank Conservatism in the Late 19th Century', *Explorations in Economic History,* no. 32, pp. 409–20.

Cassis, Y. (1997) *Big Business: The European Experience in the 20th Century* (Oxford: Oxford University Press).

Edwards, J. and Ogilvie, S. (1996) 'Universal banks and German Industrialisation: A Reappraisal', *Economy History Review*, vol. xlix.

Friedman, M. and Schwartz, A. J. (1963) *A Monetary History of the United States* (Princeton, New Jersey: Princeton University Press, for NBER).

Holmes, A. R. and Green, E. (1986) *Midland: 150 Years of Banking Business* (London: Batsford).

Neuberger, H. and Stokes, H. H. (1974) 'German Banks and German Growth, 1883–1914: An Empirical View', *Journal of Economic History,* vol. xxxiv, no. 3.

Ross, D. (1992) 'Bank Advances and Industrial Production in the UK. During the interwar xxx years: A Red Herring?', in P. L. Cottrell, H. Lindgren and A. Teichova (eds), *European Industry and Banking Between the Wars* (Leicester: Leicester University Press).

Schubert, A. (1991) *The Credit Anstalt Crisis of 1931* (Cambridge: Cambridge University Press.

Watson, K. (1996) 'Bank and Industrial Finance: The Experience of Brewers, 1880–1913', *Economic History Review,* vol. xlix.

Comments on 'What Kind of Stability Helps Industry? Contrasting Experiences with British and German Banking', by Forrest H. Capie and Geoffrey E. Wood

Benedikt Koehler

The material presented by Professors Capie and Wood has its special merit in that it first examines, and then challenges, a familiar, widely-held preconception of industry in the UK and in Germany. I would like first to consider the observations made in their chapter, and then offer some suggestions on the direction of further discussion.

There is a widely held consensus to explain the gap in industrial growth rates registered in both countries over the past half century, which lays at least part of the blame on the unwillingness of banks in the United Kingdom to lend long-term. The chapter refutes this view on several grounds. The track record of the Midland Bank, for example, illustrates how a major clearing bank would prop up a corporation under financial stress irrespective of whether loans were committed long-term or on overdraft. Then, the chapter goes on to introduce into a comparison of banking in the UK and in Germany the role and contribution of central banks. The chapter explains how discrete and timely involvement of central bank authorities would sway lending policies in favour of defusing a commercial crisis, and makes plain that the contribution of the financial community to a sound and lasting framework for industry must be judged by its ability to withstand crisis. This is a key determinant of performance, often overlooked in discussions of the relative performance of British and German industry. In addition to questioning consensus opinions regarding the performance of the financial sector, the chapter also quotes recent research showing that at least in that segment of industry comprised by the country's largest corporations, industrial performance in Britain actually matches, and often exceeds, comparable companies in Germany.

This chapter has challenged conventional wisdom, and by introducing central banks into the debate, widens the discussion about industrial performance in the UK and Germany. This is, I feel, where the chapter most contributes to further discussion. A comparison of German universal banks with Britain's commercial banks has so far not been carried out on a level playing field. I would like to explain why I think so, and that the reasons lie in differences of historical development.

Germany reached statehood comparatively recently, in 1871; the history of German industry and the economic history of Germany tends to begin with that date. At that time, the City of London was already acting as a worldwide centre of financial information and a turntable for transactions throughout the British Empire and around the globe. Indeed, the City of London is often blamed for its internationalism which led to a neglect of industry on its own home territory. At this time, the indisputable centre for financial decision-making in Germany was Frankfurt.

Indeed, the way business was transacted in Frankfurt had a great deal more in common with the way business was transacted in the City, than with other regional centres in Germany. Until Germany, through industrialisation, began to offer opportunities for investment rivalling those achieved elsewhere, Frankfurt bankers concentrated their resources on the finance of international trade and investment. They saw no reason to concentrate their funds on the growth of the economy in Germany, unless there were sound business reasons for doing so. Banking in Frankfurt until German unification, to be sure, was conducted on a smaller scale than in the City of London, but it was every bit as international and efficient. The Rothschild family, after all, used Frankfurt as the hub of their international network. This changed when in 1871 Germany became a single market, and Berlin as a centre of banking and industry grew to be a serious contender for the title of Finanzplatz. It was only after 1871 when Germany became a vast single market, that the great universal banks, Deutsche Bank, Dresdner Bank, Commerzbank and many others, flourished along with the emergent multinationally-orientated powerhouses of German industry, such as Siemens, Mannesmann and Krupp. One of the reasons why the major German banks grew hand-in-hand with German major corporations, is because they both started at about the same time.

Things were different in Britain. When Britain's great commercial banking institutions came into being, many aspects of finance and investment were already the domain of well-established, international merchant bank groupings. Before the great engines of industrial growth of the nineteenth century, steam and electricity, were harnessed for corporate benefit, banks such as Barings and Rothschild were already well-established businesses with long traditions. So when the corporate appetite for investment required ever-increasing loans of lengthening maturities, merchant banks needed to invent new lines of business, and gravitated towards the business of providing and arranging equity. They also, in an early example of disintermediation, expanded the market for corporate bonds. Commercial banks, comparatively speaking late-comers to the financial market, were left with the task of specialising in corporate lending.

This is why, in my view, a comparison of the relative benefits provided by the financial communities in Britain and in Germany to their countries' industries needs to compare the financial sectors of each country as a whole, rather than limiting the comparison to individual segments of the financial industry. From the outset, a German universal bank encompassed all the services provided in the City of London by a range of institutions: merchant banks, stockbrokers as well as commercial bankers. In Britain, on the other hand, a far more mature financial industry had already developed a degree of specialisation, which lasted until the Big Bang of 1987.

The chapter focuses on the issue of crisis and of response to crisis situations, and I think it points the way to asking what other criteria might apply for assessing financial systems. I would like to submit another criterion of industrial adaptability: the ability to promote and adjust to innovation. One of the major distinctions between industry in Germany and in Britain, in my view, is the longevity of Germany's list of premier corporations. I am not a business historian, but I would suspect that a list of Germany's top 25 corporations would feature far less change in composition than the comparative list for Britain. Indeed, it is astonishing that after the wholesale deconstruction of German industry in the 1920s and the 1940s, there should still remain an almost intact list of internationally-orientated concerns dating back a century. There are in Germany families who now for four or five generations have been employed by Siemens or by Daimler Benz; I doubt Britain has had an equivalent experience. Conversely, and almost astonishing considering the high savings rate of the German private sector, Germany even today has *not* succeeded in developing a flourishing venture capital industry, whereas in Britain, where the savings rate is notoriously low, the willingness to take a long-term view, and risk equity on a long shot, remains unimpaired, irrespective of the relative decline of national wealth compared to other countries. Lastly, one wonders why Germany even today has a remarkably small corporate bond sector. I think this chapter offers the benefit of placing bank-lending into an overall context of financial systems.

Allow me to summarise. The chapter argues against a strand of orthodox thinking which runs along these lines:

German industrial performance has its lynchpin in three sectors: equipment, chemicals and automobiles. Each of these have long lead times in product development and investment, and to match the planning horizon of companies in these business sectors, it stands to reason that they require long-term funding. The reason that in the UK the automobile industry, chemicals and equipment could not over time match the performance of their competitors in Germany, is often held to be the responsibility of a structural weakness of Britain's banking industry. Whereas German bankers would be prepared to match the life-cycle of long-term assets, by extending and committing loans for long-term production cycles, in Britain, home of the overdraft as the principal form of commercial lending, industry could not with the same assurance as their peer group in Germany look to implement investment programmes stretching across a long-term budgeting horizon. This is a commonly held view why, together with a few other reasons, British industry has been lagging behind industry in Germany. The chapter shows that this view is flawed and does not stand up to close scrutiny.

Finally, I would like to place this chapter in the context of the conference from which it derives. The question to which the chapter leads is not only about industrial efficiency. There exists a tacit assumption that commercial banking in Germany, because it is seen to lend for the longer term, in a crisis is more prone to have a cooperative rather than an adversarial approach to problems. This makes not only for an efficient working relationship, but is also more fair to industry and thus to employees. Long-term lending, in this view, is part and parcel of a stakeholder society. Giving the diversity of financial institutions in Britain, I wonder whether this view can be upheld. From my own point of view, I would like to add another question to the debate about the social responsibility of bankers: are bankers accountable for the ways in which they deal with the interests of borrowers, or are they primarily accountable for protecting the interests of their depositors? This question of fairness, in a moral rather than a strictly commercial sense, is a particularly relevant challenge considering the large-scale reconstruction of European business in a globalised economy.

5

Financial Competition, Risk and Accountability: The Role of Trust Banks

Jan A. Kregel

Classical economics has produced conflicting interpretations of the responsibilities of individual agents engaged in market competition. Although it is widely accepted that it is the competition of individuals that produces the economic efficiency associated with free markets, Lionel Robbins has warned that 'the pursuit of self-interest unrestrained by suitable institutions, carries no guarantee of anything except chaos' (Robbins, 1952, p. 56). More recent analysis, on the other hand, suggests that while 'millions of greedy, self-seeking individuals in pursuit of their own ends and mainly uncontrolled in their pursuits by the State, seem to common sense a sure recipe for anarchy', it is in fact the very basis of the economic efficiency of the market (Hahn, 1980, p. 123).

Robbins argued that the basis for market efficiency was to be found in the broad economic policy framework that set out the constraints within which self-interested individuals were allowed freedom to compete. These constraints would not arise naturally, they were the result of active government policy legislation. On the other hand, giving full rein to unbridled self-interest implies the absence of general constraints. On this view, policy intervention should be limited to precise prohibition of clearly aberrant behaviour, rather than a general framework of regulations. Obviously, the application of either of these two alternatives could lead to malfunction of the competitive process. An overall framework of regulations might become so extensive as to stifle the efficient operation of the pursuit of individual self-interest, while particular regulations of specific aberrant behaviour could evoke a change in that behaviour that is even more pathological than that being regulated.

While both approaches accept that the benefits of economic efficiency resulting from market competition require the pursuit of self-interest, there is ambiguity surrounding the definition of this self-interest. For example, a strong argument can be made that the efficiency of the market is also dependant on relations based on trust and reciprocity. Although Adam Smith argued that it is not from the benevolence of the butcher, the baker and the brewer, but from their self-interest that we benefit, he nonetheless based his idea of market competition on empathy and informed altruism.

Why should we be worried about the interests of the baker and the butcher? Smith's answer was that in an economy characterised by extensive division of labour, which he believed was the cause of the 'wealth of nations', economic actions were interdependent. If I specialise in making boots I will be dependent for my physical sustenance on the actions of those individuals who specialise as butchers and bakers.[1] Even more importantly, I will be dependent on the willingness of the butcher and the baker to provide the subsistence that I cannot produce in exchange for my boots. Thus, to ensure my physical survival, it is in my self-interest to cut the boots I produce to suit the desires of my butcher and baker clients, not to my own whimsy. Smith argues that by making the interest of others your own, you benefit your own interests. Now, if this is the case, it follows that it is not in the self-interest of individuals to misrepresent or otherwise act unethically.

The successful operation of the market mechanism may then said to be based on trust. Trust that the goods offered by the seller are what they are represented to be, that the means of payment offered by the buyer have equivalent value to the agreed price of the goods, that the boots I produce will wear well, and that the bank note I accept for them can be converted at its par value. But, Smith argues, no individual can know the intentions of others. The creation of trust that is required for the successful operation of the market is a question of the accumulation of information by experience leading to confidence. The necessary information to form confident beliefs about the behaviour of other market participants can be acquired either through experience, or the result of a regulatory framework.

This aspect of market exchange has two diverse interpretations. In the case of greedy self-interest, the acquisition of information by experience is costly, and private. The consumer that buys contaminated meat from a dishonest butcher will not do it again; the dishonest butcher will eventually have no more custom. But, such learning experiences may be terminal, and are best anticipated – through specific regulations, such as minimum sanitary conditions for butchers.

On the other hand, if the incentive structure is set up such that each individual is known to operate in the other's self-interest, then no contaminated meat would ever be sold. The information to be acquired through personal experience would be implicit in Robbins's general regulatory framework and is thus essentially costless to the individual, although Robbins would have conceded that there would be some costs in framework implementation.

Whatever position we take on the roles of greed and trust in determining the efficiency of market exchange, it is common to represent exchange in financial markets as based on trust. This is due to the fact that the completion of such exchange usually takes place over an extended period. Thus, future outcomes cannot be known. But there is little difference between the trust involved in purchasing a bond which is expected to pay interest and repay principal at distant futures dates without default, and the purchase of a toaster which is expected to furnish breakfast toast over a lifetime without breakdown.

Just as market exchanges are regulated by laws of contract, there is a considerable jurisprudence relating specifically to the trust relationship in financial exchange. A legal relationship of trust implies a fiduciary responsibility of care and custody in which individual self-interest is subservient to that of a beneficiary, under penalty of personal liability. The penalty is to indemnify any loss to the beneficiary resulting from actions taken by the fiduciary trustee. In simple terms it is recognised that a trustee faces a potential conflict of interest (often called moral hazard) between personal interests and the interests of the beneficiary – the personal liability penalty is to discourage self-interested, greedy behaviour. But, not only must the fiduciary avoid actions that clearly benefit his own self-interest, he must also take positive actions to further the self-interests of the beneficiary. This seems very close to Smith's motivation for market exchange given above.

Legislation originally governing trust deeds required specification of either the individual securities to be purchased by the trustee, or a schedule of permitted investments. This aspect of the trust relationship appears to be in contrast to Robbins's characterisation of classical economic policy as allowing broad action within a framework of constraints. British and US law specified the individual investments; they were usually restricted to government securities, and no risk or speculation was admitted. This changed in the 1830s when regulation of trust relationships more compatible with Robbins' idea were introduced in what has come to be known as the 'prudent man' rule. This rule replaced the specification of particular investments and directed the fiduciary to 'observe how men of prudence, discretion and intelligence manage their own affairs, not in regard to speculation, but in regard to the permanent disposition of their funds, considering the probable income, as well as the probable safety of the capital to be invested' (quoted in Longstreth, 1986, p. 3).[2]

It is not only individuals who may take on fiduciary trust. A wide range of financial institutions have been formed with the aim of undertaking the fiduciary responsibility of trusteeship. In an attempt to encourage and provide a safe investment for worker savings, 'trustee savings banks' were set up in the UK to operate under the direction of a board of trustees on behalf of depositors. They were eventually joined by the National Post Office Savings Bank, which functioned in roughly the same way, investing in government debt securities under the trusteeship of the National Debt Commissioners.[3] Another example is the British unit trust, which is based on a trust deed governing the management of investments for the beneficiaries by trustees.

The savings bank based on a trust deed was common in the US, where it was known as a 'mutual' savings bank.[4] Following the English example, the investments of the savings banks were primarily undertaken through joint-stock banks, rather than through direct purchase of government securities. The concept was further extended through the formation of 'trust companies'. Somewhat ironically these non-bank financial institutions were initially justified 'to promote public interests by affording to the owners of capital not engaged in business many of the advantages secured by our savings bank system for the savings of labor' (Barnett, 1911, p. 14). They were individually incorporated financial institutions formed to take on the fiduciary responsibility of trustee; they were most always chartered separately from banks, and were usually forbidden the use of 'bank' in their name. The idea was that they could better carry out the fiduciary responsibilities of trusteeship for investments than could private individuals. In addition to trust business, it was common for a trust charter to grant powers to insure lives, grant annuities, insure the fidelity of persons in positions of trust, insure titles to land, provide safe-deposits, receive deposits of money in trust and loan money. Despite their name, and the fact that the actions of the owners of the trust company were subject to the law governing fiduciary responsibility of private trusts, these institutions were hardly distinguishable from ordinary deposit-taking, discounting banks (cf. Barnett, *ibid.*). This was because it was common for ordinary banks to have a 'trust department' carrying out the same activities as the separately chartered 'trusts'. Although trust departments were separated by a 'chinese wall' from ordinary banking business, they usually operated in combination with the bank's bond department.

There is no precise German equivalent to the trustee savings bank movement in Britain or mutual savings banks and trust companies in the USA. One reason is that local and regional governments provided a very similar alternative in the form of the public law 'sparkasse'. These savings banks enjoyed the unlimited liability guarantee of their government organisers, and had the ability to act as trustees for trust accounts. Investments were mainly in local and regional government debt. Their balance sheets would look very similar to the trustee savings bank, with savings deposits as liabilities and government debt as investments.

The nearest equivalent to the mutual society is the co-operative bank[5] or *Volksbank* which was organised in two different forms distinguished by geographical coverage. The banks operating in urban areas were organised on the Schultze–Delitzsch principle, and those in rural areas were organised on the Raiffeisen principle. Both are non-equity organisations in which the member-depositors are the beneficiaries of the investments made by the accountant-administrators. Both the savings banks and the two forms of co-operative bank have been involved in a wider range of banking business than their British or US counterparts; in particular they have traditionally been able to accept deposits from non-beneficiaries. The co-operative banks differ in that their creation was motivated more by the need for sources of lending than for securing the investment of funds on trust.

The German savings and co-operative banks are organised to offer the same services as universal banks through their national Giro system and are an active and important part of the financial markets. In the USA, most of the trust banks quickly extended their activity to general banking business and soon became indistinguishable from commercial banks. Most of the mutual savings banks were converted to joint-stock charters in the savings and loans crisis of the 1980s. Only in the UK has the transformation process via the conversion of the trustee savings bank and the building societies to joint-stock been delayed until the present.

The main characteristic of all these various sorts of financial institution based on trust is that the 'beneficiaries occupy [the same] place in the sphere of private trusts, as shareholders do in that of business corporations' (Longstreth, 1986, p. 23). There is a clear identification of the beneficiary, and legislation governing the relation between the trustee and beneficiary. This continues to hold true whether the organisational form is a private or a corporate trust. As noted regulation of trustees has shifted from the precise specification of permitted investments to specification of the framework in which these investments are made. The organisation of these institutions provides a guideline for the analysis of the relationship between competition producing economic efficiency and individual responsibility. As the evolution of these institutions into more or less fully-fledged commercial banks shows, other forms of bank organisation (such as private banks, joint-stock banks etc) would not have been necessary to achieve full-scale deposit and investment banking. If modern banking systems had evolved from trust banking, then all financial institutions would have been regulated through restrictions on acceptable investments. Capital requirements would have been unnecessary.

In a traditional limited liability company formed under commercial or civil law, the corporate charter replaces the trust document, management takes the place of the trustee, and the shareholder takes the place of the beneficiary.[6] The principles which regulate the behaviour of management with respect to the welfare of the owner-shareholders are based on the 'business-judgement' rule which is much less strict than the 'prudent-man' rule, nor are the managers of a company held personally liable to the owner-shareholders for losses due to their actions in administering the capital of the company.

Most of the financial institutions that we today recognise as 'banks' were organised under Royal or commercial charter. They were owned and operated for the benefit of their owners. It was the case that only highly infrequently did the owners supply the capital which was to be exploited by the company. Even in the case of the Bank of England, the capital was only partially paid and delivered in specie, with the remainder supplied in bank notes, that is by the owners of the bank borrowing it from the general public. Commercially chartered banks were generally formed by borrowing the initial capital, whereas trust banks administered capital held in trust.[7]

The way private banks usually raised capital by borrowing from the public through the issue of 'deposit receipts' or notes against the deposit of specie is similar to a trust relationship.[8] The specie was clearly given for safekeeping. Early Venetian money scriveners issued '*contado di banco*', while goldsmiths issued receipts against precious metal in their safekeeping. Initially it is clear that these were trust relationships of the type '*depositum non est mutuum*'. They were deposits of particular items which were to be returned. In the middle ages, the prohibition of the payment of interest encouraged this idea.

In the absence of precise trust regulations, it was common for the deposits to be used for commercial purposes rather than held as a fiduciary, that is for personal self-interest, rather than the interest of the beneficiary. The examples of such abuse are legion, from the Venetian private bankers to the raids of Charles I and Charles II on the Tower and the Exchequer deposits of the goldsmith-bankers. The generalised failure of these safekeeper fiduciaries to meet their trust responsibilities led to the cry for bank reform. In Venice the Rialto Bank and the Banco del Giro, in Germany giro banks were founded in Hamburg in 1619 and Nuremburg in 1621, in the Netherlands, the Bank of Amsterdam. The major justification for formation of what became the Bank of England was to provide a giro bank for deposit safety. These banks were fiduciary banks in the sense that they could only hold deposits, not employ them. But, not only did they provide safekeeping of specie and plate for individuals, they provided payment services. They functioned as clearing houses, and created a linkage between the trust or fiduciary relationship and the transfer of ownership, now better known as means of payment services. However, for most of these banks the transactions services were strictly 'in bank'. The individual depositors had to present themselves before the money scrivener to effect a transfer (each party to the transaction had to verify that the physical property being transferred was that which had been originally given or received).

The Bank of Amsterdam provided a technological advance by providing a common, abstract unit of account for these transfers, 'bank money', which was uniform and non-existent. It did not initially offer receipts which could function as means of payment. So in the early stages the giro banks were *de facto* trust or fiduciary banks, but they did not create fiduciary money in the form of bank notes that could be redeemed by the bearer rather than the original creditor. This was the real innovation by the Bank of England granted, according to Clapham, as an afterthought to the draft of the Act creating the bank.[9]

And it was an innovation, for the issue of notes allowed the creation of a bank without the owners providing the initial capital. The bank could lend by issuing notes against the collateral of the shares issued to the owners. Instead of representing a trust holding the specie given by a depositor to a safekeeper, the issue of notes represented the trust holding of (unpaid) shares in the capital of the bank. In simple terms, the bank was a trust holding unpaid IOUs. Here '*depositum non est mutuum*' has become a contradiction in terms; what is held by the bank is a loan. The presumption was that the bank would produce enough income to repay the loans and thus constitute the bank's capital. The issue of notes to form the capital of the bank was then a discounting operation, which made future income present income, and made the present income liquid as a means of payment. What was being capitalised was in effect the business value of the bank charter.

But, this system was rapidly extended to the discounting of other projects offering expected income and making them liquid. This is what becomes the normal loan business of the bank. And it is what recommended the institutions to most governments that approved banks. It is clear in the attempt to create a Land bank at the same time as the Bank of England; land owners could see no reason why they could not capitalise the value of their real estate assets into liquid bank notes in the same way that the financial assets of the owners of the Bank of England had been turned into current purchasing power. The same attraction motivated most state governments in the USA, who looked upon banks as a way of creating the capital needed for their development without pledging anything more than future possibilities. They perfected the practice of creating banks without any paid-in capital in the form of specie. Yet, these same institutions continued to issue notes against specie, and to make their notes payable in specie. This was called a 'fiduciary' issue of money because it was presumed that the bank held specie in trust against the notes, when in fact what little specie it had was usually employed in the self-interested operations of the bank's owners.

However, the conjunction of the holding in trust of specie and creating notes or deposits against bank advances creates an additional moral hazard independent of the separation of ownership from managerial control. Even if management acts in the interests of the owners, rather than its own, there may be a conflict between the interest of the owners and the external creditors of the corporation. Under normal corporate law this difficulty is not difficult to overcome, for indentures to credit documents may be written which place effective legal controls on the behaviour of management to insure the interests of senior external creditors. This is a practice that goes back to the beginning of corporate form in the USA.[10] Bondholders can write what is the equivalent of a trust document which limits the ability of management to employ the funds which have been entrusted to them through the bond indenture. This is why they are said to provide 'senior' debt. But in a bank, the major source, and sometimes the sole source, of capital is from the issue of bank notes, the fiduciary issue, and it is the use of notes in lending which is the major source of earnings. The noteholder, who is not a borrower or an owner, is thus the senior, unsecured, creditor of the bank.

Obviously, the same arguments apply to financial systems in which the note issue has been consolidated in a single bank, usually the

National or State bank (the idea of a central bank or a monetary authority is a more modern one), leaving the rest of the system to issue deposits. It is the depositor of funds, who is neither owner nor borrower, that provides the capital of the bank. However, since banks are generally regulated by commercial charter, or a special version of the commercial charter dealing with banks, the depositor does not enjoy the same protection as a bond holder or as the beneficiary in a trust. As a result, the depositor is subject to the hazard that the bank is operated in the interests of the equity owners, which may conflict with the interests of depositors.

Within this framework it is clear that action to increase competition in the banking sector with the aim of increasing efficiency and shareholder value may exacerbate the conflict between the interests of unsecured depositor-creditors and residual owner-shareholders of the bank. The position that one takes on the appropriateness of bank regulation to control this moral hazard or conflict of interest will depend on whether the depositor is considered to be more like a beneficiary to a trust and the bank more like a fiduciary, or whether the depositor more resembles a short-term unsecured creditor and the bank more a business firm that has as its principle objective the maximisation of shareholder value. It seems that depositors are considered by legislators to be similar to beneficiaries, while banks are considered by economists and management consultants to be ordinary business firms. However, the regulations which are required to realise the former restrict the possibility of achieving the latter. In such conditions increased competition by its very nature produces moral hazard in bank management, the managers are being asked to act at the same time in the interests of depositors and shareholders. The regulatory legislation that has been introduced to make depositors more like beneficiaries is of two types. One seeks to insure the full capitalisation of non-trust, joint-stock banks at adequate levels, the other seeks more directly to force banks to behave as fiduciaries towards their depositors.

Traditionally, company charters did not specify minimum levels of capitalisation, or impose terms for the payment of capital subscriptions. Thus, specific legislation for the incorporation of banks usually involved the creation of a special charter for banking institutions, and specified, inter alia, higher capital standards than applied to normal commercial companies, increased personal liability for owners of banks and set special conditions on payment of bank capital subscriptions. The result was that the chartering of banks became the granting of monopoly powers (as the Bank of England continuously sought to convince Parliament) and which became a source of corruption in the early US financial system.

The second type of regulation required banks to hold specie reserves against deposit liabilities, that is to behave more as fiduciaries. An early example was the 1844 Bank Act which sought to insure that specie and Bank of England notes were 100 per cent substitutes, but not complements, so that '*depositum non est mutuum*', although specie was fungible to this requirement. This concept was extended in the USA to providing 'security' for bank deposits. It was usual for specie reserves against deposits to be substituted or supplemented by holdings of lists of safe securities, usually local or federal securities, as in a trust act.

These two types of regulation were often considered to be interchangeable. In the United States the era of free banking, which abandoned special chartering of banks on the grounds that it encouraged monopoly and impeded competition, was based on the idea that the imposition of 100 per cent reserve requirements would make the business so onerous that only suitable persons would operate banks and would employ capital appropriate to their operations. Special charter provisions were considered unnecessary.[11] As a result of complaints from bankers, even the requirement of reserves of securities of 100 per cent of deposits was quickly reduced, but the principle of a security reserve composed of an officially approved list of securities remained. Today, that list has been reduced to one item, deposits with the central bank, while the concept of an approved list of securities has been extended to the banks' entire investment portfolio.

This extension occurred in the USA after the 1933 Bank Holiday, when banks that continued to acquire credit via deposits were required to limit their activities to a list of acceptable investments, primarily the underwriting and investment of local and federal government securities and commercial and industrial short-term collateralised advances.[12] Not only were the equivalent of specie reserves required, the bank's portfolio was now designed to provide security for depositors.

This extension of the 'index of approved investments' to the investments of a bank represented an attempt by United States authorities to impose on the system the 'Banking principle' in the form of the real bills doctrine. This had formed the basis of the Federal Reserve Act, and most experts blamed the 1930s banking crisis on the fact that the majority of banking activities had been in the underwriting and financing of speculation in private company liabilities, rather than loans to finance real productive activity. Thus, the new legislation was a compromise which was meant to provide security for depositors similar to that of a 100 per cent reserve system, while it retained real bills by restricting the use of bank funds to the financing of commercial and industrial activity or riskless government lending.[13]

In the postwar period a US commercial bank was subject to virtually the same type of regulations as a fiduciary in a private trust before the introduction of the prudent-man rule. The difficulties facing commercial banks arose because of a failure of banking authorities to adapt a similar mechanism to prudent man, leaving banks to experiment individually in order to discover what the relevant regulatory authorities considered acceptable investment behaviour. The ink was barely dry on the 1933 Bank Act before commercial banks started to transgress the list of approved investments, providing term loans with maturities to 15 years to commercial borrowers – not really the stuff real bills are made of (cf. Trescott, 1963, p. 212). One of the reasons, of course, was the collapse of the equity market and the difficult conditions faced by investment banks, but the pressure of competition as banks attempted to replace their bond departments and security affiliate business was present. After the war the competition from government securities reduced their corporate core deposits, while other forms of corporate borrowing, such as commercial paper, reduced the bank's natural commercial and industrial (C&I) clientele. Banks were forced to push beyond the boundaries of their official list of investments to more risky activities in order to survive in market conditions in which deposits were becoming more costly while borrowers were becoming ever more scarce. The story of the 'deregulation' of banking has been that of extending the official list of approved banking activities and the creation of 'section 20' affiliates that are free from the restrictions which limit maximisation of return on bank equity.[14]

There was an alternative to the approach taken in the 1930s legislation. At the same time as the shift to free bank chartering was occurring, the state of Louisiana in 1842 introduced the 'Forstall system' based on the principle that the primary role of a bank was to provide means of payment, and thus should limit investments to short-term, self-liquidating assets (cf. Kregel, 1996). This is not much different from the real-bills doctrine, except that, in addition, banks were required to separate their 'deadweight' loans, that is loans defined as longer-term credits secured by stocks or mortgages, from 'liquid' loans against assets maturing in less than 90 days and could only increase deadweight lending if their note and deposit (only Massachusetts and Louisiana had limitations on deposits) liabilities were secured by one-third in specie and two-thirds in paper liquidating in less than 90 days. This was similar in effect to the 1844 Bank Act, and kept the deposit and the investment sides of banking separate within the same bank. This is similar to the approach that has been used in Germany since the 1934 reform of the bank law. By setting up broad maturity-matching for fiduciary activity and the bank's own investment activities, it provides much greater freedom than the specification of a list of admissible securities (cf. Kregel, 1997a).

The German regulatory system more resembles the shift to the application of the prudent-man rule, as it leaves open the investment decisions of banks. Indeed, when the 1934 reform law retained universal banking, it was justified as simply codifying good banking practices. It does place restrictions on bank investments, but these are more designed to insure that long-term exposures to risk are matched by similar funding sources. Although the postwar German system provides for reserve requirements, they are conceived as serving monetary policy purposes rather than prudential or security purposes,[15] and only recently has a system of deposit insurance been considered necessary.

The continuous decline in the application of the trust principle through the erosion of the specified lists of investments has led bank regulation back to an emphasis on capital adequacy. But, this recent emphasis on capital requirements tends to undervalue or completely ignore the aspects of the trust principle that have evolved naturally as constituent parts of the framework, or better the structure, of the financial system that provides for the security of depositors funds.

A good example of a financial structure providing implicit stability is Italy, which introduced reforms similar to the USA in March 1936, placing the entire financial sector under the direct or indirect control of the government. The reform was the culmination of the experience of 20 years of government rescues of small and large banks, and the clear aim was to provide a mechanism for safeguarding private savings. It was based on the idea that the collection of public saving and its investment, that is the exercise of credit, constitute a function considered to be in the public interest and subject to government scrutiny and control. This approach was aided by the existence of a fascist government seeking centralised control of the economy. All credit institutions were placed under the control of the *Ispettorato per la difesa del risparmio e l'esercizio del credito* (Inspectorate for the Defence of Saving and the Exercise of Credit) which was expressly created for the central planning of saving and investment (cf. Guarneri, 1988, p. 573). The reform created the equivalent of US commercial banks, the 'Aziende di Credito', as the standard form of deposit-taking institution, separated from the 'Istituti di Credito Speciale' responsible for the long-term finance of industrial investment through the issue of debt securities. As in the USA, the Italian ordinary credit banks soon found their limited investment opportunities excessively restrictive and started to expand their activities into longer-term lending to firms, the restricted province of the special credit institutes. This was aided by the fact that the government control of the investment banking activities of these institutes effectively eliminated the development of a private market for financing firms' longer-term debt commitments.

In this context the Italian system provided the continued protection of savings by promoting what has come to be called the system of 'dual intermediation'. In the words of the then Governor of the Bank of Italy, and the main architect of this process:

> When the banks spread into the field of long-term credit, this means that they finance fixed capital formation by loans which, so far as the borrowing company is concerned, supplement or replace self-financing and funds raised on the capital market. ... Recent experience both in Italy and elsewhere shows that the banks are spreading into the long-term field both through direct loans for fixed capital formation and through larger security portfolios. ... However, the two forms in which banks may enter the long-term field are very different from the point of view of risk selection and ultimate risk distribution.
>
> As regards the first form [i.e. direct financing of capital formation], we in Italy have had our bitter experience in this century. ...
>
> In the second form, when the banks acquire bonds of large direct issuers, the risk is limited both to the extent that such bonds may be government-guaranteed and that they can be more easily sold on the stock exchange.
>
> When the banks buy the bonds of special credit institutes, the two intermediary stages through which savings thus pass on their way from households to investing firms bring about an aggregation of selected risks which is akin to insurance. When the banks buy securities and so keep intact the deposits which the public might have used for the same purpose, depositors are in effect relieved of the risk of price fluctuations. When they buy bonds issued by the industrial credit institutes, the banks acquire securities which guarantee a higher degree of liquidity, even though this may involve price fluctuations, and which have a built-in compensation of risks among different firms and sectors.
>
> In the end, when the banks expand their intermediation by offering higher rates to savers with no definite preference as between deposits and securities, they do not fundamentally alter the division of labour between banks and special credit institutes in our system, provided the larger deposits find their counterpart in security invest-

> ments and are not simply a forced attempt to make good a failure to reduce banking costs; nor do the banks thereby create conditions in which their assets are in danger of freezing, so that ultimately they can turn only to the central bank.
>
> But the amount of bonds which can be placed with the banking system has its limits, and it is hard to see how these limits can be transgressed if we want to have a market in which bond prices, and hence yields, remain free to oscillate. Without a margin for oscillation, bonds would become like money, and we would lose variations in the rate of interest as one of the mechanisms by which the demand for funds can be balanced with their supply. Even if the monetary authorities intervene to keep the oscillations within a narrow range, the banks may still be afraid of losses and hence limit their purchases. (Carli, 1993, pp. 166–8)

This system, which made formal deposit insurance redundant, was in place until the late 1970s. As Carli noted, there are limits to the amount of bonds that can be placed with the banking system, and the increasing government deficits soon produced government debts that passed this limit. The decision to join the EMS and the greater need to control interest rates for currency stability brought about the so-called 'divorce' between the Bank of Italy and the Treasury. The result was a shift by the public from deposits to government debt, the introduction of a bank-organised deposit insurance fund and increased emphasis on the Bank of Italy's role in bank supervision.

Germany was spared the legislative reactions typical of the USA and Italy in the 1930s, but its concern to protect savings within the banking system was no less evident. It is common to identify the German system as one in which equity financing is unimportant. But it is completely unjustified to present the German financial system as one in which securities markets play no role. It would be more correct to say that in postwar Germany the bond market, and in particular bank bonds, replaced the equity market as the dominant security market, and households restricted their asset holdings to bank deposits (cf. Kregel, 1995). The share of deposits in family assets has been around 50 per cent for the postwar period (rising as high as 60% in the 1960s). Sight deposits (again taking the mid-1980s as a reference) were around 10 per cent of households' annual savings flows with time and passbook-savings deposits accounting for around 40 per cent, (with the shares of the two shifting back and forth from around 3 to 1 depending on the interest rate environment). The deposits are primarily held through the government-guaranteed regional banks (for mid-1980 around 30%), local Sparkassen (10%) and the co-operative banks (20%), rather than in the larger banks (the big three account for only around 10%). On the other hand, firms financed their postwar expansion primarily from internal funds, supplemented initially by short-term bank borrowing, which soon evolved into *de facto* or *de jure* long-term lending commitments from banks.

Taken as a whole, the banking system carried on its balance sheets the price risk that in Italy was diversified through the system of double intermediation described by Carli. But, if one looks more closely, the majority of small private deposits were held with the local savings and regional government. These are the local and regional savings banks which invested primarily in government debt or with the co-operative banks which lent primarily to their local individual members at very low risk. Any excess funds were transferred through the two girozentral systems to the regional and then the national level, where they could be used in financing industrial and commercial borrowing. It is the national Giro institutions for the cooperatives and the regional savings banks that provide competition with the big universal banks. Thus, there was a similar type of risk diversification to protect the funds of small savers (cf. Kregel, 1997a).

The larger banks were the primary lenders to large industry, and it is on the balance sheets of these banks that the mismatch between borrowing through deposit-taking and lending long-term to industry may appear. It is at this stage that the regulatory structure of the German system becomes important. Through a system of liquidity and capital ratios which had been in operation since the 1930s, German banks were subject to broad balance sheet controls which required matching of short-term liabilities with equivalent term assets and long-term liabilities with long-term assets.

As the postwar recovery progressed, banks found that the demands for long-term loans was outstripping the long-term resources required to meet the regulatory standards, since these resources were composed primarily of family savings deposits with terms over four years. With a falling share of equity in household portfolios and a stagnant equity market, it was not possible to raise equity. Banks started to issue bonds in order to generate long funding for their lending to firms. Initially these bonds were sold to other banks with portfolio mismatches or to insurance companies (after deposits, families held around 20% of their assets in insurance policies) which held almost all of their assets in bonds. It is important to recall that, unlike now, the German government was a net creditor through most of the postwar period, so that bank bonds found a ready home in insurance company portfolios.

Only in the 1970s did households start to hold bonds directly. Long-term bank lending to firms, intermediated through the bank bond market, came to replace the role of the equity markets in providing capital finance to German firms.

Despite the regulatory differences, the Italian system of double intermediation is remarkably similar to the German system. On the one hand, the separation of the ordinary credit and the special credit institutes of the Italian system is maintained in Germany via the separation of the maturity matching requirements of the long and short section of the balance sheet, and of the local sparkassen from the national giro bank. The use of bank bonds provides a dispersion of the risk of the price fluctuation of long-term bank loans, and the separation of deposit-taking through savings banks from the long-term lending to industry through the big private limited liability banks and the National giro banks has a similar effect.

Britain is unique in the group of USA, Italy and Germany in that it did not experience a major banking crisis in the 1930s. It escaped the more radical measures of separating industrial-investment banking and deposit banking. Both regulation and structure remained relatively stable until the 1970s. One is tempted to describe the British system as one of natural division of labour between deposit banking and industrial banking. The clearing banks did not engage in large-scale industrial lending, and behaved very much as if they were following the real-bills doctrine. For much of this time their deposit business was linked to commercial firms and their investments were in bills and commercial loans. The discount houses played a crucial role in rendering bills and government securities liquid, which represented a crucial difference from the New York money market where call money was lent by commercial banks to stockmarket firms. Merchant banks and private investment houses provided for trade financing and investment underwriting. The deposits of the labouring public, as noted, were placed in savings banks which invested in government securities. The basic form of long-term capital finance was retained earnings and the stockmarket, where the investment trusts and other financial institutions such as mutual insurance companies played a crucial role (recall Keynes' battle to make equity a suitable investment for life companies).

Financial institutions still hold from 40 to 50 per cent of the equity in the British market. The major impact of competition and credit control in 1971 was to give the clearing banks a larger share of the small retail depositor market and entry into the building societies' preserve of mortgage lending. Despite the fact that there is no formal impediment to clearing banks acting as universal banks, they were never tempted to do so. But, the banks that experienced the greatest difficulty were merchant banks, heavily dependent on foreign business, that found themselves in great difficulty when England went off gold in 1931. The predominant use of investment trusts and other forms of institutional investment as the basis for capital market financing is just what the 100 per cent reserve plans proposed by Henry Simons (Simons, 1948) and Irving Fisher (Fisher, 1935) had ordered. The clearing banks, although they did not keep 100 per cent reserves, did have a very good record of keeping their cash ratios above 10 per cent of deposits through the worst years of the 1930s. Thus, in all of these different national financial systems, trust banks contribute to overall stability by offering low-risk deposits and management which does not pursue maximum shareholder participation through leveraged loan and investment portfolios.

Competition from non-trust financial institutions to provide satisfactory returns to their equity owners has been an important force in changing the overall financial framework that has provided inherent protection for depositors via the coexistence of various types of bank ownership. Given that joint-stock banks can operate on the principle of leveraging their earnings, returns to equity on such banks are higher than the returns to beneficiaries of trust banks. This has led to a belief that trust banks could be made more efficient by being transformed to equity-owned profit-maximising banks. But such a comparison loses sight of the fact that the goals of trust-based banks are different from those of equity banks. It also overlooks their contribution to financial stability when they exist in combined financial systems.

Recent regulations placing minimum limits on capital in bank charters may be considered as a substitute for the specification of a schedule of acceptable investments. But they also represent a shift in logic to exclusion of combined financial systems because a capital requirement for a trust bank is a contradiction in terms – a mutual bank has no equity capital, only the funds of its beneficiaries, and in general it will not be engaged in leveraged lending but simply managing the investments of its members' funds.[16] The move towards increased reliance on capital requirements to insure depositor protection suggests that regulators operate on the presumption that trust-banking organisations do not exist or that they should be eliminated as inefficient. Yet, the history of most banking systems suggests there are positive benefits from a symbiotic coexistence of trust-based and profit-based banking organisation. Indeed, throughout much of history the role of providing protection for small savers' deposits has been borne by some form or other of general framework in which trust-based institutions played a central role. This suggests that financial systems are likely to behave much differently without them, and that capital requirements may be less efficient at providing systemic stability because they ignore the importance of the appropriate balance between trust and self-interest in financial market exchange.

Notes

1. Smith is concerned to show the viability or an economy based on the division of labour, and is not linked to a separate discussion concerning the 'invisible hand'. (Cf. Kregel, 1985.)
2. The actions aimed at the preservation of capital, either in nominal or real terms, is not specifically mentioned, although nominal preservation was eventually introduced and some courts have considered a policy to offset inflation as prudent.
3. Similar to US money market mutual funds introduced in the 1970s to allow small savers to invest in government bonds normally sold in $1 million minimum size.
4. The mutual concept was used in the formation of life insurance companies which were the property of the policy-holders. Pension funds, credit unions, friendly societies, building societies and building and loan banks are in this category.
5. Not to be confused with the Cooperative Wholesale Society in the UK which offered limited financial services to members of its wholesale merchandising operations, but equivalent to 'people's banks' in other European countries.
6. When charters were temporally limited, the shareholders of record at winding up take the place of the remainder man in a private trust.
7. There were early banks formed on the basis of capital represented by an income earning asset. The best known surviving example is the Monte dei Paschi di Siena.
8. The discussion here is based on arguments in Kregel, 1996a.
9. Clapham says the charter made no explicit provision for the Bank to issue notes. Clause 28 of the Act, joined to the original bill as a separate schedule, makes reference to 'Bills obligatory and of credit under the Seale of the Corporation' and makes these 'sealed notes' assignable by endorsement. The Bank quickly started to issue them, along with Cashier's Notes, paying 2^{d} per cent per day, in an amount equivalent to the government debt it had agreed to acquire in exchange for the Bank Charter. Some notes were used by the members of the Compania to complete their initial subscription for shares. Clapham (p.20, p. 305) notes that the 'Bonds' of 'subscribers', a sort of over-the-counter personal IOU, were accepted in lieu of the stipulated cash payments. They represented bank advances to shareholders and it is impossible to discover how much hard specie the government received from the Bank, but it was certainly less than a quarter of the sum stipulated in the Act. The balance was financed by the credit created by the bank.
10. Cf. Lyon in a book on corporate finance: 'Organizers of a corporation may contract out to holders of other classes of securities some of the control exercised by the stock, and to that extent place control with the other classes of securities' (p. 11) ... 'the corporate mortgage has become the most

elaborate document, and through it the bondholders secure to themselves very substantial amounts of actual present control ... [through] limitations, in favor of the bondholders, on the power of the shareholders' (Lyon, 1916, pp. 29–30).

11. According to contemporary (1827) comment by Professor John McVickar, who argued that specialised charters conferred monopoly rights which created moral hazard for the legislator, the reserve conditions should prove to be so onerous that 'banking would lose all its attraction except to the honest, the economical and the persevering; it would have no surplus profits to tempt the needy and the speculative, nor any cover for bankruptcy to allure the unprincipled' (quoted in Madeleine, 1943, p.159).
12. There was a movement in the US to introduce trust legislation via 100% reserving. This was to be accomplished by allowing the banks to sell their investment portfolio over time and 'After this substitution of actual money for securities had been completed, the bank would be required to maintain *permanently* a cash reserve of 100% against its demand deposits. In other words, the demand deposits would literally be deposits, *consisting of cash held in trust for the depositor.'* (Italics added) (Fisher, 1935, p. 10). This implied the separation of deposit banking from investment banking: 'If our bankers wish to retain the strictly banking function – loaning – which they can perform better than the Government, they should be ready to give back the strictly monetary function which they cannot perform as well as the Government.' (Ibid., p. 20).
13. In the absence of a formal document providing security for depositors, banks were required to acquire malpractice insurance (in the form of deposit insurance) and to prevent the moral hazard thus created, were forbidden from competing for deposit funds.
14. Although the Federal Reserve still limits the proportion of the gross returns that the affiliate can derive from these activities.
15. There is a substantial difference between a security reserve, such as that implied by the 1844 Bank Act, or the free banking legislation in the US and the use of variations in reserve requirements as an instrument of monetary policy. This latter role seems to have been first contemplated in the US in 1916 and only fully introduced in the 1935 Bank Act. It was about this time that it was first considered in Germany. It has never been used, although recommended by the Macmillan Commission, in the UK.
16. This is less true of the German savings and cooperative banks, since they accept funds from non-members. Nonetheless, it does make the trust aspect of their operations more onerous. This is in part offset by the use of government guarantees in the provision of capital to these banks, reducing their capital costs. Private German banks are requesting the European Commission to ban this as anti-competitive. It is offset for all types of trust banks that limit their investments to government securities which are given zero risk weighting in the capital requirement formula.

References

Barnett, G. E. (1911) *State Banks and Trust Companies since the Passage of the National-Bank Act* (Washington, D.C.: Government Printing Office).

Carli, G. ((1993) 'Concluding Remarks for 1965', in *Concluding Remarks to the Annual Reports of the Bank of Italy, 1960–1974* (Special Issue of the Banca Nazionale del Lavoro *Quarterly Review).*

Clapham, J. H. (n.d.)*The Bank of England, I* (Cambridge: Cambridge University Press).

Fisher, I. (1935) *100% Money* (New York: Adelphi).

Guarneri, F. (1988) *Battaglie Economiche fra le due Guerre* (Bologna: il Mulino).

Hahn, F. H. (1980) 'General Equilibrium Theory', in *The Crisis in Economic Theory,* special issue of *The Public Interest.*

Kregel, J. A. (1985) 'Is the "Invisible Hand" a "Fallacy of Composition"?', *Cahiers d'Economie Politique,* nos. 10–11, pp. 33–49.

—- (1992) 'Universal Banking, US Banking Reform and Financial Competition in the EEC', *Banca Nazionale del Lavoro Quarterly Review,* no. 182, September, pp. 231–54.

—- (1985) 'Market Form and Financial Performance', *Economic Notes,* vol. 24, no. 3, pp. 485–504.

—- (1996) *Origini e sviluppi dei mercati finanziari* (Arezzo: Banca popolare dell'Etruria e del Lazio / studi e ricerche).

—- (1997a) 'The Role of 1930s Regulations in the Development of Financial Markets in Post-war USA, Germany and Britain', in D. J. Forsyth and T. Notermans (eds), *Regime Changes: Macroeconomic Policy and Financial Regulation in Europe from the 1930s to the 1990s* (Boston: Berghahn Books Inc.).

—- (1997b) 'Corporate Governance of Banks: Germany', *Banca Nazionale del Lavoro Quarterly Review* (Special Issue, supplement to no. 200, March).

Longstreth, B. (1986) *Modern Investment Management and the Prudent Man Rule* (New York: Oxford University Press).

Lyon, H. ((1916) *Corporate Finance,* complete edition (New York: Houghton Mifflin).

Madeleine, M. G. (1943) *Monetary and Banking Theories of Jacksonian Democracy* (Philadelphia: Sisters, Servants of the Immaculate Heart of Mary).

Robbins, L. (1952) *The Theory of Economic Policy* (London: Macmillan).

Sarcinelli, M. (1977) 'Bank Governance: Models and Reality', *Banca Nazionale del Lavoro Quarterly Review* (special Issue, supplement to no. 200, March).

Simons, H. (1948) 'Positive Program for Laissez Faire', in *Economic Policy for a Free Society* (Chicago: Chicago University Press).

Tonveronachi, M. (1997) 'The Corporate Governance of Banks: Alternative Solutions for Coherent Structures and Control', *Banca Nazionale del Lavoro Quarterly Review* (special Issue, supplement to no. 200, March).

Trescott, P. B. (1963) *Financing American Enterprise: The Story of Commercial Banking* (New York: Harper & Row).

6
The Dynamics of Change and Risk in Corporate and Wholesale Finance

Barry Howcroft

Introduction

The traditional function of commercial banks has been to act as financial intermediaries between deficit and surplus sectors (Heffernan, 1996) but fundamental to this process has been the assumption that banks can intermediate at lower costs than those prevailing in direct financing arrangements (Gurley and Shaw, 1960). Developments in corporate wholesale financing over the past twenty years or so have, however, significantly undermined this 'cost imperative' for large national and international companies. This has resulted in significant disintermediation of commercial banks by large companies and raised the question as to whether this development signals merely another evolutionary phase in modern banking or something far more fundamental which could herald the ultimate demise of commercial banking (Gardener and Revell, 1988).

Commercial banks have responded to these changes by becoming more investment bank oriented (Rybczynski, 1996). Traditional on-balance-sheet services for large companies have, therefore, been largely replaced by the off-balance-sheet activities of providing investment advice, making placements and the provision of standby facilities, and so on. These fundamental changes in business activity have had a marked effect on the commercial banks' principal sources of income, but perhaps, just as important, on the risks inherent in the business. Equally, these changes have had an effect on the banks' business philosophy and how they conduct their business which have quite marked social and economic implications which impinge far beyond wholesale banking.

An historical perspective: the growth within wholesale financial intermediation

Before these sorts of issues and their implications for modern-day banking can be discussed in detail, it is important to take an historical perspective in order to understand why there has been this shift away from wholesale financial intermediation. The biggest impetus to commercial banks' corporate wholesale activities and, therefore, perhaps the logical starting point, was the quintupling of oil prices in 1974. This resulted in massive deficits in the current accounts of OECD and non-OPEC less-developed countries (LDCs). An insight into the sheer magnitude of these imbalances and the enormity of the financing problem is revealed by the fact that the combined current account deficits of these two country groupings increased from $2 billion in 1973 to $52 billion the following year. Subsequent hikes in the price of oil in 1978 ensured that these imbalances continued, eventually peaking in 1981 at $105 billion! The brunt of the adjustment process, however, fell on non-OPEC LDCs whose current account deficits alone totalled $85 billion during 1981. The traditional providers of international finance, namely the International Monetary Fund (IMF) and the World Bank, simply lacked the resources to finance imbalances on this scale, and as a consequence the vacuum was filled by the world's private commercial banks (United Nations, 1991).

History bears testimony to the fact that between 1974–82 private commercial banks were only too willing to participate in wholesale business. The growth in syndicated bank lending, for example, was quite spectacular, increasing from 226 announced deals with a total value of $7.4 billion in 1972 to 1070 deals with a total value of $131.5 billion at its peak in 1981. Similarly, throughout the period 1974–78 the Eurocurrency market was growing at an annual rate of approximately 25 per cent per annum, suggesting that participating banks could double the size of their balance sheets over this four-year period. As profits did not keep pace with this growth, capital inadequacy emerged as a serious problem for the banks and eventually undermined shareholder confidence. The reasons underpinning the private commercial banks' willingness to enter these new markets are varied, but perhaps it would be unfair and probably untrue to suggest that they were simply awash with deposits and were desperate to on-lend these funds. Banks, like conventional businesses, think strategically in terms of asset growth rather than liability growth. In other words, they decided by how much they wanted to see assets grow, which markets they wanted to be in, what products they wanted to be associated with, and so on, and then sought to finance their expansion plans via deposit acquisition. For about three to four years after the initial oil price hike, private commercial banks gave every indication of wanting OPEC deposits by actively competing against each other and increasing bid prices. This suggests that they had clear ideas regarding how and where these resources were going to be deployed. The new markets presented by the financing requirements of LDCs emerged at exactly the time when the banks' traditional domestic markets, triggered by the oil crisis, were going through deep recession. As such, they presented the banks with an opportunity to enter new markets and diversify their business. The herd instinct, so strong in banks at the best of times, prevailed and almost all banks, irrespective of size and experience, were eager to take advantage of the new opportunities which the new markets presented. This 'follow-my-leader' attitude was also facilitated by syndicated lending which allowed relatively small and inexperienced banks to join international syndications as participants.

In order to get a foothold in these new LDC markets, there is also strong evidence to suggest that commercial banks adopted a loss-leader strategy or were, at least, prepared to lend on extremely attractive terms. Maturities on syndicated lending, for example, increased from an average of 6.57 years in 1972 to 8.71 years by 1979, and spreads (using spreads as a proxy for price) decreased from 1.56 per cent in 1975 to 0.71 per cent in 1981. When account is taken of the bid rates prevailing at the time, it becomes very clear that the private banks were operating on extremely fine margins and offering terms which, in many respects, were more attractive than the official sector (Edwards, 1984).

This encouraged excessive consumption of private bank finance which, combined with the vagaries of balance of payments financing and the ensuing capital flight (spurred on by cheap borrowing and high-earning, relatively risk-free bank deposits) began to make the private commercial banks feel increasingly uncomfortable. Consequently, from about 1978 there was a perceptible shift away from sovereign lending and balance of payments financing towards project financing with its emphasis on collateral and repayment from the future dedicated cash flows of projects. This change in the mode of financing facilitated a continuation of wholesale financing to LDCs until 1983 when, rather than incur the stigma (and wrath of the banks) of outright default, several major debtor countries rescheduled their debts. During this year $63 billion, approximately 9 per cent of outstanding private debt, was rescheduled and this signalled a virtual end to the wholesale financial intermediation of the previous nine years and the beginning of a new era in wholesale banking.

Several initiatives, notably from Secretaries Brady and Baker of the US government, attempted to persuade private banks to initiate new advances to the most heavily indebted developing countries, but the success of these plans was modest (Kaletsky, 1985). As a result, from 1984 through to 1990 capital flight combined with interest repayments on outstanding debt meant that there was an implied net transfer of resources from developing countries to the lending banks located in the industrialised countries. Concerns about the ability of the principal debtor countries to control their respective economies and repay outstanding principal persisted throughout the remainder of the 1980s, and a high proportion of internationally renowned banks had their triple-A credit rating reduced by Standard and Poor's and Moody's. Not only did this adversely affect the propensity of investors to place international deposits with the banks, but it also reduced shareholder confidence. Consequently, in 1986 the international banking fraternity, led by the example set in America, began attempting to strengthen their balance sheets by making substantial provisions for bad and doubtful Third World debts.

In 1987, the UK's four main banks' (Barclays, Lloyds, Midland and NatWest) total exposure to LDC debt amounted to £14.7 billion, and in the instances of Lloyds and Midland their exposures were greater than their total capital. Consequently, when provisions ranging from 28–25 per cent of outstanding debt were made during that year, Lloyds and Midland saw their hitherto substantial profits reduced to losses of £248 million and £505 million respectively. This rather painful action was thought necessary to strengthen the banks' balance sheets, but there was undoubtedly a certain amount of politicking between the UK banks aimed primarily at Midland Bank, whose balance sheet position had already been weakened, notably by the acquisition of Crocker. In any event, the better performance of Latin American countries, especially towards the end of the 1980s, saw provisions being eventually clawed back into profits and, to some extent, this offset bank losses which were incurred in the early 1990s. The ability to securitise Latin American debt and repackage or transform essentially illiquid financial assets into liquid securities also helped to resolve the problem of bank exposure as did their ability to sell Third World debt (Bray, 1984; Editorial, *The Banker*, 1991).

With retrospect the obvious question to ask is: was the financing option the best solution to non-OPEC LDC deficits? From the perspective of industrialised countries, so-called 'recycling' could not prevent economic recession, but at least it avoided a world depression by facilitating relatively high volumes of international trade at fairly buoyant prices. Within industrialised countries, financing of external deficits by the banking sector also meant that the problem became a relatively short-term problem for the other sectors in the economy. The exception, of course, was the banking sector itself which was to inherit Third World debt problems for the next fifteen years or so. From both a political and economic viewpoint, however, 'sacrificing' the banks in this way was probably a reasonably price to pay when viewed against the lack of alternative solutions and the possibility of world depression. It is perhaps also worthwhile reflecting on the fact that governments under pressure find it politically expedient to periodically criticise or penalise the banking system, and the 1970s was no exception.

From the perspective of non-OPEC LDCs, they undoubtedly bore the brunt of the industrialised countries readjustment process despite being worse-placed to afford it. From an economic perspective, however, financing the balance of payments deficits did alleviate much of the short-term hardship which otherwise would have resulted in these countries. Moreover, if bank finance which was released into the private entrepreneurial sectors in Latin America had been used to develop their respective economies, as was the case in Korea and Taiwan, for example, they too would have emerged from the crisis much stronger. In the event, much of the finance released to the private sector resulted in capital flight attracted by the high rates and low risks prevailing on bank deposits at the time. As a result, Latin American governments became virtually bankrupt, whereas a minority of private entrepreneurs became extremely wealthy. This served to further polarise the economic and social dualism which has always existed in these countries. Finally, from a political perspective, financing the deficits was extremely efficient because governments typically elected for three to five years could borrow in excess of ten years and, therefore, need not concern themselves about eventual repayment and the economic and social hardships which this might entail.

Securitisation and disintermediation: the implications for commercial banking

Since 1983 the OPEC surpluses, the counterpart of non-OPEC LDC deficits, have been replaced by deficits and the position which OPEC occupied through the 1970s, as the world's surplus sector, has been taken over by Japan. This structural change in the world's balance of payments together with changing perceptions about the riskiness of banks brought about a significant change in investor-demand preferences. In contrast to OPEC investors' risk-aversion and preference for liquidity, characteristics which are generally associated with bank deposits, the profile of the emergent investors was more sophisticated with a preference for direct investment in capital market instruments. It is important, however, to recognise that many of the innovations which have liquefied or securitised the Euromarkets were also supply-led in the sense that the banks themselves initiated some of the changes. Banks have responded and, in some instances, anticipated gaps in the supply-and-demand disequilibrium in financial markets. This gap, which is referred to in the literature as 'the financial preference gap', exists when market participants either require a new form of intermediation or would purchase new financial investments if they existed. The process of liquefaction, therefore, involves the identification of gaps or latent demand in the market and a response to the expressed requirements and desires of market participants. In this respect, it is important to remember that both the dynamics of supply and demand in the Eurocurrency markets have been responsible for innovations in financial and capital-market investments (Feeney, 1987).

Securitisation has generated a wide range of new instruments (Henderson and Scott, 1988), but for the purposes of this chapter attention will be focused on those shown in Table 6.1, namely bonds and euronote facilities. Even with such a limited focus, it is important to recognise that the actual process of securitisation can be discussed at two broad levels (Gardener and Revell, 1988). The first, or primary level, involves commercial banks (and financial institutions) securitising existing illiquid portfolios by repackaging the assets in an acceptable form and selling them on as securities in the open market. In the United States, in particular, large markets have developed in loan-asset backed securities for car loans, mortgages and a wide range of other bank assets. The common purpose in all of these markets, however, remains the same, namely to resolve the problem of excess demand for loans at prevailing interest rates and existing levels of capitalisation relative to given levels of deposits. Although this type of securitisation involves what Gurley and Shaw (1960) refer to as 'direct finance' between the capital market and the banks, it also allows the banks to supplement their deposits which have been depleted by changes in investor demand preference. To some extent, therefore, this type of securitisation can also be regarded as a form of 'indirect finance' or financial intermediation.

Table 6.1 International financial activity (US$bn)

	1981	*1982*	*1983*	*1984*	*1985*	*1986*	*1987*	*1988*	*1989*	*1990*	*1992*	*1994*	*1996*
Securities markets instruments:													
Fixed-rate bonds (straights)	32.1	56.4	50.0	65.5	108.6	172.6	163.6	160.0	149.9	166.5	275.3	296.1	351.0
Floating-rate bonds (FRNs)	7.8	12.6	15.3	34.1	55.9	47.8	12.0	23.5	23.4	42.1	42.8	92.7	76.4
Euronote facilities inc underwritten faculties (NIFs, RUFs, etc)	1.0	2.3	3.3	18.8	5.3	57.2	37.3	10.6	10.3	3.0	10.2	–	–
Medium-term notes (MTNs)	–	–	–	–	–	–	–	16.3	12.2	22.1	22.6	157.0	223.9
Euro-commercial paper (ECP)	–	–	–	–	–	13.9	46.1	19.9	5.3	11.8	0.9	36.4	41.1
Total securities market	40.9	71.3	68.6	118.4	214.8	291.5	259.0	230.0	201.1	245.5	350.0	582.2	92.4
Announced eurocurrency syndicated loans	131.5	88.2	38.1	31.3	19.0	29.8	87.9	101.8	149.0	165.2	68.7	248.6	530.0

Source: Bank of England, *BIS Annual Reports*.

The secondary level of securitisation represents a serious challenge to commercial banking because it is exclusively concerned with direct financing and, therefore, involves the process of bank disintermediation, whereby flows through financial instruments are displaced by flows through capital markets (Kasi, 1990). Table 6.1 provides an insight into this trend over the period 1981–96 showing that at the beginning of this period Eurocurrency-syndicated lending was approximately 320 per cent greater than securities market activity, but that from 1983 onwards these positions were reversed (BIS, 1997). Despite the continued dominant position of capital market activity over bank lending for well over a decade, the past few years have witnessed a revival in bank-syndicated lending (Howcroft, 1998; Garrity, 1997). To some extent, however, this revival has been secured on the back of reduced margins to high-rated names and this serves to illustrate the importance for banks in linking this business to more lucrative or complicated services and also seeking higher returns through loans to smaller companies and personal customers (Garner, 1997).

Apart from the changing demand preferences of investors, the growing importance of the securities markets also reflects how innovative banks have been in responding to latent demand and the requirements of market participants. Bond financing has accordingly evolved from exclusive reliance on fixed-rate finance in the 1960s to floating-rate notes and instruments which incorporate convertibility and a variety of warranties. The best examples of innovation and growth over a relatively short period have, however, come from euronotes which were first introduced onto the markets in 1978 (BIS, 1986). The notes themselves are basically short-term bearer promissory notes issued for a set maturity, usually on a discount to yield basis, and denominated in a variety of currencies but usually in US dollars, ecus and Hong Kong dollars. Face values and maturities are similarly varied; for example, the face value of individual notes range from US $10 000 to US $500 000 and maturities range from 7 days to up to one year, although issues up to five years are not unusual and some medium-terms notes (despite the word 'medium') have had maturities in excess of 30 years.

In addition to the flexibility of the notes themselves, the success of euronote facilities has also been due to the responsiveness of the banks in changing the issuance mechanisms to reflect the various and sometimes conflicting needs of market players. As a consequence, the Revolving Underwitten Facility (RUF) was replaced by the Note Issuance Facility (NIF) in the early 1980s. As Figure 6.1 shows, the RUF

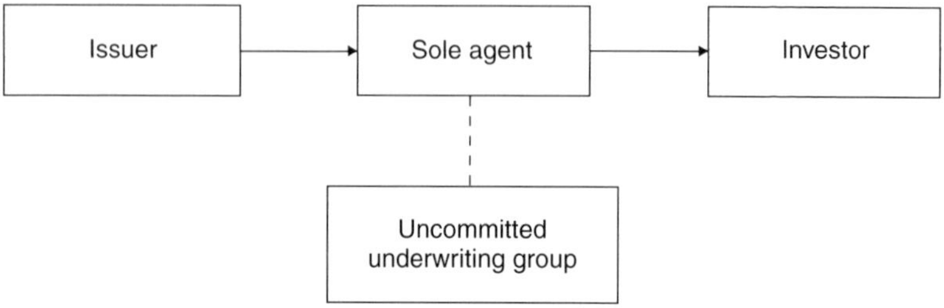

Figure 6.1 Revolving underwritten facility (RUF)

was a sole-placing-agent mechanism in which bids were made at an agreed fixed rate and the underwriting group had no opportunity to acquire notes until they were called upon to underwrite. Settlement took about 10 days and this raised concerns amongst issuers that just one bank acting on their behalf, that is the sole agent, did not have the necessary international network to quickly get the best deal for the customer or even sell the entire issue. Moreover, as bids were at an agreed fixed price, any windfall gain emanating from higher than expected investor demand went to the sole agent rather than the issuer.

Apart from the issuer's concerns, the underwriting group was also dissatisfied because they were prohibited from bidding for the notes and, therefore, did not have an opportunity to purchase them until they were called upon to underwrite the issue. This situation usually occurred when there was low investor demand typically caused by overpricing of notes or concerns about the creditworthiness of the issuer. As a direct consequence of these concerns, the NIF, shown in Figure 6.2, replaced the sole agent mechanism with a tender panel which could incorporate as many as 100 banks competitively tendering for notes within an agreed floor and ceiling price.

Any windfall gains (or at least a fair proportion) were, therefore, passed on to the issuer, and because the mechanism involved a relatively large number of bidding banks the commensurate increase in geographical spread and international networking reduced settlement time to about five days. Finally, as the tender panel usually incorporated the underwriting banks (it could also include banks who were not committed to underwrite), they were given the opportunity to bid for notes at the outset of placement.

Both RUFs and NIFs represent investment rather than commercial bank activities, and show the banks acting as agents on behalf of

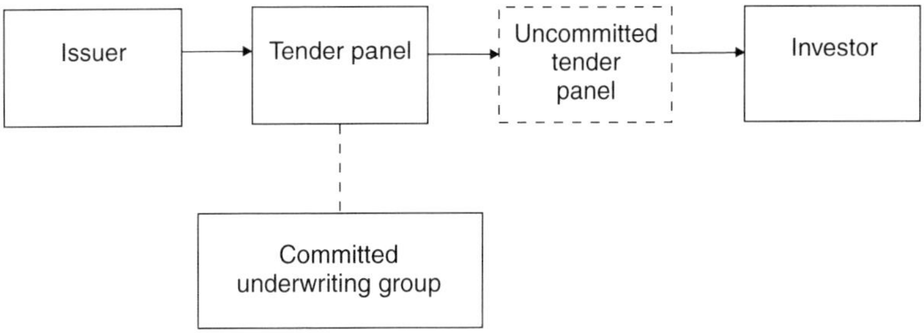

Figure 6.2 Note issuance facility (NIF)

clients rather than as financial intermediaries. As such, these activities do not appear on-balance sheet, but rather appear off-balance sheet as contingent liabilities in respect of underwriting commitments. Prior to the 1980s, the contingent liabilities readily associated with banking were limited to guarantees, acceptances and documentary credits, and so forth, and these were taken into account by the central authorities in calculating adequate capital. The emergence and unprecedented growth in euronote facilities, however, saw central banks effectively lagging behind market practice until 1987, when the introduction of new regulations on capital adequacy brought the underwriting of euronotes into account when calculating reserve asset ratios (Bank of England, 1987).

This reregulation was fairly unique in an era of unprecedented deregulation and had a marked effect on euronote business (see Table 6.1). It directly gave rise to Euro Commercial Paper (ECP) and, as Figure 6.3 shows, the emergence of ECPs heralded another distinctive change in wholesale activity. Under this mechanism the banks do not act as agents on behalf of investors, but rather are acting as dealers or principals in their own right, either holding the notes until maturity or operating a book and selling them in a secondary market. Equally significant is the fact that this business in on-balance sheet, there being no underwriting facility, with the notes typically appearing as 'investments' in the bank's balance sheet.

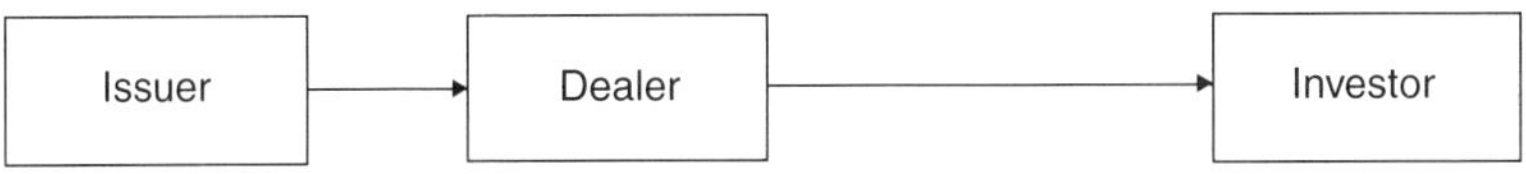

Figure 6.3 Euro commercial paper (ECP)

LIBID (cost of money)	+	MARGIN (overheads)	=	LIBOR (selling price)	+	SPREAD (risk factor)
↓		↓		↓		↓
4.5%		0.5%		5%		5.5%

Figure 6.4 Hypothetical example of costs associated with euronotes and conventional bank borrowing

The emergence of euro-medium-term notes (EMTNs) represents the final stage in recent wholesale-market innovation by combining some of the features of bonds and euronotes. Like bonds they can be underwritten, but they confer much greater flexibility than traditional bond issues. Placement through dealers, for example, represents a discrete way of testing market acceptance for new borrowers compared with traditional eurobonds. For regular borrowers, EMTN facilities provide a quicker and cheaper way of accessing different pockets of investment demand as they allow the introduction of tailor-made instruments which can often better capture arbitrage opportunities or regulatory loopholes compared with standalone international bonds. The attraction of euronote facilities for companies is undoubtedly the additional flexibility they confer on corporate treasurers, combined with their relative cheapness compared with more traditional forms of bank finance.

Bank borrowing is, for example, typically priced to risk around LIBOR (5.5% in Figure 6.4), whereas euronotes without the margin associated with financial intermediation are usually priced around LIBID plus a maximum (normally) of about 20 basis points i.e. $^{2}/_{10}$ ($4^{7}/_{10}$ in Figure 6.4). For top-rated companies, designated A_1^+ by Moody's credit rating agency and P_1 by Standard and Poor's, euronotes have been priced at sub LIBID. Similarly, euronote investors can earn yields in excess of LIBID and, therefore, in excess of prevailing interest rates on bank deposits. For representation purposes, the hypothetical example in Figure 6.4 does probably exaggerate the differences in costs and returns between euronotes and traditional financial intermediation, but even slight differences are sufficient to attract investors and borrowers.

To some extent, this reduction in costs and increase in returns is offset by a commensurate increases in risks. In essence, innovations in euronote facilities have separated all of the various functions and roles which were undertaken by the banks in classical syndicated lending. Accordingly, credit risk, funding risk and pricing risk and so on, which were normally assumed by banks, have been 'unbundled' and are now directly carried by either borrowers or investors. For example, with unwritten facilities credit risk is directly assumed by investors, and funding and pricing risks by borrowers.

Increased risk should also be considered against the fact that although euronote facilities constitute direct finance, in the sense that investors invest directly into companies, there is no 'relationship' between the two parties. This means that if a particular company goes through a crisis, or even a difficult trading period, the investor will be inclined to liquidate his investment to avoid any significant capital loss. In reality, a bank too would call in the liquidator if a company's trading position became impossible, but the important question of timing, that is when to liquidate the investment or to appoint the liquidator, would be quite different. This is because although a bank, like a private investor, is interested in ultimate return and needs to safeguard the investments of its depositors and shareholders, it is in the business of managing risk and within corporate financing this involves creating a banker – customer relationship and, therefore, by definition taking a longer-term perspective than the private investor. To some extent, too, there is a social and economic responsibility placed on banks to support corporate customers through times of crisis, which most definitely does not apply to the private investor.

Nevertheless, the success of euronote facilities has been primarily driven by reduced costs to borrowers and increased returns to investors, rather than concerns about increased risks. As Table 6.2 shows, disintermediation has been taking place for some time in the United Kingdom and France.

In the United States, which has always been regarded as a capital market system, net withdrawal of funds from the banks amounted to US$65 billion in 1990 (Llewellyn, 1994). This suggests that not only

Table 6.2 Percentage of net funds raised by non-financial companies

	1970		*1980*		*1990*	
	Banks	*Other*[1]	*Banks*	*Other*[1]	*Banks*	*Other*[1]
France	90	10	60	40	25	75
UK	95	5	80	20	20	80
USA	45	55	55	45	(–65)	(70)
Germany	100	0	95	5	80	20

[1] Bonds, shares and short-term securities; billions of US dollars.
Source: Llewellyn (1994).

are large US companies raising large amounts of direct finance on the capital markets (amounting to US$70 billion in 1990), but that they are also engaged in actively withdrawing funds from the banking system presumably either to finance themselves or to invest in capital market instruments. In Germany, which in contrast to the USA is regarded as a bank-oriented system with a long tradition of close banker–customer relationships, the same trend in disintermediation, albeit on a smaller scale, is taking place. This serves to emphasise that if large national and multinational companies want to compete in the world economy, they must be competitive and this means financing themselves in the most cost-effective markets which are no longer necessarily traditional bank or even local domestic markets. In other words, as companies become increasingly international, their funding operations must take on an equally globalised perspective.

As large national and international companies increasingly raise finance on the world's capital markets, the amounts borrowed from banks will continue to decline and this has significant implications for bank loan portfolios. On the assumption, made in bank-pricing strategy, that large companies are usually less risky than small companies, disintermediation will have a tendency to reduce profitability and increase portfolio risk by increasing the incidence of small companies and businesses. To some extent, these considerations, combined with the structural changes which are taking place in most western economies, explain why banks placed greater emphasis on the volumetric targetting of small businesses and the personal sector in the 1980s. The magnitude of this change is vividly put into perspective by the fact that in 1976 personal lending accounted for approximately 10 per cent of NatWest's loan portfolio, but by 1994 this figure had increased to 40 per cent.

The commensurate emergence of the 'hard-sell' in banks is not to be encouraged. The overheating of consumer demand and the ensuing economic recession and record high bank debt-provisioning bears testimony to this statement. Moreover, selling bank products is quite different from selling a pair of shoes or a shirt where quality is easily ascertained. In contrast, bank products can be complicated and are not readily understood even by sophisticated corporate treasurers. Consequently, there is an element of trust usually placed in banks which is not normally present in the conventional buyer–seller interchange. In contrast to the evolution of euronote facilities, where bank and customer needs were fairly evenly matched and where the customer benefits were readily discernible, developments in derivative and other sophisticated bank corporate products do raise the question as to whether this trust has been misplaced in an endeavour to simply get new business.

The change in bank business, with an increased emphasis on small companies and personal-sector lending, has also arguably made commercial banks more susceptible to cyclical changes in their domestic economies. Figure 6.5, which examines the UK commercial banks' returns on assets compared with annual growth rates in gross domestic product suggests that over the period 1984–94 bank profitability has become more closely linked to the performance of the domestic economy. This in itself, however, does not necessarily make the business of banking more risky as bank performance from 1982–86 reveals the folly of an internationally-diversified portfolio in the form of excessive lending to non-OPEC LDCs. Almost intuitively, however, there does seem to be some sense in the argument that an internationally-diversified portfolio, or at least a portfolio with internationally-diversified customers, can allow a bank to buck the trend in the domestic economy.

Figure 6.5 reveals that this was the case in the late 1970s and early 1980s when bank profitability remained relatively buoyant despite the economic recession. The significance of this is that it allowed the banks to continue financing fundamentally sound businesses which otherwise could have been placed into liquidation. This is in stark contrast to the recession of the late 1980s and early 1990s when bank profitability closely tracked economic performance and reduced the ability, rather than the willingness, of banks to nurture businesses through the

Figure 6.5 Banks' profits and the economic cycle

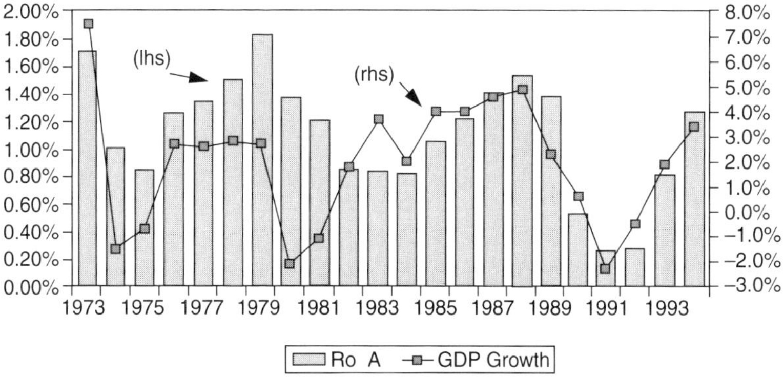

recession. Although there are a number of other factors, changes in the profile of the banks' loan portfolios is, therefore, an important factor in explaining why the economic recession of the late 1980s and early 1990s was unprecedented both in terms of its depth and speed.

Securitisation and the commensurate disintermediation associated with corporate wholesale finance has, therefore, had an important impact which goes far beyond wholesale banking. The considerations which have been discussed in this chapter, combined with other forces which are bringing about unprecedented change in the banking industry, have seen not only commercial banks become more like investment banks, but investment banks become more like commercial banks. From the commercial banks' perspective, however, there has been a strong imperative to develop what was traditionally regarded as 'ancillary business' and so by definition the traditional core services have changed bringing about an equally marked change in income structure. Greater emphasis is now placed on fee rather than interest income; for example in 1979, 28.6 per cent of commercial bank income in the UK was generated from fees, but by 1995 this had increased to 43.3 per cent (BBA, 1996), and for some commercial banks fee income is now greater than interest income.

It has been argued (Gardener and Revell, 1988) that this change in income generation increases bank risk because pricing in financial intermediation is based on the sort of cost-plus basis (shown in Figure 6.4) usually associated with conventional industries, whereas fee income is more susceptible to the vagaries of tendering for business. This might be the case, but it must not be forgotten that commercial banks have always found it difficult to accurately ascertain their costs and price to risk. Moreover, the change in emphasis to fee income does confer some advantages in the sense that most fees are paid upfront and this represents a 'timing' advantage compared with interest income. Perhaps, however, the most important advantage associated with fee income is the fact that it is tangible and readily understood. In this respect, it affords commercial banks an opportunity to introduce explicit pricing policies and hopefully resolve the myth of high bank charges. Finally, for large companies (and to some extent companies generally) good service is necessarily associated with a close relationship between the bank and its customer. It must not be forgotten, however, that an effective banker–customer relationship is expensive to operate and, therefore, its success is dependent upon banks extolling the very tangible advantages which banking relationships confer. This will help banks to charge appropriate fees in the knowledge that customers understand both the resource implications in providing relationship banking as well as the benefits to themselves.

Conclusion

Although there is nothing to necessarily suggest that developments in corporate wholesale banking herald the 'beginning of the end' for commercial banking, the changes discussed in this chapter do have serious implications for banks. The chapter has described and attempted an evaluation of some of the apparent changes in corporate wholesale banking and in the process has contrasted the indirect financing, associated with bank financial intermediation, with the direct financing more readily associated with capital market activity. The most pertinent conclusion from this comparison is, however, that although the discussion focuses ostensibly on banks and changes in corporate wholesale finance, the effects of these changes have been felt in a very tangible sense in other bank markets and in the economy as a whole.

References

Bank for International Settlements (1986) 'Recent Innovations in International Banking' (Basle: BIS).

Bank for International Settlements (1997) *67th Annual Report* (Basle: BIS).

Bank of England (1987) 'Convergence of Capital Adequacy in the UK and US', Banking Supervision Division, January, pp. 1–5.

Bray, M. (1984) 'Developing a Secondary Market in Loan Assets', *International Financial Law Review*, October, pp. 22–5.

British Bankers' Association (1996) *Annual Abstract of Banking Statistics*, Vol. 12 (London: BBA).

Editorial (1991) 'Bulls Buoyed by Brady Bonanza', *The Banker*, October, pp. 50–4.

Edwards, S. (1984) 'LDC Foreign Borrowing and Default Risk: An Empirical Investigation', *American Economic Review*, vol. 74, no. 4, pp. 726–34.

Feeney, P. (1987) *Loan Securitisation: Euronote and Eurocommercial Paper Markets*, Institute of European Finance, Research Monograph no. 1.

Gardener, E. and Revell, J. (1988) *Securitisation: History, Forms and Risks*, Institute of European Finance, Research Monograph no. 5.

Garner, J. (1997) 'What Price Credit Worthiness?', *Chartered Institute of Bankers*, February, pp. 39–42.

Garrity, B. (1997) 'Loan Syndications Set Another Volume Record', *Investment Dealers Digest*, vol. 63, no. 4, pp. 16–17.

Gurley, J. G. and Shaw, E. S. (1960) *Money in a Theory of Finance* (Washington D. C.: The Brookings Institute).

Heffernan, S. (1996) *Modern Banking in Theory and Practice* (Chichester: Wiley).

Henderson, K. and Scott, J. P. (1988) *Securitisation* (Cambridge: Woodhead Faulkner).

Howcroft, J. B. (1998), 'International Bank Syndicated Lending: Some Practical and Legal Issues', *Accounting and Business Review*, vol. 5, no. 1, pp. 123–40.

Kaletsky, A. (1985) *The Costs of Default* (New York: Priority Press).

Kasi, V. (1990) *The Impact of Securitisation on UK Bank Corporate Lending*, Institute of European Finance, Research Paper no. 19.

Llewellyn, D. T. (1994) *Cyclical, Structural and Secular Pressures in Swedish Banking*, LUBC Research Paper no. 81.

Rybczynski, T. M. (1996) 'Investment Banking: Its Evolution and Place in the Financial System', in E. Gardener and P. Molyneux (eds), *Investment Banking Theory and Practice*, 2nd edn (London: Euromoney Books).

United Nations (1991) *Transnational Banks and the International Debt Crisis* (New York: UN).

Comments on 'The Dynamics of Change and Risk in Corporate and Wholesale Finance', by Barry Howcroft

Bernd Zugenbühler

In recent years, corporate lending markets could be characterised by a highly increasing number of developments and changes: globalisation, securitisation, deregulation, computerisation are only some of the most important and most influencing tendencies leading to drastically changed environmental conditions. Detailed studies and in-depth analyses underline this changing environment in corporate lending markets and, moreover, the changing role of commercial banks in these markets.

Thus, the question arises as to what really has changed during recent years, and, even more important, what will change during the years to come. Within the following remarks, some thoughts and reflections concerning this issue will be outlined. However, due to the complexity and the number of current developments, as well as the increasing speed in which these changes take place, only a brief idea about the subject can be given. This might even lead to the fact that more questions will be raised than answered and fragments will be presented rather than final solutions.

Disintermediation in corporate lending markets

Working through newspapers and statistics, the process of disintermediation in corporate lending markets becomes obvious. Especially looking at large international corporates with favourable credit standing, there is a certain tendency of directly addressing capital markets instead of raising funds through the intermediation of commercial banks.

As the access to capital markets is restricted to highly rated companies, corporates with a lower credit rating generally continue raising funds by addressing intermediates. Thus, it is often argued, commercial

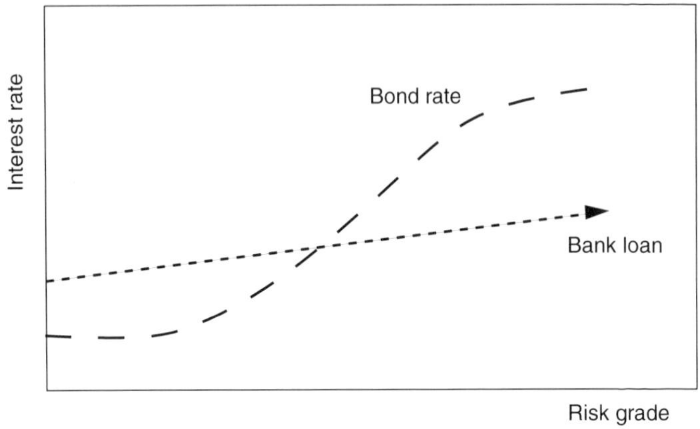

Figure 6.6 Bank loan interest rate dependence on risk

banks are facing the potential risk of deteriorating credit portfolios and decreasing margins.

Disintermediation as a result of inflexibility?

When looking for reasons and backgrounds for this development, which took place over years, there is a big bundle of potentially influencing factors. However, at first sight, the question might arise whether a certain inflexibility of commercial banks might have led to the above mentioned tendency in the corporate lending market. This hypothesis might be emphasised especially by comparing large commercial banks to much more flexible investment banks.

However, a comparison that differentiates only between flexible investment banks on the one hand and inflexible commercial banks on the other hand, rather seems to represent a usual stereotype than the complex reality of changing environmental conditions. Especially when looking at commercial bankers who are dealing with international and multinational banks, non-bank financial institutions, corporates or treasuries on a daily basis, this stereotype generally does not fit at all.

For this reason, a diligent examination of potential reasons and backgrounds has to be carried out starting with a basic comparison of interest rates versus risk, as shown in Figure 6.6. The figure shows that interest rates for bank loans vary in dependence on the inherent amount of risk in a transaction. The better the credit standing of the customer, the lower the risk margin and, by this, the interest rate that he will be charged by the bank. However, comparing the course of the interest rate charged for bank loans to the corresponding interest rate for bonds, it is rather obvious that the bond rate is much more sensitive to the underlying risk of a transaction.

As a result, in the part of the market where risk of transactions is low, bank loans offered to customers are often more expensive than the respective prices charged for bonds. And, vice versa with regard to transactions entailing a higher risk grade, bond rates seem to be unfavourable compared to interest rates charged for bank-loans.

Risk oriented pricing as a reason for disintermediation

As outlined above, within capital markets pricing is strongly linked to the inherent risk of the transaction. By contrast, in the past risk used to be taken into account only to a certain extent by commercial banks when fixing interest rates for loans, especially not in a way directly linked to rating-grades/risk-categories and the resulting default risk. Thus, highly-rated companies could take advantage by raising funds at the capital market directly instead of borrowing money from commercial banks. This inevitably leads to the tendency of avoiding intermediaries for refinancing.

Cherry picking

On the one hand, bond rates are highly attractive to customers of a high credit standing. On the other hand, customers with a lower credit rating, with a higher risk of not being able to service their debts, only have limited access to capital markets and are offered rather unfavourable rates.

Thus, as pricing policies of commercial banks were not that risk-oriented, for more risky customers interest rates charged for bank loans are generally lower than prices charged for bonds. As a result, highly-rated international companies are frequently more attracted by capital markets, whereas corporates with a low credit standing keep on raising funds through intermediaries.

The important role of collateralisation

In addition to this, there is another crucial factor for lower-rated companies being granted more favourable interest rates in corporate lending markets than in capital markets. In general, ratings for issuing companies are based on the underlying credit standing without taking into consideration any collateral available.

By contrast, within the corporate lending market, collateralisation is often crucial for the customer's rating and any loan decision. Commercial bank loans are usually covered by a number of different securities such as real estates, savings deposits, marketable and other securities, guaranties, cash, and so on. Depending on the type of collateral, lending values are established normally on a case-by-case basis.

As recovery values of collateral reduce the amount of expected loss in case of default, commercial banks also account for collateral available when establishing a corporate client rating. Thus, though primarily looking at the company's earnings and financial position, commercial banks might improve ratings due to the underlying collateralisation of a transaction which, consequently, is influencing the bankís margin and pricing decisions.

Quality of risk assessment

The basis for risk-oriented pricing is the adequate assessment of risk. As far as commercial banks are concerned, internal ratings have been established for the analysis of their customers' credit standing. In case there is no commercial bank acting as an intermediary, external rating agencies often provide ratings of issuing companies for the customers investing in securities. Thus, the process of disintermediation also leads to an increasing importance of public high-quality risk assessment and therefore to a growing market for external rating agencies.

The quality of risk assessment is dependant on several factors, such as the availability of detailed and reliable information, the experience and know-how of analysts, the rating methodology, and so forth. As the quality of credit ratings of external rating agencies is crucial for the efficiency of capital markets and the improvement of capital allocation, highly demanding standards of quality have been established for risk assessment by external rating agencies. In order to be able to meet these standards, rating agencies frequently work together very closely with the issuing companies. Thus, rating agencies often obtain information from issuing companies which is not publicly available otherwise, guaranteeing a high level of accuracy and impartiality.

On the basis of these external ratings which classify transactions according to their inherent level of risk, risk-oriented prices are fixed for respective transactions.

As important as external ratings for capital markets, there are internal ratings used by commercial banks for the assessment of their loan portfolios. In recent years, sophisticated scoring and rating methodologies – frequently based on mathematical and statistical approaches – have been developed by commercial banks for internal assessment purposes. As these internal ratings are the basis for a bank's credit portfolio management and control, highest standards of quality of methodologies and of the experience of analysts have to be ensured.

In addition to this, internal rating systems have to fulfil the highest standards of flexibility. Efficient credit-risk management requires all customers of the bankís portfolio to be classified. Thus, internal-rating methodologies are frequently required to cover a very large number of customers which generally exceeds by far the number of companies classified by external rating agencies. Moreover, rating systems often have to be adapted to fit to different types of customers such as industrial corporations, banks, non-bank financial institutions, and so on; to various industries; as well as to different types of transactions, for example commercial bank loans, project financing, or structured financing.

As a result, the accuracy and reliability of both internal and external ratings, is crucial for appropriate pricing policies in the corporate lending market and the capital market. Inadequate assessment of risk automatically leads to inadequate interest rates, prices and margins. When wrong margins are fixed, not only might too little be earned, but, additionally, in the worst case too much might be lost.

The steady upward trend in the capital markets

The tendency described above of large international companies to take advantage of favourable rates at capital markets for raising their funds is one reason for the increasing importance of capital markets. Due to capital-consuming transactions and the rising number of innovative financial products, the importance of financial markets will continue to grow.

In addition to this, globalisation – that is, growing internationalisation, decreasing borders and time differences in financial markets and growing interdependence of capital markets supported by improved communication and information technology – as well as deregulation and liberalisation increase the attractiveness of capital markets and lead to a steady upward trend.

The cost of equity as a factor to be taken into account

As outlined above, differences in interest rates granted by commercial banks compared to capital markets are due to differences in the risk assessment and risk orientation. However, there are of course various other factors influencing the pricing methodologies of banks and markets. A crucial factor to be taken into consideration is the necessity for banks to hold a certain amount of capital intended to act as a protection against potential losses.

- The Banking Regulation defines the regulatory capital which is the minimum of capital to be guaranteed by banks mainly depending on the bank's counter-party exposure. It represents the amount legally prescribed, and is roughly risk-dependent.
- Within the Capital Adequacy Directive (CAD) further types of transactions to be cushioned by capital have been stipulated; especially transactions covered by a bank's trading-book.

The availability of the amount of capital necessary has to be guaranteed as it is to act as a buffer against unexpected losses. Thus, the requirement of capitalisation constitutes an additional expense to banks which has to be reflected in additional basis points and in the interest rates charged for loans.

Regulatory costs

However, costs arising due to the necessary capitalisation are only part of the expenses caused by regulatory requirements. In general, banks are subject to strict and complex regulations imposed by supervising authorities for the protection of customers and investors, and in order to fulfil these standards they have to invest into appropriate systems and structures, as, for example, with regard to reporting needs.

Again, these additional expenses have to be taken into consideration when calculating interest rates as they increase prices charged for loans in relation to prices within capital markets where regulatory costs are only of marginal effect.

Tendencies in the corporate lending market: credit portfolios as the basis of innovative financial products

Parallel to tendencies in the capital market, disintermediation and securitisation also had impacts on the corporate lending market. As a result of increasing requirements of capitalisation and the costs incurred, secondary markets for bank loans have been developed. A number of appropriate financial products such as 'asset-backed securities' or 'credit derivatives' have been generated which, placing assets aside from the bank's balance sheet, enable commercial banks to reduce capital requirements and to improve their liquidity.

On the other hand, non-banks also started to take advantage of these developments: the traditional, old-fashioned plain-vanilla lending became attractive for insurance companies and other institutions searching for credit portfolios. Some of the these innovative financial products based on traditional bank loans are briefly outlined below:

- Asset-backed securities. In the case of an asset-backed securities transaction, a financial institution sells part of its loan portfolio to a company which has been established for this or similar transactions. This company refinances the transaction by issuing securities which are then called asset-backed securities. When the securities fall due they are redeemed by repayments arising out of the loans by which they are covered. In general, the selling bank maintains service functions for the loans sold.

  The most suitable assets for these transactions are receivables from a larger number of debtors which are rather homogenous and characterised by low default rates. In characteristic asset-backed securities transactions, credit solvency of securities issued is separated from the seller's credit standing.
- Credit derivatives. These are intended to enable banks to separate the risk arising out of a credit from the client relationship. This means that the risk component is passed on to the market, whereas parts of the earnings component as well as the intangible benefit of the client-relationship itself is kept by the bank.

  Any credit derivative products are characterised by very similar basic structures: they constitute a transaction between a credit-protection buyer which is interested in transfering credit risk in exchange for paying a premium, and a credit-protection seller willing to accept that credit risk in exchange for being paid that premium. On this basis, several types of credit derivatives have been developed, some of the most important being:

  - the credit default swap representing a typical plain-vanilla type of credit derivative: the credit-protection buyer pays the seller a premium to protect himself against a contractually-defined credit and its specific underlying risk.

- the total return swap in which the credit-protection seller pays out the total return of an asset to the credit-protection buyer which includes interest payments and capital depreciation. In return, he receives a floating-rate payment, usually based on Libor. At maturity a payment is made to one party by the other, as a function of the market value of the reference asset.
- credit spread options in which the credit-protection buyer is offered spread protection on a specific asset in exchange for paying a premium.

The development of secondary loan markets and the growing number of transactions with credit derivatives, asset-backed securities and so forth will have several positive effects on commercial banks, especially with regard to their increased capacity to dynamically steer their credit-risk portfolios.

Summary

Through an increasing awareness that the price of a loan or a bond includes additional elements – certainly a premium to cover the risk of default – pricing resulting from the neglect of such factors may be reduced. As a very important consequence, the capability of a bank or an investor to do a reliable risk assessment on a corporate customer and its loan or its bond is regaining the vital role it formerly had in banking. Only those who evaluate a credit risk ahead of the market in a reliable way can take additional advantage of the changing environment.

7

Risk Management and the Ethics of New Financial Instruments

Justin Welby

Introduction

Option theory, swaps and securitisation are the massive changes of the last twenty years in the financial markets. Of these only the first is 'new', relying principally on the mathematics of the model developed by Black and Scholes. However, swaps and securitisation have had such a radical and creative effect on the way in which finance is considered that they have changed the whole landscape of large-scale, especially corporate, financing. Everything else is basically derivative, with the scale of dealing being the only reason to attract attention. By contrast, the long and widespread history of futures is demonstrated by my regular discussions in the local undertaker's hearse with one of the bearers, whose main job is farming, on the futures prices in potatoes, which have varied from £0.70–£5 per bag in the last two years.

New financial instruments continue to develop and the major forms of derivative continue to expand. Recent studies report an increased use of derivatives in the USA since Proctor & Gamble; 66 per cent. of middle-sized companies in the USA are using derivatives more than in 1994. Since 1990 the outstanding principle value of interest-rate swaps has risen by $725 bn to $11.8 trillion, and foreign exchange (FX) swaps by $262 bn to $5.6 trillion.[1]

There is a proliferation of further forms of derivative, involving not only asset packaging but the breakdown of risk into smaller and smaller discrete units. These include the securitisation of credit guarantees, the swapping of credit risk, economic hedges through a swap of total return on an investment, and in the insurance market loan issues with a put option for the buyer in the event of defined catastrophes. The list could be extended. One feature unites these developments;

risk. New financial instruments are driven less by the simple need to raise finance (although that must be somewhere in the foundations), but by the desire to manage risk. At the heart of almost all the instruments is a more calculated analysis of risk, and an attempt to divide it more cleverly so that parties take the risks they want and lay off the ones that they do not.

There is also the aspect of risk arbitrage in which an issuer or buyer gains an advantage by using the different understandings of risk found in different markets, such as debt and insurance. In the case of options or futures, risk management is obviously central, and the same is true for many of the securitised products.[2] Securitisation is often more the delivery of differentiated risk than asset packages.

This chapter assumes that most readers are familiar with the basic terminology of derivatives, and defines it only briefly in the Appendix. It will concentrate on the ethics of risk management before applying this to some aspects of new financial instruments.

The nature of risk management with new financial instruments

> Risk is ever present in Treasury. Indeed, it is the treasurer's *raison d'ĕtre*. The treasurer's job is not just to identify risk but to manage it. The aim is to protect his or her organisation from an unacceptable level of loss and, where prudent and authorised, to take advantage of the risk:reward ratio to enhance returns.[3]

This simple statement of aim obscures the real issues. In corporate finance almost all action beyond the plain vanilla buy–sell, borrow–lend leads to complexity. The expression 'enhance returns' takes for granted the debate as to whether the Treasury is a profit centre or cost centre, and has little to do with risk management. At times one feels that the treasurer's profession and the corporate finance sector in the City are engaged in a mutually rewarding process of finding ever more complicated ways to manage the ever more complex risks that their methods are creating ever more prolifically.

All complexity leads to obscurity The ethical struggle is to seek transparency of risk so that both management and those innocents who deal with the corporate entity know whom they face. The importance of this is shown clearly both with the losses from options trading of the National Westminster Bank in 1996–97 and, supremely, with the Barings Bank failure. The former case has led to little more than embarrassment, the loss of some bonuses, and an effect on the share price. In the latter case there remain a number of investors who thought, perhaps naïvely, that they were buying the bonds of a bank and did not realise the far higher risks they were running, with or without Leeson, the derivatives trader responsible. Although he was the final cause of the fall, Barings' increasing reliance on high levels of dealing in volatile and complicated products was effectively changing both its risk profile and its corporate ethos.

In the late 1970s, a new Treasurer was often given a 150–page book written by the then head of Hambro's foreign exchange. After reading it he or she had learned most of what mattered in FX. The big problems were settlement and dealing practice. Forwards and forward-forwards were the height of strategy. Today there are a series of exams, and lengthy articles in 75 per cent. of the issues of the *Treasurer* magazine (the publication of the Association of Corporate Treasurers) which cover only the foothills. Complexity grows exponentially. Risk management is the buzz term in Treasury and its practice is an increasingly black art.

The risks of risk management

All action to resolve risk creates risk. Yet in financial markets inaction is in itself the adoption of a risk profile. For a portfolio manager, either to invest or to leave reserves in cash are both risk choices. In foreign exchange (FX) management to engage in the use of option strategies creates many risks; not to do so creates others. Even boards of directors have begun to recognise this, as the risks of risk management have loomed larger in professional thinking. In response to the Leeson affair, Procter & Gamble, Orange County and lesser-known events, the burden of managing risk management has grown, to the point where its consumption of resources in non-financial firms must begin to pose ethical questions even in consequentialist terms.

Stewart Hodges, Director, Financial Operations Research Centre at the University of Warwick, pointed out in a complicated article dealing with the effects of delta hedging using the Black–Scholes model[4] that: 'the risk exposure is constantly adjusted in response to market movements', and that this leads to very high turnover (thus costs and transaction risks): 'In fact the expected level of turnover is proportional to the square root of the number of revisions [of the hedge following market movements], becoming unbounded in the limit.'[5]

The Futures and Options Association have published guidelines for non-financial corporate users on the use of derivatives.[6] They establish six principles:

1. the Board produces 'effective policy for use of derivatives';
2. senior management (SM) 'establish clear written procedures for implementing the derivatives policy';
3. creation by SM of an 'effective framework of internal controls and audits';
4. SM establish 'a sound risk management function for... controlling all aspects of risk';
5. procedures in place for 'a full analysis of all credit risks'; and
6. procedures for 'management of legal risk'.[7]

The document recognises that derivatives may be used for hedging but some transactions which are thought to be hedging 'may only modify the organisation's risk exposure',[8] for example an interest rate swap. It is questionable, incidentally, whether this is a valid distinction. All hedging modifies risk, and very little removes it. The more important distinction is between speculative trading, where there is no underlying commercial risk to justify use of a derivative, and hedging, modifying a risk exposure.In the commentary on the principles, 1-4 above and especially 3 and 4 require considerable use of management time and energy. The impression given is of a highly dangerous activity that builds considerably more risk into the operations of the company that will need much senior management time, and staff recruitment, to control.

The question must be asked whether it is ethically justified to use resources in this way. Risk is inherent in life; new financial instruments are often loosely thought of as hedges when they are risk management tools.There is a responsibility for managers who use them to recognise the true nature of what they are doing. Given that most instruments are copious users of energy and other intangible resources of the business, as well as having a risk-profile deriving from their use at all, they must be justifiable in terms of consequence, rule or virtue. Of these it is clear that the last two place risk management as one sensible preoccupation among others, without giving it primacy.

Should we try to manage risk?

Risk can be defined in two principle ways, either 'an expected distribution of outturns around a mean', that is both up and downside; or 'a feared outturn'; 'financial theory concentrates on the former, insurance theory on the latter sense of "risk"'.[9]

Justice in relative power

In general terms this is obvious in the normal running of life. I should take normal precautions against harm provided that they do not lead to harm to someone less able to protect himself or herself. It is ethical to test the strength of ice before walking on it, but not to do so by putting my children on it first, on the grounds that their earning power is less than mine and they are therefore more expendable.

In retail finance this is seen in the 1980s and 1990s legislation on Investor Protection. The burden of risk in ensuring that a product is suitable for the purchaser has shifted dramatically from a *caveat emptor* approach to fall squarely on the seller. Thus in any sale of life products the majority of the paperwork is less about the product than whether the purchaser has had all the legal and prudential warnings. It is recognised that a life company is in a far better position to assess risk than an individual, and must make sure that the investor has had the risk management carried out on their behalf. Legislation directs that more weight is given to an ethical than market-driven distribution of risk.

The parallel with usury

A classical and Thomist challenge would pose questions in terms of the ethics of making money out of money, similar to the issue of usury. The effect of many new financial instruments, especially where there are options embedded, is so out of proportion to the capital employed in their use that one may argue that it is unethical. However, the risks are balanced; a dealer or initiator of such structures may lose money as easily as make it. There is an equivalence of risk and reward that marks a distinction from the abuse of power and wealth inherent in usury.

The distribution of understanding

Is there then an unjust distribution of risk? The question here must focus on options. Futures and swaps (see Appendix) are the exchange of equivalent rights and obligations. With options the seller (technically writer) acquires an obligation of potentially unlimited cost and the buyer a right of unlimited potential benefit in exchange for the payment of a premium. Unlike insurance there is no fixed value to be compensated. This can clearly lead to an abuse of power, especially where the option is embedded in another instrument which is the main focus. Convertible bonds would be an example. If the value of the option is not properly reflected in the price of a retail product that would be unethical. Similarly, if the balance of risk is only properly understandable by sophisticated dealers, but is sold at the retail level, then there is injustice.

The best example of this was the Proctor & Gamble affair, and other matters involving the US bank Bankers Trust in the mid-1990s. Bankers Trust were selling large corporate and institutional clients very complicated packages of options. So long as everyone made money there was no argument, but when Procter and Orange County lost large sums they sued on the grounds that they had been led into dealing in matters beyond the understanding of a mere company rather than a clever bank. One is tempted to be a little cynical. However, Bankers Trust has since set procedures to prevent dealing by companies without sufficient understanding. This shows an ethical attempt (however motivated) to provide a balance of justice, and confirms the rule that ethics demand responsibility by the expert in new financial instruments even when dealing with powerful counter-parties.

Equitable allocation of risk

The rule of responsible justice also has a positive side for new financial instruments. Derivatives have at their best enabled a far more sophisticated division of risk through the financial markets. If they are accessible to a wide range of users of finance the allocation of risk may become more just rather than less. For example, in the United Kingdom the ability to use swaps and options in the management of a mortgage portfolio enables lenders to offer fixed rate or low start finance to house buyers. The history of housing since 1980 show that retail borrowers are both the most vulnerable to rising interest rates and have had least access to protection from them. Derivatives have changed this with the interest-change risk moving to the financial markets where they can best be handled. The borrower can use the most suitable form of finance, and the lender has to deal with the financial consequences. This is an ethical division of risk.

The problem with any rule-based approach is that it may rapidly become out of date and says little about the intrinsic ethical value of derivatives. Are they good, bad or neutral? The financial services industry (see below) argues that new financial instruments have no intrinsic merit or evil, but are ethically the result of how they are used. For that one has to look to an ethics of virtue.

An ethically virtuous basis for risk management

Courage

An ethics of virtue raises questions when risk management becomes obsessive, and behaviour such as cowardice is first held in contempt and then treated as pathological in extreme cases. It is recognised that an obsession with risk paralyses action, and that there is a proper balance between recklessness and terrified immobility. An honest living with the fact of risk and its consequences is seen as a good.

Any attempt commercially to enter into a transaction involving risk, but to lay off all the risk involved while still retaining a profit is ethically questionable. Since the risk–reward ratio is a law of unswerving severity, this approach is also likely to be commercially unsuccessful. All other things being equal we rightly admire the entrepreneur who creates a new industry with ingenuity and courage, producing jobs and economic development.

Prudence

A key virtue in Aristotle and Aquinas, linked to wisdom, justice and charity. Within the Christian Bible the Wisdom tradition calls for a prudent middle-way that does not draw undue attention through ambition.[15] However, within the Bible there is a tension between faith in the ultimate goodness of God in all circumstances,[16] and an avoidance of recklessness that tests providence and faithfulness.[17] Prudence is commended in parables such as the unjust steward, but sacrifice of oneself is also demanded.[18]

This tension is also reflected in common law in the Anglo-Saxon system with the tests of reasonable care and contributory negligence. The search for risk free life is seen in such absurdities as the famous McDonald's coffee law-suit in the USA, where a jury initially awarded damages of $2 000 000 (reduced on appeal) to a woman who was scalded while simultaneously driving and trying to drink a hot cup of coffee. In legal ethics such cases are seen as increasingly indefensible. The opposite extreme is found at the Pont du Gard, near Nîmes in France, an unrailed and crumbling Roman aqueduct with a vertical drop of over 100 feet. Anyone can walk across, if they dare, the only caution being a rusty sign saying 'Les vents puissent s'enlever', perhaps translatable as 'Gone with the wind'! Particularly for the non-financial corporate user new financial instruments permit a far more prudent approach to risk. This is perhaps the ethical answer to the challenge of the Modigliani–Miller case which states that investors will manage their own risk through portfolio diversification, and therefore companies should neither diversify nor hedge in order to manage risk by other means than the normal operating procedures of their industry (although the latter point is made less strongly). This is also covered to some extent in the section on transparency below.

Prudence is a virtue when it leads to a proper assessment of risk, and the use of reasonable means to mitigate those risks which can reasonably and economically be avoided. Thus in the 1980s, as a company treasurer, I used to buy foreign exchange options because the premium paid to avoid the majority of the potential losses that the company might face was small compared to the massive disruption that would be caused by unprotected exposure to that risk.

Prudence encourages self-awareness, considered as a virtue from before Aristotle. New financial instruments compel a proper and well-balanced view of the nature of the company and its outlook; they encourage a willingness to resist the fatalistic approach to the future that diminishes the significance of human free will.[19] Like health and safety rules they support the management of risk, and thus help to focus an organisation on its proper objectives.

Finally, they incite a proper balance of risk; leading management to take the risks it should, and to transfer others to those better able to carry them. An oil exploration and production company may hedge interest rate and foreign exchange risk, buying certainty in contrast to the vagaries of the drill-bit which it is in business to face.

Transparency

Both in the secular philosophical and religious traditions of European thought, transparency is thought of as a virtue. Iago may be clever, but is nevertheless a villain because of his dissembling. In the Wagnerian Ring cycle one may feel that Siegfried is a musclebound idiot, but still a hero because of his transparency. Candide is naïve, but Voltaire sees his transparency as virtuous. John's first epistle has the famous exhortation to 'walk in the light' with one another and with God. King David's uniqueness is not his moral uprightness but his honesty and openness in his walk of faith, expressed most clearly in Psalm 51 or 32. Straightforward dealing is a City virtue (*dictum meum pactum* etc.) and is enshrined in legislation and regulation.[20]

The virtue of transparency is not only ethical but also a management aim in order to understand risk. Its perceived benefits lie behind reforms in accounting, the break-up of conglomerates, the fashion for mission statements that control priorities, and concern over derivatives. We cannot manage what we cannot see. A recent Accounting Standard Board discussion paper on financial instruments aims for this: 'The issue is that, whatever basis [of accounting] is used, it should be unambiguous, universal and simple'.[21]

Transparency is not only for self-preservation, in that false information leads to false markets, but applies even when there is no obvious consequential harm, as is often seen in insider trading. Transparency is a virtue even of consenting adults in private, as well as in the open market, and its importance is being reinforced. At the back of much of the underlying unease that dominates public discussion of new financial instruments is a concern about transparency. The FOA guidelines are designed to ensure that there is at least internal transparency, so that the highest levels of management understand the risk-profiles of the company for which they are responsible. All new financial instruments create fog; as the following three examples illustrate:

- *What do we owe?* A company issues a 7 per cent £250 million loan note with a 25-year maturity and fixed coupon. Its lenders, its board, its shareholders and, were they to think about it, its employees, its customers and its suppliers know that provided it can pay the interest of £8.75 million twice a year its material obligations are complete for the foreseeable future.

  But then the treasurer notes that since the issue interest rates have risen, a swap can be taken out to make this a floating rate obligation at LIBOR–1 per cent. His fear of the opportunity loss if long-term interest rates fall encourages him to act. A few years later, the issuer buys a company in the USA, and to hedge its translation exposure part of the issue is swapped from floating rate sterling into a mixture of floating and fixed rate dollars.

  The result of these actions is a totally different risk-profile for the company, and a series of FX, interest rate and counter-party risks that neither shareholders (nor probably the board) will have clearly identified. The balance sheet will show the Loan Note, with a complicated and lengthy note about swaps.
- *What do they earn?* An alternative (and equally true example) would be that of an oil exploration and production company based in the UK. With almost all its costs in £, almost all its revenues are in US$. It is also mercilessly exposed to the oil price. Fearing a fall in the price and a rise in £, it enters into a series of options and forward transactions the sum result of which is to provide a graded and diminishing participation in £ oil-price increases, and considerable protection against falls. The shareholders will not know about this until the next annual report; the banks and analysts may only find out by accident. The Prudential and the Pearl (major UK life insurance companies) think they are investing in well-managed $ oil exposure; the reality is that they have a temporary utility with more or less fixed prices. The market is false.

- *Who am I dealing with?* A company enters into a syndicated loan with 12 banks, contributing varying amounts totalling US$350 million, in a multi-currency, multi-option, and fully-revolving form. The banks are chosen on the basis of their significant levels of business with the company, familiarity with its kind of business, the geographical spread of their activities and credit strength. The treasurer of the borrower has a moment of inattention as the lawyers wade through the terminally dull pages on assignment and intra-syndicate obligations. Two years later, at a time when business is tight and the company struggling, a routine roll-over produces a shortfall of the Spanish peseta equivalent of US$10 million because one of the 12 has sold a securitised sub-participation of the loan to a regional Japanese bank that is having funding problems. In the negotiations that follow, as the company's liquidity drains away towards default, the treasurer finds herself facing 17 banks, eight of whom she has never met before, and with whom there is neither relationship nor understanding. Different kinds of case could be given for retail mortgages that are then packaged and securitised, or credit card receivables.

New financial instruments in practice

Six thousand word theories of ethics are all very well, but they are unlikely to be read and discussed in the average dealing room or corporate treasury. One is reminded of the court case in rural Warwickshire not far from my parish where the accused was on trial for receiving stolen property. The judge asked his lawyer, 'does your client not know the principle' *Nemo dat quod non habet?* ' [No-one may give what he does not own]. The lawyer replied dryly, 'My Lord, they talk of little else in the pubs of Warwickshire.' Dealers in new financial instruments do not talk much about Aristotle, Aquinas or deontology, at least in my experience.

So what are the practical steps that can be suggested both to the financial corporation dealing and making markets in these instruments, and the corporate treasurer seeking to use them as part of the management of the company's cash-flow?

For financial corporations the inevitable presence of derivatives poses three issues. First, will the active management of our positions created by this activity result in a change in the nature of our business, and, if so, has this been clearly communicated to the world around? Secondly, are they intrinsically valuable or so complicated that no client could use them and monitor the new exposures involved?

Thirdly, do they result in an equitable distribution of risk between the parties involved, given their relative sophistication and understanding?

All three questions are relatively easy to apply. The first is inward-looking. It can be measured by the proportion of profit for any material unit in the Group that is generated from these instruments. What profile do they have in management reporting? How much time is spent on the monitoring of the risk and at what level of the hierarchy? The more significant the answers the more likely it is that at least part of the company is seeing a cultural change to a much higher level of risk being tolerated as normal. Such a change may be acceptable, but it must be communicated to all those with an interest in the organisation, including staff and customers, as well as obviously to creditors and shareholders. It should never be a careless slip from being one sort of place to being another, which is not accompanied by changes in management style and public perception.

The second question links to the issue of virtue. An instrument should have some clear purpose in enabling the user to operate better, focused on the risks inherent in his or her business. The seller should balance the creation of fog and the desire to do a deal. In some cases the user may be able, with the creation of new systems, to monitor the incremental risks created, but still find that the essential effect of using a new derivative strategy is less rather than more transparency. It is at this point that the normal pull of business and human instincts is strongest. Restraint of this kind is hard to justify in terms of benefits or management. Transparency is costly for individuals and for corporate entities that are more exposed to criticism as a result. This demand is especially strong when dealing with a retail sector that may understand the transaction result (a fixed rate mortgage), but have difficulty assessing the long-term risks and implications.

The third question is partly one that life insurers already face, and banks now routinely consider. Any decision to sell new financial instruments to a customer must involve satisfaction that this instrument in this form is capable of being understood and monitored. For the purchase of options that is very simple. Before the creation of complex structured financings, or the use of options embedded in other instruments, a more complicated due-diligence exercise would be required. However, the problem goes beyond a box-ticking exercise. As with private placements in the USA that are not registered with the SEC, there should be a form of sophisticated investor test. It cannot be ethical to lead any client into using instruments that require such developed systems and consume so much management time that the company is consumed by the process. In one sense this is an echo of the culture point. The seller must ask whether the client is the sort that should try to use these instruments. For many smaller companies the answer will be no. Engaging in financial operations of that sort will create a force more powerful than they are.

For non-financial corporations the ethical question is one of motivation. Herd instinct operates in financial management as well as anywhere else. If a competitor is doing these things, and its treasurer is in the press and reputed as 'innovative' then a company will worry in case it is losing an edge, and *its* treasurer will want some reputation as well. Ethical financial management will pose many of the same questions as for financial corporations; in principle it will be suspicious of any new instrument that complicates its business. The claims of potential user departments like Treasury should be taken with a large pinch of salt.

The company management is primarily responsible to the shareholders and the first question to be answered is whether the use of these instruments will in any fundamental way change the nature of the risk that they feel they hold. Given the shareholding structure of most UK companies, there is here an implicit responsibility to the wider community of indirect investors through pensions and savings schemes. Secondly, is there a justification of prudence or transparency that outweighs the necessary complexity? The buzz of the financial markets is often more alluring than the mundane routines of ensuring health and safety, environmental protection and responsibility to the communities where the company operates. Without clear justification, allowing distractions from these issues is often wrong.

Conclusion

The widespread and elaborate use of new financial instruments among corporate entities and financial institutions requires justification. It faces the charge of increasing both the level and complexity of risk in the financial system under the pretext of reducing it. It is prodigious of management resources and IT, and it obscures the integrity of the nature of the non-financial user.It is not mere academic argument to question the ethics of some instruments. Both in the USA and the UK, certain forms of financial instrument are deemed too risky to be used by all and sundry.[22] Other forms of instrument may be banned outright, even though many financial professionals will be perfectly capable of measuring the risk involved.[23]

The force of this attack is recognised in the financial industry. One defence frequently put forward is similar to that of the National Rifle Association in the USA about guns. It is the users, not the product, that are the problem. 'One misconception is that derivatives are risky instruments that are used for speculation. It is more accurate to say that derivatives are instruments that can be used to alter risk profiles'.[24]

The mere fact of an instrument existing is no reason to use it. The biggest advocates of exotic options are bankers. Practising treasurers spend much time seeking to distinguish between the fascinating idea that the bank's rocket scientist wants to try, and the derivative that will genuinely benefit the company.The fact that many of these instruments are harmful or spurious does not mean they should be banned, but neither does the absence of a ban make them ethical. The ethical question to ask for all corporations is to do with the proper balance of courage, prudence, transparency and justice. Will this instrument enable the company to carry out its proper task with more focus and self-awareness, or is it an attempt to neutralise the proper risks that it is there to take? Does it manage risk at the expense of leaving it with others less able to bear it, whether retail purchasers, smaller companies or primary product producers?

On reading this again I am once more struck by a remark made to me by a clergyman long before I was ordained: 'What is an ethical Treasurer?' One of the major challenges in the field of finance ethics is the development of an adequate, and clearly communicated, measure of the intrinsic ethics of finance. Since the collapse of the condemnation of interest as usury in the majority of Christian thought, nothing has taken its place.

Appendix: basic derivative terminology

A 'futures contract' is an obligation for one party to deliver and another to take a given quantity and quality of a certain financial instrument or other commodity on a set date in the future at a price set now. It is a way of removing price uncertainty from seller and buyer.

An 'option contract' is the sale and purchase of a right or obligation to take or deliver a given quantity and quality of a certain financial instrument or other commodity on (or sometimes before) a set date in the future at a price set now. One party has an obligation (to sell or buy), the other a right, which they may or may not exercise. The price of the option is the value of that right. If it is exercised the full, agreed price of the thing under option will be exchanged. The price of an option is determined by two elements. How close is that price to the present price of the commodity? How volatile is the price of that commodity? The mathematics is very complicated, and a seller of an option (who thus receives a payment and takes on an obligation) may 'delta hedge'; that is, constantly buy and sell the commodity to minimise the risk.

A 'swap' is an exchange of rights and obligations. Thus a company that has borrowed £100 million for 10 years at 8 per cent may swap the interest obligation with another company that has borrowed the same amount at a variable rate of interest. They both retain their obligations to their lenders, but acquire extra obligations to each other.

Futures and options are traded on public markets like LIFFE in London, MATIF in Paris and the Chicago Board of Trade, and 'over-the-counter', that is directly between the parties, often on a bespoke basis.

This is a very simplified view. Derivatives combine any or all of these basic instruments, or apply the theory (especially option theory) to other sorts of risk. The importance of option theory can scarcely be exaggerated; it claims to be a way of measuring financial risk so as to permit a better analysis of the components of that risk.

Notes

1. *Treasurer,* December 1996, p. 8 ff.
2. The development of asset-backed bond financing was initially driven by a desire to free capital for further funding. In the UK this was seen in the Sterling Floating Rate Note market with large issues by major building societies in the 1980s. In the United States, where these instruments were developed by the vehicle finance subsidiaries of the major automobile manufacturers, almost any receivable can be packaged and sold in a bond. However, the technique is now more widely used, for example in project finance, to break up the risks in a project, with different lenders or sponsors retaining only certain risks. An example would be the funding of the Second Severn Crossing in part by an indexed linked bond at RPI + 6 per cent. The structure of the loan meant that the lenders were taking the risk on traffic-flow projections more than on the construction of the new bridge.
3. 'Risk – the Treasurer's *Raison d'être'*, Stuart Leadill, Treasurer of Balfour Beatty, *Treasurer,* Dec. 1996, p. 31.
4. The most widely accepted model for pricing options. Black has recently received the Nobel prize for economics.
5. *Treasurer,* November 1991, 'Current Research on Derivative Products', pp. 6, 9.
6. *Managing Derivatives Risk Guidelines for End-users of Derivatives,* Futures and Options Association, Dec. 1995.
7. *Ibid;* pp. 7–10.
8. *Ibid;* p. 11.
9. Alfred Kenyon (visiting Professor, City University Business School), *Treasurer,* September 1991, 'Protection or Speculation?', pp. 7 ff.
10. Behind this issue is the whole philosophical argument over the nature of planning, which is, of course, not the subject of this chapter.
11. Report in *La Tribune,* 29 August 1997, on a book by Marc Potters and Jean-Philippe Bouchaud of the CEA, *Théorie de risques financiers.*
12. *Treasurer,* April 1995, Editorial.

13. *Ibid.*
14. 'Risk', *New Dictionary of Christian Ethics*, SCM, p. 557, see also *The Common Good*, Catholic Bishop's Conference 1996, para. 77, p. 19
15. For example, Ecclesiastes 4–5.
16. For example, Daniel 3:17–18 and Romans 8:28.
17. For example, Deuteronomy 6:16 and Matthew 4:7.
18. Matthew 5:43–8.
19. The basic argument in an article by Gay Evans, Chairman, International Swaps and Futures Association, in *Treasurer,* October 1996, 'The Great Contradiction', p. 30.
20. Stock exchange listing regulations, especially obligations on disclosure of material facts, insider trading legislation and Takeover Panel rules about concert parties would be three examples.
21. *Treasurer*, October 1996, David Creed, Group Treasurer Tate & Lyle PLC, 'A Personal View of the ASB's Financial Instruments Discussion Paper', p. 16
22. Investing in private placements in the USA, and the 'sophisticated investor' test under the FSA.
23. Pyramid-selling schemes.
24. Gay Evans, *op. cit.*

8
Business Ethics in the Banking Industry: Some Remarks

Andreas Wagner

Incentives as the basis of business ethics

Individual banks as well as the banking industry as a whole are facing broad public unease because of a wide range of scandals such as insider trading, money laundering and misuse of funds for personal gain. In this climate, in the United Kingdom just as in Germany, ethical questions have become more relevant for banks especially because there is an awareness that only the tip of the iceberg of illegal and unethical dealings has been exposed. As a consequence, for a larger part of the public, banking business and moral principles are considered to be more and more antagonistic. Regarding these developments, banks seem to need some good advice on how to cope with their ethical problems, in order to regain public acceptance.

The research activities in business ethics at universities as well as the scale of ethics programmes in practice in this decade continued to expand worldwide. By now in the USA virtually all major companies have some kind of ethics programme in place or plan to have one in the immediate future (Center for Business Ethics, 1992). Yet in Europe, although it is expanding, formalised programmes will not be found to that extent. One determining factor for the performance of business ethics in the USA has been the enaction of the USA Federal Sentencing Guidelines, which do not focus on the personal responsibility of managers, but on punishment for criminal conduct of organisations, such as bribery, environmental destruction or insider dealings. Hereby it is spelled out that it is seen as a mitigating factor if the corporation has implemented measures to prevent and detect violations of the law (Rafalko, 1994, p. 627). In other words financial fines can be reduced significantly, if the company has institutionalised a business ethics programme. Companies consequently are regarded as 'moral agents', that is they have their own moral and legal responsibility. It is quite obvious that legal arrangements are setting the incentives to initialize ethical considerations.

The fact that there is a whole variety of approaches towards business ethics[1] leads to my own point of view of a modern business ethics theory for banks. It is necessary therefore to get back to the philosophical distinction between individual and institutional ethics.

Undoubtedly in modern economies and businesses the individual ethics of actors, for example of bank managers or employees, is still of high importance and even plays the decisive role in some cases, even in the usage of new financial instruments. But modern business ethics in my opinion is, from a methodological point of view, not that of ethics of the individual or of virtue, as are the ethics of duty by Kant. It has to be the institutional ethics of incentives, or of rules appropriate to the corresponding moral questions it should answer (Homann, 1995, p. 9). Like the ethics of medicine or biology, business ethics should solve practical problems and not create lasting values. Thus, ethical categories have to be translated into economic terms, because the market system simply does not understand the original ethical code but only economical ones. Neglecting this fact would mean, that under the conditions of competition, the moral bank or bank employee would be punished continously by the market if there exists only one less moral competitor who does not hesitate to do the business. In other words: even the most upright individuals can become desensitized if they see people around them getting away with wrongdoing (Ettore, 1996, p. 14). That is particularly true for young investment bankers who are constantly exposed to pressure to achieve high performance. In the end, furthermore, the original moral intention often does not become fulfilled, because, especially in global competition, competitors fill the breach, and so high moral standards are in danger of becoming increasingly weakened.

As a consequence, the increase of disastrous incidents in banking is neither necessarily evidence for decay of morals in banking, nor does it show the need for a moral rearmament. It is much more likely that the structural incentives are wrongly placed in the sense that immoral behaviour pays out and moral considerations are being punished.

In regard to those circumstances, business ethics in financial institutions has to concentrate on the arrangement of incentives for moral behaviour. That means, corresponding to the legal framework that contains moral intentions of the whole society, the framework within

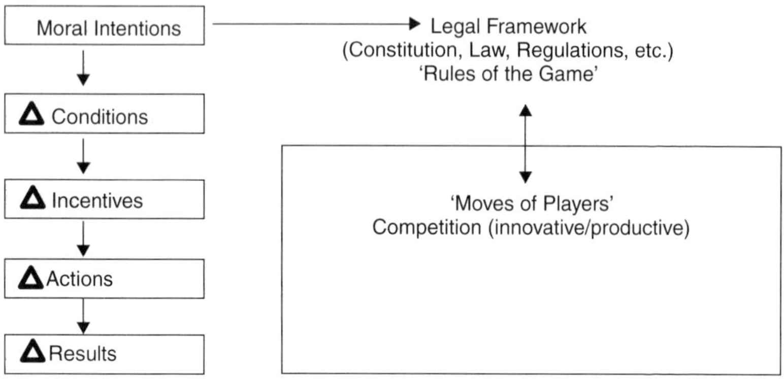

Figure 8.1 Levels of frameworks for economic and ethical behaviour

any bank has to be arranged in such a manner that, for those employees that consider moral standards, it is possible to behave morally without facing any disadvantages in salary or career perspectives (see Figure 8.1).

It therefore has to be pointed out, that bank managers who fail to put into operation systems that facilitate ethical conduct share responsibility with those who conceive, execute and knowingly benefit from corporate misdeeds. Bank managers have to acknowledge their role in institutionalising business ethics and seize this opportunity to create a moral climate that can strengthen the reputation on which their banks success depends (Paine, 1994, p. 106).

Restructuring ethical problems of banks in three dimensions

The description and recording of ethical questions in banking business receives its theoretical foundation by the theory of contracts (Hart and Holmström, 1987).[2] In this respect ethical problems of banks are interpreted as the result of opportunistic behaviour within incomplete contracts (Homann, 1995, p. 18; Wagner, 1997, p. 60). The default of implict contractual obligations happens in three different types of incomplete contracts that banks usually put into effect (see Figure 8.2).

Thomas Hobbes states that moral behaviour shows primarily in keeping contracts (Hobbes, 1651/1989, p. 110). Interpreting moral problems of banks as a default of implicit obligations is a proper means to reduce the complexity of moral questions in the field of banking. This is especially adequate because most of the banking businesses are

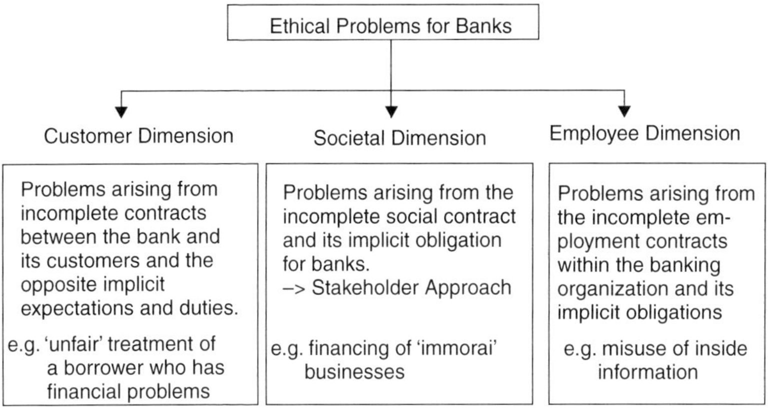

Figure 8.2 Restructuring ethical problems of banks in three dimensions

based on a long-term relationship that, because of unforseen contingencies, is incomplete in many respects. Bank – customer relationships, therefore, are so-called relational contracts (Williamson, 1985) which require trust on the one hand and morality to keep implicit obligations on the other.

Motives for a bank to implement a business ethics programme

In the same way as it must make economic sense for a bank to behave morally at least in the long run, the application of a business ethics programme has to be beneficial in the end (see Figure 8.3).

Reputation

Due to their business structures banks more than other industries are in need of good reputations as there is a wide range of informational advantages that can be used to the prejudice of their clients. Besides various other kinds of reputation (such as for professional competence in complex financial transactions, technical competence in electronic payment systems or simply for financial strength), a good reputation for fair and moral behaviour therefore gains in significance, especially in the financial markets. With this in mind, for a bank to invest in corporate ethics is the same as investing in a strategic competitive advantage to attract customers or other financial partners. Reputation for integrity is not primarily a result of affirming to behave in a fair

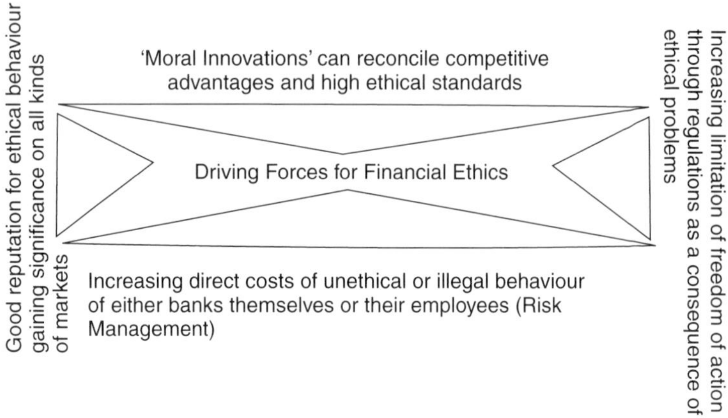

Figure 8.3 Motives for the implementation of an ethics programme in banks

manner; it emerges from the costly institutionalisation of mechanisms that detect own opportunistic behaviour, which is ultimately a business ethics programme.

Risk management

It is especially global players in the financial industry that have to face the fact that teams for complex financial projects, as for project financing, financial mergers or in the field of derivatives, are increasingly a mixture of very much culturally-diverse employees (Wagner, 1997, p. 70), probably with different values and moral standards with regard to loyality or honesty. On the other hand, it becomes more and more important for banks to promote cultural diversity in order to stimulate innovation and creativity in solving complex financial problems. Furthermore, companies nowadays cannot expect every employee to be fully socialised or brought up with the same firm moral standards. A bank's preference for moral values documented in an ethical code of conduct or by training ethical scenarios is an alternative to manage and to control the risk potential that results from complex financial instruments. It also prevents employees from moral overcharge if they know precisely what moral standards a bank stands for and that an ethics officer can be contacted if necessary. In this connection it has to be pointed out again that managing a bank by ethics, based on trust, individual freedom of action and joint values, can only work on an economic basis that guarantees the reward of ethical behaviour! This is expecially true for the field of derivatives, where executive managers often know less about the instruments, than do the new younger recruits, who are highly qualified but inexperienced.

Moral innovations

Creating a moral climate within a bank can also be the basis for the development of moral innovations in banking such as affinity credit cards, ethical investment products (Cowton, 1994) or probably the use of new financial instruments for ethical purposes. It should be absolutely legitimate to support moral issues in the economic system by economic instruments, such as derivatives. It just depends on how they are handled and on whether the incentives are set in a way to deal with them morally!

Prevention of financial sanctions and regulations

The consequences of scandals in the banking field are widespread and in most cases serious. Apart from financial losses that can lead to bankruptcy, banks have to face financial compensation for their clients, and in many cases a rise in financial regulation and banking supervision for the whole industry.[3] Furthermore the US Sentencing Guidelines are discussed as an appropriate model also for European companies (Heine, 1996, p. 213). Especially in the investment banking business, young and highly qualified but rather inexperienced people can blow up and devastate a whole bank. The responsibility to teach them legal and ethical issues is a burden that no other industry has to the same extent (Ettore, 1996, p. 15). As a result, bank executives who ignore ethics run the risk of personal and corporate liability in today's increasingly tough legal and regulatory environment (Paine, 1994, p. 106).

Cornerstones of a business ethics management for banks

When it comes to the question of business ethics in banking practice, three aspects can be distinguished (see Figure 8.4) in implementing an ethics management (Wagner, 1997, p. 71).

1. *Substantial aspects* As to the contents of a business ethics strategy it is necessary to establish the corporate values in the ethical code of conduct. It seems remarkable that in a recent empirical study carried out by the author among German and British banks, it was shown that most of the major British banks are in possession of a code of conduct which explicitly refers to ethical questions,[4] whereas practically all of the major German institutes have none

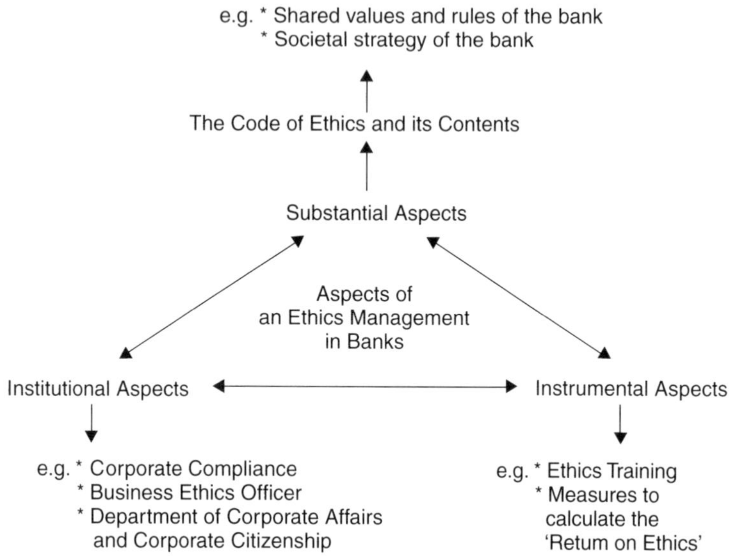

Figure 8.4 Aspects of an ethics management in banks

or only a very general code of conduct (Wagner, 1998). Regarding also the intense US tendency towards banking codes of ethics,[5] it leads to the insight that we find in the Anglo-Saxon area a code of conduct tradition, whereas German banks obviously trust in the unspoken rules of integrity.

2. *Institutional Aspects* One of the most important cornerstones for institutionalising business ethics in banks is the compliance office.[6] But providing bank employees only with a compliance rule book, as practiced in many institutes, will do little to address the problems underlying unlawful conduct. In order to foster a moral climate that encourages exemplary behaviour, a comprehensive approach is required that goes beyond the legal compliance status (Paine, 1994, p. 106). Legal clearance does not certify the absence of ethical problems, as the cases of Leeson of Barings, Milken of Drexel Burnham, Young of Deutsche Morgan Grenfell or Iguchi of Daiwa have shown. An integrity-based approach to financial ethics therefore combines a concern for the law with an emphasis on the managerial responsibility for ethical behaviour (Paine, 1994 pp. 106–7).
3. *Instrumental Aspects* Various banks in the United Kingdom, the USA and Canada have recently been starting to use ethical training

programmes as an instrument within their ethics management. In this respect, ethical scenarios present situations which help put the bank's code of conduct into an everyday working context. Furthermore, plenty of research is still necessary in order to develop instruments for the measurement of the effects of a bank's ethical behaviour on their reputation and financial success.

A recent Harvard study about ethical dilemmas of young managers, among them several managers from financial institutions, produced the following implications for an integrated ethics management (Badaracco and Webb, 1995, pp. 23–5):

- Codes of ethics can be helpful, particularly if they are specific about acceptable and unacceptable behaviour and provide advice on handling 'grey areas'.
- Young managers are much more likely to believe that a code means what it says if the code is enforced. This means punishing individuals who are guilty of violating the code; it also means letting the organisation know that these infractions have been punished. In contrast, when violations go unpunished, codes become simply another wall decoration or filing-cabinet filler.
- Furthermore if the leading managers are not going to make an unremitting effort to high ethical standards, and if they will not investigate and discipline violators of the code of conduct, they should abandon creating ethics credos or announcing their personal dedication to high ethical standards. They may simply be setting themselves up to be viewed with suspicion and cynicism. This also means that moral leadership by bank managers is a key success factor for the bank's moral climate!

Financial ethics is on its way

Having gone through a period of underdevelopment combined with a lack of theoretical foundation (McHugh, 1997, p. 34), financial ethics today, both in theoretical research and in banking practice, seems to be gaining in significance. But still the concept and the possible competitive advantages of an integrated ethics management are quite unknown. A decision of a London court probably showed the way to business ethics for banks – 'two former employees of the Bank of Credit and Commerce International were given leave by a London judge to sue the liquidators of the corrupt bank, on the grounds that their own reputation had been adversely affected by working for a dishonest company. Integrity not only of persons but also of organisations seems to gain more and more significance as an implicit part of employment contracts' (*EBEN-Newsletter*, no. 2, 1997, p. 8).

Notes

1. While in Anglo-Saxon business ethics research nowadays, the ethics of virtue seems to play a major role, institutional ethics in Germany operates through being a state of art see Homann (1995) for Germany.
2. For a survey on theoretical approaches to the problem of finance ethics, see Schuster (1997), pp. 12–15, and Wagner (1999), pp. 28-32 and 38–41.
3. For recent examples see the cases of Barings and Deutsche Morgan Grenfell; Prudential Securities, the US broker had to pay the second largest fine ever to the US Securities and Exchange Commission for the unsuitable sale of more than US$8 billion in limited partnerships to unsophisticated investors. The financial result for Prudential Securities was: a US$300 million pool for damaged investors; a US$26 million fine to state securities regulators; and a US$5 million fine to the National Association of Securities Dealers (Caccese, 1997, p. 10); and for a survey on some recent regulatory developments for financial institutions, see Frowen (1995), pp. 40–42.
4. For example, see NatWest Group (ed.) (1993), *It's Good Business – The Nat West Group Code of Conduct.*
5. For example, see Citibank (ed.), *Code of Conduct and Ethical Policies.*
6. For a more detailed discussion on institutional aspects of an ethics management in banks, see Wagner (1999), 346–366.

References

Badaracco, J. L. and Webb, A. P. (1995) 'Business Ethics: A View from the Trenches', *California Management Review,* vol. 37, no. 2, Winter, pp. 8–28.

Caccese, M. S. (1997) 'Ethics and the Financial Analyst', *Financial Analyst Journal,* vol. 53, no. 1, Jan.–Feb., pp. 9–14.

Center for Business Ethics at Bentley College (1992) 'Instilling Ethical Values in Large Corporations', *Journal of Business Ethics,* no. 11, pp. 863–7.

Cowton, C. J. (1994) 'The Development of Ethical Investment Products', in A. R. Prindl and B. Prodhan (eds), *Ethical Conflicts in Finance* (Oxford: Blackwell), pp. 213–32.

Eben Newsletter (1997), vol. 2.

Ettore, B. (1996) 'Temptation of Big Money', *Management Review,* February, pp. 13–17.

Frowen, S. F. (1995) 'The Functions of Money and Financial Credit: Their Objectives, Structure and Inbuild Deficiencies', in S. F. Frowen and F. P. McHugh (eds), *Financial Decision-Making and Moral Responsibility* (London: Macmillan; New York: St Martin's Press), pp. 31–46.

Hart, O. and Holmström, B. (1987) 'The Theory of Contracts', in T. F. Bewley (ed.), *Advances in Economic Theory,* papers presented at the Fifth World Congress of the Economic Society in Cambridge, Mass. (Cambridge: Cambridge University Press), pp. 71–155.

Heine, G. (1996) 'Die strafrechtliche Verantwortlichkeit von Unternehmen: Internationale Entwicklung-nationale Konsequenzen', in *Österreichische Juristen-Zeitung*, vol. 51, no. 6, pp. 211–19.

Hobbes, T. [1651] (1989) *Leviathan*, ed. I. Fetscher, 3rd edn (Frankfurt-am-Main: Suhrkamp).

Homann, K. (1995) *Gewinnmaximierung und Kooperation – Eine ordnungsethische Reflexion*, the Kiel Institute of World Economics (ed.), Kiel Working Papers, no. 691.

McHugh, F. P. (1997), 'Of Tombstones and Financial Ethics', in L. Schuster (ed.) *Die gesellschaftliche Verantwortung der Banken* (Munich: Beck), pp. 33–49.

Paine, L. S. (1994), 'Managing for Organizational Integrity', *Harvard Business Review*, March-April, pp. 106–17.

Rafalko, R. J. (1994), 'Remaking the Corporation' *Journal of Business Ethics*, pp. 625–36.

Schuster, L. (1997) 'Die gesellschaftliche Verantwortung der Banken – Überlegungen zu einer 'Gesellschaftsorientierten Bankbetriebslehre'', in L. Schuster (ed.) *Die gesellschaftliche Verantwortung der Banken* (Munich: Beck), pp. 2–22.

Wagner, A. (1997), 'Unternehmensethik – ein Thema auch für Banken', in L. Schuster (ed.) *Die gesellschaftliche Verantwortung der Banken* (Munich: Beck), pp. 51–82.

Wagner, A. (1999), *Unternehmensethik in Banken* (Vienna: Orac).

Wieland, J. (1993), *Formen der Institutionalisierung von Moral in amerikanischen Unternehmen* (Bern: Paul Haupt).

Williamson, O.E. (1985), *The Economic Institutions of Capitalism: Firms, Markets, Relational Contracting* (New York: The Free Press).

9

The Savings-Ratio Behaviour in Globalised Money and Capital Markets: A Comparison of the UK and German Experiences

Stephen F. Frowen and Elias Karakitsos

Introduction

Deregulation, liberalisation and globalisation of financial markets in the 1980s and the 1990s has meant more reliance on prices (interest rates) as the clearing market mechanism. Moreover, central banks throughout the world are making much heavier use of interest rates to control monetary aggregates and the other ultimate targets of economic policy. These structural changes imply much larger volatility in interest rates than before which, in turn, causes a more stressful adjustment for the corporate, personal and financial sectors. This adjustment is not uniform. Small businesses are hit more than large ones, and the consumer is hit even harder when interest rates rise, thus raising general issues on the preferred method of the conduct of monetary policy and the effects of deregulation, liberalisation and globalisation.

Deregulation especially in the Anglo-Saxon countries induced consumers and small businesses to accumulate debt. Throughout the 1980s the personal sector debt-to-disposable-income ratio soared (in most Anglo-Saxon countries it more than doubled). In contrast, Germany and continental Europe have not yet followed these trends. This has made the consumer much more vulnerable and prone to boom-and-bust asset cycles in the Anglo-Saxon than the continental countries. But the trend even on the continent may be changing. In this chapter we illustrate the mechanism through which the consumer adjusts in these boom–bust asset cycles. In particular, we show that contrary to the accepted view, as epitomised in the life-cycle–permanent income hypothesis, the adjustment of the saving ratio is counter-cyclical rather than pro-cyclical.

Monetary policy in the UK and Germany

It is of some interest to contrast the differences between the conduct of monetary policy in the UK and Germany, and to draw some conclusions from this analysis for assessing monetary ethics in both countries during the postwar period.

Looking at the UK first, we find a history of final and intermediate economic objectives, which is less consistent than in Germany. Thus, the 1950s and 1960s were the heydays of Keynesian demand management in the UK with the principal macroeconomic objective being full employment via high rates of economic growth and simultaneous external equilibrium. Aggregate demand was controlled mainly by an anti-cyclical fiscal policy. Interest rates at that time were kept low to keep the budget deficits at a sustainable level, which was important considering the size of the UK national debt. Thus the financial sector could only support fiscal policy actively by direct credit controls. These consisted mainly of qualitative restrictions on both bank lending and hire-purchase agreements, as well as controls on capital issues. There was no money supply target as such, but rather a target for the growth of bank lending at times.

This policy was successful during the 1950s and part of the 1960s. Full employment was achieved, growth rates were high, but external disequilibrium often caused problems. On the whole one could say that the Keynesian demand management policy at that time achieved the objectives of an ethically justifiable economic policy, although the achievements were often accompanied by higher inflation rates (see Frowen and Karakitsos, 1997).

Towards the end of the 1950s doubts began to emerge about the efficiency cost of the British monetary system, and the Radcliffe Committee on the working of the monetary system was set up in 1957, concluding in their report in 1959 that the structure of interest rates rather than the supply of money is the centrepiece of the monetary mechanism; yet by the late 1960s the first steps were taken in the UK towards money-supply targeting. This policy was linked by the late 1960s to a greater flexibility in interest rate policy. All this was instituted after radical changes to the regulation of the British monetary system, following the Bank of England document *Competition and Credit Control* in September 1971.

Short-term Keynesian stabilisation policy was finally replaced by a more convinced monetarist policy in the form of a medium-term anti-inflation policy, based largely upon monetary control measures, in

May 1979 by the newly-elected Conservative government. Money-supply targets were set but seldom achieved. Extensive deregulation and financial innovations made them obsolete and they were replaced by an exchange-rate target within the framework of ERM. After leaving the ERM in September 1992 came the introduction of a single-stage strategy of direct inflationary control by means of preannounced medium-term inflation targets (set by the Treasury in May 1997 at $2^1/_2$ per cent).

The achievement of this inflation target by means of interest-rate policy became the responsibility of the Bank of England's Monetary Policy Committee established in May 1997, with the power of setting base rates having been transferred by the new Labour Government from the Treasury to the Bank of England at the same time.

To control short-term interest rates, the UK has always relied on the discount window or standing facilities combined with open-market operations, with the emphasis on the latter for smoothing money-market operations. This is in contrast to Germany where open-market operations have only lately started playing the dominant part they always did in the UK where there has never been a shortage of suitable short-term paper for this purpose.

Post-war monetary policy in Germany has taken quite a different course. At the end of the Second World War, the Allies themselves set up an independent decentralised central bank system in West Germany following the currency reform of 1948 by means of which the Reichsmark was replaced by the Deutschemark and the inflationary overhang eliminated. It also meant the cancelling of a huge government debt. The new central banking system was a two-tier system with the Bank deutscher Länder, starting its operations in September 1949, being the upper tier, and the legally independent land central banks being the lower tier. It was replaced by the Deutsche Bundesbank by means of the Bundesbank Act of 1957, still retaining the land central banks.

In contrast to the UK, German postwar economic policy has been marked by a consistent monetary policy conducted by an independent central bank, its principal objective being the stability of the Deutschemark. In fact, this is the Bundesbank's main mandate laid down by law in the Bundesbank Act. Supporting the general economic policy of the federal German government – another obligation laid down by the Bundesbank Act – comes second. These arrangements resulted in Germany achieving one of the lowest inflation rates among the major industrial countries virtually throughout the postwar era, with the exception of a brief period during the immediate years following the German currency union of 1990.

However, changes did take place in the application of German monetary policy instruments. With virtually no government debt left as a result of the currency reform of 1948, there was no room for sufficient open market operations and the Bank deutscher Länder and subsequently the Deutsche Bundesbank had to rely on the traditional instruments of monetary policy, that is rediscount and lombard policy supported by an active and complex minimum reserve policy. The application of monetary instruments by the Bundesbank began to change when regaining control over the money supply as a result of the breakdown of the Bretton Woods system in 1973, but the most dramatic changes came following the globalisation of financial markets since the early 1980s, making a total insulation from international financial influences an impossibility.

West Germany never had direct credit controls and cartel arrangements of the type popular in the UK during the 1950s and 1960s, and also went in for early liberalisation of the financial system. This facilitated the Bundesbank's response to financial globalisation. Most important was a shift of emphasis from traditional refinancing policy to open-market policy, which became the centrepiece of day-to-day money-market operations. The previous more traditional instruments remained, but were assigned modified functions. Rediscount policy provided basic funding of the banking system, lombard policy supplied lender-of-last-resort facilities, while minimum reserve policy supplemented open-market policy in meeting the demand for base money and also constituted a liquidity buffer in the money market. Thus the whole system had adjusted to fine-tuning of the kind always prevalent in the London market. Most of the German open-market operations now consisted of securities repurchase agreements where either the banks determined the individual allotment rate, or, by means of a fixed-rate tender, where the Bundesbank set a specific (uniform) rate – the so-called repo rate.

Looking at both the UK and German (now ECB) shape of monetary policy, the fact is that – in line with the USA – it is interest rate policy, the determination of short-term interest rates, which has become a vital variable because if it changes it affects directly (through valuation) or indirectly (through other macro-variables) all components of the personal sector net wealth. Thus in periods of high interest rates the value of bonds falls, house prices and the value of shares decline, servicing the debt increases or the value of debt increases through the restructuring of loans.

Accordingly, consumer net wealth declines as the value of assets falls, whereas that of liabilities increases. Consumer wealth falls short of its target prompting consumers to spend less and rebuild their wealth by saving more as they feel poorer. In contrast, in periods of low interest rates the value of bonds rises, house prices and the value of equities increase, servicing the debt becomes easier or the value of debt is reduced through the restructuring of loans. Accordingly, consumer net wealth exceeds its target prompting consumers to lower their savings ratio.

The adjustment of consumption in the business cycle

The wider macroeconomic implications of the developments in the financial sector can be established if we investigate in some depth the changed consumption patterns in the business cycle.

The consumer's utility function depends on the level of consumption in each period t of her time horizon. Thus, for T periods ($t = 1, \ldots, T$) the utility of an individual consumer is:

$$U = U(C_{t+1}, C_{t+2}, \ldots, C_T) \qquad (9.1)$$

with $\partial U / \partial C_{t+j} > 0$, $\partial^2 U / \partial C^2_{t+J} < 0$. The positive first partial derivative implies that the marginal utility is positive (that is, more consumption always increases utility). The negative second partial derivative implies diminishing marginal utility (that is, as consumption increases the marginal utility decreases).

The consumer's budget constraint is:

$$V_{t+1} = (1 + r)V_t + YL_t - C_t \qquad (9.2)$$

where V is real wealth, YL is labour income, C is consumption and r is the real interest rate earned on wealth. The budget constraint states that wealth next period is equal to the wealth in this period, plus the return on wealth between t and $t + 1$, plus the addition to wealth in this period due to savings, $(YL - C)$.

Alternatively, the budget constraint (9.2) can be defined as the total resources, R, available to the individual for current and future consumption. These resources consist of current real wealth and the present discounted value of current and future labour income. Total lifetime resources are thus defined as:

$$R_t = V_t + \sum_{s=0}^{\infty} \left(\frac{1}{1+r} \right)^{s+1} E_t YL_{t+s} \qquad (9.3)$$

The lifetime resources can alternatively be defined not in a stock form, as defined previously, but in a flow form. The flow form defines permanent income, or the annuity value of wealth. Thus permanent income, *YP*, is defined as:

$$YP_t = r\left[V_t + \sum_{s=0}^{\infty}\left(\frac{1}{1+r}\right)^{s+1} E_t YL_{t+s}\right] \tag{9.4}$$

In the infinite-horizon problem the consumer chooses consumption in each period, C_t, ($t = 1, \ldots, \infty$) in order to maximise the expected value of the discounted present value of her future utility,

$$E_t \sum_{j=0}^{\infty}\left(\frac{1}{1+r}\right)^{j} U\left(C_{t+j}\right) \tag{9.5}$$

subject to the budget constraint (9.2); where E_t denotes the mathematical expectation of (.) conditional on information available at *t*.

It can be shown (see Zeldes, 1989a; Flavin, 1981; Yaari, 1964) that for any concave utility function with variable but non-stochastic future income, the maximisation of (9.5) subject to (9.2), (9.3) or (9.4) gives rise to a consumption function which is proportional to permanent or lifetime income,

$$C = \kappa\, YP \tag{9.6}$$

Consumption is proportional to the expected present value of lifetime resources, which consist of human and non-human wealth. Human wealth is the present discounted value as of time *t* of expected future labour income. The constant of proportionality κ is equal to the amount one could receive in the remainder of the lifetime by giving up one dollar or sterling today. When $r = 0$, κ is simply equal to $1/(T - t + 1)$, that is the inverse of the number of periods in the remainder of the lifetime. Yaari (1964) showed for a certainty model that if the proportionality hypothesis holds (for all *r* and δ), then the utility function must be a constant relative risk-aversion utility function. When $r = \delta$, the proportionality hypothesis holds under certainty for any concave utility function, see Zeldes (1989a).

Permanent income can be thought of as the constant resource flow which, conditional on expectations in period *t*, can be sustained for the rest of the individual's life while maintaining her total wealth intact. Thus if $\kappa = 1$ and expectations are rational, in which case the expectation of next period's revision in expected future labour income $(E_t + 1 - E_t)\ YL_t + s$, and the expectation of unanticipated capital gains from real wealth $V_t - E_t - 1V_t$ are equal to zero, then permanent income is a martingale (see Hall, 1978), namely, it has the property:

$$E_t\ YP_{t+1} = YP_t \tag{9.7}$$

For $\kappa < 1$, permanent income is a non-stationary first-order autoregressive process,

$$YP_{ts} = (1 - \kappa)\ YP_{t-1} \tag{9.8}$$

According to the life-cycle – permanent income hypothesis LCH/PIH (see Friedman, 1957; Ando and Modigliani, 1963), consumers smooth their consumption patterns in the business cycle by basing their expenditure on their estimate of their permanent or trend income. Hence, saving should rise in a boom and fall in a recession as consumers interpret the fluctuations in current income as temporary. In a boom consumers regard the high current income as temporary and save the excess over permanent or trend income for the rainy days. In a recession consumers regard the drop in their current income as temporary and try to safeguard their standard of living by drawing down their savings (wealth). Thus, the saving ratio (the fraction of saving over disposable income S/YD) moves pro-cyclically. (A variable is said to fluctuate pro-cyclically if it rises in the upswing of the cycle and falls in the downswing).

These premises can easily be derived by combining the PIH, equation (9.9), with the definition of disposable income, equation (9.10):

$$C = C_y\ YP \tag{9.9}$$

$$YD = C + S \tag{9.10}$$

where YD = disposable income; S = saving.

With a simple substitution of (9.10) into (9.9) the behaviour of saving (saving ratio) in the course of the business cycle can be assessed:

$$\frac{S}{YD} = 1 - C_y \frac{YP}{YD} \tag{9.11}$$

In a boom, current income exceeds permanent income and the ratio *YP*/*YD* falls which leads to a rise in the saving ratio *S*/*YD*. In a recession current income falls short of permanent income and the ratio *YP*/*YD* rises which leads to a fall in the saving ratio.

However, the conclusion that the saving ratio fluctuates pro-cyclically is not robust in models of uncertainty as the empirical evidence for some countries suggests. If income is stochastic (that is, there is uncertainty about future labour income) then the influence of human and non-human wealth should be separated to allow for revision in permanent income in view of changes in current income. Thus the combined PIH/LCH under conditions of uncertainty implies,

$$C = C_y\ YP + C_v V \tag{9.12}$$

where *YP* is now redefined as permanent labour income, and *V* = private sector non-human wealth. This form of the consumption function follows if income is stochastic (see, Zeldes, 1989a; and Flavin, 1981), whereas the standard form is derived under the condition that income is variable but non-stochastic. In his original work, Friedman (1957, pp. 16–17) conjectured that the introduction of income uncertainty should cause consumption to depend positively on the ratio of non-human wealth to permanent income. Under conditions of uncertainty the proportionality rule breaks down.

Substituting (9.10) into (9.12) the saving ratio is obtained:

$$\frac{S}{YD} = 1 - C_y \frac{YP}{YD} - C_v \frac{V}{YD} \tag{9.13}$$

It is clear from the above relationship that the saving ratio depends not only on the ratio of permanent to current income in the business cycle, but also on the wealth–income ratio. Thus, although in a boom the permanent to current income ratio falls, the wealth–income ratio may rise sufficiently to cause a fall instead of a rise in the saving ratio. Hence, in order to analyse the behaviour of the saving ratio in the business cycle we must examine the determinants of the wealth–income ratio.

Wealth is created by the accumulation of past savings. Thus, if saving commenced *n* periods ago, the value of wealth in period *t* (today) is:

$$V = \sum_{i=t-n}^{t} S_i \tag{9.14}$$

Table 9.1 The personal-sector balance sheet

Assets (A)	*Liabilities (L)*
Financial assets	Bank loans
Notes and coins	Mortgages
Bank and other deposits	Consumer credit
Bonds and equities	Other credit (e.g. credit cards)
Physical wealth	
Land and property	
Net wealth = *A* – *L*	

But wealth is kept or invested in various assets (tangible and financial) and consumers can additionally borrow, using as a collateral their assets, in order to increase the value of their wealth through investment. Thus, wealth is properly defined as *net* wealth which is the value of assets less the liabilities of consumers. The value of assets and liabilities can increase or decrease as their prices change through time thereby altering the net wealth of consumers.

Table 9.1 provides a schematic framework of the personal-sector balance sheet which determines net wealth. The assets consist of two major items, physical and financial. The latter consists of cash, all forms of bank deposits and deposits with other financial institutions, government as well as corporate bonds and shares. Physical wealth consists of land and property, including owner-occupied houses. The liabilities of the personal sector consist of bank loans for house purchase (mortgages), consumer credit for big ticket items such as consumer durables, and other consumer credit such as credit cards. Table 9.2 shows the UK personal-sector balance sheet at the end of 1990.

How, therefore, would consumers respond in the course of the business cycle? At any point in time they would have a target wealth which is computed on the required consumption for the remainder of their life expectancy taking into account that one of the spouses may outlive to become very old, the bequests consumers would like to leave to their heirs, and the amount of precautionary saving in case they are faced with large medical bills during retirement. Since the target level of wealth would finance future consumption for themselves or their children, consumers would use the PIH/LCH to estimate their permanent or lifetime resources and the desired level of consumption.

Table 9.2 The UK personal-sector balance sheet, end of 1990

Assets (A) £2342 billion	*Liabilities (L) £440 billion*
Financial assets (£1127 billion)	Bank loans (20%)
Notes and coins (1%)	Mortgages (65%)
Bank and building society deposits (28%)	Consumer credit (2%)
Equities (15%)	Other credit (13%)
Unit trusts (2%)	
Equity in LAPFs (43%)	
National savings (2%)	
Other (8%)	
Physical wealth (£1215 billion)	
Land and property	
Net wealth = £1902 billion	

However, actual wealth would fluctuate around its target level as asset prices fluctuate in the course of the business cycle and consumers take advantage of low or high interest rates to borrow or repay their debts. Moreover, other variables like consumer confidence influenced by the level and rate of change of unemployment, inflation, wage-settlements and interest rates, the length and depth of the recession or the extent of the boom may affect the level of precautionary saving and consumers' estimates of their permanent income. In good periods, like a boom in the property or the equity market, wealth may exceed its target prompting consumers to spend more thereby reducing their savings ratio as they feel wealthier. The situation may be accentuated if economic activity is buoyant in which case consumer confidence is rising prompting consumers to borrow more as their estimate of their permanent income is also rising.

In bad periods, after a bust in the property or equity market or because their debt has increased, wealth may fall short of its target prompting consumers to spend less thereby raising their saving ratio as they feel poorer. The situation may be aggravated if falling wealth is accompanied by a recession in which consumer confidence is eroded, precautionary saving is increased and the estimate of their permanent income is reduced thereby prompting consumers to repay their debt. Hence, the adjustment of the saving ratio in the course of the business cycle requires an evaluation of all components of net wealth as well as the factors which affect permanent income.

In this framework, the interest rate becomes a vital variable because if it changes it affects directly (through valuation) or indirectly (through other macro-variables) all components of the personal-sector net wealth. Thus, in periods of high interest rates the value of bonds falls, house prices and the value of shares decline, servicing the debt increases or the value of debt increases through the restructuring of loans. Accordingly, consumer net wealth declines as the value of assets falls, whereas the liabilities increase. Consumer wealth falls short of its target prompting consumers to spend less and rebuild their wealth by saving more as they feel poorer. In contrast, in periods of low interest rates the value of bonds rises, house prices and the value of equities increase, servicing the debt becomes easier or the value of debt is reduced through the restructuring of loans. Accordingly, consumer net wealth exceeds its target prompting consumers to lower their savings ratio.

The savings ratio in UK business cycles

Figure 9.1 shows the UK personal-sector savings ratio (saving as a per cent of personal disposable income) in the course of the business cycles between 1960 and 1996. The savings ratio was relatively stable in the 1960s fluctuating around 8.5 per cent. However, from the beginning of the 1970s onwards the fluctuations have been very large with a maximum at 13.5 per cent in 1980 and a minimum of nearly 5.5 per cent in 1988. What are the causes of these large fluctuations in the savings ratio from the 1980s onwards? Are these large fluctuations a new permanent feature or is it likely that we shall return to the relatively stable environment before the 1970s?

A cursory look at Figure 9.1 suggests that most of the time the savings ratio fluctuates counter-cyclically – rising in a recession and falling in a boom. (The main exception to this rule was in the early 1970s – the so-called 'Barber boom' – in which the savings ratio moved pro-cyclically. The boom was caused by easy monetary policy through the relaxation of hire-purchase controls. The consumer went into a spending spree financed by credit. Imports soared, the balance of payments went into deficit and a year later monetary policy had to be tightened again. Hence, in spite of the rise in the savings ratio consumers increased their spending by raising their debt-to-income ratio. In the sharp and quick downswing of the cycle the savings ratio continued to rise resuming its counter-cyclical adjustment.) This is at odds with the LCH/PIH which predicts that since consumers smooth their

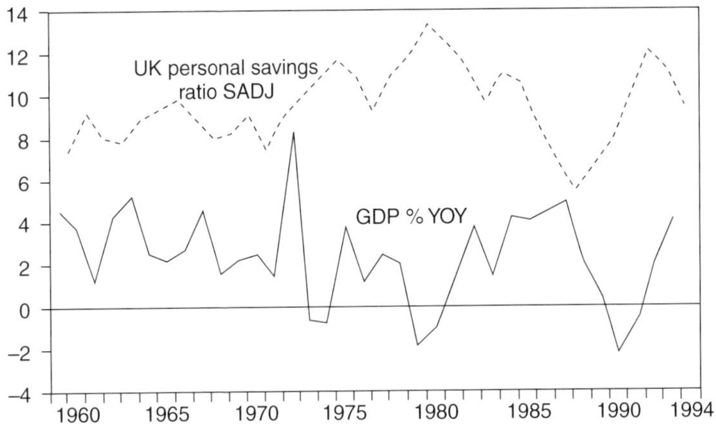

SADJ = seasonally adjusted.
YOY = year-on-year.
Source: Datastream.

Figure 9.1 UK personal savings ratio in business cycles

consumption over their lifetime the savings ratio should move pro-cyclically – rising in a boom and falling in a recession. The implication of a counter-cyclical movement in the savings ratio is that consumers increase the amplitude of the business cycle – when their income is falling they attempt to save more thereby making the recession worse. When their income is rising they run down their savings making the boom more pronounced. This makes the case for activist policies – in which the policy-makers attempt to dampen the amplitude of the business cycles – even stronger. How, therefore, can such a behaviour on the part of consumers be explained? The quick answer is that financial deregulation and liberalisation, as discussed below, has made the large fluctuations in the savings ratio a permanent feature, and that the counter-cyclical pattern of the savings ratio is the product of a complicated adjustment between the net wealth-income ratio and the ratio of permanent to current income according to equation (9.13) which involves an evaluation of all the constituent components of the personal-sector balance sheet in Tables 9.1 and 9.2. The long shot requires an explicit definition of the relevant variables and their time profile.

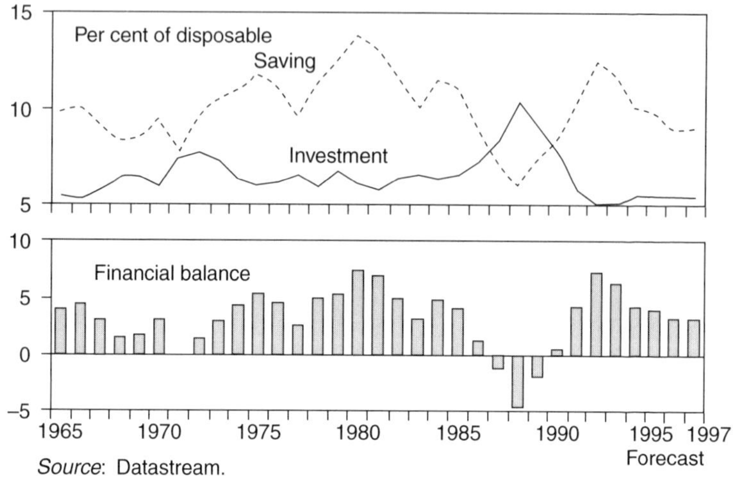

Figure 9.2 The personal-sector financial balance

The UK national accounts define the personal sector not only as households but also as unincorporated business, charities and the life assurance and pension funds (LAPFs). *Personal saving* is defined as the difference between personal disposable income and consumer expenditure, according to equation (9.10):

$$S = YD - C \tag{9.15}$$

Savings can be used to invest in physical and financial assets. Investment in physical assets (called simply *investment, I*) includes purchases of new houses, land and existing buildings as well as spending on improvements and maintenance of houses. The difference between saving and investment defines the personal-sector *financial balance*. The personal sector is said to be in *financial surplus* when its saving exceeds its investment, and in *financial deficit* when its investment exceeds its saving. The financial surplus can be used to acquire financial assets or repay debts, *net acquisition of financial assets, NAFA*, where

$$S - I = NAFA \tag{9.16}$$

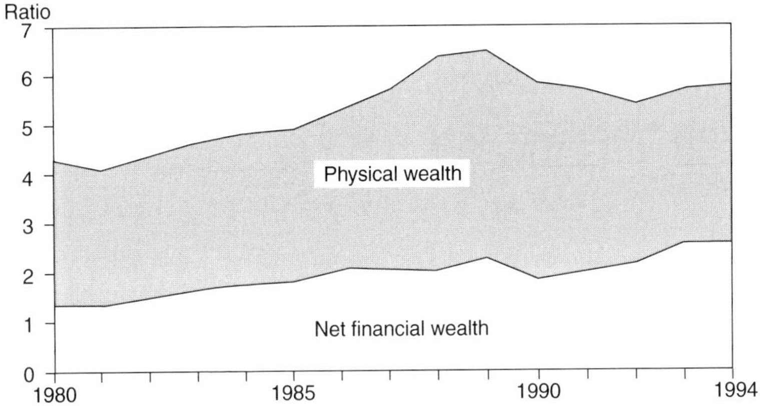

Source: Datastream.

Figure 9.3 Personal-sector net wealth–income ratio

Figure 9.2 shows the saving, investment and financial balance of the personal sector from the late 1960s onwards. The personal sector, with the exception of 1986–88, has been running a financial surplus. In spite of these surpluses, its net financial wealth, the accumulation of *NAFA*, declined in the 1970s. However, net wealth increased as the value of physical assets (houses) more than offset the decline in financial wealth. Figure 9.3 shows the total net wealth split into physical wealth and net financial wealth according to the definitions of Tables 9.1 and 9.2. Net financial wealth is equal to assets less liabilities. Figure 9.4 shows the personal-sector debt burden in a stock and flow form. In a stock form, which follows from the balance-sheet definitions of Tables 9.1 and 9.2, the debt burden is defined as the stock of outstanding debt relative to disposable income. The stock concept is more relevant for the long term. The flow form is more relevant in the short run as it is restraining the cash flow of consumers and is defined as the interest payments relative to disposable income (that is, the proportion of income which is allocated for servicing the debt). If interest payments rise, then consumers have less income for consumption. Finally, Figure 9.5 shows the house price–earnings ratio. House prices have varied substantially since the 1970s thereby affecting the valuation of physical wealth. Such fluctuations in asset prices play a key role in the adjustment of the savings ratio in business cycles.

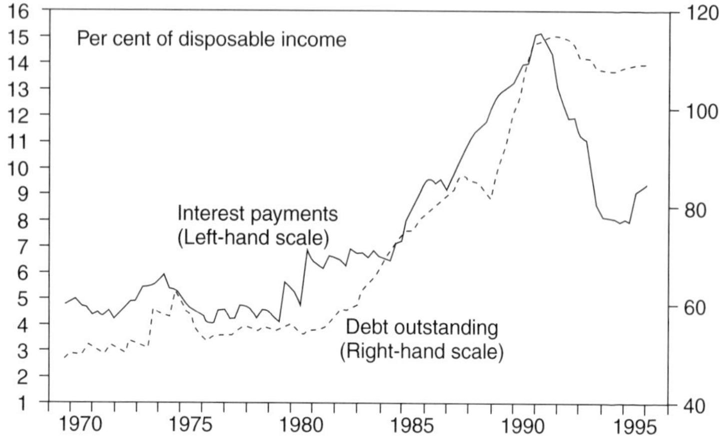

Source: Datastream.

Figure 9.4 Personal-sector debt burden

With this information as a background we can attempt to answer why the savings ratio varies counter-cyclically. Consumers have a target level for their wealth so that they can finance their own future consumption as well as that of their children in the form of bequests. Hence, households determine the optimal rate of their annual saving on the basis of their expectations about future income, asset prices, interest rates and inflation. In addition consumers take into account their precautionary saving – for the rainy days. If plans turn out as expected there is no need for adjusting their savings rate. However, if wealth is rising faster than expected their need to save is reduced, while if wealth is falling short of its target then consumers need to save more. Wealth can rise faster than expected if asset prices increase or income is growing faster or if inflation falls more than anticipated. Hence, the savings ratio varies in a way to achieve the target wealth in the face of unexpected developments in the main determinants of the future path of wealth.

Consider now the causes of the counter-cyclical fluctuations in the savings ratio in the 1980s. First, as house prices increased faster than income (see Figure 9.5) consumers felt wealthier (wealth increased) and reduced their savings ratio. Second, as inflation abated in the 1980s the real value of their financial wealth was restored, hence again prompt-

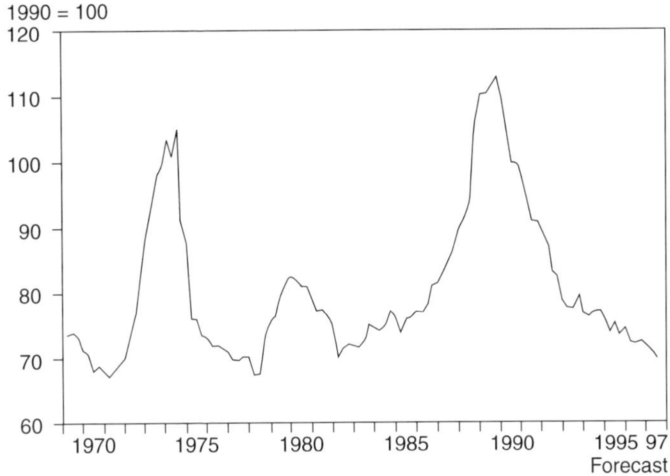

Source: Datastream.

Figure 9.5 House price–earnings ratio

ing consumers to reduce their savings ratio. Third, large increases in equity prices until October 1987 further boosted financial wealth again contributing to a fall in the savings ratio. Fourth, rising incomes reduced precautionary saving. Fifth, rising house prices and the possibility of capital gains prompted households to invest more in the property market thereby inducing them to increase their debt to income ratio, see Figure 9.4. Sixth, rising incomes made those extra debts affordable in the sense of being able to service higher levels of debt. This trend was exacerbated as interest rates fell and consequently interest payments were made more affordable. Hence, as net wealth rose consumers were willing to accumulate more debt. All these factors did not operate independently but were mutually reinforcing.

However, this is a recipe for a boom–bust asset cycle. Consumers' expectations are self-fulfilling. The more consumers are willing to accumulate debt the more their wealth is rising, and in the late 1980s consumers expected these trends to last forever. This was evident in the unprecedented deficit that the personal sector incurred in 1986–88 in which investment in houses exceeded savings. Obviously consumers got up to their necks with debt on the expectation that house prices would continue to rise.

The catalyst to this process is monetary policy. As soon as interest rates start to climb, the demand for credit declines and banks become less willing to extend credit. Hence, the upward trend in asset prices is reversed, wealth falls and consumers' expectations are shattered. Indeed, interest rates not only in the UK but in all major economies in the late 1980s increased as the boom in domestic demand led to overheating and inflation started to climb. The most sensitive component to changes in interest rates is equity prices which were the first to give in as interest rates started to rise in the October 1987 world stock-market crash.

With a lag, property prices are also hit. In a boom both property developers and consumers are willing to accumulate debt as house prices rise and the banks are willing to finance both the demand and the supply in the property market. Banks are willing to finance property developers when house prices rise as the balance sheet of the banks looks healthy on the back of rising developers' profits. Banks are also willing to finance the demand for houses since the collateral of consumers (the price of houses) is also increasing. This is a spiral causing a boom in the property market as banks, developers and consumers enjoy profits. This situation persists as long as interest rates remain low, but such a boom is unsustainable if it is financed by credit. As soon as interest rates start to climb both property developers and consumers find it difficult to service their debt. The appetite to accumulate more debt diminishes and the demand for houses falls. House prices then decline not only because demand is weakening but also because developers lower prices as they face cash-flow problems. Falling asset prices reduce wealth. The deteriorating cash-flow position of consumers and property developers induces banks to restrict credit thereby further accentuating the downturn.

At the initial phase of this adjustment process consumers do not overreact as their incomes continue to grow and therefore they can still service their debt. However, as interest rates continue to rise the economy decelerates, disposable income is reduced and consumers find it difficult to service their debt. The restructuring of the personal-sector balance sheet aims at rebuilding wealth by increasing saving and repaying debts. This retrenchment takes many years to unwind, and hence the ensued recovery is anaemic – less buoyant than usual. Indeed, in the USA, Japan and the UK, which all experienced a boom–bust cycle in asset prices with considerable variations in net wealth and increased indebtedness, the recovery was anaemic because of the retrenchment not only of the personal sector but also of the corporate and financial sectors.

In addition, as the recession deepens consumer confidence is eroded because of rising unemployment, declining wealth and falling income which reduces estimates of permanent income. Accordingly, precautionary saving increases. Moreover, more people find themselves liquidity-constrained as banks restrict credit (credit crunch), see Jappelli (1990), Wilcox (1989) and Zeldes (1989b). Thus, more people base their consumption expenditure on current rather than permanent income. This leads to a rise in the aggregate savings ratio. Hence, contrary to the common belief the wealth effect in consumption is very slow but very pronounced. This was, perhaps, best expressed in the aftermath of the October 1987 stockmarket crash according to which the belief of a sizeable wealth effect led forecasters to predict a dramatic slowdown in the economy and policy-makers to pump liquidity into the system and lower interest rates to avoid a 1930s-style recession. The subsequent meagre impact on consumption and the quick reversal of policies was interpreted as evidence that the wealth effect is negligible. However, this is not true! The wealth effect took years to unwind as consumers had to restructure their balance sheets in the face of falling asset prices and unsustainable levels of debt and debt-servicing because of lower incomes.

The wealth effect is therefore slow but very pronounced, and is triggered by changes in interest rates. Thus, contrary to the other common belief, interest rates have a significant effect on consumption, but it is unleashed gradually through the changes in wealth and the consequent restructuring of the personal-sector balance sheet.

Financial deregulation and liberalisation – UK and other countries

Other countries, in particular the USA, Japan, Canada, Australia and a number of Nordic countries experienced similar boom–bust cycles in asset prices and hence large swings in wealth and the savings ratio. The worst hit was Japan in which both land and stock prices rose at a frenetic rate in 1986–90, and then fell rapidly in the first half of the 1990s. However, it was not the personal sector which suffered most from these large fluctuations in asset prices but the corporate and financial sectors as these were the ones who invested heavily in these markets. Hence, the savings ratio of the personal sector did not fluctuate wildly in the 1980s – it moved in the range 15–18 per cent. The Nordic countries – Finland, Norway and Sweden – experienced the second largest fluctuation in asset prices with large swings in the savings ratio. The UK was somewhere in between with the USA affected even less.

In all these countries the fluctuations in the savings ratio reflected an adjustment to offset the variations in wealth relative to its target as a result of unexpected developments in asset prices, inflation, interest rates and incomes in the manner described above for the UK. However, the severity of this adjustment has varied among these countries. Apart from country-specific factors, two major forces have contributed to this variation – first, the stance of monetary policy; and, second, financial deregulation and liberalisation.

The stance of monetary policy determines the level of interest rates. If monetary policy is accommodative then interest rates are low and this encourages consumers and property developers to acquire credit and banks to provide it. Thus one reason why asset prices rose more in some countries than others is because interest rates were very low, for example in Japan and to a lesser extent in the UK.

Financial deregulation and liberalisation lifts hire-purchase controls and other credit restrictions, widens the range of activities permissible to banks and building societies, opens up money and capital markets to small savers and makes credit more easily and generally available, as mentioned above. In the UK, financial deregulation and liberalisation began in the early 1970s and has continued almost uninterruptedly until the early 1990s. Before deregulation monetary tightening affected the supply of credit to households and businesses through the banking system. Banks, in effect, rationed the quantity of credit as reserves were withdrawn from the system at the will of the central bank. Credit rationing after deregulation is less important because there are now many alternatives to bank lending. Hence, after deregulation credit markets are relying for clearing much more on the price-adjustment mechanism (mainly interest rates). This reasoning provides the answer to our second question, namely whether the large fluctuations in the savings ratio, observed in the 1980s, will become a permanent feature from now on. Deregulation has made consumers much more sensitive to changes in interest rates because of the high levels of debt. Hence, there will be large fluctuations in the savings ratio in response to changes in incomes, asset prices and indebtedness triggered by swings in interest rates, unless monetary policy is assigned to asset-price stability. In some countries, like Japan, asset-price stability has become one of the targets of monetary policy, following the boom–bust cycle of the last 10 years, and in many countries asset prices are used as indicators of the stance of monetary policy.

The effect of deregulation should be a once-and-for-all step-increase in the debt to income ratio and a corresponding permanent drop in the savings ratio as consumers are now able to meet their desired debt ratio which previously they could not because of credit rationing. In the UK, demand for credit surged after financial deregulation in the 1980s, and the indebtedness of the personal sector rose from 55 per cent of disposable income in 1975 to 120 per cent in 1990. However, not all of that surge in debt represented a permanent increase because of financial deregulation. Part of it was cyclical caused by the forces described above which led consumers to increase their debt and reduce their savings ratio as they felt wealthier. But there is no doubt that a significant proportion of the increase in debt and the resulting fall in the savings ratio from 13.5 per cent to 5.5 per cent between 1980 and 1988 can be accounted for by financial deregulation.

Although more empirical work is required if the importance of deregulation and the cycle is to be quantified, the experience of other countries can throw some light. In the USA where financial deregulation preceded that in the UK, the debt to income ratio has stabilised at around 100 per cent of disposable income. In the UK the debt to income ratio declined to 110 per cent by the end of 1995. Therefore, the UK may have reached a new steady state with the appetite for new credit having been saturated. Other countries, such as Japan and Canada, are also converging to the same debt ratio of 100–110 per cent. If the new steady state is somewhere in this range then most of the increase in debt and the drop in savings ratios in the UK in the 1980s can be accounted for by financial deregulation. Moreover, from now on as interest rates vary in the business cycle the debt-to-income and the savings ratios may fluctuate wildly around their new steady states.

The role of fiscal and monetary policy in personal-sector balance-sheet adjustment

The previous analysis suggests that deregulation has probably made the large fluctuations in the savings ratio observed in the 1980s a permanent feature in the Anglo-Saxon countries and one that will emerge in continental Europe and the rest of the world as deregulation spreads. Consumers are now much more sensitive to changes in interest rates because of the high levels of debt which are used as a leverage to boost asset prices. What is the role of fiscal and monetary policy in this new framework of deregulation and increased globalisation?

In the era of credit rationing and regulation, consumption used to have a stabilising influence on the business cycle through the concept of consumption-smoothing as suggested by the PIH/LCH. In the new era of deregulation, liberalisation and globalisation of financial services the personal sector is as destabilising as the corporate sector. Fiscal and monetary policy as the two most important instruments of demand management should be actively used to dampen the amplitude of the business cycles. Thus the private sector is the source of instability and the role of fiscal and monetary policy is to offset such instability. Globalisation means that shocks from the rest of the world will become more important than in the past. In this framework, although both fiscal and monetary policies can be equally successful in dampening business cycles, the latter is more focused on the roots of the problem. The large fluctuations in the savings ratio are caused by large swings in the stance of monetary policy. Low interest rates encourage a surge in credit which boosts asset prices and prompts the consumer into a spending spree thereby aggravating the upswing of the business cycle; high interest rates trigger a collapse in asset prices and create cash-flow problems for the personal, corporate and banking sectors. The retrenchment of the personal and corporate sectors accentuated through the credit crunch of the lending institutions makes the downswing of the business cycle deeper, longer and the recovery anaemic. Thus it is extremely important that large swings in the stance of monetary policy should be avoided. Fiscal policy should not be the cause of instability in the conduct of monetary policy. If fiscal policy is destabilising as it was in the aftermath of German reunification, then monetary policy would have to be tighter than otherwise to offset it, thereby inducing large fluctuations in the savings ratio. In this new era of deregulation there is more need for synchronisation and harmonisation of fiscal and monetary policy.

Although the target of monetary policy should continue to be price stability in goods and services, developments in asset prices should be of concern to central banks. Thus the best way forward is to include asset prices in the indicators of the stance of monetary policy. Japan in the 1980s provides a good lesson. CPI-inflation was extremely low, but asset inflation was extremely high. The Bank of Japan ignored developments in asset prices for a long time thereby fuelling the bubble. When it finally tightened monetary policy it triggered the burst of the bubble, but set in motion a spiralling retrenchment effect in the corporate and banking sectors which has crippled the economy until now.

Asset prices should be monitored but not targeted as this would interfere with the free functioning of market forces. Moreover, there is no obvious target rate of growth in asset prices especially in a period of rapid deregulation, liberalisation and globalisation in world financial markets. Restricting the rate of growth of asset prices would also interfere with the worldwide problem of the pensions of an ageing population. Thus market forces should be allowed to determine the optimal rate of growth of asset prices. Nonetheless, asset prices should be monitored by central banks for signs of excessive consumer spending. The comments made by Greenspan in 1996–8 relating to the 'irrational exuberance' of financial markets can be put in perspective only as a statement that the Fed is monitoring asset prices not *per se*, but in relation to their effect on consumption.

Conclusions

In this chapter we have shown how the counter-cyclical adjustment of the savings ratio can lead to a more stressful adjustment for the consumer when interest rates rise. We have also shown how more reliance on prices (interest rates) as the clearing market mechanism in financial markets may lead to a boom–bust cycle in asset prices. Such a pattern seems to have been prevalent in the Anglo-Saxon countries and in Japan in the 1990s. This adjustment explains the depth of the downturn in the early 1990s and why the recovery was anaemic. It also provides an explanation for the causes of the speculative bubble boosting in Japan. This type of adjustment did not occur on the Continent in the 1990s. Nonetheless, there may be a change in the trend there, too.

References

Ando, A. and Modigliani, F. (1963) 'The Life Cycle Hypothesis of Saving: Aggregate Implications and Tests', *American Economic Review*, vol. 53, pp. 55–84.

Flavin, M. A. (1981) 'The Adjustment of Consumption to Changing Expectations about Future Income', *Journal of Political Economy*, vol. 89, pp. 974–1009.

Flemming, J. S. (1992) 'Financial Innovation: A View from the Bank of England', in S. F. Frowen and D. Kath (eds), *Monetary Policy and Financial Innovations in Five Industrial Countries: The UK, the USA, West Germany, France and Japan* (London: Macmillan; New York: St Martin's Press), pp. 120–8.

Friedman, M. (1957) *A Theory of the Consumption Function* (Princeton, N.J.: Princeton University Press).

Frowen, S. F. (1995) 'The Functions of Money and Financial Credit: Their Objectives, Structure and Inbuilt Deficiencies', in S. F. Frowen and F. P. McHugh (eds), *Financial Decision-Making and Moral Responsibility* (London: Macmillan; New York: St Martin's Press), pp. 31–51.

Frowen, S. F. and Karakitsos, E. (1997) 'An Evaluation of Inflation Targeting in Germany and the UK', *Kredit und Kapital*, vol. 30, no. 4, pp. 501–32.

Hall, R. E. (1978) 'Stochastic Implications of the Life Cycle – Permanent Income Hypothesis: Theory and Evidence', *Journal of Political Economy*, vol. 86, pp. 971–87.

Jappelli, T. (1990) 'Who is Credit Constrained in the US Economy?', *Quarterly Journal of Economics*, pp. 219–34.

Wilcox, D. W. (1989) 'Social Security Benefits, Consumption Expenditure, and the Life Cycle Hypothesis', *Journal of Political Economy*, vol. 97, pp. 288–304.

Yaari, M. E. (1964) 'On the Consumer's Lifetime Allocation Process', *International Economic Review*, pp. 304–17.

Zeldes, S. P. (1989a) 'Optimal Consumption with Stochastic Income: Deviations from Certainty Equivalence', *Quarterly Journal of Economics*, pp. 275–98.

Zeldes, S. P. (1989b) 'Consumption and Liquidity Constraints: An Empirical Investigation', *Journal of Political Economy*, vol. 97, pp. 305–46.

10

The Conduct and Ethical Underpinnings of Monetary Policy in the United Kingdom and Germany

Eric Owen Smith

Introduction

This chapter originated as a few discussant remarks on the Frowen and Karakitsos contribution to this volume (Chapter 9) (hereinafter F&K1). I was subsequently invited by the editors to expand my remarks into a self-standing chapter. The working title of F&K1 was 'A Comparison of the Conduct and Ethical Underpinnings of Monetary Policy in the United Kingom and Germany'.

Given that the Bank of England was granted a degree of independence by the newly elected Labour Government in May 1997 to conduct monetary policy as required by EMU, I must confess that my first – and last – thoughts have concentrated on the phrase '*Conduct and Ethical Underpinnings of Monetary Policy*', which implies that we are concerned with our perceptions about what is right and wrong in terms of the moral obligations of monetary policy-makers to the community. It is little wonder that the dedication page of Paprotzki's thesis (1991) bears the following quotation from Friedman and Schwarz: 'money is a fascinating subject of study because it is so full of mystery and paradox'. Indeed, it is incumbent upon me to demonstrate that within the Friedman paradigm *neither* governments *nor* bankers are to be entrusted with controlling the supply of money. The policy and ethical implications of such a policy stance were obvious to Friedman and they too must be explored below. Keynesians, on the other hand, are far more relaxed about money. They do not accept the Classical dichotomy. The quantity of money, the rate of interest, saving, investment and, of course, income are all interactive. In this sense they determine one another. But the Friedmanite and Keynesian frameworks are not well brought out in F&K1. Whereas they imply that critical features of post-war central banking in Germany have been conveniently neglected by its proponents, they do not fully cover either its theory or its influence on the *conduct* of monetary policy, particularly in the EU. Yet its origins and effects are often obfuscated by exaggerated claims.

If, as seems to be the case, monetary policy now dominates fiscal and social policies in the EU, then its *ethical underpinnings* are of even greater relevance to the implications of macroeconomic policy-making. This by no means implies that I am in disagreement with what the authors say about:

- the counter-cylical nature of the savings ratio in the UK, and
- the effects of large variations in *short-term* interest rates on the housing market and other long-term rates in the UK, and on economic stability.

On the contrary: there are two valuable inferences which one can draw from these factors, both of which relate to the *conduct* and *ethical underpinnings* of monetary policy in the UK *and* Germany. First, the manipulation of short-term interest rates for electoral advantage in the UK was grist to the mill for the advocates of central-bank independence. It is nothing short of amazing that the two worst perpetrators – Barber and Lawson – were in effect rewarded by the financial markets with lucrative jobs in the City (see also F&K1, p. 147). A system which can justify such an ethical approach to policy-making is surely beyond contempt. Moreover, there was something contradictory in the UK's (post-Keynesian era) policy-goal of eliminating public-sector deficits but at the same time inducing large rises in private and foreign sector debt. Since the former is lucidly analysed in F&K1, and I wish to add the latter, I shall return to this policy contradiction. But note that the figures in their chapter are concerned only with the UK. I shall therefore want to add German data, mainly drawing on my 1994 book. It will also be necessary to add a Figure 10.1 (p. 186) to complement their Figure 9.1.

A further contradiction in terms of the ostensible policy stance in the UK was writing off the debt of some industries and/or increasing their prices prior to privatisation. I wish also to mention this in another context below. Secondly, the general effects on the real economy of monetary policy are dramatically demonstrated by the disaggregated example of the housing market. The UK's monetary policy reaction to the housing boom of the late 1980s, along with entering the ERM at an overvalued nominal exchange rate DM2.95 = £1, caused the second serious recession in the period 1979–97.

The arguments therefore proceed as follows. In the first section, the general interaction of central banking, economic policies and real economic performance is reviewed. This is followed by an overview of the economics of central banking. A concluding section then examines the behaviour of the savings ratio.

Central banking, economic policies and *real* economic performance

Indeed, the dramatic differences in the macroeconomic performance of the postwar British and German economies might, on a perfunctory analysis, be attributed to the presence – and ethical superiority – of an 'independently' conducted monetary policy endowing an unassailable comparative advantage to West Germany. In other words, democratically elected governments are not suited to the task of conducting monetary policy. If this argument is accepted, there is a critical policy inference: independent central banking – partially the product of some German governments historically creating enormous monetary overhangs through a subservient central bank – is ostensibly the alchemy of a successful economic policy. It is conveniently overlooked that:

- these overhangs were truly enormous;
- unconstrained government borrowing which began during the First World War, combined with the wholly unrealistic demands for reparation payments, culminated in the 1923 overhang and a completely unsustainable balance of payments crisis;
- the 1945 overhang created by the despotic Nazi regime necessitated the Allied draconian currency reform which was preceded by the creation of an independent central bank in March 1948 (Bank deutscher Länder – BdL); the establishment of the democratic Federal government followed eighteen months later.

If these historical phases are to be used for postulating an ethical framework, generations of ethicists have completely wasted their intellectual efforts.

A little detail on these differences in macroeconomic performance is therefore appropriate. I shall rely not only on my own past work in this field, but also on current research I am undertaking with a German colleague (Owen Smith, 1993, 1994, 1997, 1998a, 1998b, 1998c, 1999a and 1999b; and Owen Smith and Funk, 1998):

- The consumption function is lower in Germany than Britain, investment (in both physical and human capital) has therefore been higher. A higher R&D ratio in Germany added a valuable qualitative dimension to investment. Factors of production and products in the UK and Germany are certainly non-homogeneous! Both the neoclassical and the Keynesian models have serious shortcomings in this sense, and, in addition, given differing consumption functions, the implementation of the locomotive theory attempted at the Bonn and Louvre summits was misconceived Keynesianism.
- Economic growth has been export-led in Germany, thereby positively contributing, along with investment, to the determinants of GDP. In this sense, West German policy-makers created, for the most part unwittingly, a near perfect Keynesian model. Moreover, in spite of Professor Walter's aside, I still consider this export propensity to be an economic virtue. Naturally, a trade-deficit country such as the UK – with its 'flexible' labour and 'globalised' financial markets developed in the period 1979–97 – is required to fund this deficit, which since the mid-1980s has contained a significant net deficit item (manufactured goods), yet enjoyed a positive contribution from North Sea Oil. Given that we are concerned with a long-run period, this must surely be a critical acid test of the supply-side, or post-Keynesian era. In short, German exports are robust, bolstered by favourable price and income elasticities. Predictably, there was some inevitable but short-term trade diversion as a result of German monetary, economic and social union (GEMSU).
- The current account deficits in the first half of the 1990s were the products of the UK's trade deficit, but deficits on foreign travel (stimulated by a strong DM), net transfers to the EU and remittances by foreign workers in Germany. (See Hölscher *et al.* (2000) on how the German current account may be posting surpluses towards the end of the 1990s and note that the British deficits will increase. Notice also that the costs of GEMSU had relatively little direct impact in this context.)

It is particularly important to note that all these indicators – apart from the 'globalised' financial markets – pertain to the *real* economies. In other words, we are concerned with the creation of wealth and not its manipulation. Privatisation in the UK is a case of the latter *par excel-*

lence. Similarly, a policy scenario which induced house-owners to regard their property as a speculative asset rather than an investment – as in Britain in the 1980s – was a recipe for ultimate financial and economic instability. I return to this latter topic below.

There are, moreover, important differences in the conduct and ethical underpinnings of monetary policy in Germany and the UK. As is pointed out in F&K1 (p. 149), the 1948 currency reform in Germany eliminated the monetary overhang and cancelled the 'huge government debt' – a fact all too often overlooked by contemporary observers. I would like to add some implications. It is ironic in the extreme that the Deutsche Bundesbank (BBk) – an institution which owes its degree of independence to the 1948 reforms – should overlook this exercise in debt elimination and play a major role in endowing the post-Maastricht era of fiscal rectitude. The painstaking analysis of the post-GEMSU debt in East Germany was symptomatic of this approach, not to mention the ethics of the G8's conscious policy decision not to write off the sovereign debt of less-developed countries. Moreover, with virtually no government debt left as a result of the ethics of 1948 approach to monetary policy, there could be no open-market operations. There was no need for the equivalent of the Radcliffe Committee: the BBk developed policy virtues out of its enforced use of short-term interest rates and complex minimum reserve policies. The former instrument was ultimately used to target some (necessarily nebulous) proxy for the money supply, while the latter became insignificant in operational terms. Ostensibly, it seemed that the goal of price stability was being achieved by monetary policy, whereas in reality it was *productivity* gains (in the *real* economy, of course) which contained, indeed even over-compensated for, the inevitable rise in nominal wage costs. Real unit labour costs were therefore constrained, thus retaining a highly competitive real exchange rate – in spite of the effects of the (self-fulfilling?) expectation on the part of speculators that the nominal exchange rate would be revalued. This is all the more remarkable when one compares the (enforced) revaluation of the DM with the (enforced) devaluation of sterling. Yet there was virtually no difference in real unit labour costs in the two economies in 1997 (1991 = 100; EC, 1997, pp. 130–1).

It is equally apposite to note that wage inflation was more problematical in the UK. Nominal unit labour costs in Germany and the UK were identical in 1997, yet in national currency terms, again where 1991 = 100, the index number for Germany in 1960 was 30.8, but for the UK 8.8 (*ibid.*, 128–9). A reasonable policy inference is that Britain's productivity growth has therefore lagged spectacularly behind

Germany's. Speculation in Germany's case followed the clear undervaluation of the DM during the 1950s, a period during which West Germany significantly regained her export prowess. This was only one, albeit significant, feature of the happy constellation of events during the period 1948–60 which were a combination of good luck and macroeconomic management. The inevitable internationalisation of the DM obliged the BBk to ultimately create its own money-market paper in the 1970s. In the meantime, government debt was being funded by other parts of the financial system. Again, notice that the costs of GEMSU are not mentioned here – they were met, even in an era when fiscal policy is considered unorthodox, by fiscal transfers, the magnitude of which would have been unsustainable in Britain.

F&K1 similarly give (pp. 147–48) an accurate caricature of British monetary policy, or rather its absence, in 'the heydays of Keynesian demand management' in the 1950s and 1960s. But, again, an analysis of the policy implications of the exchange-rate regime is conspicuous by its absence. Even 'short-term Keynesian stabilisation policy' cannot be appraised without an appraisal of Bretton Woods and the unjustifiable opposition to the two enforced devaluations of 1949 and 1967. Nor is it necromancy to assert that Keynes himself would have taken a very dim view of policies which required the domestic economy to sustain an overvalued nominal but fixed (more accurately, *managed*) exchange rate, rather than adjusting the exchange rate to achieve the 'objectives of an ethically justifiable economic policy' (*sic*). Moreover, the domestic economic policy implications of attempting to retain the Sterling Area and international defence commitments were clearly regarded as acceptable. But Keynesian economic policies were not responsible for the growing underlying weakness of the British economy. Indeed, the general collapse of Bretton Woods was perfectly predictable within the Keynesian paradigm: the system permitted the French to convert their US$ reserves for (Fort Knox) gold, a facility which the BBk did not avail itself of – presumably in the interests of attempting to sustain the regime. In this sense the growth in world trade was limited by a crude latter day gold standard – and Keynes's views on such a regime are on record. So 'full employment was achieved, growth rates were high, but external disequilibrium often caused problems'. As I have now made clear, that disequilibrium was fuelled by both low productivity and an overvalued nominal exchange rate (cf. Hölscher et al. 2000).

The virtual monetary policy interregnum of the 1970s (in the sense that neither the exchange rate nor the money supply was targeted) saw

Britain outside of the Snake yet attempting to withstand the inflationary impact of both the Barber boom and, ironically in view of the subsequent policy attitude to the Snake, entry into the EEC. The very misnomer of Common Market went uncorrected, even after the Single European Act 1986 which was eventually introduced at the beginning of 1993 – twenty years after the British accession. In fact the inflationary impact of British entry was due to the fact that the EEC was a Customs Union with a scandalous protection of French and German agriculture, the costs of which for British consumers in welfare terms were enormous. It meant leaving the straightforward and uninflationary system of deficiency payments for what is now euphemistically known as the European Agricultural Guarantee and Guidance Fund. In such conditions, the Competition and Credit Control Measures (1971) were to prove as inadequate as the various attempts at enforcing real consumption wage cuts by, in particular, the £6 and 5 per cent nominal wage growth limits in the mid and late 1970s respectively. That said, the trade union response was to lend legitimacy to the (understandable) introduction in the first half of the 1980s of statutory limits on picketing and the closed shop, as well as pre-strike ballots. In Germany, the latter were voluntarily introduced by the trade unions themselves in the early 1950s. The less understandable infringes of civil/human rights which were also introduced in the UK (trade union derecognition, regulating internal union governance and the abolition of minimum pay legislation) masqueraded as trade union reform but were inconsistent with the EU's Social Charter, as it was then known. Such infringement would have been unconstitutional in Germany. Opposition to the Charter (and, even more so, the later otherwise legally binding Chapter) was in theory perfectly consistent with a supply-side policy stance. But in practice the Charter/Chapter were an antidote to the inevitable process of concentration in product markets which would inevitably follow the Single European Act. In other words, ignoring the growth in imperfect competition and information, always the butt of criticism of Keynesian economics, also played a contradictory role in the supply-side era.

The 1980s ushered in money-supply targets which were predictably subjected to continual redefinition and, in common with the BBk's experience, 'seldom achieved'. Howe's deflationary budgetary policy had more effect. His use of short-term interest rates was also deflationary demand management. In addition, North Sea oil came on-stream. In consequence, sterling's nominal exchange rate was driven upwards. (The Falklands' war paradoxically diverted electoral support to a government mismanaging the economy. For that matter, chauvinism was later to lead the German electorate to accept their government's undertaking that GEMSU would be a costless exercise). Record unemployment for the postwar period characterised the first half of the decade in the UK. It was reduced only by the Lawson boom, resuming 1979 levels by 1990. Inflation, which fell below the average for 1950–96 in 1983, exceeded that average again in 1989 and 1990. Although there had already been an implicit policy of shadowing the DM, this became the explicit monetary target when Britain entered the ERM (1990–92). The economy had already been moving into recession, yet high short-term interest rates were necessary to maintain the pegged exchange rate of DM2.95 = £1. Unemployment rose and inflation fell, the latter leading the prime minister to predict that the elusive goal of price stability had been achieved and that sterling would replace the post-GEMSU DM as the ERM's anchor. He was disabused of this unrealism by the fiasco now known as Black Wednesday. Free international capital movements, another product of the supply-side era, endowed foreign-exchange speculators with sizeable windfall gains. Of even greater significance here is the fact that leaving the ERM meant that sterling could float and the inflation rate could be then targeted. 'Float' is not to be taken literally, of course: since leaving the ERM sterling's exchange rate initially fell dramatically, only to peak at DM3 = £1 in early 1998.

The costs to the real economy of this exchange rate voyeurism in 1990–98 have been at least as serious as in the 1950s and 1960s, notwithstanding the fact that some observers believe that high nominal exchange rates induce productivity gains in manufacturing industry. Be that as it may, the Monetary Policy Committee (MPC) of the Bank of England currently has the policy remit to target an average annual underlying inflation rate of 2.5 per cent in an economy where the headline rate averaged 6.4 per cent annually in the period 1950–96. This compares to Germany's 2.8 per cent for the same period. Like all mean values, no account is taken of variations here (see my remarks about the 'patterns' of inflation and unemployment below). Equally, extrapolating trends to demonstrate that the UK has reached a permanently lower 'natural' rate of inflation hardly squares with the MPC's increases in short-term interest rates immediately on taking office. True, in the absence of crude oil and EEC-entry price shocks, the average inflation rate fell in the 1980s and again in the 1990s. On the other hand, the domestic consumer booms fuelled by housing (1980s) and demutualisation (1990s) inevitably produced short-term interest rate rises when fiscal factors (1980s) or responses (1990s) were respectively a major cause or unorthodox. Money clearly mattered: not as the sole determinant of the absolute price level, but rather within a system in which its quantity interacted with interest rates and the low levels of investment and savings.

The economics of independent central banking

This leads me to a point where I must draw on another work by Frowen and Karakitsos (1997 – F&K2). Using a quadratic objective function (*ibid.*, p. 21), they show that policy-makers can have different priorities on inflation ('hard-nosed') and unemployment ('wet'). There are several caveats that both these authors and/or I would want to enter. First, note that this phraseology is sufficiently rigorous to allow for the fact that neoclassical economists do not accept a straightforward trade off between these two variables. They ultimately rely on the assumption that real product and factor prices determine resource allocation. Expectations dominate the Phillips curve, which is vertical and coincides with the natural level of unemployment. It is consistent with zero inflation where their version of the trade-off cuts the horizontal axis. However, hysteresis makes this 'natural' level unstable: it depends on unemployment in the past; it may also be influenced by variables over which the wage bargainers have no influence. Fiscal policies and exchange rates are two probable examples. Meanwhile, the independence of an inflation-averse central banker or institution is seen as crucial for the credible implementation of monetary policy to achieve the bank's inflation targets (Hamburg, 1997, p. 7).

This all said, it is tempting to associate the BBk with a 'hard-nosed' policy stance and the UK authorities with a 'wet' approach. Yet there are two factors which make it difficult to prove that this is the case in practice (F&K2, p. 22). I would like to think that I have dealt with both factors. First, there is a built-in assumption that revealed preference shows optimal points in the function. But the constraints in the optimisation problem are different in Germany and the UK. Quite apart from the real economy differences referred to above, cyclical behaviour in the economies is neither synchronised nor even compatible in terms of the pattern of both unemployment and inflation (see the next paragraph). In the longer run, it would be far easier to compensate for the latter problems – synchronisation and pattern – in estimating the objective function. Second, the priorities of the policy-makers change through time. For example, there was an overt attempt at Keynesianism in Germany in the late 1960s and the early 1970s, whereas in the UK there was a putative supply-side revolution during the 1980s. Admittedly, it would be extremely easy to exaggerate the extent to which policy-makers and their advisers espoused either Keynesianism or the Friedmanite monetarist counter-revolution (Riemer, 1983, p. 80). The truth is that the West German brand of Keynesianism was not suddenly superseded by Friedmanism in the early 1970s, nor was there wholehearted support for the supply-side revolution in the 1980s. This lack of a clear-cut macroeconomic approach exacerbated the problems generated by unification (Owen Smith, 1994, p. 124).

There is a fundamental difference in the pattern of unemployment and inflation in the two economies. The rate of change in unemployment has displayed increasingly serious fluctuations ('stop–go' characteristics) in the UK. Admittedly, the peak in the early 1990s was not quite as high as in the mid-1980s (on Eurostat definitions, 10.4 per cent in 1993 compared to 11.5 per cent in 1985 and 1986 – EC 1997, p. 69). But from an ethical point of view both peaks must be of policy concern, especially given the costs of the social upheaval ushered in by 'flexible' labour markets, a central feature of the supply-side revolution. Germany's unemployment rate, on the other hand, was above but converging on the UK's during the catch-up period of the 1950s, briefly and marginally in 1975, again on the contemporaneous misleading British definition in the late 1980s and, of course, the average for *unified* Germany has been higher since 1990. On a Eurostat definition, West Germany's rate was on average below the UK's during the three decades 1961–1990. In both cases, however, this average rate grew in each decade: from 0.7 per cent (1961–70) to 6.0 per cent (1981–90) in Germany; from 1.7 to 9.8 per cent in the UK (EC, 1997, 68–9). But cyclical fluctuations in Germany are less of a policy problem than the ratchet effects observable following the rises in unemployment which were initiated by the first two crude oil price shocks and GEMSU (1973, 1980 and 1990). The third crude oil price shock significantly contributed to the disinflation which culminated in a fall in prices 1986 on 1985, whereas the first two shocks and, to a lesser extent, GEMSU had exacerbated inflationary pressure. Some caution is necessary here: inflation in Germany exceeded the UK average for 1950–96 only in 1952, 1973 and 1974.

In general, short-term interest rates have been correspondingly lower in Germany but have unambiguously risen steeply to combat inflationary pressure. Wage bargaining has been the focus of the BBk's attention in the domestic economy. In addition, the ratchets in unemployment growth may have been the result of capital substitution in manufacturing industry as the growth in real product wage rates changed relative factor prices (the neoclassical approach). As a result, business sector profitability (always above UK levels) recovered and rose (the Marxian approach). Keynesians would argue, however, that supply-side factors are not alone in affecting the level of unemployment; additionally and importantly there is the effect of *investment* on unemployment (Arestis and Biefang-Frisancho Marischal, 1997, p. 2). Along with other factors, a *capital shortage* in both the UK and Germany may have been responsible for the persistent level of unemployment (*ibid.*, p. 12). German real consumption wage rates, on the other hand, were squeezed by relative wage restraint at a time of rising prices, taxation and social insurance contributions. Moreover, the German economy, unlike the UK's more 'flexible' model, has not been able to create the widening of the real pay structure necessary to generate low-paid, service-sector jobs. From the ethical point of view, however, it is crucial to note that neither model has eradicated long-term unemployment.

But can an independent central bank alone influence the rate of inflation? Crude evidence which assumes that the inflation rate is functionally related to the degree of central bank independence generally indicates that this may be the case (*The Economist*, 2 February 1991, quoted by Pugh and Carr, 1993). In this scenario Italy, with one of the worst average inflation records (1973–86), had one of the least independent central banks, while Germany had the most independent central bank and, along with Switzerland, enjoyed the lowest inflation rate. Heylen and Van Poeck (1996: particularly p 55), on the other hand, estimate a more complex model for the period 1970–89. They show that the gains from a more independent central bank are not fixed. They are larger in countries with unstable governments, not committed to fixed (pegged?) exchange rates ('no commitment to shadow the DM'), and in countries where 'left-wing' parties had a strong position. The effect of increasing central bank independence is also shown to depend on the level of the natural unemployment rate and the slope of the short-term Phillips curve.

Above all, the number of right-hand-side variables should be noted. Empirical evidence refutes the *a priori* assertion that independent central banks automatically produce lower inflation rates. Posen, for example, treats such independence as an endogenous variable, in the sense that a high public aversion to inflation may produce an independent central-bank; similarly, Cukierman found that there may be a reverse impact of inflation on the degree of central bank autonomy

(Hamburg, 1997, p. 17; Heylen and Van Poeck, 1996, p. 45). The general evidence of the effect of independence on both inflation and economic growth seems to be mixed (Hamburg, 1997, tables 1 and 2). The choice of criteria, as well as their weighting, is subjective and the ranking of central banks could be changed by varying these factors; for example, Italy varies between rank 11 and 4 in work done prior to the statutory changes required by the ESCB (*ibid.*, 20 and table 6). Moreover, additional explanatory variables are included and dropped without explanation, while outlier countries are excluded (*ibid.*). If outlying values are subjected to 'smoothing' and more robust measures of inflation for the period 1871–1988 are adopted, they significantly demonstrate that Germany, ignoring the early 1920s, has similar inflation behaviour under both dependent and independent regimes (Wood, Mills and Capie, 1993, pp. 22, 24 and 28–30).

There are also important theoretical differences between a pure Friedmanite stance and the BBk's approach to monetary policy. I have chosen to cite the original version of Friedman's seminal 1960 essay which appeared in an edited volume by Yeager (1962), rather than the (1968) reprint of both this and some of his other essays. This is because the title of the 1962 volume demonstrates the problem addressed by its contributors. All the contributors shared a roughly similar conception of the 'good society' and regard the decentralised organisation of economic life by means of markets, money and prices as indispensable to human freedom (Yeager, 1962, p. 1). We are not told who enjoys this freedom and for what purpose. Will poverty decrease? Will monopoly power increase? That is probably why the following page warns about policy recommendations hinging on specific value judgements and not resting solely on positive analysis. Nonetheless, the volume indicates the extent to which the USA inspired the founding of the BdL, the British having just previously nationalised their central bank. In the view of some commentators this step undermined the independence of the Bank of England (Wood, Mills and Capie, 1993, p. 18).

Friedman is logically consistent and lucid on the issue of freedom. A rigorously defined independent central bank (see below) is *rejected* because it would not be tolerable in a democracy to have so much power concentrated in a body free from any kind of direct, effective political control (Friedman, 1962, p. 237). He goes on to pose the question of how else a monetary system can be established that is stable, free from irresponsible tinkering and incapable of being used as a source of power to threaten economic and political freedom (*ibid.*, p. 239). For Milton Friedman, the control of monetary policy is a potent tool for controlling and shaping the economy (*ibid.*, p. 219). Three solutions are considered. First, a commodity standard, notably the gold standard – which is somewhat disparagingly rejected. Next, an extension of the separation of powers so as to include an independent central bank is considered but rejected – rightly so because it would necessitate a highly controversial constitutional amendment. It could be added that where a senior part of the judiciary is charged with interpreting the constitution, it cannot be controlled by the executive or the legislature. In effect, the constitutional court would become arbiters of monetary policy! The European Central Bank (ECB) is thus the *only* constitutionally independent central bank, its having been established by EU Treaty (Hamburg, 1997, pp. 22–3). In any case, Friedman is rightly sceptical about those central bankers who have historically pursued an implicitly dictatorial and totalitarian doctrine (Friedman, 1992, pp. 228–9). Conversely, weak personalities in such posts can have an equally damaging effect. In addition, it would be necessary to concentrate all debt-management powers of the fiscal authorities in the hands of the independent monetary authority.

Finally, Friedman points out that such an independent institution would almost inevitably give undue emphasis to the point of view of bankers (*ibid.*, pp. 236–8). Money would be created as a result of the extension of credit, and monetary and credit policy would become confused. After all, Friedman had advocated the reduction of monetary-policy instruments to *quantity*-orientated open market operations and the introduction of *high* (even 100 per cent) minimum reserve requirements (Paprotzki, 1991, p. 56 – my emphasis). On the other hand, MRRs became increasingly identified as a major factor undermining the competitiveness of German banking (see the *Finanzplatz Deutschland* section of chapter 7 in Owen Smith, 1994). Another departure from the Friedmanite model was the absence of flexible DM exchange rates (Paprotzki, *ibid.*). As already seen, however, exchange-rate treaties made by politicians, especially the EMS, constrained the discretion of the Bundesbank's Council in this respect. The introduction of monetary targeting in 1974 should not therefore be confused with the received theory of monetary control at that time. The BBk acted on the *demand* for money, not its *supply*. Perhaps the most apt metaphor is that it was a case of Hamlet without the prince (Owen Smith, 1994, p. 165). In other words, Friedman had a deep distrust of the power enjoyed by the commercial banks when it came to the creation of money. Government debt should be sold to non-banks. Above all, the banks possess the initiative to re-discount in a re-discounting system; in such a system, it is *extremely difficult to predict* the effect a *change* in the discount rate, let alone its effect *on the stock of money* (Paprotzki, 1991, pp. 56–7, my emphases).

I would add that this lack of predictability in the use of short-term interest rates leads one to infer that such a policy tends to be *indiscriminate* in its effects on the capital markets, particularly in the UK as F&K1 so lucidly demonstrate. However, a basic issue is oversimplified by Friedman: defining the monetary aggregate to be targeted and then controlling its growth is not an easy task. Moreover, it has been shown that the pure Friedmanite model of controlling the money supply and introducing flexible exchange rates was eschewed by the BBk's policy-makers (Owen Smith, 1994, p. 147). True, Friedman favoured a monetary rule to constrain central bankers, but that monetary rule was *not* the achievement of a target rate of inflation. Rather, the central bank would be required to control the growth of the stock of money (Friedman, 1992, pp. 242–3). Either way, a credible monetary policy aiming at long-term price stability requires detailed and extensive expertise to define adequate measures and choose and apply appropriate policy instruments (Hamburg, 1997, p. 9). Long-run stable and low inflation rates are seen as critical in the context of reducing economic risk when planning investment and long-term wage contracts; lower risk premiums on long-term interest rates are then sought (*ibid.*, pp. 8–9). Keynes also emphasised the role of expectations on the propensity to invest.

There is already an emerging body of evidence which gives insights into the differences between the BBk and MPC models of independent central banking. The BBk Act (1957) confirmed the basic function of aiming to safeguard the currency independently of instructions from the Federal government. (Federal ministers may attend Council meetings as observers and the President of the BBk must be consulted by the government on important monetary policy matters.) The BdL endowed the BBk with complete autonomy in domestic monetary policy. The evolution of its instruments was summarised above and its sole goal has been price stability. The deliberations of its Council are confidential and its decisions were announced as if they enjoyed unanimous support, although a wide range of publications still provide detailed commentaries and background material on economic, fiscal and financial indicators. On the other hand, the British Treasury still sets the inflation target which is the ultimate policy goal. The MPC publishes the minutes of its deliberations and voting pattern following each meeting. Its members are appointed for only three years as opposed to eight years in the case of the BBk. Moreover, MPC members appear before

Parliamentary committees, notably the Treasury Select Committee – a system in principle similar to the practice in the United States. It is also intended that the Bank of England's *Annual Report* will be debated in Parliament. An *Inflation Report*, introduced when Britain left the ERM and began inflation targeting, is seen as a means of increasing openness and transparency in the conduct of monetary policy. (An important ethical problem was raised by the opposition in an issue of the latter Report to a minimum wage for adults because it *may* be inflationary; at least that is better than the afterglow of supply-side economics which asserts that it *will* be inflationary. Following the orthodox policy stance, controversial high earners – notably directors, including privatised and demutualised organisations – receive less attention.)

In both economies, then, short-term interest rates can, in 1998, be used for demand management to target the inflation rate, either *via* the intermediate target of the money supply (Germany) or directly (the UK). Exchange rate targeting is unnecessary: the DM is the anchor of the ERM and sterling is a floater. Before it is even launched, there are ominous rumblings to the effect that the euro must be a 'strong' currency. It remains to be seen whether in practice the ECB will target the euro's exchange rate with, say, the US$, or the (mean?) inflation rate in member countries. Either way, monetary policy will be too tight for some members and too loose for others. Even before the ECB's Council met, moreover, it was envisaged that its deliberations would be secret and its decisions would purport to be unanimous. Speculation will therefore be rife as to which ESCB members are supporting which view. The composition of the MPC, on the other hand, has been criticised on the grounds that its members are largely drawn from central bankers or academics. These critics advocate more representation from industry, although industry's role in the UK is viewed with contempt by an increasing number of commentators. Moreover, the ECB will have both an inflation and a monetary target. Its accountability and transparency will be opaque. Duisenberg is willing to appear before the (powerless) European Parliament, but not before the (still powerful) national parliaments (Wood, 2000). Records of its proceedings will be published only after 16 years have elapsed, and not even a general indication of voting (so many for, so many against) will be made available. Admittedly, a precise disclosure of voting patterns by members of the ECB's council would severely weaken its independence since politicians in a member state where unemployment is rising would expect the Council's member from their region not to support any proposed increase in interest rates. Yet the ECB has the power to counter both fiscal and social policies which remain the responsibility of the member states (Owen Smith, 1998a and 1998c). It will have exchange-rate competency not even enjoyed by the Bundesbank (Hamburg, 1997, p. 23). In short, it is the world's first constitutionally independent central bank, responsible to no democratically elected body and it has still to make its precise policies clear. Not even the advocates of central bank autonomy seem happy with this arrangement. But they have only themselves to blame: they have endowed this approach to monetary policy with a mystique, rather than a careful appraisal of the theoretical and empirical evidence.

The behaviour of the savings ratio

Short-term interest rates have not only been determined differently in Britain and Germany during most of the postwar period. The term structure has also behaved differently. It is also viewed quite differently from a policy standpoint. The determination of short-term interest rates in Britain has therefore 'become a vital variable because if it changes it affects directly (through valuation) or indirectly (through other macro-variables) all components of the personal sector's wealth' (F&K1, p. 149). Moreover (pp. 149 and 163):

> Thus in periods of high (short-term) interest rates the value of bonds falls, house prices and the value of shares decline, servicing debt increases or the value of debt increases through the restructuring of loans ... The wealth effect is slow but very pronounced, and is triggered by changes in [short-term] interest rates. Thus, contrary to the other common belief, interest rates have a significant effect on consumption, but it is unleashed gradually through the changes in wealth and the consequent restructuring of the personal-sector balance sheet.

There are three things missing: the speculation in commercial property by 'property developers' (yet see p. 164); the completely unpredictable (random?) effect of changes in short-term interest rates *at any point in time* on all the (long-term) assets mentioned; and the exchange-rate effects of movements in short-term interest rates, especially since exchange controls were abolished to facilitate what was termed 'free capital movements'. This is mainly the bitter harvest of regimes during the period 1979–97 which avowedly wanted 'free' market forces to operate but in effect gave speculators in the finance markets their heads. One aspect of globalisation is that these speculators are now beyond control, as many central bankers at least privately admit. It is rationalised by such phrases as 'not bucking the markets'. 'New Labour' has also embraced 'competitive' markets. But none of the theories outlined above would condone such limp mitigations of the problems created by a 'free' financial system. Without regulation, markets are inherently destructive.

Moreover, the savings ratio is (necessarily?) considered in nominal terms until the implied real effects in the passage quoted. Nonetheless, the useful detail on the composition of the personal sector balance sheet in Table 9.1, followed by its quantification for the UK in Table 9.2, leaves no doubt how the phenomenon of negative equity arose in the UK's housing sector. This is where, at times of high interest rates, the value of a house – proxied by its (falling) price – fell below the outstanding (and rising) mortgage debt. Two other factors exacerbated the situation on the demand side. First, financial liberalisation included the relaxation of controls on mortgage lending (see also F&K1, pp. 163–5). First-time house buyers could obtain average loans of 86 per cent of the purchase price by 1986, compared to 76 per cent in 1980 (Griffiths and Wall, 1997, p. 327). A 100 per cent advance even became more feasible. Secondly, in order to further increase owner occupation the government retained housing subsidies in the form of MIRAS. Continuous warnings were given about the inequity and inflationary nature of this subsidy. In its heyday interest relief was paid at the taxpayer's highest marginal rate and multiple claims per household were possible. This relief was gradually reduced to 10 per cent in the 1990s, and relief has been restricted to single claims per household throughout this period. Presumably for electoral reasons, however, notice was given when the latter provision was introduced, thereby inducing a period of high housing demand. In the net wealth context it is instructive to note that the rising value of property and higher incomes have outstripped the utility of the 10 per cent tax relief, not least because it is limited to the first £30,000 of a mortgage. But given the rise in owner occupation, oscillations in short-term interest rates will be rapidly reflected by changes in mortgage interest rates, especially given that the majority of the large building societies have converted to profit-orientated banks.

It is little wonder therefore that savings in the UK are countercylical – and are likely to remain so for the foreseeable future. Interestingly, Japan is the only industrialised country with a higher net equity in housing to GDP (*ibid.*, p. 305; see also F&K1, p. 163). Here, it seems,

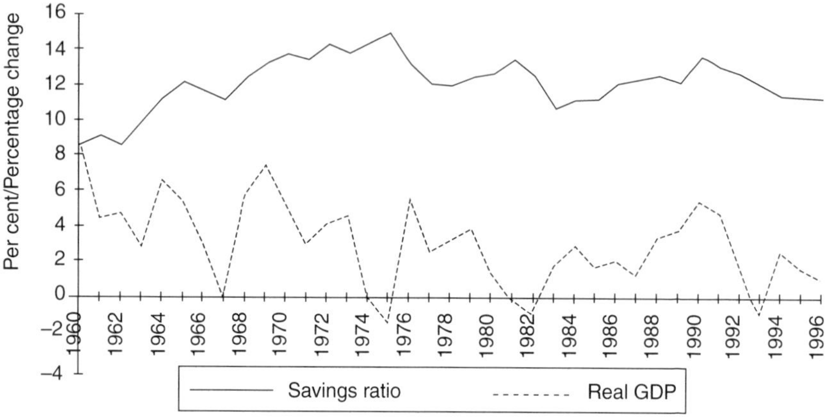

Figure 10.1 German cyclical behaviour patterns
1. 1960 plotted at origin in original
2. 1967 is –0.2 per cent (Real GDP)
3. 1975, 1982 & 1993 are –1.3, –1.1 and –1.2

savings have also started to increase during recessions, even when taxes are cut. Not surprisingly, the lucid explanation for the counter-cyclical behaviour of the savings ratio proffered by F&K1 probably also holds for Japan where financial instability is exacerbated by bad debt. In spite of the absence of radical financial deregulation in Germany, however, Figure 10.1 indicates that the first two crude oil price shocks caused the phenomenon of a counter-cylical savings propensity to emerge.

More precisely, real GDP fell on the previous year in 1975, 1982 and 1993. The first *negative* trough coincided precisely with a peak in the saving ratio, the ratio peaked one year prior to the second *negative* trough, whereas the 1990 peaks and 1993 troughs were pro-cyclical. Hence, before and after the first two crude oil price shocks the relationship was of a well-behaved pro-cyclical nature. One compelling explanation is probably that the sharp rise in short-term interest rates which accompanied the first two oil shocks in both the UK and Germany affected expectations in the manner intended by the policy-makers. The net wealth effect in the above quotation from F&K1 operated accordingly. But in the absence of radical deregulation, the pro-cyclical behaviour of the two variables in question returned in the later 1980s in Germany, whereas in the UK it became, if anything, more seriously counter-cyclical. In any case, house prices are relatively so high in

Germany that *two* different types of mortgages are required, one of which requires contracted savings for a number of years prior to purchase. Correspondingly large differences in the *institutional* framework constrain the scope for the type of competition between lenders in the UK which fuelled the housing boom in the 1980s. Moreover, the (large) German rented sector has also received generous government subsidies. Last, but no means least, the BBk has the explicit policy aim of reducing inflation to '... an acceptable level in order to avoid setbacks in the capital market ... [which] would hit borrowers harder than any easing short-term interest rates, for longer-term funds account for 83 per cent of all bank lending ...' (quoted by Owen Smith, 1994, p. 153).

References

Arestis, P. and Biefang-Frisancho Marischal, I. (1997) 'Wage Determination, Capital Shortage and Unemployment – A Comparison between Germany and the UK', *IGS Discussion Papers*, no. 97/3, Institute for German Studies, The University of Birmingham, UK.

EC European Commission (1997) *European Economy*, Directorate-General for Economic and Financial Affairs, EC.

Friedman, M. (1962) 'Should there be an Independent Monetary Authority?', in L. B. Yeager (ed) *op. cit.*, pp. 219–43, Republished in M. Friedman (1968) *Dollars and Deficits* (London/Englewood Cliffs, New Jersey: Prentice-Hall, pp. 173–94).

F&K2-Frowen, S. F. and Karakitsos, E. (1997) 'A Framework for the Comparison of Inflation Targeting in Germany and the UK', *IGS Discussion Papers*, no. 97/19, Institute for German Studies, The University of Birmingham, UK. Subsequently published under the title 'An Evaluation of Inflation Targeting in Germany and the UK', *Kredit und Kapital*, vol. 30, no. 4, 1997, pp. 501–32.

Griffiths, A. and Wall, S. (eds) (1997) *Applied Economics*, 7th edn (London: Longman).

Hamburg, B. (1997) 'Central Bank Independence and the European Monetary Union', *IGS Discussion Papers*, no. 97/15, Institute for German Studies, The University of Birmingham, UK.

Heylen, F. and Van Poeck, A. (1996) 'Central Bank Independence: Only Part of the Story', *The Economist*, 144(1), pp. 45–61.

Hölscher, J., Owen Smith, E. and Pugh, G. (2001) 'The DM's Undervaluation and West Germany's Economic Performance', in J. Hölscher (ed.) *Fifty Years of the German Mark. Essays in Honour of Stephen Frowen* (London and New York: Palgrave).

Owen Smith, E. (1993) 'The German Economy', in *Western Europe*, 2nd edn (London: Europa Publications).

—— (1994) *The German Economy* (London: Routledge).

—— (1997) 'Incentives for Growth and Development', in S. F. Frowen and J. Hölscher (eds), *The German Currency Union of 1990: A Critical Assessment* (London: Macmillan; New York: St Martin's Press.).

—— (1998a) 'The German Model and European Integration', in K. Larres (ed.), *Germany since Unification: The Domestic and External Consequences* (London: Macmillan; New York: St Martin's Press).

—— (1998b) 'The Determinants of German Socioeconomic Policies', in T. Lange and J. R. Shakleton (eds) *The Political Economy of German Unification* (Providence and Oxford: Berghahn Books).

—— (1998c) 'Economic Aspects of German Unification: Lessons for European Integration', in J. Hölscher and A. Hochberg (eds) *East Germany's Economic Development: Domestic and Global Aspects* (London: Macmillan; New York: St Martin's Press), pp. 166–84.

—— (1999a) 'The German Economy: sectors, prospects and problems', in *Western Europe 2000* (London: Europa Publications).

—— (1999b) 'The British Third Way: some macro and microeconomic aspects', in Lothar Funk (ed.), *The Economic and Politics of the Third Way: Essays in Honour of Eric Owen Smith.* VWL Schriftenreihe, vol. 30 (Hamburg: Lit Verlag).

Owen Smith, E. and Funk, L. (1998) 'A Comparison of German and British Macroeconomic Performance', *IGS Discussion Papers*, No. 98/20, Institute for German Studies, The University of Birmingham, UK (reprinted with minor amendments in 1999, also published (same year) as SAM- *Diskussionsbeitrag*, No. 70, University of Trier, FBIV, April): page references in this chapter are to the reprinted version.

Paprotzki, M. (1991) *Die geldpolitischen Konzeptionen der Bank von England und der Deutschen Bundesbank* (Frankfurt Main: Peter Lang).

Pugh, G. and Carr, D. (1993) 'The Monetary Consequences of German Reunification', *Economics and Business Education*, 1(3), pp. 116–23.

Lange, T. and Pugh, G. (1998) *The Economics of German Unification: An Introduction* (Cheltenham: Edward Elgar).

Riemer, J. M. (1983) *Crisis and Intervention in the West German Economy: A Political Analysis of Changes in the Policy Machinery During the 1960s and 1970s*, PhD thesis, Cornell University Microfilms International, Ann Arbor, Michigan.

Wood, G. E., Mills, T. C. and Capie, F. H. (1993) *Central Bank Independence: What Is It and What Will It Do For Us* (London: Institute of Economic Affairs).

Wood, G. E. (2001) 'Is the European Central Bank Too Independent?, in J. Hölscher (ed.), *Fifty Years of the Deutsche Mark. Essays in Honour of Stephen Frowen* (London and New York: Palgrave).

Yeager, L. B. (ed.) (1962) *In Search of a Monetary Constitution* (Cambridge, Mass.: Harvard University Press).

11
The Role of Central Banks in a Global Competition Environment

Norbert Kloten

Introductory remarks

The topic of this chapter is of immediate interest. The recent crisis of financial markets in Southeast and East Asia and the spectacular devaluations of currencies involved once again raises the question of the role of the leading central banks in today's world.[1] Of course, the US$ and the euro are not challenged immediately. The third major currency, the yen, is weakened by domestic factors. The world financial centres are touched but not destabilised. Waves of financial transactions signal irritation and anxiety, but have left no deep distrust in the international financial system. At stake are the financial markets of the industrialised countries, the relationship between their international credits and debits, the efficacy of their monetary policies and the reputation of their governments. The crisis has exposed the vulnerability of emerging financial markets, the carelessness of borrowing and lending, and the propelling force of financial flows in creating speculative bubbles and exacerbating the crisis. The interrelations between waves of capital movements and structural distortions in the real economy have become obvious.

Even central banks took part in the game. I remember – some time ago – a meeting with the governor of a Southeast Asian central bank. He was proud of billions of US$ he had turned to profit by interventions in foreign exchange markets, making use of information obtained from other central banks about intended operations. Not long afterwards unexpected moves by big central banks caused him to realise huge losses. He had to resign. The crisis we are now observing reflects political failures as well as inherent instabilities, and a lack of national capacity to handle downward trends. The financial turmoils together with the impact of the failure of Russia and other East European countries to progress properly on the road to transition fuels worldwide apprehensions about what might come next.

But before I deal with the crisis and its implications I have to clarify some more general effects of financial globalisation on central banks, and the role of central banks nationally and internationally. The answers have to bear in mind:

- the nature of structural changes observed;
- the impact of financial flows on exchange rates and real transactions;
- the relations and connections between central banks and international monetary institutions, above all the International Monetary Fund (IMF); and
- the split of opinions among academics and in political and financial circles.

Definition of globalisation

Globalisation is a trend phenomenon stimulated by liberalised capital and money markets, by a modern communication network, by innovative market products and by rapidly growing volumes of disposable financial assets. The integration of financial markets around the globe intensifies from year to year as well as competitiveness, while sensibility to market signals increases. All this is well-known and often discussed. Less clearly stated are the interrelations between the new formations in the worldwide scale of financial transactions and the real economic world. The following statements are beyond question:

1. Today´s national economies are more and more influenced by international market processes, and national economic circumstances are becoming increasingly part of international economic realities. The impact of world markets limits the scope for any counter-directed shaping of national economic states of affairs by national political authorities.
2. The accelerating growth of disposable means searching for profitable investments in bonds, shares and funds as well as new market techniques and innovative sets of futures forces the volumes of financial transactions to explode. They grew by about 20 to 30 per cent annually. Financial transactions compose about 95 per cent of all transactions in foreign exchange.

3. Exchange rates in our modern world are widely determined by financial transactions instead of being bound to real transactions in the form of exports and imports of goods and services as in the past.

Erich E. Streissler, a well-known Austrian economist, reported at a meeting of the Committee of Monetary Theory and Policy of the Verein für Socialpolitik in the Spring 1997 on the determinants of exchange-rate levels. He compared competitive theoretical approaches, and his findings supported the view that financial transactions can generate sizeable and long-lasting deviations of nominal exchange rates from relevant purchasing power parities. Adjustment processes can continue for quite some time – up to a decade or more – and they may coincide with new speculative waves, often leading to overshooting in the opposite direction. Central banks may feel obliged to stabilise markets by interventions, but they never know for certain whether what they are defending is a manifestation of market equilibrium or not. And by means of official statements or by selling and buying operations central banks may give speculative transactions an unwanted lead. Should they intervene? How? On their own or jointly with other central banks? What in any case are the implications for monetary policy?

The role of central banking

I shall concentrate on the past policies and operations of the Deutsche Bundesbank. I shall then proceed to outline what Europe and the world might justifiably expect from the European System of Central Banks (ESCB), and we will ask whether the Federal Reserve's Policy has been influenced by the new global environment. I will conclude with some remarks regarding the international monetary system and the implications of the financial crisis in Asia.

The traditional role of central banking, expressed plainly, is to provide the country concerned with central-bank money and to safeguard the purchasing power of the domestic currency. If we accept this, a central bank has a foremost inward-looking responsibility, supplemented by reasonably outward-looking responsibilities. Implications of this state of affairs on the exchange markets have to be born in mind as well as the spreading of financial tremors.

Until the final breakdown of the Bretton Woods system in early Spring 1973, German monetary policy was repeatedly undermined by an unwanted influx of foreign currency, specifically of US$. On the one hand, the undervaluation of the deutsche mark by the official US$ parity stimulated the export drive and the propensity to invest, but on the other hand was a source of overheating, overemployment and price rises difficult to control effectively by demand management. The commercial banks could not be guided properly by the traditional policy approach of the German central bank, which for a time had been focused on so-called 'free liquidity reserves'.

The failure of the famous 'Law on Stability and Growth' of 1967 (Kloten, 1989) gave rise to arguments in favour of a new concept of stabilisation policy. The basic idea of the 'New Assignment' – labelled as such by the Council of Economic Experts – was to return to monetary policy its leading role in the efforts to stabilise domestic economic growth, employment and international trade, leaving fiscal policy to fulfil its traditional role of providing the economy with public goods, thus withdrawing from an anticyclical fiscal policy as the hard core of the above-mentioned law. The Council – of which at that time I was still a member – advocated in 1974 a money supply-side concept (Geldangebotspolitik). The Central Bank Council of the Deutsche Bundesbank finally decided to apply its own version of a new type of monetary policy (von Hagen, 1998). In December 1974 the Bundesbank set its first annual money-supply target, in this case for 1975, in terms of the so-called central-bank money stock (that is, M1, comprising coins, bank notes and commercial banks' deposits with the Bundesbank, especially those arising from minimum reserve requirements). The calculated growth rate of this key currency item (interim target of economic policy as well as central monetary indicator) referred (1) to the forecasted growth rate of the overall production potential, (2) the expected change of money velocity and (3) a component, which could be considered as an 'unavoidable' – later named 'normal' – inflation rate. Additional monetary indicators were taken into account. The conceptual key element of monetary targeting, the expected growth rate of the production potential, introduced a trend element into the determination of monetary policy (Kloten, 1992).

Generally speaking, German monetary policy proved to be succesful despite half of the published money supply targets not being realised. The definition of the targets (annual rate versus current rate; targets with and without a band; wide band or small margin; 'unavoidable' or 'normal' inflation rate) changed; in 1988 the money stock M3 (currency plus sight deposits, short-term time deposits and savings deposits at three months´ notice) became the accepted monetary target

(Schmid, 1998, pp. 36–40). The realised rates of inflation varied more than was compatible with the stable money criterion. Sometimes German monetary policy was regarded as expansive, sometimes as contractive. Critics at home and abroad never ceased to put the blame on the Bundesbank. But what counts most in the context of this chapter is the consistency of German monetary policy in general, its trustworthiness, and the fact that it primarily focused on national data. German money-supply targeting found general acceptance, and quite a few countries began setting money-supply targets, usually calculated to satisfy their own requirements. But already in the 1970s and even more so in the 1980s some central banks began abandoning money-supply targeting, either finding it difficult to realize the targets set, or being subjected to external shocks. This then led to a search for alternative targets such as in the UK (see Frowen and Karakitsos, 1997b). The discussion of the pros and cons of alternative indicators of monetary policy became intense. Among the proposals were a medium-term target instead of an annual one. The German model was also challenged by proposals to focus monetary policy on a targeted growth rate of gross national product, or a targeted inflation rate, or a special mix of monetary indicators and feedbacks.

The Bundesbank reconsidered its policy stand as well as alternative approaches, but it went on to adhere to the conceptual key elements of its policy. The German Central Bank Council accepted neither an international exchange rate agreement nor any binding of its monetary policy decisions by political authorities. As a member of the German Central Bank Council myself at the time, I vividly remember how decisively initial attempts by representatives of the German government of exerting political pressure on the Bundesbank were rejected. The Council regarded even tentative first steps towards a systemic targeting of exchange markets as not compatible with its own preference for money-supply control. Most Council members did not believe in the virtues of defined 'target zones' for exchange rates, not to speak of the thus generated interventions in foreign exchange markets. The Bundesbank was not prepared to go further than to regard trends on the foreign exchange markets as monetary indicators. Extreme volatility of foreign exchange rates were identified as a clear overshooting and served as an argument in favour of common interventions by selling or buying foreign currencies, particulary if there were convincing signs of already staggering markets.

In the 1980s and even more in the 1990s, it became obvious that German monetary policy did not match the deliberations and suggestions of other members of the European Monetary System (EMS). After German unification they complained rightly that the high interest rate policy of the Bundesbank exerted an unsuitable pressure on their economies (see Frowen and Hölscher, 1997). That was regretted by German authorities, but nevertheless German monetary policy did not deviate from its track. The crises of the European Exchange Rate Mechanism (ERM) in 1992 and 1993, respectively, were regarded as unavoidable adjustments to real economic fundamentals[2]. Already in 1989 on the occasion of my von Thünen lecture at the Verein für Socialpolitik in Berlin, I raised the question whether the time has come for a change in the paradigm of German monetary policy (Kloten, 1988a, p. 165). I examined the pros and cons on that occasion and also in a later paper (Kloten, 1988b) and argued that the time for such a change was not yet ripe. Today it is widely acknowledged, especially in Europe, that the Bundesbank, thanks to its stubbornness (Kloten, 1995 and 1998), paved the way towards the now existing European Monetary Union (EMU) in which the German central bank as well as the central banks of all other participating countries have been downgraded to merely executive entities, with the exception of the 11 central-bank presidents forming a powerful group in the policy-making European Central Bank Council.

What do we have to expect from the ESCB? Will it be prepared to respond more to the changing global environment than the Bundesbank? The statute of the ESCB as well as all its decisions since its first meeting in June 1998 indicate that the ESCB will not do so – at least not for the time being.

The conduct of European monetary policy to be executed by the European Central Bank (ECB) and the national central banks taking part in EMU, had already been structured by the European Monetary Institute (EMI) in its publication entitled *Uniform Monetary Policy in Stage 3 of European Monetary Union* (January 1997). The EMI evaluated alternative monetary strategies and rejected the monetary targeting of foreign exchange rates (pp. 8–11). Negatively assessed, too, were a targeting of interest rates as well as a targeting of nominal national product. Regarded as reasonable was the targeting of the money stock and the direct focusing on inflation targets. The EMI had already agreed on the following key elements of future European economic policy:

- A quantitative definition of the final target of price stability;
- Additional intermediary targets to evaluate the performance of monetary policy;

- The publishing of the leading elements of applied policy;
- Detailed information about monetary aggregates; and
- The application of an appropriate method of forecasting.

In September 1998, the ECB published the final commitments of ESCB´s Central Bank Council, entitled *The Single Monetary Policy in Stage 3. General Regulations about the Monetary Policy Instruments and Procedures of ESCB*. And at its meeting on 13 October the ESCB pinpointed the major elements of the European monetary policy strategy to ensure the realisation of the monetary stability of the euro. The Council's decision came out in favour of a money-stock approach as the primary intermediate target with an inflation target as a subsidiary item; both will be supplemented by a set of relevant indicators. The money-stock target (for the time being called 'reference rate') will be published as a growth rate of an 'extended M3' within a band, hence as a target zone. The inflation target is regarded as a forecasted but unpublished inflation rate used only for internal opinion-forming. Price stability is assumed to be realised if the harmonised index of consumer prices within the currency area of the euro increases by less than 2 per cent per annum during a medium-term period.

With these provisions the ESCB acccepted widely conceptual elements of the proven German monetary strategy. No doubt, the monetary policy of the ESCB will be first of all of an inward-looking type. It will serve primarily European needs. Efficiency of monetary policy is regarded as a prerequisite of gaining international credibility of the euro as a requirement for a smooth transition from Deutsche Mark and other eurozone national currencies to the euro on international markets. External and not least global aspects will be born in mind but not at the expense of the defined European objectives of domestic monetary stability. This expectation is backed by the outspoken refusal (for example, by Will Duisenberg and Hans Tietmeyer) of exchange rate agreements to establish target zones, not to speak of a systemic approach towards a new global system of fixed exchange rates. Such a basic position does not contradict the willingness to respond properly to worldwide financial challenges and to participate in safeguarding the operations of the IMF and the World Bank.

A unique role on the global scene has always been and will continue to be played by the US Federal Reserve. Even after the breakdown of the Bretton Woods System in the early 1970s the Fed remained the most influential central bank around the globe. In collaboration with the US Treasury it was a driving force behind any major international operation or even its initiator. I refer to the Plaza Agreement (1985) and the Louvre Agreement (1988) and to the enduring pressure on Japan and Germany to cooperate with the United States trilaterally. The rescue operations in the crisis of the Mexican peso or the relief operations of the IMF in the Asian financial crisis are all marked by US points of view. On paper it is always up to the IMF (quite often supported by the World Bank) to negotiate and to define impending operations or to impose programmes such as for tight money, stabilising efforts of fiscal policy, debt management and so on. But whatever will be put forward by the IMF has to be in line with the interests of the United States by the USA keeping rigid financial reigns on both the IMF and the World Bank. Notwithstanding discernible splits of opinion between the US Treasury and the Fed in the course of decision-making processes, the Fed's activities will ultimately always be focused on what serves the USA and the US$ best. The IMF quite often drew attention to the limits of its financial means, and sometimes it even exposed itself to moral hazard. Of course, the IMF refuses to be regarded as the sole lender of last resort, urging in case of need the big central banks, especially in the past the German Bundesbank, to contribute adequately.

I say this with an appreciative undertone. The United States are politically as well as economically the hegemonial power on a world-wide scale. They have to take the lead and they have to handle international affairs in a way which coincides with national concerns. What bothers many, though only occasionally, are their rough manners on the one hand, and an obvious priority of pragmatic, even opportunistic solutions on the other. Political procedures on a global level support the Fed in its endeavour to act as an autonomous decision-making central bank, concentrating on home affairs. It is difficult to detect any distinct lasting influence of financial globalisation on the Fed´s monetary policy. In other words, the mixture of today´s monetary policy operations and of US activities in shaping the international financial scene confirms impressively the maxim: the United States and the rest of the world.

The main message of my deliberations might be surprising to many: both leading central banks, the Fed as well as the Bundesbank, acted in my view more or less continously as autonomous national institutions, foremost trying to realise their specific monetary policy concept. The Bank of Japan operated more in the background of international monetary affairs, showing solidarity with initiatives of both the IMF and the Fed, without of course, neglecting to serve Japan's national needs.

Central banks as well as the IMF were aware of the obvious changes in flows and applied adequate techniques on international financial markets. These were regarded primarily as an endogenous fallout of globalisation, finally to be welcomed as propelling forces behind intensifying market dynamics. In this case, it is first and foremost up to market participants, to commercial banks and to investment houses, to match the new challenges by adequate business operations as well as by strategic concepts and appropriate tactics leading to higher market shares. Neither the IMF nor central banks recommended restrictive capital flow controls. They stressed almost anonymously the bright prospects of globalised markets. Of course, the monetary authorities did not fail to detect political implications, as globalisation requires new schemes of worldwide cooperation, especially in banking supervision. This point and the desperate need for a decision-making supranational supervisory authority was stressed by Stephen Frowen as early as 1992 at a Von Hügel Institute Cambridge Conference (Frowen, 1995, p. 44).

The scene mutated with the financial crisis in Southeast and East Asia. The question was raised whether the impact of the globalisation of financial markets and intensified competition on them were underrated, and whether the IMF reacted adequately. What is really at stake is the complexity of the modern financial world and the adequacy of global monetary order as well as the proper relationship between private commercial operations and surveillance by national and international authorities. Competitiveness is one element of a complex entity. Thus it is not sufficient to focus on it without taking into account some essential issues of a wider spectrum.

How should we respond to financial challenges in a globalised world?

The political implications of the swift evolution of international financial markets will be discussed for years. Countries, especially major ones, are increasingly affected by each other's economic affairs:

> Domestic financial and monetary developments have an immediate impact on other nations. Financial markets' volume and volatility have increased. Exchange rates have become sensitive and their movements are sometimes extreme, as market attitudes, perceptions and expectations change. There have been prolonged periods of

> misalignment along the major currencies. (Bretton Woods Commission, 1994, p. A-4)

Exchange rate misalignments have created uncertainty and added to protectionist pressures from vulnerable industries. Fixed exchange rate regimes temporarily practised by unilateral decisions of governments and central banks or institutionalised via currency board arrangements are exposed to speculative capital movements. They are further threatened by deviations between nominal rates and real economic data, by arbitrary political decisions as well as by the spillover of financial and political crises at home or abroad.

These facts led to the establishment of the Bretton Woods Commission in 1992, set up on the initiative of the Bretton Woods Committee, New York (Kloten, 1996). In 1994 on the occasion of the 50th anniversary of the Bretton Woods Conference it published a Report entitled *Bretton Woods: Looking to the Future*. The report was supplemented by a Staff Review and Background Papers, submitted by experts to the Commission.

The Commission focused its deliberations on identified problems of the international monetary system, recommending (besides achieving a more efficient macroeconomic policy at home) 'arrangements for global economic cooperation' between the major industrial countries and the designing of an 'improved international monetary system' (p. A-5). It was proposed to establish 'a more formal system of coordination, involving firm and credible commitments', to support 'greater overall macroeconomic convergence' and to avoid 'excessive rate misalignments and volatility' (p. A-4). 'The IMF should be given a central role in coordinating macroeconomic policies and in developing and implementing monetary reforms' (p. A-5). The *Staff Review* made evident that most members of the Commission were prepared to follow – at least in principle – the Williamson–Bergsten (1994) approach, but the Commission as a whole refrained from any open commitment to this model.

In particular, the German members of the Commission – including myself – had argued that the time had not yet come for a Bretton Woods II, and that especially the major countries were not prepared to accept any binding scheme limiting the scope for operations under their own responsibility and putting them formally under the governance of the IMF.

In his Foreword to the Proceedings of the Bretton Woods Conference, 21/22 July 1994 in Washington, Paul Volcker, the

Chairman of the Bretton Woods Commission, underlined the existing split of opinions (p. 2):

> A number of participants endorsed the Commission's recommendation to move toward a more formal system of exchange rate coordination over time, and to give the IMF a central role in that process. Some would have moved faster. Others were quite sceptical. Interestingly, officials from Germany, Japan and the United States were clearly not prepared to support the idea, nor did they seem eager to undertake reform of the monetary system in other respects.

The resistance of central bankers and government representatives to a worldwide initiative to set up a new international monetary order also became evident at the IMF/World Bank Conference 'Fifty Years after Bretton Woods. The Future of the IMF and the World Bank', held in Madrid, 29–30 September 1994.

With the refusal of generating a new global monetary system, the wide range of unresolved problems of the present 'non-system' has to be further handled by loose *ad hoc* operations of leading central banks, by G 7 provisions, and by specific IMF and World Bank programmes.

The Asian crisis (Hesse and Auria, 1998; Frowen and Karakitsos, 1997a) had not been foreseen. Even in its Annual Report for the year ended April 1997, the IMF was unaware of the huge potential for discrepancies in financial markets and in the interaction of real economies, of mismanagement of governments and central banks. According to the Executive Board of the Fund the 'conditions remained favourable for the continued satisfactory expansion of world output and trade' (p. 21). The board anticipated for Asia 'that the pace of expansion would slow to a more sustainable, though still robust, rate following a tightening of policies in several countries' (p. 23). For Japan, the board expected 'a phase of recovery' (p. 46). Hong Kong was viewed as having 'a strong protection for further high growth over the medium term' (p. 57). Thailand was praised for her 'remarkable economic performance and the authorities' consistent record of sound macroeconomic policies'. Critical remarks concerned the current account deficit and the level of short-term capital inflows regarded as a source of 'Thailand's vulnerability for economic shocks' (p. 91). Welcomed in the report is Korea's 'continued impressive macroeconomic performance' (p. 59). The Report stressed Indonesia´s 'impressive record of economic development' and recommended 'further substantial reforms' and appropriate measures 'to resolve the problems of insolvent banks', 'to reduce the vulnerability of the economy to shocks' and to provide more 'transparency in policy implementation' (pp. 80–1).

The directors of the Executive Board agreed that 'globalisation had contributed enormously to global prosperity' (p. 24), and that it limits 'the scope for countries to pursue politics incompatible with medium-term financial stability' (p. 25). The constraints imposed by globalisation are, according to the board, best dealt with 'not by imposing restrictions' but 'by adopting sound, transparent, and sustainable macroeconomic policies' (p. 25).

Today, much of all this is seen in a different light (Cieleback, 1998). For example, the Bank for International Settlements (BIS) maintains in its 68th *Annual Report* (1998, p. 13) that the turbelances and the looming crises were indicated by a lot of alarming signs, notably capital movements and fading solvency of commercial banks. Traditional evaluation prevented a sober in-depth analysis of the total complex network of economic relations in Asia, of the central role of Japan´s failure to solve its structural problems, of propelling engagements, economic and financial defects in Southeast Asian countries, of their institutional weaknesses, of the ambiguity of fixed exchange-rate arrangements in cases of crisis, of the likely virulence of contagious effects produced by intensifying turbulences, of the impact of switching capital flows within the business and financial sector, and so on (OECD, 1998, pp. 9–21). What happened is well-known. The IMF (Fischer, 1998, and IMF staff members, 1998) reacted by demanding a mixture of macroeconomic tightening, financial restructuring and structural reforms. The recipe included the closure of insolvent banks and re-capitalisation of surviving ones, the tightening of fiscal policy aiming at budget surpluses, rebuilding foreign exchange reserves, imposing restrictive monetary reigns, credit ceilings and high real interest rates. The demands of the IMF 'amount to a transformation of the economic system in a decidedly Anglo-Saxon direction' (M. Feldstein, quoted by Wolf, 1998, p. 8). The markets reacted with panic. Previously high net private inflows in the case of countries most damaged by the crisis turned within one year into huge outflows. The combined current accounts of Indonesia, Malaysia, South Korea, Thailand and the Philippines shifted from a deficit of $55 billion in 1996 to a surplus in 1997:

> *The real villains are the commercial banks, whose net lending jumped from $24 billion in 1994 to $56 billion in 1996 before turning into net repayment of $21 billion last year.* (Wolf, p. 2)

> *The exchange rate adjustment [after the breakdown of fixed exchange rate arrangements] exceeded any reasonable estimate of what might have been required to correct the initial overvaluation of the affected currencies.* (S. Fischer, 1998, p. 4)

The rating agencies put fuel in the fire by pre-cyclical evaluations. Not only were the financial markets severely damaged, but also the real economies. Recovery is expected but will still take some time to materialise.

I cannot dwell on details, but must limit myself to some salient facts:

- The IMF and to a lesser extend the World Bank operate with financial programmes based on their disposable means. Hans Tietmeyer, the President of the Deutsche Bundesbank at that time, as well as others, reproached the IMF for having spent too much money too quickly to the benefit of the commercial creditor institutions involved.
- The IMF acted in concordance with the US Treasury 'which appeared to be the Fund´s absolute master' (Wolf, 1998, p. 6). At stake was the role of the US$ which was to be protected against financial turmoils.
- By and large, the Asian crisis affected some of the South American countries and depressed the mood on international financial markets, but did not severely touch the United States' economy and the economic situation in Europe, which at the time was still setting up the European Monetary Union (EMU), a task now accomplished.

Meanwhile, worldwide discussions and negotiations at different levels finally led to the Declaration of the G 7 Ministers of Finance and Central Bank Governors of 30 October 1998. Accordingly, the IMF gets additional means (US$90 billion); also agreed is an increased transparency (of global financial transactions) based on new statistical data. Further points cover an effective governance by the IMF, an intensified supervision of commercial financial institutions, an institutionalised cooperation between the different supervisory authorities, better risk management of commercial banks, an effective set of sanctions in case regulations are disregarded by commercial banks and investment houses, and so forth. It is intended to make appropriate responses to the given challenges, to avoid future crises, to consolide reforms of the global financial system and to add additional competences for the IMF. The agenda of what is at stake is impressive, but anxiety as well as cautious suspicion still dominate the scene.

Concluding remarks

Globalisation will continue to progress, nor can it be stopped. The same is true of the competitive environment of monetary policy. The world will integrate further economically and, with ups and downs, political integration will not be far behind (Ramphal, 1998).

The Asian crisis has proved that even efficient financial markets are not balanced, they tend to overshoot and to overreact to external shocks. The measures agreed upon are remarkable and justify steps towards a better performance of financial markets and of the national and international institutions involved. Yet, as things stand and regarding the complexity of the economic and political network, the supremacy of national competences and the limits of sanctions imposed in case of misguided actions or simple political impotence, the situation in total remains labile.

The best warranty against defective market performance is stability in the domestic economic and political situations, specifically in major industrialised countries. This is especially true of the United States. During the Asian crisis, the US$ remained strong but vulnerable. With the merger of the deutsche mark in the euro and the yen´s loss of credibility as an international reserve and transaction currency, the US$ has to bear a burden which must be a source of concern. The paramount position and responsibility of the US$ justify the obvious claim of US authorities to play a dominant role in all international efforts, in order to cope properly with any economic and monetary problems. But the world has a right to expect that solutions proposed and carried out by the US Treasury and the IMF are not only shaped according to US models and yardsticks; what is decided upon should also be appropriate to the needs of emerging market economies in Asia, Latin America or Africa. The detail has to serve the whole.

It is to be hoped that the euro will quickly take the place previously occupied by the deutsche mark on the international financial scene. A strengthening of the euro supported by an increasing credibility may lead to a new triangular set-up together with the US$ and a yen again reflecting a balanced Japanese economy. A strong euro would give the US$ a chance of burden-sharing; although the US$ and the euro are bound to be competitors as well as partners (see Frowen and Karakitsos, 1998). Sterling will probably fade out, as rather volatile exchange rates may speed up Britain's entry into EMU.

Due to the crisis, the increasing weight of Third World countries and the still noteworthy impact of former centrally-planned economies has become obvious. The crisis in many Asian countries endangered the world´s financial system and provoked global actions; and bankrupt Russia now overshadows the mood worldwide, especially in Europe. The economic world is more than a trilateral affair. Reforms of all kind, not least in the field of institutional restructuring to achieve international standards, are to be pushed forward. National consolidation and international participation should, first and foremost, be the fruits of countries' own efforts and not of impositions from outside.

The time is not yet ripe to effect a new fixed exchange rate system, a kind of Bretton Woods II. A policy of reregulation of financial markets, widely but vaguely recommended at present, has little chance of being implemented. Representatives of the Fed as well as of the ECB have strongly rejected German and French ideas of target zones for exchange rate management as counterproductive, although the idea is still being pushed by both countries at G7 meetings and elsewhere. It will, anyhow, take time to establish the big bundle of precautions contained in the manifesto of the G7. For the time being, energies should be concentrated on this common concern. Adequate institutional and/or functional regulations as well as signs of solidarity in political behaviour can be regarded as steps paving the way to a new international financial and monetary order. Contemplation of alternatives or phases for realising such a complex approach is welcomed. Much has already been considered in the past; what in the future will adequately ensure a stable international montary system we may still have to discover.

Notes

1. For an account of the causes of the Asian crisis and for a model of currency risk that accounts for the volatility of capital flows, see Frowen and Karakitsos (1997a).
2. For a defense of the German position during the ERM crisis of 1992, see Frowen (2000).

References

Bank for International Settlements (1997) *67th Annual Report* (1 April 1996–31 March 1997) (Basle: BIS), pp. 1–220.

Bergsten, F. and Williamson, I. (1994) 'Is the Time Ripe for Target Zones or the Blueprint?', in Bretton Woods Commission: *Bretton Woods: Looking to the Future* (Washington D.C.).

Boughton, I. M. and Lateef, K. S. (eds) (1995) *Fifty Years after Bretton Woods: The Future of the IMF and the World Bank,* Proceedings of a Conference held in Madrid, Spain, 29–30 September 1994 (Washington D.C.: International Monetary Fund World Bank Group), pp. i-vii and pp. 1–280.

Bretton Woods Commission (1994) *Bretton Woods: Looking to the Future: Commission Report* (pp. A1–10), *IMF Staff Review* (p. B1–36), Background Papers (pp. C1–322), (Washington D.C.)

Bretton Woods Commission (1994) *Bretton Woods: Looking to the Future. Conference Proceedings* Washington D.C., 20–22 July 1944, pp. 1–89.

Cieleback, M. (1998) 'The Asian Crisis – Was it Really so Unexpected?', *Intereconomics*, vol. 33, no. 5, pp. 223–9.

European Monetary Institute (1997) 'Die einheitliche Geldpolitik in Stufe 3. Festlegung eines Handlungsrahmens' (Frankfurt Main: EMI), pp. 1–110.

European Monetary Institute (1998) 'Die einheitliche Geldpolitik in Stufe 3. Allgemeine Regelungen für die geldpolitischen Instrumente und Verfahren des ESZB' (Frankfurt Main: EMI), pp. 1–125.

Fischer, S. (1998) 'The Asian Crisis and the Changing Role of the IMF', *Finance and Development*, vol. 35, no. 2, pp. 2–5.

Frowen, S. F. (1995) 'The Functions of Money and Financial Credit: Their Objectives, Structure and Inbuilt Deficiencies', in S. F. Frowen and F. P. McHugh (eds) *Financial Decision-Making and Moral Responsibility* (London: Macmillan; New York: St Martin's Press).

Frowen, S. F. (2000) 'Unjustified British Critique of the Bundesbank', *Central Banking*, vol. x, no. 3, 1999–2000, pp. 40–45 (reprinted in Deutsche Bundesbank, *Auszüge aus Presseartikeln*, no. 12, 8 March 2000, pp. 15–17.

Frowen, S. F. and Hölscher, J. (eds) (1997) *The German Currency Union of 1990: A Critical Assessment* (London: Macmillan; New York: St Martin's Press).

Frowen, S. F. and Karakitsos, E. (1997a) 'The Capital-Flows Theory of Financial Crises', *Public Finance*, no. 1, pp. 64–88.

Frowen, S. F. and Karakitsos, E. (1997b) 'An Evaluation of Inflation Targeting in Germany and the UK', *Kredit und Kapital*, vol. 30, no. 4, pp. 501–32.

Frowen, S. F. and Karakitsos, E. (1998) 'A Strategic Approach to the Euro Prospects', *Public Finance*, vol. 53, no. 1. also published as *IGS Discussion Paper*, no. IGS2000/8, by the Institute for German Studies, University of Birmingham.

G 7 (1998) 'Leader´s Statement on the World Economy', 30 October, in Deutsche Bundesbank, *Auszüge aus Presseartikeln*, no. 65, 2 November 1998, pp. 4–5.

G 7 (1998) 'Erklärung der G 7 Finanzminister und Notenbankgouverneure' of 30 October 1998, in Deutsche Bundesbank, *Auszüge aus Presseartikeln*, no. 65, 2 November 1998, pp. 1–4.

Hagen, J. von (1998) 'A New Approach to Monetary Policy (1971–8)', in Deutsche Bundesbank (ed.), *Fifty Years of the Deutsche Mark: Central Bank and the Currency in Germany since 1948* (Oxford: Oxford University Press), pp. 403–38.

Hesse, H. and Auria, L. (1998) 'The Financial Crisis in Southeast Asia: Causes and Effects on the Global Economy', *Economics*, vol. 57, pp. 45–70.

International Monetary Fund (1997) *Annual Report* (1 May 1996–30 April 1997) (Washington, D.C.: IMF), pp. 1–284.

IMF Staff (1998) 'The Asian Crisis: Causes and Cures', *Finance and Development*, vol. 35, no. 2, pp. 18–21.

Kloten, N. (1988a) 'Paradigmawechsel in der Geldpolitik', *Zeitschrift für Wirtschafts- und Sozialwissenschaften*, vol. 108, pp. 1–24.

Kloten, N. (1988b) 'The Impact of Innovations and Globalisation of Financial Markets on Monetary Policy: The German Case', in P. Arestis (ed.),

Contemporary Issues in Money and Banking. Essays in Honour of Stephen Frowen (London: Macmillan), pp. 69–84.

Kloten, N. (1989) 'Das Stabilisierungsproblem: Konzeption und wirtschaftspolitische Praxis', in *Währungsreform und Soziale Marktwirtschaft,* Schriften des Vereins für Socialpolitik, N.S., vol. 190 (Berlin: Duncker & Humblot), pp. 79–112.

Kloten, N. (1992) 'The Control of Monetary Aggregrates in the Federal Republic of Germany under Changing Conditions', in S. F Frowen and D. Kath (eds) *Monetary Policy and Financial Innovations in Five Industrial Countries: The UK, the USA, West Germany, France and Japan* (London: Macmillan; New York: St Martin Press), pp. 32–58.

Kloten, N. (1993) 'Tracks towards a Common Monetary Policy in Europe', in S. F. Frowen (ed.), *Monetary Theory and Monetary Policy: New Tracks for the 1990s* (London: Macmillan; New York: St Martin's Press), pp. 1–17.

Kloten, N. (1995) 'European Monetary Union: Sovereignty and Hegemony', in S. F. Frowen and F. P. McHugh (eds), *Financial Decision–Making and Moral Responsibility* (London: Macmillan; New York: St Martin's Press), pp. 197–206.

Kloten, N. (1996) 'Die Bretton Woods Commission: Zur Zukunft der Internationalen Währungsordnung', in Zohlnhöfer (ed.), *Zukunftsprobleme der Weltwirtschaftsordnung* (Berlin: Duncker & Humblot), pp. 133–170.

Kloten, N. (1998) 'German Unification: A Personal View', in S. F. Frowen and R. Pringle (eds), *Inside the Bundesbank* (London: Macmillan; New York: St Martin's Press), pp. 110–119).

OECD (1998) *Economic Outlook*, no. 63, June (Paris), pp. 1–288.

Ramphal, S. (1998) 'Global Governance. Die Notwendigkeit einer Weltordnungspolitik', *Internationale Politik*, vol. 53., no. 11, pp. 3–9.

Schmid, P. (1998) 'Monetary Policy: Targets and Instruments', in S. F. Frowen and R. Pringle (eds) *Inside the Bundesbank* (London: Macmillan; New York: St Martin's Press), pp. 32–44.

Wolf, M. (1998) 'Global Capital Flows and Emerging Economies: Lessons of the Asian Crisis', *Address to the Trilateral Commission 1998 Annual Meeting in Berlin,* 21–23 March 1998, pp. 1–12.

12
Bank Supervision in the Context of Global Competition

John G. Ellis

My role in the Bank of England currently has three dimensions. First, I am a supervisor of banks. Secondly, I am heavily involved in the design of the new single financial services supervisory agency, which the government announced in May 1997 it wished to create. This will be known as the Financial Services Authority (FSA). (At the time of the Conference, the agency was known by its provisional title of NewRO.) It will encompass the banking supervision currently done at the Bank of England, the work of the City regulators set up under the Financial Services Act, the supervision of Building Societies and Friendly Societies and the regulation of the Insurance industry. Thirdly, I am the Bank's Business Ethics Adviser. I therefore propose to focus my remarks on issues that both affect the FSA and have an ethical dimension. However, all these views presented are my personal ones and should in no sense be taken as an official statement either by the Bank of England or by the future management of the FSA.

So why did the British government feel it necessary to reform banking supervision in the UK? One significant trend is the way that financial institutions are spreading their activities beyond their traditional boundaries. Commercial banking, investment banking and insurance activities are not necessarily now carried out by separate institutions. There is therefore some obvious appeal in bringing the supervision of all these activities into one organisation. This is perhaps the main reason offered to the public for the creation of the FSA.

An equally prominent argument within the supervised community is the burden from the increase in the total regulation they have experienced and a desire to reduce costs and duplication. I believe we have to be careful with the argument on costs. Sometimes, when a bank comes to me to propose moving into a new business line, I respond that they seem to have appropriate management expertise and controls, but warn them to factor into their cost–benefit analysis the increased supervisory costs. I may well require extra information which may cost them time and money to produce. I cannot fulfil my responsibilities as a supervisor for a bank in sophisticated derivatives markets using the same information as would be adequate if they were merely extending overdrafts to corner shops. In other words, the costs of supervision should be proportionate to the risks in the enterprise being supervised, and increased costs where an institution moves into more complex business are not necessarily a sign of inefficiency on the part of the supervisory regime.

Nonetheless, duplication of supervision is an inefficiency. It is quite possible at present for banks in the UK to find an area of their business supervised by one part of the Bank of England under the Banking Act, by a different part of the Bank of England under the Financial Services Act, and also by the Securities and Futures Authority under a different part of the Financial Services Act. The FSA is intended to simplify this structure.

The key elements that the FSA intends to offer the supervised institutions include the following. First it will provide a 'Lead Supervisor', who will provide a single point of contact in the FSA for all the activities of a given financial group in the UK. Within the FSA, the lead supervisor will have a role in ensuring much closer coordination of all the elements of supervision relevant to the group. Secondly, the FSA offers clearer accountability. All UK supervision will be under one management and subject to one Act of Parliament. Thirdly, the FSA hopes to deliver some economies of scale. Present budget forecasts suggest it will have 2000 staff, and to make an organisation of that size run efficiently is not a trivial task. Nonetheless, the FSA has set itself the challenge of identifying savings relative to the existing structures.

I would now like to turn to some of the issues about the FSA which are still subject to lively debate. These are part of the British response to the evolving global banking industry. My first question is 'Whom should the FSA be protecting?'

At the time the Banking Act 1987 was drafted, the specific task given to UK banking supervisors was to protect depositors. The ethical basis for that is that the innocent should be protected from loss: members of the public cannot expect to have the information to assess complex financial institutions and supervision can provide them with some reassurance. At least since the Industrial Revolution, the Church has encouraged thrift as a virtue, and to protect people's savings is in line with that tradition. An older strand in Judaeo-Christian ethics, however, is found in the Old Testament emphasis on the need to protect borrowers. The ethical argument is that those who borrow were usually in desperate circumstances and the imbalance of power left them subject to exploitation. Therefore the state had to provide protection.

In the FSA, the first high-level aim is to protect consumers of financial services. If applied directly to banking supervision this appears to extend the brief beyond just depositors. It is possible that the FSA could have a responsibility to those who have borrowed £200 from Barclays just as much as to those who have deposited £200 there. The breadth of the aim also raises questions about whether all consumers should be treated the same. If global financial players are arranging bilateral deals between themselves, what is the ethical justification for a regulator interfering in the terms that they choose? Cannot sophisticated players look after themselves? This is generating a lively debate about how far wholesale and retail business can be defined as distinct categories and how far the supervision should then differentiate between them.

However, long before there was any Banking Act establishing a statutory framework for British banking supervision (the 1987 Banking Act replaced the 1979 Banking Act, which first gave a statutory basis for UK banking supervision), the Bank of England watched the activities of the London banks. This was because of the systemic implications of bank problems. Some would argue this is the most fundamental task of banking supervision. Now that all the statutory supervisors are being plucked out of their existing organisations and put in one coherent new one, we create the novel problem of lender-of-last-resort facilities and the traditional functions of the central bank being in a separate organisation, and under a separate management, from the supervision of individual institutions. The FSA has to work on how to avoid this separation making swift action in a crisis more difficult.

The second cluster of practical questions for the FSA revolves around the issue of identifying who holds responsibility in the banks. The ethical maxim is that power should not be exercised without responsibility. By extension, in a powerful organisation there should be individuals who are accountable for the firm's actions and accept that responsibility. The existing Banking Act worked well for a small British bank with a chairman and board of directors all based in London, and clear lines of responsibility to separate divisions of the bank.

Supervisors vet and approve the directors and senior management and everyone accepts that they are then responsible for the teams who work to them.

With the globalisation of banking, this simple model does not reflect reality for a growing number of the supervised banks. Foreign exchange business in an international bank, for example, may have no home base but operate 24 hours a day moving around the globe from Tokyo to London to New York and back to Tokyo in each daily cycle. It then becomes more difficult for the supervisor in any specific location to identify who is responsible for that activity. Similarly, I have UK-incorporated banks who have American parents who wish to appoint as chairman of the UK bank someone resident in the US. Should I be persuaded that someone who is not in London can be sufficiently aware of the nuances of day-to-day life in his London operation to be effectively in control and to spot issues before they become problems?

One solution proposed in the face of such complications is to follow the course of the non-banking supervisors in London and register individuals down through all levels of a bank's organisation. It is argued that the supervisor can then more easily hold particular individuals responsible however complex the management structure above them. This approach is not entirely straightforward either. For a start it hugely increases the number of individuals the banking supervisors have to track, and there are doubts about whether this is the best use of supervisory resources. In addition, the globalisation of bankers' careers mean that many people taking up positions in London may have no track record in the domestic marketplace. Any information on career histories outside the UK is often harder or impossible to assess objectively and so the decision to approve more junior staff can be subject to greater error. This is just one small illustration of the general problem that supervision remains organised nationally while the banking industry is organised internationally.

More fundamentally, however, there is an ethical question about whether registering individuals at every level in a structure and bringing any sanctions against them personally does not implicitly reduce the responsibility that properly belongs to senior management.

A third FSA topic area with an ethical dimension is that of punishment. Often the pattern of supervision exercised by the City regulators operating under the Financial Services Act is to set out clear rules and if firms or individuals breach them, then to levy fines; to impose reputational damage by publicising the fines; and in some cases also to prohibit individuals from the industry or parts of it. The Bank of England's approach to banking supervision is to issue policy notices which in many respects give more generic and informal guidelines. Discussions with those who stray beyond acceptable limits will take place behind closed doors with no publicity of the discussion or the agreed actions. The supervisors have some ways of imposing additional costs on errant banks but these remain confidential. There are certainly no automatic intermediate penalties for minor offences below the nuclear options of restricting or closing a business, or finding individuals not fit and proper to continue in their jobs.

Now it is often argued that transparency is one of the characteristics of ethical behaviour. In the present context it has certainly been argued that it would be unrealistic, given the philosophical underpinning of the introduction of the FSA, to expect Parliament to give the Authority a mandate to operate the very confidential style of supervision that the Bank evolved in a previous generation. To address the ethical question, however, we need to ask why this confidentiality occurs.

One reason is doubtless the British obsession with secrecy, especially in the public sector, but that is not the whole story. It is important to note the objective of banking supervision. Almost without exception when discussions take place about problems in a bank, the objective is to reform the institution so that it becomes a healthier part of the financial community. Regulators of other constituencies may adopt a different set of priorities. Very often for the other City regulators, the client is a small firm whose success or failure has no noticeable impact on the financial system or interest to the national media. There may be no third parties financially at risk. In some cases, the regulator may have such occasional contact with the institution that the regulator will have difficulty checking on whether the institution followed an agreed action plan even if one were established. Very often, therefore, the approach of these regulators is principally to punish without undue qualms about the consequences.

Typically for banking supervisors, the institution being dealt with is larger and there will be depositors at risk. Action may be sought by supervisors to head off possible threats to depositors which would escalate rapidly if rumours of concern began to circulate. In some cases there could be systemic implications of actions taken or reputations tarnished. There will always be very frequent contact between the supervisor and the institution. In these circumstances the approach is likely to be to persuade the institution to acknowledge its problems and then to facilitate its own identification of how to reform itself. The glare of publicity may make reform much more difficult to achieve rather than assist it.

The objective of reform can certainly find support in ethics. In Christian doctrine, the best route for a sinner is to repent and then be helped to lead a new life. Why should this not be a legitimate ethic for the financial sector? Is transparency in all discussions such a superior ethical goal that it should override maximising the possibility of reforming the institution?

As well as an ethical argument, there may be good economic reasons for supporting confidentiality in some circumstances. We are reminded of the long-term stability of the British banking system and its remarkable ability to avoid crises. Part of the reason for this may be that the crises were simply hidden from view; or, more precisely, the potential crises were dealt with out of sight and never became full-blown financial crises. On a number of occasions over the time period discussed in this volume there may have been quite frenetic activity inside the windowless walls of the Bank of England with the objective of securing the future of particular banks. The lack of transparency at those critical moments may have proved greatly to the benefit of the financial system in the longer term.

I hope I have given some tasters of the current British response to the challenge of bank supervision in the context of globalisation of the banking industry. I entirely endorse the thesis that the markets evolve rapidly and banking supervisors must make strenuous efforts to evolve at least as fast in their techniques and organisational structures. I hope I have also demonstrated that, as we rush to maintain supervisory credibility, what at first sight may look like the desirable ethical solution can be misleading. On further reflection it may not seem the best route to the fundamental objectives.

13

Economic and Monetary Union: An Ethical Issue?

*Martin Donnelly**

In 1848, John Stuart Mill deplored 'the barbarism of most civilised nations' who 'assert their nationality by having, to their own inconvenience and that of their neighbours, a peculiar currency of their own'. One hundred and fifty years later the arrival of Economic and Monetary Union in Europe generates great passion among supporters and opponents. What is it about EMU which makes it of more than technical importance? What is the ethical dimension to decisions on EMU – indeed is there one at all? This chapter seeks to approach the key issues raised by EMU and their wider implications for the group of European countries embarking on a new form of economic relation between sovereign states.

First of all we need to consider what ethics means in the context of a choice of monetary systems. I put the question to a non-European economist who paused, frowned, and then said 'ethics is about who wins and who loses'. So it may be useful to begin by looking at the arguments for and against economic and monetary union from the perspective of potential winners and losers. But before doing so we need to recall what EMU involves. Former European Commission President Jacques Delors recently stated that 'EMU is not an end in itself', and we cannot separate discussion of EMU from wider political choices about the type of European cooperation being sought. We can, however, define a *monetary* union along the accepted lines: it involves a single monetary policy under one monetary authority, a single short-term interest rate, a single exchange rate and, certainly over time, at least some currency notes accepted throughout the monetary area at par value.

* Views expressed in this paper are those of the author only.

The definition of *economic* union is more difficult. The Treaty of Rome talks in terms of freedoms: freedom of capital, freedom of labour, freedom of goods, freedom of services within a single economic area. The European Union has largely though not entirely achieved this, most notably through the efforts to complete the single market following agreement on the Single European Act of 1986. The United States of America has also largely but not entirely achieved it. It is, for example, significantly easier to provide banking services between countries of the European Union than between states of the USA. But we would generally describe the USA as an economic union, not least because of a certain centralisation of the main levers of economic power, a centralisation which exists to a much lesser extent in Europe.

So the 'E' of EMU is a potentially more slippery concept (see p. 194). But it is important not to redefine EMU as simply a single currency. It is not, and never has been. In all probability a single currency without a wider economic structure to complement it would not be politically achievable in Europe, for reasons which are based in the history and objectives of the European integration process over the last half century, and indeed in the culture of European nations themselves.

The arguments for EMU

EMU removes an element of uncertainty and cost in transactions between areas which previously used different currencies and therefore makes markets work better. Prices become more transparent. Businesses can sell across frontiers more efficiently, without exchange-rate risk or extra bank charges. Customers are offered a wider choice, and investors can compare business opportunities more easily. EMU extends and consolidates the single market within Europe.

Who gains from this? Consumers, and the most efficient businesses. Those firms which are already efficient can increase further sales, profits, production and investment. And inevitably their less-efficient competitors must lose – profits, employment, perhaps their very existence. The economic adjustment process already at work within Europe is speeded up. The last local currency barriers to the continuing process of economic globalisation within Europe are removed.

Economic theory tells us reasonably confidently that the winners will generate more overall welfare. But economic theory is much less forthcoming in explaining how best to redistribute these net welfare gains to compensate the losers. So those who are already doing well should do better under EMU. Those having problems are likely to find those problems worsened unless they can take action more rapidly than hitherto. While there is a potential for public authorities to compensate the losers from the additional wealth created, recent social experience in most European countries suggests that increased output is also accompanied by higher levels of inequality, at least in terms of initial income distribution.

Such inequality may not necessarily be unethical, or it may be defended as an unavoidable element in a wider system of greater prosperity. It is in any case arguable that it is the forces of economic globalisation, rather than currency structures, which exert pressure towards inequality of incomes, and over time of wealth.

The individual as consumer should benefit from the EMU process , and will certainly do so initially. How far the customer continues to benefit will depend on how rigorously *competition rules* are enforced. A successful company naturally looks to consolidate its position through a quiet life. And within this newly transparent internal market complemented by a single currency, maintaining a vigorous competitive environment is inevitably a European rather than a national responsibility.

The original 1957 Treaty of Rome provides power in Article 85 to control a broad range of price-fixing, market-sharing or other anti-competitive agreements. Article 86 prohibits abuse of a dominant market position; and Article 90 more controversially includes public sector enterprises within these rules. The effective implementation of these treaty powers has taken a generation since the European Commission first received the power to carry out 'all necessary investigations' in 1962, and to enforce fines of up to 10 per cent of annual turnover. EMU makes the effective implementation of this policy even more necessary. Indeed the role of national competition authorities is likely to become increasingly focused on local competition issues which do not justify central intervention. In general, regions within a monetary union, even important ones such as Bavaria or Scotland, do not have their own competition authorities. It is likely that, post-EMU, the majority of those involved in competition and market regulation will be working in a more fully-integrated European structure of competition law enforcement.

On this basis, European firms should become relatively more competitive globally than without EMU. They should therefore generate more business and more jobs – though how many is difficult to predict – than would otherwise have been the case. European companies may simply lose less jobs to competitors in third countries than hitherto; but in both cases the outcome should be better than it would otherwise have been.

So we have efficient firms and customers, if well-protected by competition legislation, as gainers from the EMU process. What of the wider impact of EMU?

On a macroeconomic level EMU prevents its component member states from seeking to shift the burden of adjustment onto other countries within the European Union through the impact of sudden exchange rate movements. It also prevents these exchange rate movements being brought about by market pressures. It removes the possibility of speculation between currencies. Again we need to look more closely at how the benefits and costs of this change are likely to be distributed.

If it is no longer possible to speculate on intra-European exchange rate movements what happens? Foreign exchange dealers are able to buy fewer Porsches out of the profits they would have made from the transaction costs, but any underlying pressures for adjustment between the national economies remain. They have simply not been expressed through changes to relative exchange rates. Ending the speculative option undoubtedly removes the possibility of disruptive and unnecessary speculative exchange rate movements. But it also increases the importance of adjustment to any fundamental imbalances taking place through alternative routes. Either the prices of labour and other products must change relatively, or adjustment will take the form of resources left unused, in particular through greater unemployment.

A similar lesson of the impact of EMU therefore emerges in macroeconomic terms as applies on a microeconomic level. EMU is likely to benefit further those economies which are flexible and able to adapt rapidly. It will intensify the pressures on protected sectors and rigid wage structures and so make reform more likely. EMU rewards successful countries.

This argument has to be nuanced, however. The accelerated adjustment process we see all around us – rapid technological and organisational change, the exposure to competition of previously sheltered sectors of employment, the general decrease in job security – stems from the increased openness of the European economy through the internal market and developing global trading patterns. The empirical evidence of the last thirty years suggests that flexible exchange rates do not in practice always encourage adjustment to these structural trends. Indeed, by appearing to reduce the need for real adjustment through a temporary increase in price competitiveness they may on occasion make such adjustment more difficult; and depreciation tends to increase inflationary pressures which are then slow and costly to remove from the economic system.

Other things being equal, a more rigid economy is likely to face a higher level of unemployment inside EMU. But it may nonetheless be better off than seeking illusory competitive gains through devaluation outside EMU, where the result may be both higher unemployment and high inflation. The United Kingdom experience of high and variable inflation levels in the 1970s suggests that the money illusion effect induced by devaluation is evanescent – diminishes over time; and the assumption by those setting prices and wages that inflation is likely to continue makes a subsequent return to price stability increasingly costly to achieve in terms of output foregone.

Economic adjustment and the role of speculation

Nonetheless, the question of whether renunciation of the ability to adjust exchange rates is sensible for any given country or group of countries is clearly in part a technical issue. Since the collapse of the Bretton Woods system there is a range of evidence on which to base a judgement. There are circumstances in which devaluation or revaluation can help to correct underlying imbalances when combined with appropriate fiscal or structural measures. It can also be misused and make the achievement of underlying stability more difficult.

But EMU also contains a non-economic, moral dimension of fairness. It is undoubtedly the case that more powerful countries can seek to avoid adjustment, or at least postpone it, at the expense of weaker countries. Moreover in Europe, the exchange rate mechanism of the European Monetary System (set up in 1979) increasingly functioned through acceptance of the Bundesbank's leading role in setting monetary policy. Others then set interest rates to maintain currency parities with the mark. Since the mid-1980s this led to the emergence of a core bloc of currencies, including the French franc, linked to German monetary policy.

There is a wide consensus that a stable internal market in Europe requires low inflation and stable trading relations. But the constitutional role of the Bundesbank had been to maintain price stability in Germany, not more widely (see Frowen and Pringle, 1998). The Bundesbank came to perform a wider European monetary stabilisation role while the members of its Governing Council had specific regional responsibilities only within Germany; and the market tensions in the early 1990s following German reunification illustrated clearly the limitations of such a system (see Frowen and Hölscher, 1997).

EMU therefore represents an attempt to bring institutional structures in line with actual responsibilities within Europe's current level of economic integration; and in so doing made particular demands of Germany. For while this pre-EMU system may have been unstable, it conferred significant power on the Bundesbank. The German willingness to share this power in a wider structure can be justified on grounds of improving economic welfare everywhere within Europe including in Germany itself. But it represented a significant commitment to European solidarity and a rejection of economic realpolitik.

A disproportionate degree of economic power allows either an organisation or a country the ability to distort competitive conditions to its short-term advantage. On a national level, a member state can seek to set international standards and to bend rules concerning state subsidies. These measures may in the long run be self-defeating, but they can ensure that the short-term impact of adjustment is pushed on to others. Examples abound, from the refusal of the United Kingdom in the 1960s to allow the EFTA system to limit UK state subsidies to the aluminium industry, to arguments over international environmental norms today.

Devaluation remains the key example of such behaviour. It may not lead to long-term economic gains for anyone. But in the short-term it can ensure that companies trading in price sensitive sectors find that markets for their products disappear due to an unplanned or unexpected exchange rate change. Countries have considered the impact of exchange rates sufficiently important to seek a series of methods of dealing with their implications, from Bretton Woods through to the Plaza and Louvre indicative agreements, and of course the EMS exchange rate mechanism.

There are two responses by national authorities to an exchange rate shift, for example the devaluation of the lira and to a lesser extent sterling, in 1995. One is to argue that it is part of the nature of things, determined by market forces and not by governments, and if unjustified it will unwind. The transitional costs are simply one element of the wider benefits of a market system. The other is to argue that the exchange rate tends to reflect domestic monetary policy and is therefore ultimately under the control of the member state. If it is used as a means of gaining short-term competitive advantage this is not merely economically sub-optimal but politically unacceptable. It is therefore reasonable for others to respond with protectionist measures to counteract the effects of such an exchange rate change.

An interesting example of this type of response occurred in the autumn of 1992. Following sterling's departure from the exchange rate mechanism in September 1992, its subsequent 20 per cent devaluation had a major impact on some sectors of the Irish economy, very open to the UK. In particular, the Irish textile sector found itself unable to compete with such an immediate price advantage. The European Commission competition authorities gave exceptional approval to a temporary export subsidy scheme designed to ease the transition for Irish firms exporting to Britain. This type of measure is not, however, easily compatible with the single market, and illustrates the difficulty of maintaining a fair adjustment process in response to exchange rate changes.

Unless all countries and sectors affected are prepared to live with the consequences of unplanned exchange rate movements there is inevitably pressure for a protectionist reaction to them, driven by arguments of fairness and equity as much as economic welfare. There is a widespread political perception in Europe that economic competition should be transparent. Exchange rate-induced changes in competitiveness can have a large impact on vulnerable sectors, and can take place very quickly. Even if temporary they can disrupt production in price-sensitive sectors. And exchange rate shifts are easier to reverse than the factory closures or layoffs which they can trigger. They therefore disrupt the agreed ethical framework of fairness on which the European internal market implicitly depends.

The extent of this effect is disputed, and the macroeconomic significance of devaluation probably limited. But it is a political reality within the European Union that unplanned exchange rate movements between participating member states do cause major political and social tensions. A depreciating national currency may encourage other member states faced with very rapid or unforeseen adjustment pressures to retaliate through tariffs or other less-transparent trade barriers despite the legal rules forbidding such behaviour; or at least to seek countervailing policy sanctions through the European negotiating process. This must therefore influence our approach to the wider debate about economic and monetary union.

It is clear that EMU helps to make the economic adjustment process more transparent. By eliminating an element of uncertainty it reduces the need for speculation to deal with that uncertainty and also reduces the risks and rewards attached to that speculation. Speculation can of course have a stabilising role to play in providing a market to deal with uncertainty in financial matters, and commercial issues more generally. But it cannot be argued that speculation is *per se* a good thing. Where uncertainty can be removed, and conflicting pressures for economic adjustment dealt with in more straightforward ways this must be a better way forward.

To argue this is not to present EMU as an anti-market solution, nor to criticise the inevitable and often positive role of speculative behaviour within market systems. But the risks attached to speculative behaviour – a focus on immediate gains and losses to the exclusion of any wider concept of social or personal responsibility, an inevitable distance between a transaction and its consequences for individuals or even whole societies, and the risk of corrupt behaviour which inevitably associates itself with such potentially large gains – should clearly be minimised. A monetary union offers the opportunity to achieve this without sacrificing the welfare of those societies involved, nor the export of adjustment to others.

Exchange rates and international financial structures

Clearly EMU will have a major impact on the international financial environment, and the market signs of this are already apparent. The euro is widely expected to become the major competitor of – and to complement – the dollar. Perhaps one-third of world transactions may ultimately be invoiced in euros. The euro will become a major world reserve currency, and its existence is likely to reduce the global need for reserves, particularly of dollars.

From a European point of view this brings clear gains. The willingness of governments and private individuals in other countries to hold more euros allows firms and governments in Europe to invest and sell their debt more cheaply. It will provide significant seigniorage gains to the ECB, as the world stock of euros is in effect an interest-free loan to the European authorities. European firms will increasingly be able to buy raw materials, probably including oil, in euros rather than dollars, removing another exchange rate risk and uncertainty from the productive process.

There are wider potential gains which depend on the behaviour of European and other monetary authorities. There is scope for a degree of cooperation between the authorities in Europe, the United States and Japan to agree on economically sensible target zones for the three major currencies. To be effective this must work with and not against the underlying economic pressures in the market. But it is often forgotten that markets themselves respond positively to coherent government statements about the direction of policy, when these are backed up by consistent policy actions to support them.

Again this in no way undermines the legitimate and constructive role of speculation in assisting the process of trade and market activities. But it can help to remove unnecessary speculation from the system. The euro therefore offers the opportunity for a clearer and more balanced organisation of world currency markets. When this is combined with freedom of capital movements a combination of effective market forces within the necessary framework of stability provided by national governments and monetary authorities should lead to an increase in global welfare.

It is of course possible that this potential for concerted market intervention by the principal currency blocs would be misused. But this is not an argument against Europe giving itself the ability to influence the global financial system in the direction of fairness and transparency.

The responsibility of national authorities within EMU

Acceptance of Economic and Monetary Union means that individual member states' governments renounce even the possibility of a separate monetary policy. There will inevitably be circumstances in which the renunciation of an autonomous interest rate policy will lead to monetary conditions being less than optimal in the member state involved, just as regions or sectors within a national economy now might benefit from a tighter or looser monetary policy than that actually pursued by the national central bank. Governments of course also lose the ability to increase inflation through an irresponsibly loose monetary policy, providing an unambiguous gain for their citizens.

In terms of national policy-making, therefore, the same pressures apply to governments as apply to firms or individuals. Those most successful at achieving adjustment and developing a more skilled and flexible workforce are likely to benefit; those countries or regions or sectors, including the public sector, which remain more rigid will find their problems increase substantially. EMU must therefore imply an acceptance of the problems caused by the need for economic adjustment, including wages, levels of taxation and provision of public services, and their integration into national policy-making. While EMU does not itself cause additional structural adjustment – just as it has no immediate effect on a nation's wealth or income distribution – it makes the cost of slow adjustment very clear, and it may also involve temporary acceptance of a sub-optimal monetary policy, as already discussed.

While key budgetary and supply-side decisions – on most taxes, on regulation, on infrastructure and so on – will remain national responsibilities, there is likely to be political pressure for a more coordinated

European response to wider economic difficulties. Can the political structures within Europe satisfy the demands for increased macroeconomic management and coordination which are likely to be placed on them? Is it responsible to go forward with the monetary union on the basis of the current European level of economic policy integration and with only a rudimentary legal structure for cooperation set out in Articles 102 and 103 of the Treaty? Alternatively, will Europe seek to over-centralise economic policy, leading to needless constraints on national policy-making and, perhaps worse, on overall policy decisions?

There are certainly no traditional budgetary tools available at the European level. The Community budget has no discernible countercyclical influence. Indeed arguably many of the transfer payments related to the common agricultural policy make adjustment more difficult, and often involve a transfer of resources from poorer urban to richer rural areas.

Within EMU, fiscal policy remains a national responsibility, within certain broad limits. The Stability Pact is designed to ensure that countries do not freeride on the wider monetary stability provided by the ECB to borrow excessively at interest rates which might reflect the credibility of the ECB rather than their own fiscal policies. This is a sensible constraint. But no single member state works internally on the basis of so minimalist a coordination between fiscal and monetary policy at present, suggesting that there is at least scope for effective further coordination at a European level.

It is in principle possible to seek to coordinate the cyclical impact of national fiscal policies without transferring resources from one member state to another. To do so successfully would be a remarkable achievement, given the loose structure of cooperation currently existing. How far will member states be willing to place their domestic fiscal policy decisions within a wider European monetary framework set by the ECB in Frankfurt? But if this coordination does not occur voluntarily, and if there is no agreed structure to supplement the simple deficit limits set out in the stability pact, EMU is likely to operate with a suboptimal policy mix, implying that interest rates may be set higher than would otherwise be necessary.

The separation of fiscal and monetary policies is also designed to allow for the clear working of the so-called no bail-out rule, whereby member states remain responsible for their own public-sector debt. The assumption is that debt markets will penalise countries prone to fiscal indiscipline with higher borrowing charges, adding a market element to the disciplines of the Treaty and multilateral surveillance. The rapid narrowing of interest-rate spreads in 1997, anticipating decisions on membership of Stage 3 of EMU from 1999, illustrates the speed with which market views can change. We will have to determine how far market perceptions of credit risk prove able to provide a sufficient framework of discipline for member states' fiscal stance after EMU.

It has been suggested that revised capital asset ratios should be used after EMU begins as a tool for supervisors to encourage banks to limit their exposure to the various sovereign risks within monetary union (see Goodhart, 1997). This is a logical reflection of the risk involved in holding financial instruments issued by authorities who lack monetary autonomy, and so become more like local or regional authorities. It is of course also true that foreign lenders face less risk in lending, since the borrower cannot resort to currency depreciation to change the loan's value.

Ensuring that European financial regulatory structures adjust to this series of challenges, not least in terms of maintaining the competitiveness of European banks in international markets, will be a major task. Again there is a learning process to be gone through by financial market-makers and also by governments within a monetary union. There is no precedent for the unification of so many independent public-sector debt markets into a single currency with its money supply controlled by an independent issuing authority.

Should supervision of Europe's unified financial sector become more centralised? For a banking and securities market which is at least in terms of regulatory structure, with home country control and universal banking, more unified than that of the United States, it is striking that there is so little central oversight, for example, of the relative competence of national supervisors, and that so much is left to informal networks. The risk of a gap developing between the integration of financial market activities within the single currency zone and more fragmented national regulatory structures poses a major challenge to market regulators. The ECB may find itself drawn to fill this policy vacuum in response to any possible future banking difficulties which affect markets in more than one member state. It should be noted in this context that the statutes of the ECB and the ESCB – the European System of Central Banks – give scope for the ECB 'to perform specific tasks relating to the prudential supervision of credit institutions'.

More generally, effective regulatory structures are also a traditional means of ensuring macroeconomic policy stability. Within that stability it is economically sensible as well as politically necessary for Europe to continue experimenting with different types of social structures, to see which provides the best overall balance of growth and equity. Some structural policies, for example competition policy, trade policy and anti-dumping policy are already effectively European in scope; and there is a broad consensus that they function most effectively at this level.

Economic union in Europe, based as it is on coordination between national authorities, needs to achieve a high degree of understanding and acceptance of the relative distribution of roles. Otherwise the temptation for policy failures on one level to be blamed on another – in practice for national policy problems to be treated as the responsibility of 'Europe' – risks undermining the wider degree of political consensus needed for the system to work.

Conclusion

A starting point for a decision on whether EMU is ethical requires a judgement on whether the potential benefits it offers are achievable; and that in turn depends on the commitment of the central banks, finance ministers and financial authorities most concerned to accept the disciplines needed to achieve a smoothly functioning monetary union consistent with greater economic prosperity. Ultimately, however, it also needs a wider commitment on the part of Europe's political parties, and economic and social interest groups, to a level of European solidarity based on equal respect – one in which decisions are taken on the basis of equity and fairness, not merely on relative financial power.

EMU requires the same act of faith as did the original European Coal and Steel Community Treaty when it spoke of the need 'to lay the foundations for institutions which will give direction to a destiny henceforward shared'. Money is to the 1990s what raw materials were to the postwar decade when European construction first took shape. Fifty years on, the economic community begun by the Treaty of Paris is widely perceived as requiring a monetary union to sustain it.

EMU offers the opportunity to create a new financial and economic structure with implications for both Europe and the world. If successful it could replace some of the uncertainty and distance of economic pressures driven by outside forces with a more transparent structure of economic adjustment freed from the risks and instability of the foreign exchange markets. EMU cannot change the underlying influence of market forces, but it can facilitate the development of an economic system in Europe which is fair, and perceived to be so, and which allows scope for greater choice about the political and social structures complementing that open economy.

EMU may therefore be taken as a challenge to restructure and develop the market economy, for the benefit of all Europe's citizens. But the stakes are high. Does the underlying political and moral commitment to what that Treaty calls 'a broader and deeper community' exist today? If it does, then EMU is right and will succeed. If it does not, then EMU is likely to falter with serious consequences for the future of the wider European construction.

References

Frowen, S. F. and Pringle, R. (eds) (1998) *Inside the Bundesbank* (London: Macmillan; New York: St Martin's Press).

Frowen, S. F. and Hölscher, J. (eds) (1997) *The German Currency Union of 1990: A Critical Assessment* (London: Macmillan; New York: St Martins's Press).

Goodhart, C. E. A. (1997) *Two Concepts of Money and the Future of Europe,* LSE Financial Markets Group Special Paper no. 96, June.

14
Capital and Credit-based Development: Lessons from the Experience of Industrial Countries for Transition Economies in Central East Europe

Stephan Herten and Jens Hölscher

Introduction

The hypothesis of this chapter is that a strategy in favour of financial liberalisation in the emerging market economies of Central East Europe will lead to Anglo-Saxon types of financial sectors, including the implantation of chronic short termism and vulnerability to speculative attacks. For economic policy we argue therefore in favour of a careful rehabilitation approach following the postwar West German example (see Grünbacher and Hölscher 1997).

This result is derived from theoretical reflections on the inter-relationship of financial systems and economic development at the micro- and macroeconomic level, which are part of this introduction. In the following section on the macroeconomics of financial systems we can unfortunately not resolve the jigsaw puzzle of finance and development, but find strong support for the assumption that the Rhenish system has the ability of building up hidden reserves in order to buffer intertemporal fluctuations of the business cycles. This finding is sufficient to support the adoption of a 'Rhenish' type of model for a theory of the transition of financial sectors in Central East Europe.

However, it will be shown later in this chapter that Central East Europe's situation is best characterised as a 'worst-case scenario' of a mix-up between both models. Due to the unresolved bad asset problem of the past we find an apparent German system on the institutional level of the surface, but extreme short-termism in the structural depth of the markets. This transitional phenomenon is a clear indicator for the ongoing transformation of the economic systems. The discussion of a rehabilitation versus a 'free entry' approach will lead to the conclusion that 'free entry' is an inappropriate policy for the promotion of sound financial sectors as long as the bad-asset problem is not resolved. On the basis of our analysis we will argue in favour of a strategy of 'semi-liberalisation', in order to use foreign participation to induce learning without giving away financial control.

Microeconomy: the dilemma of corporate governance theory

Most approaches to transition economics discuss the choice between an Anglo-Saxon type and a German type of financial system in terms of agency problems, and end up in a dilemma. Capital markets have been established but do not yet perform as a market for corporate control. Banks, often set up as finance departments of firms and burdened with bad debts, show a questionable solvency and are prone to moral hazard (see overview in Buch, 1995, or Grosfeld, 1994).

Policy advice highlights the role of monitoring, screening and restructuring of insolvent firms and emphasises either the role of banks or the role of capital markets for external funding and control. However, a contribution of the other, less-pronounced part, be it banks or capital markets, is certainly not denied. It can be assumed that the minor part shall fulfil a corrective function when, after a circular argument, the call for the principal's principal is not answered.

This unsatisfactory result of applied economics is not as surprising as it may seem. The traditional way of gaining insights into the role of institutions has to be reversed. New institutional economics, that is the introduction of transaction costs and its incorporation into the theory of finance, is a successful scientific programme, which explains the variety of existing institutions in developed market economies by their contributions to reducing the costs of controlling and enhancing contracts. It helps to assume that the existing institutions must be efficient and reduce transaction costs, otherwise they would have perished in a competitive environment. However, explaining reality, the reality of single institutions, with theory is one thing. Giving policy advice for institution-building is quite another, especially when faced with institution-building in a transition economy, which by its nature is a process of revolutionary change. A range of efficient institutions does not yet exist and implemented or evolved institutions have interdependent effects on each other. Here the premature state of corporate governance theory becomes apparent: in spite of some eclectic arguments the interaction of institutions is still puzzling. Even if the countries concerned try to imitate western systems, in what the term 'choice' suggests, they can only adapt some singular institutions. Therefore institution-building in the transition economies will remain a spontaneous process of trial and error.

Macroeconomy: empirical arguments

First attempts have been made in order to integrate the theory of finance and macroeconomics (for example, Greenwald and Stiglitz, 1993, or Bernanke and Gertler, 1989), yet these approaches are not applied to a comparison of financial systems. Empirical research might offer another argument for policy advice. Some cross-country studies demonstrate a correlation between stockmarket development and growth. This suggests that an Anglo-Saxon type of system with equity finance as the dominant form of external finance is in favour of development. But this relationship has to be viewed cautiously. Whereas rising credit at least means more intermediation, albeit not necessarily for productive means, rising equity prices need not reflect external funding in the form of new emissions on the primary stockmarket. It can be a reflex of internal accumulation or just a consequence of profit expectations. Moreover, as flow analyses by Corbett and Jenkinson (1997) shows, companies in the USA and in the UK were the net financiers on the stockmarket during the 1980s. Debt or profits have been used to buy back previously issued shares instead of being used to invest. In other words, a disinvestment/disintermediation took place with regard to the stockmarket. Not so in the emerging market economies of the Far East: there, new equity issues were the dominant source of external finance and they contributed much more to corporate growth than in developed countries (Singh and Hamid, 1992). But this was partly due to regulation and tax advantages favouring stockmarkets. More importantly: a substitutive relationship between both kinds of external financing seemed to exist; stockmarket development fostered by international diversification did not coincide with growth, but with domestic consumption and declining bank credit (Singh, 1997).

A recent controversy on finance and development can be summarised as follows:

1. a correlation between financial development (intermediation as percentage of GDP) and economic growth cannot be denied; yet the question of causality still remains open;
2. the results of liberalisation are disappointing;
3. the statistics show different pictures for individual countries; and

Unfortunately, no empirical argument in favour of a bank or financial market-based financial system is stated. Arestis and Demetriades (1997; p. 785) put it in a general way: 'the causal link between finance and growth is crucially determined by the nature and operation of the financial institutions and policies pursued in each country'. In general, cross-country studies cannot capture these differences. They therefore argue in favour of time-series analyses for each individual country separately.

In order to gain insights for a comparison of the Anglo-Saxon and German types of financial organisation, time-series analyses for each individual country are a too-restrictive approach if countries of a similar market organisation also show a similar causal link between financial development and growth. In an *ad hoc* approach a recent study finds that splitting the countries into groups of different financial systems, according to the ratio of bank credit and stockmarket capitalisation to GDP, leads to a considerable difference in comparison to general cross-country studies. It demonstrates that 'countries with relatively deeper bank credit and relatively shallower stockmarkets show a stronger relationship between bank credit and investment than do the complimentary group of countries' and vice versa (Black and Moersch 1998).

General cross-country studies which demonstrate a correlation between stockmarket development and growth, therefore, do not justify a choice in favour of an Anglo-Saxon system because the causal link depends on the system itself. In a contrary study, Steinherr and Huvenirs (1994), also using variables describing the structure of the banking system, found that 'in countries where interest rate spreads are low and/or where universal banking has been introduced, growth tends to be above average'.

Macroeconomics of financial systems

An anatomy of financial systems

In order to highlight differences between the Anglo-Saxon and German types of financial market the following arguments focus on external finance, although we admit that internal finance is the main source of investment in both systems. But having emphasised factors and macroeconomic constellations (low real exchange rate, income deflation combined with profit inflation – see for example, Hölscher, 1996) which foster internal finance, this focus can be misinterpreted as an aim to reverse the evolution of capitalism, characterised by a separation of ownership and control. So pure profits which reflect a flow disequilibrium are not considered.

Using the microeconomic arguments and the empirical results we interpret the difference between the Anglo-Saxon and German types of financial system as availability and use of long-term finance for investment. The main difference between both systems is seen in the fact that in the German system banks provide long-term finance in the form of credits to firms, whereas in the Anglo-Saxon type, long-term finance is provided by the capital market via equity. These basic assumptions characterise the prototypes. The reason for this difference might be found in the historical development, namely the evolutionary process of specialising market participants and regulation or strong competition on the liability side of banks. Certainly, in the real world, they are not exactly the same for each economy within the same group.

From a process-oriented point of view the transformation of maturities is different. In Anglo-Saxon systems the transformation of maturities takes place on the capital market. Commercial banks offer short-term finance to firms with investment opportunities which decide whether to refinance the initial amount by issuing shares (Chick, 1995). The firms therefore hold the transformational risk; liquid capital markets can reduce it and extend the flexibility of finance in principle. In the German system the banks have to bear the transformational risk; hereby the so-called 'golden banking rule' expresses the individual reduction of risk. Typically, banking supervision controls the relationship of short-term liabilities and long-term assets in addition to restricting the danger of systematic risk. Yet in both systems the initial source of finance is represented by bank credit.

The flexibility of bank credits might be welcome because it can provide purchasing power to the Schumpeterian entrepreneur, but it inherits the risk of inflationary pressure if too much money is created via bank credits and not transformed. Keynes, for example, mentions in the *General Theory* that the transformation of short-term into long-term finance is one factor that neglects the traditional link from the initial amount of money supply to prices. In addition, if the solvency of banks is in doubt the system inherits the risk of financial instability through the possible occurrence of bank runs (Diamond and Dybvig, 1983). In fact, both have been major problems in Central East Europe. Bad debts and moral hazard of banks hampered monetary policy and regenerated real money supply, so that inflation did not lower the monetary overhang. But this problem is independent of the financial system, as long as the theoretical option of narrow banking is not considered, which would neglect the evolutionary development of banks in industrialised countries (see, for example, Kregel 1996).

On the other hand, a financial system with endogenous money has the advantage that at least the supply of credit underlies a commercial bank decision on the solvency of the creditor. This arrangement relieves the central bank of a simultaneous solvency assessment for individual debtors when providing liquidity to the financial system (Riese, 1993). Bank credit leading to the creation of deposits is a similar feature of both financial systems. In contrast to narrow banking with an authority restricting the amount of money it presents a market approach towards money.

Some reflections on development aspects of different systems

As in the different finance option available for firms, households in either prototype are offered distinct asset options. In a monetary equilibrium created money has to be held deliberately in the portfolios of investors. Without internal finance the level of production is determined by the volume of assets that can be used for productive means. On the basis of the simple anatomy a first conclusion could be that the Anglo-Saxon system offers a relative advantage over the German system if inflation expectations are the main obstacle to the economy concerned. Yet equity does not represent an absolute inflation-secure asset. For example in a fixed exchange rate system, rising prices lower the international competitiveness of the economy and reduced profit expectations stop share prices from rising in line with inflation.

Moreover, inflation expectations can go hand in hand with the expectation of a future restrictive monetary policy, with a negative effect on share prices. Nevertheless, equity seems to be more inflation-secure than nominal assets. On the other hand, the German system might offer a relative advantage if asset uncertainty is the main obstacle, because banks pool projects intersectorally. Although this function can be performed through the capital market that covers all sectors of the economy, it is rather doubtful that the individual investor really participates in all assets. Moreover, if small firms are not represented on the capital market, even diversified investors unproportionally bear the risk of larger companies.

Certainly the description above does not capture some important dynamic difference between both systems. Consider rising profit expectations in the Anglo-Saxon economy. If these coincide with rising share prices a wealth effect leads to higher overall wealth and changes the relative distribution of assets for households, but without additional external finance for the firms in the first instance. The wealth effect restricts the expansions of the level of production in comparison with the German system because households have an incentive to rearrange their distribution of assets towards real or foreign assets. The opposit is true for depressed profit expectations. In support of this argument Black and Moersch (1998) find that the real exchange rate and the real interest rate show a negative correlation with investment for the German type of economies, whereas in the Anglo-Saxon system there is none. This leaves us with a simple policy advice. Insofar as this is due to the wealth effect of the share prices it can be argued that the German type of system is favourable in prosperous macroeconomic constellations in which, for example, the advantages of an exchange rate strategy can be fully exploited.

This preliminary result has certainly to be taken cautiously. A study of the Bank for International Settlement (BIS) came up with the result that monetary policy in Anglo-Saxon systems is more effective. Effectiveness, here, is not measured by a rising interest rate but by its restrictive effect on output (Bockelmann 1996). In other words: these countries can be worse off when fighting inflation is on the schedule. Nevertheless, it should be borne in mind that, first, restrictive monetary policy in these countries has a fast effect on output but the German types of economies suffer from a stronger effect after a time lag, which is transmitted via the investment channel. Secondly, the study also emphasised a paradox: although monetary policy in these countries is more effective, they were less successful in fighting inflation. Using the above argument, the Anglo-Saxon system seems to have a lower cost of inflation and therefore makes it more likely, whereas fighting inflation has higher costs in the short run. From the viewpoint of this chapter it is more interesting that this fast effect on output did not allow the economies concerned to maintain a policy of rising interest rates in the latest crises of the European Monetary System. They dropped out of the exchange rate system when the German Bundesbank took the lead in pushing up interest rates. If a higher conflict between internal and external stabilisation is a general feature of Anglo-Saxon systems, this might hamper an exchange rate strategy set up in order to support domestic development.

Finally, one important difference between both systems has been emphasised by Allen and Gale (1994, 1995). It is related to the described portfolio effects but pronounces the welfare aspects. In the German system banks build up reserves in good times and draw on reserves in bad times (see also Frowen and Karakitsos, 2000), thereby offering their creditors nearly the same payouts. The capital market cannot smooth the intertemporal risk in the same way: it cannot differentiate between an investor who is concerned with asset uncertainty because of a liquidity orientation, and an investor who is concerned with profit arbitrage. Therefore, once the system is running and reserves are built up the German system can make everybody better off. However, this intertemporal insurance for households has an obligatory character: direct investment facilities provided by a liberalised capital market offer arbitrage opportunities and undermine this feature. A larger set of alternatives, that is markets plus financial intermediaries, might not make individuals better off than intermediaries alone (Allen and Gale, 1995, p. 190) – a statement in high contrast to most advices given for transition economies. With regard to the transition economies the immediate problem is not to build up reserves, but to smooth the write-off of the inherited bad debts over time.

The Central East European background

Monetary policy, bad debts and financial institutions

By following the four-stages model for the transformation of financial systems from plan to market of Hilbers (1993), the economies of Poland, the Czech and the Slovak Republics and Hungary are, albeit national differences, in the third stage of increased liberalisation and privatisation in conjunction with market-determined interest rates and regained macroeconomic stability. Nevertheless, a fully market-based monetary policy, as characterised by the fourth stage of a developed market economy, is not achieved yet. This can be shown by three indicators of the interrelationship between the central banks and commercial banks in Central East Europe (Table 13.1).

The first indicator of the growth of central bank lending can be interpreted as stabilisation policy. Fighting inflation in the stabilisation year 1992 shows a reduction of central-bank lending, which has proved

Table 14.1 Indicators of commercial bank liabilities and receivables from the national banks in the Czech Republic, Hungary and Poland, 1989–94

	1989	*1990*	*1991*	*1992*	*1993*	*1994*[a]
Growth of central-bank lending to financial institutions (% change over the respective period of the previous year)						
Czech Republic	...	52	–8.0	–17	–41	0.5
Hungary	11.8	39	17.5	–29.7	25.7	4.6
Poland	457	251	–1.3	–35	30.1	2.4
Ratio of liabilities to central bank to total assets of commercial banks (%)						
Czech Republic[b]	...	...	(38.1)	(25.1)	6.9 (11.9)	5.6 (11.4)
Hungary[c]	23.7	25.9	19.8	12.9	14.0	12.9
Poland[c]	36.6	33.3	19.7	9.8	8.7	7.9
Excess reserves of commercial banks (in % of total deposits with the central bank)						
Czech Republic	...	...	...	42	40	27.4
Hungary	68.3	75.3	65.9	60.9	69.7	74.9
Poland	88.1	38.5	35.8	40.5	28.5	24.8

Notes: [a]June; [b]figures in brackets represent liabilities to the Czech National Bank over total deposits of clients of commercial banks; [c]data for 1989–90 and for the following years are not entirely comparable.
Source: Buch (1995).

most effective in the Czech Republic from 1991 to 1993. The second indicator, the ratio of liabilities to central banks to total assets of commercial banks, shows the maturity of capital markets in terms of the acceptance of domestic money for household savings. A sharp decrease of the central banks' share can be observed in 1991/92. This trend is continuing in Poland and the Czech Republic, whilst Hungary dropped back in 1993. In all countries financial sectors are in their infant stage compared with a ratio of 3.8 per cent in Germany.

The third indicator, the excess reserves of commercial banks in per cent of total deposits with the central bank, shows the role of the rate of interest as the price for holding liquidity. This interpretation derives from the fact that excess reserves are not interest-bearing. An exception is a certain phase in Hungary, when the central bank offered the highest interest rates in the market, a situation which nevertheless confirms the hypothesis of an infant financial sector, because this was the only way to restrict credit creation. The Czech lands and Poland have improved dramatically and Hungary has still to cope with a high non-pecuniary liquidity premium. A summary of the indicators supports the hypothesis that the execution of a sound monetary policy is still jeopardised by financial systems lagging behind. The important role of central-bank lending points towards extreme short-termism. Sound instruments have not emerged yet and the interbank market remains shallow, the banks therefore rely heavily on refinancing which is the most short-term form possible.

The stock argument of the bad loan problem (for options to resolve this problem see Tomann, 1997) offers a proper explanation for these circumstances (Winkler, 1996). The macroeconomic equilibrium is given in the state, in which profit expectations (r^*) equal the representative market rate of interest (i) equal to profits of banks. The solvency-securing interest rate spread (lending rate r_L minus rate on deposits r_D) is regarded as function of the inflation rate (p), the share of the non-performing assets of the balance sheet (k) and the requested real rate of return of deposits *rD*. Concentrating on the lending rate, which is the relevant rate for the entrepreneurial sector, it follows that:

$$r_L = f\,(p, k, r_D)$$

The importance of the bad loans for the interest-rate policy of the central bank becomes clear. A synthesis of Hilbers' (1993) four-stages model of financial markets in transition and Winkler's (1996) interest-rate-spread approach shows the result indicated in Figure 13.1.

Stage of capital market	**1** (plan)	**2**	**3**	**4** (market)
Interest rate criterion	n.a.	a) $0 > r_L > r_D > -p$ b) $r_L > r_D > 0 > -p$	$r_L > r_D$	$(r_L - r_D) = r$
Scenario	Credit administration	Subsidies instead of credits	Stabilisation (-crisis)	Market-based credit creation

Figure 14.1 Capital markets, interest rates and credit creation

During the transition period, financial sectors go through different phases of interest rates. In the planned-economy (stage 1) the interest rates are not relevant to credit creation, because money in general does not have the function of keeping resources scarce. The price mechanism for credit creation indicated by interest rates is not in place. Stage 2 represents the inflationary scenario, firstly with negative rates of interest and secondly with positive rates of interest, experienced in many countries in transition as a sequence towards stage 3. Here the overall credit creation finances the debt service on bad loans, thereby increasing their amount. New credits take the form of subsidies to maintain the liquidity of the financial sector and in most cases the enterprises as well. The flow functions of corporate control are not executed.

Stage 3 represents the stabilised economy in transition. The central bank has introduced positive real interest rates and the lending rate exceeds the rate on savings. The constellation is fragile, because the high lending rate might turn down growth of output, because the interest spread of the banking sector has to be paid by production in the 'real sector'. In the case of a stabilisation crisis, the economy is in danger of falling back to stage 2 ending up in a stop – go policy (see also Hölscher, 1997). The only difference between stage 2b and stage 3 is the absence of high inflation in stage 3. The stage of a developed capital market is represented by an equilibrium in which interest is paid by profits.

The figure shows that the lending rate for credits is higher than necessary due to the non-performing assets. Banks have to maintain high interest rate spreads to cover their insolvency risk. Interest rate policy of central banks has a multiplied effect on market rates, a fact that is particularly crucial in stage 3, where 'monetary policy can react only by raising interest rates again and again' (NBH, 1994 p. 16). This policy alone leads to an increase of new bad loans, because originally good loans become doubtful as a consequence of a higher lending rate.

Some general observations of the institutional level can be made on the basis of the very diverse material (see Appendix). The absence of institutional investors like pensions funds leaves the emerging capital markets in a fragile condition in terms of transaction volume and number of market participants. The overall picture shows the Rhenish-style universal banking system on its surface as a consequence of restructuring policy. The structure of the financial market is oligopolistic, which alone would lead to rent-seeking behaviour with a higher lending rate than necessary. There are still very few well-equipped bank offices which offer the full range of financial services. Systems of clearing and payments are inefficient and slow; geographical differences are enormous. Apart from the capitals the CEECs are still 'underbanked' and suffer from a huge disproportion in household deposit collections in the countryside and lending in the centres.

We find a combination of universal banking and a high interest rate spread, both as a result of restructuring. Yet universal banking alone is hardly the criterion for a German type of financial system. The refinancing structure of the banks shows the Anglo-Saxon feature of short-term liabilities, but due to the bad-debts problems monetary policy is not as effective. In short: Central East Europe seems to be the worst of both worlds.

Rehabilitation versus liberalisation

In all of the four countries attempts were made to separate the problem of bad assets from the problem of privatisation of those enterprises which represent the bad assets. This went along with the improvement of the capital basis by consolidation bonds or privatisation. (The first Hungarian bank privatisation even provides a case of a mix between both variants plus a foreign strategic investor plus a state stake (Komendi, 1996). Meanwhile Hungary's privatisation of the big commercial banks of the financial sector has been successfully completed.) The state still holds a huge stake in the financial sector due to the 'negative net worth hole' (Kormendi and Snyder, 1996, p. 3). Meanwhile all countries have introduced special state banks, with the task of collecting the 'bad assets' of the commercial banks. This rather new policy rejects the previous idea of a revenue-oriented privatisation of state banks. The burden of the increasing indebtedness of the state as a consequence of this new move has to be balanced against the benefits of a functioning financial sector. Another observation is the increasing number of joint ventures with foreign institutions throughout Central East Europe. At first glance this is a clearly optimistic signpost, because it indicates the 'marketisation' of the financial sectors. On the other hand it could be regarded as a consequence of the hopeless attempts to set up domestic financial markets.

As the empirical picture clearly underlines the necessity to reform the banking system, the question is which approach should be followed. A discussion of this question usually distinguishes between a *new entry* or *rehabilitation* strategy (see Claessens, 1996). The countries under observation obviously pursue a rehabilitation strategy even though 'choosing the rehabilitation approach strategy when faced with a weak institutional legacy can thus be a poor policy as progress is slow' (Claessens, 1996, p. 21). The alternative to such a 'poor policy' would be to set up a new financial sector with the help of foreign institutions. This would provide a solution for the flow functions of the system, but as the stock problem causes the major macroeconomic problem of the economies, this phenomenon also has to be addressed. Given all other conditions as equal, the new entry approach calls for a higher tax rate. Instead of the banks, the state would have to take over in one form or another the burden of the bad assets.

Lessons from financial repression teach us that financial reform and liberalisation may lead to 'an explosion in government debt, economic instability and lower economic growth' (Fry, 1997, p. 768) without fiscal reform incorporating either a reduction of government spending or increased tax revenue. Neither of these possibilities seems to be a realistic policy under the fragile circumstances of the transition economies (see Hölscher, 1997). Therefore, the new entry approach in the Visegrad countries would most likely initiate a return to the inflationary scenario of stage 2. This could even destroy growth and introduce political instability.

The alternative of the rehabilitation approach assumes growth as a necessary condition. If the economies are growing it is justified to introduce a strategy wherein the bad debts are written off by the quasi-rents of the banking sector. The higher the quasi-rent, the faster the progress. Most important in this scenario are profit expectations of the entrepreneurial sector. A Schumpeterian strategy would allow a higher lending rate as long as profit expectations of entrepreneurs are high enough to increase investment. This policy option builds on factor augmentation rather than on factor allocation.

Of course this approach does not say anything about the improvement of the inefficient allocation of savings and the distribution of lending. But from a macroeconomic point of view it is sensible to separate this problem from the transition of the banking sector as such, rather than to externalise it to new entry candidates. The aim must be to prevent the creation of new bad loans, which are not a consequence of the past but a consequence of bad management. This situation calls for tough supervision with a proper accounting system. Recent banking failures show a backwards movement, because the new bankrupt banks in the Czech lands are again under direct supervision of the Nationalbank, a tendency of 'back to the monobank'.

The financial sector is still in its infant state in Central East Europe due mainly to the bad-asset problem, but also to other distortions. The conventional 'infant industry argument' applies to the banking sector in transition. As long as the circle of 'bad assets–privatisation–negative value' is not unwheeled, a solution for a sound financial sector is not in sight. The alternative, to leave the old institutions to their own fate and start from scratch with newcomers, who would mainly come from outside, ignores the destabilising effects of the existing distortions. The way of extracting the bad assets into a state pool or fund seems to be a viable possibility, but with regard to the four stages it is in principle nothing other than a more sophisticated way of interest subsidisation.

Conclusion: in favour of semi-liberalisation

On the basis of the above characterisation we argue in favour of a careful rehabilitation with foreign participation. This suggests a policy option in between the two radical solutions of 'free entry' and full rehabilitation. Figure 13.2 summarises the different policy options for the restructuring of the banking system and demonstrates the crucial link between a liberalisation strategy and the bad-debt solution.

A flow solution of the bad-debt problem seems to be only feasible without a far-reaching liberalisation. CEE banks with bad assets are less competitive than new or foreign institutions, because they cannot offer competitive rates. Therefore the rebuilding of the bad debts must have an obligatory character; it does not allow for new competitors. Direct investment facilities provided by a liberalised capital market also offer

	Level of liberalisation			
Bad-debt solution	Rehabilitation	Joint ventures with banks	Capital market liberalisation	Free entry
State solution	Domestic German type	German type	(Domestic) Anglo-Saxon type	Anglo-Saxon type; failures of domestic banks likely
Flow solution	Domestic German type	German type	Feasibility doubtful, danger of banking crises	Not feasible

Figure 14.2 Liberalisation and bad-debt solutions

arbitrage opportunities and undermine the feature of intertemporal smoothing. A flow solution of the bad asset problem calls for a German type of financial system with the additional opportunity to exploit favourable macroeconomic constellations. Economic growth is necessary to write off the bad debts. In the light of a missing banking history the typical arguments in favour of a full rehabilitation strategy, which builds on local knowledge and an existing link between the banking and productive sector, look quite weak. Instead, joint ventures in the banking sector may lead to a contribution of foreign capital and management experience within this process, but certainly foreign investors will only contribute if the profit expectations are really high.

Within an Anglo-Saxon system of liberalised capital markets a flow solution of the bad-asset problem is not feasible. Even if the domestic capital market takes over the role of funding for investment and the banks´ role is restricted to offer payment facilities, a banking crisis is very likely to occur. Sooner or later the bad debts end up on the state's balance sheet. Free entry for foreign banks and foreign competition would show an immediate effect. Most importantly, a liberalisation of the capital market is already a predecision for the development of the financial system because banks lose the ability of building up hidden reserves in order to buffer intertemporal fluctuations of the business cycle. As policy-makers are hardly aware of this fact, the future might verify Hayek´s verdict of Anglo-Saxon systems in Central East Europe as a result of human action, but not of human design.

Note

The extreme assumptions in the above discussion are supported by the non-existent relationship between the stockmarket and investment in Germany. The stockmarket does not steer capital in the most promising direction. In addition there seems to be no equity premium. This prize puzzle might be explained through the assumption that the stockmarket really works as a market for corporate control. But instead of hostile take-overs as the ultimate measure to sanction management there seems to be a non-pecuniary premium towards shareholders, at least towards the banks which use equity to control their credits, or other interlocked owners. Although in the UK no regulation forbids commercial banks to offer long-term credit with fixed interest rates to firms, they have from early-on specialised in deposit facilities. Probably fierce competition on the liability side leads nowadays to a prohibitive risk in engaging in long-term credit (Wilson Committee, 1980).

Appendix

Table A14.1 Hungary: empirical findings, 1992–94

(a) Bank assets according to the level of risk involved

	1992		1993		1994	
Qualification	*31 Dec. Ft billion*	*per cent*	*31 Dec. Ft billion*	*per cent*	*30 June Ft billion*	*per cent*
1. Problem free	1451.0	88.5	1294.7	70.9	1409.0	71.8
2. (a) To be watched	–	–	122.8	6.7	148.2	7.6
(b) Below average	38.7	2.4	52.3	2.9	47.5	2.4
(c) Doubtful	63.2	3.9	111.1	6.1	101.8	5.2
(d) Bad	84.5	5.2	244.9	13.4	255.1	13.0
Total (a + b + c + d)	186.4	11.5	531.2	29.1	552.6	28.2
Grand Total (1 + 2)	1637.4	100.0	1825.9	100.0	1961.6	100.0

(b) Development of the total assets of financial institutions (billions of forints)

	1990	*1992*	*1993*	*1994**	*Index for 1994 1994/90 1990 = 100*
Large banks	1381	1826	1982	2014	146
Small and medium-sized banks	91	185	194	218	240
Jointly-owned banks	136	230	329	396	292
Specialised financial institutions	5	22	27	28	560

Table A14.1 Hungary: empirical findings, 1992–94 – *continued*

(b) Development of the total assets of financial institutions (billions of forints)

	1990	*1992*	*1993*	*1994**	*Index for 1994 1994/90 1990 = 100*
Investment bank	0	0	20	22	n.a.
Savings co-operatives	79	127	138	145	184
Total	1692	2390	2690	2823	167

* 15 September 1994 status.

(c) The number of financial institutions

	1992	*1993*	*1994**
Commercial banks	35	35	37
of which:			
Hungarian-owned	20	17	17
Jointly-owned	15	18	20
Specialised financial institutions	6	7	5
Investment banks	0	0	1
Savings co-operatives	257	255	254
Total	298	297	297

Table A14.1 Hungary: empirical findings, 1992–94 – *continued*

(d) Subscribed capital of financial institutions (billions of forints)

	1992	*1993*	*1994*
Large banks	73	166	185
Small and medium-sized banks	13	38	42
Jointly-owned banks	29	33	38
Specialised financial institutions	8	7	6
Investment bank	0	10	12
Savings co-operatives	1	2	2
Total	124	256	285

Source: National Bank of Hungary.

Table A14.2 Poland: empirical findings, 1986–93

(a) *Structure of credits granted to the non-financial sector by Polish commercial banks, 1989–93 (per cent)*

Item	*1989*	*1990*	*1991*	*1992*	*1993*
All banks	100.0	100.0	100.0	100.0	100.0
State-owned banks[a]	95.9	89.4	81.4	77.8	68.3
Four largest banks	50.1	44.4	42.3	43.1	43.3
Banks separated from NBP in 1989[c]	45.5	43.3	37.3	34.6	25.0
Other	0.3	1.6	1.9	0.1	0.1
Private sector banks[d]	4.1	10.6	18.6	22.2	31.7
Created since 1989[e]	0.2	3.2	9.1	12.5	16.3
Co-operative	3.9	7.4	9.5	8.4	7.0
Privatized[f]	–	–	–	1.3	8.3

[a] Including Bank Gospodarki Zywnosciowej (Agricultural Bank), a state co-operative partnership.
[b] Bank Handlowy w Warszawie S.A., Bank Polska Kasa Opieki S.A., Powszechna Kasa Oszczednosci-BP (State Savings Bank) and Bank Gospodarki Zywnosciowej (Agricultural Bank).
[c] The 'nine' banks until 1992. In the 1993 figure the two privatised banks are excluded.
[d] All co-operative banks included.
[e] On the basis of the 1989 Banking Act.
[f] In 1992 – Bank Rozwoju Eksportu S.A.; in 1993 – Wielkopolski Bank Kredytowy S.A. and Bank Slaski S.A.

Source: National Bank of Poland; from Polanski, in Hölscher *et al.* (1995).

Table A14.2 Poland: empirical findings, 1986–93 – *continued*

(b) Active banks in Poland, 1986–93 (selected years)

Item	*1986*	*1989*	*1990*	*1991*	*1992*	*1993*
Total	4	21	53/1716[a]	76/1743	87/1752	90/1754
State-owned banks	3	16	15	15	14	12
Central bank	1	1	1	1	1	1
State banks	–	11	11	2	2	2
Joint-stock companies	2	4	3	12	11	9
Private sector banks[b]	–	4	37	60	71	74
of which:						
Foreign banks	–	–	3	6	6	7
Branches of foreign banks	–	–	–	1	2	2
State-co-operative bank[c]	1	1	1	1	1	1
Co-operative banks	1662	1662	1663	1667	1665	1664
Integrated into the BGZ structure	1662	1662	1578	1575	1481	1270
Outside the BGZ structure	–	–	85	92	184	394
Privatized banks	–	–	–	–	1	3

Notes: The data in the table refer to active entities, i.e. banks which were really conducting banking operations and reporting to the NBP. Thus their increases from 1990 are not equal to the number of licenses issued each year by NBP.

[a] Since 1990 the second figure includes all cooperative banks.

[b] Created on the basis of the 1989 Banking Act.

[c] Bank Gospodarki Zywnosciowej (BGZ) (Agricultural Bank). In 1993 54% of its shares were held by the State and the remaining 46% by the co-operative banks.

Source: National Bank of Poland and Ministry of Finance/Polish Development Bank (1993); from Polanski, in Hölscher *et al.* (1995).

Table A14.3 Slovakia: empirical findings

Overview of banking sector in Slovakia

No.	*Bank*	*Assets)* *(Sk billion)*	*Equity* *(Sk million)*	*State* *ownership (%)*	*Branches* *(number)*	*Credits* *(Sk billion)*
1.	VUB*	134.7	4078.1	47.8	177	95.0
2.	SLSP	133.2	2134.0	100.0	689	48.4
3.	IRB*	45.7	1 000.0	36.0	43	36.0
4.	Consolidation bank	30.7	2357.0	100.0	n.a.	30.0
5.	Polnobank	13.8	800.0	8.3	25	10.4
6.	Tatrabank	4.4	401.7	0.0	3	3.8
7.	Slovak Guarantee Bank	3.9	376.2	100.0	2	n.a.
8.	Postbank	2.3	600.0	0.0	1622	1.3
9.	Istrobank	2.5	1000.0	0.0	1	1.0
10.	Peoples Bank**	3.9	300.0	0.0	1	1.1
11.	Industrial Bank*	2.9	1001.0	35.7	2	1.9
12.	Slovak Credit Bank*	1.4	823.0	0.0	1	0.3
13.	First Housing Savings Bank	1.2	300.0	0.0	5	n.a.
14.	First Comunal Bank	0.8	444.6	0.0	18	0.8
15.	Devin Bank, Co.**	1.5	640.0	0.0	2	1.0
16.	Housing Savings Bank Wustenrot	0.4	300.0	0.0	n.a.	n.a.
17.	Credit Lyonnais Bank Slovakia	n.a.	300.0	0.0	n.a.	n.a.

n.a. data are not available.

* increase in equity during 1994.

** Ludova Bank – increased ownership equity to Sk 448 million at the beginning of 1995.
Devin Bank – increased ownership equity to Sk 800 million at the beginning of 1995.

Source: NBS, 1994 Annual Reports of Banks; from Pilkova and Blecha (1995).

Table A14.4 Czech Republic: empirical findings

Commercial Banks in CR (number of commercial banks which have commenced operations)													
Year	*1990*		*1991*				*1992*				*1993*		
Monthly data	1.1	31.12	31.3	30		31			30	31.12	1.1	1.4	1.6
	1.0	31	31	0.6	30	0.1	31	30	0.9	31	1.0	1.0	1.0
	1	0.1	0.3	30.6	0.9	2	0.3	0.6		0.1	1	4	6
		2			30.9	31.12	31.3	30.6	30.9	2			
Total	5	9	17	24	24	28	32	33	34	38	40	43	39
State financial institutions	4	4	5	5	5	5	1	1	1	1	1	1	1
Banks with decisive state participation	1	1	1	1	1	1	5	5	5	5	4	4	4
Banks with decisive domestic private participation	0	3	8	10	10	13	14	15	15	17	16	18	18
Banks with foreign participation <50%	0	0	0	0	0	0	1	0	1	1	4	4	4
Banks with foreign participation >50%	0	1	2	5	5	5	5	5	5	5	4	4	4
Banks entirely foreign owned	0	0	1	3	3	4	6	6	6	7	7	8	8
Branches of foreign banks in the CR	0	0	0	0	0	0	0	1	1	2	4	4	5

Source: Czech National Bank; cuba and Skolkova in Hölscher *et al.* (1995).

References

Allen, F. and Gale, D. (1994) 'Limited Market Participation and Volatility of Asset Prices', *American Economic Review*, vol. 84, pp. 933–55.

Allen, F. and Gale, D. (1995) 'A Welfare Comparison of Intermediaries and Financial Markets in Germany and the US', *European Economic Review*, vol. 39, p. 179–209.

Anderson, R. W., Berglöf, E. and Mizsei, K. (1996) 'Banking Sector Development in Central and Eastern Europe', *Economic Policy Initiative,* no. 1, London.

Arestis, P. and Demetriades, P. (1997) 'Financial Development and Economic Growth: Assessing the Evidence', *Economic Journal,* vol. 107, no. 442, pp. 783–800.

Balassa, A. (1995) 'Transformation and the Situation of the Hungarian Banking System', in J. Hölscher *et al.* (eds), *Conditions of Economic Development in Central and Eastern Europe,* Vol. III: Field Studies on Transition (Marburg: Metropolis).

Bernanke, B. and Gertler, M. (1989) 'Agency Costs, Net Worth, and Business Fluctuations', *American Economic Review,* vol. 79, March 1989, pp. 14–31.

Black, S. and Moersch, M. (1998) '*Financial Structure, Investment and Growth,* Paper presented at the conference 'Which Way Ahead for European Financial Markets. The German or the Anglo-Saxon Model?', American Institute for German Studies, The John Hopkins University, Washington D.C., Second Annual Conference 1996, in S. Black and M. Moersch (eds), *Competition and Convergence in Financial Markets. The German and Anglo-American Models* (North-Holland: Elsevier Science).

Bockelmann, H. (1996) 'Unterschiede in den nationalen Finanzstrukturen und ihre makroökonomische Bedeutung', in D. Duwendag (ed.) *Finanzmärkte, Finanzinnovationen und Geldpolitik,* Schriften des Vereins für Socialpolitik, Neue Folge, Bd. 242, Berlin.

Buch, C. (1995) *Monetary Policy and the Transformation of the Banking System in Eastern Europe,* Kiel Institute of World Economics, Working paper no. 676.

Chick, V. (1995) *Finance and Investment in the Context of Development: A Post Keynesian Perspective,* DP 95–13, University College London, Department of Economics.

Claessens, S. (1996) *Banking Reform in Transition Countries.* Policy Research Working Paper no. 1642 (Washington D.C.: The World Bank).

Corbett, J. and Jenkinson, T. (1997) 'How is Investment Financed? A Study of Germany, Japan, the United Kingdom and the United States', *The Manchester School Supplement,* vol. LXV, pp. 69–93.

Desai, R. M. (1995) *Financial Market Reform in the Czech Republic, 1991–1994, The Revival of Repression?,* CERGE-EI Working Paper no. 86, Prague.

Diamond, D. W. and Dybvig, P. H. (1983) 'Bank Runs, Deposit Insurance and Liquidity', *Journal of Political Economy,* vol. 91(3), June, pp. 401–19.

Drabek, Z. (1993) *The Capital Markets in Central Europe,* CERGE-EI Working Paper no. 43, Prague.

Frowen, S. F. and Karakitsos, E. (2001) 'The Savings-Ratio Behaviour in Globalised Money and Capital Markets: A Comparison of the UK and German Experiences, in S. F. Frowen and F. P. McHugh (eds) *Financial Competition, Risk and Accountability: British and German Experiences* (London and New York: Palgrave) pp. 146–168.

Fry, M. J. (1997) 'In Favour of Financial Liberalisation', *Economic Journal*, vol. 107, no. 442.

Gerschenkron, A. (1962) *Economic Backwardness in Historical Perspective: A Book of Essays* (Cambridge, Mass.: Harvard University Press)

Greenwald, B. and Stiglitz, J. (1993) 'Financial Market Imperfections and Business Cycles', *Quarterly Journal of Economics*, vol. 108, February, pp. 77–114.

Griffith-Jones, S. and Drábek, Z. (eds) (1995) *Financial Reform in Central and Eastern Europe*, London and New York (London: Macmillan, New York: St. Martin's Press).

Gros, D. and Steinherr, A. (1995) *Winds of Change – Economic Transition in Central and Eastern Europe* (London and New York: Congnan).

Grosfeld, I. (1994) *Financial Systems in Transition: Is there a Case for a Bank-Based System?*, Centre of Economic Policy Research, discussion paper no. 1062, London.

Grünbacher, A. and Hölscher, J. (1997) *From Aid to Development Finance: The German Example of Marshall Fund Use*, Discussion Papers in German Studies, no. IGS97/17, The University of Birmingham.

Guba, M. and Skolkova, M. (1995) 'Transformation and Development of Monetary Policy in the Czech Republic', in J. Hölscher *et al.* (eds) *Conditions of Economic Development in Central and Eastern Europe*, Vol. III: *Field Studies on Transition* (Marburg: Metropolis).

Hilbers, P. H. (1993) *Monetary Instruments and their use during the Transition from a Centrally Planned to a Market Economy*, IMF Working Paper, Washington D.C.

Hölscher, J. (1996) 'Privatisierung und Privateigentum', in J. Hölscher *et al.* (eds), *Bedingungen ökonomischer Entwicklung in Zentralosteuropa*, Bd. 4: *Elemente einer Entwicklungsstrategie* (Marburg: Metropolis).

Hölscher, J. (1997) 'Economic Dynamism in Central-East Europe: Lessons from Germany', *Communist Economies and Economic Transfomation*, vol. 9 no. 2.

Hölscher, J., Jacobsen, A., Tomann, H. and Weisfeld, H. (eds) (1994–96) *Bedingungen ökonomischer Entwicklung in Zentralosteuropa* (Conditions of Economic Development in Central and Eastern Europe), vols. I-V (Marburg: Metropolis).

Komendi, R. C. and Schnatterly, K. (1996) *Bank privatisation in Hungary and the Magyar Kulkereskedelmi Bank Transaction*, The William Davidson Institute at the Michigan Business School, Working Paper no. 3 (presented at the 1996 EACES conference in Grenoble).

Komendi, R. C. and Snyder, E. A. (1996) *Bank Privatisation in Transitional Economies*, The William Davidson Institute at the University of Michigan Business School, Working Paper no. 1 (presented at the 1996 EACES conference in Grenoble).

Kregel, J. (1996) 'Transformational Development, the Problem of Inflation and Financial Structure', in J. Hölscher *et al.* (eds), *Conditions of Economic Develpoment in Central and Eastern Europe*, Vol. V: *Economic Policy and Development Strategies in Central and Eastern Europe* (Marburg: Metropolis).

Myers, S.C. and Majluf, N.S. (1984) 'Corporate Financing and Investment Decisions when Firms have Information that Investors do not have', *Journal of Financial Economics*, vol. 13, pp. 187–221.

NBH (National Bank of Hungary) (1994) *Financial Sector and Monetary Policy in Hungary*, note for the OECD, mimeo.

Pilkova, A. and Blecha, L. (1995) *Banking in Slovakia*, CPHR Working Paper, May, Bratislava.

Polanski, Z. (1995) 'Building a Monetary Economy in Poland', in J. Hölscher *et al.* (eds), *Conditions of Economic Development in Central and Eastern Europe*, Vol. III: *Field Studies on Transition* (Marburg: Metropilis).

Riese, H. (1993) *Bagehot versus Goodhart: Warum eine Zentralbank Geschäftsbanken braucht*, Diskussionsbeiträge zur gesamtwirtschaftlichen Theorie und Politik, Neue Folge no. 22, Universität Bremen.

Singh, A. (1997) 'Financial Liberalisation, Stockmarkets and Economic Development', *Economic Journal*, vol. 107, no. 442, pp. 771–82.

Singh, A. and Hamid, J. (1992) *Corporate Financial Structures in Developing Countries*, International Finance Corporation Technical Paper, no. 1.

Steinherr, A. and Huvenirs, C. (1994) 'On the Performance of Differently Regulated Financial Institutions: Some Empirical Evidence', *Journal of Banking and Finance*, vol. 18 (2), pp. 271–306.

Tomann, H. (1997) 'Options for resolving the ''Bad Asset Problem'' ', in S. F. Frowen, and J. Hölscher (eds), *The German Currency Union of 1990: A Critical Assessment* (London: Macmillan; New York: St. Martin's Press), pp. 101–115.

Winkler, A. (1996) *Conditions of Macro-economic Stabilisation in Transition Economies: The Role of the Financial System*, University of Birmingham, Institute for German Studies, Working Paper no. 4/1996.

Wilson Committee (1980) *Committee to Review the Functioning of Financial Institutions*, Final Report, London.

Comments on 'Capital and Credit-Based Development: Lessons from the Experience of Industrial Countries for Transition Economies in Central East Europe', by Stephan Herten and Jens Hölscher

Mathias Moersch

Introduction

This is a wide-ranging chapter in which the authors present several distinct strands of the macroeconomic literature with the aim of giving policy advice concerning the organisation of the financial system in Central East Europe. The three topics which I want to comment on are first, the relationship between financial development and economic growth, second, the relationship between financial structure and macroeconomic policy and third, the bad-debt problem in Central East Europe.

Financial structure and real economic growth

Any policy advice concerning the financial system must first address the relationship between financial development and growth. If financial development merely follows real economic growth, there is little reason to worry about optimal financial market design. Fortunately, recent research on the observed correlation between financial development and growth indicates that finance is an important precondition for growth. In other words, financial development leads economic growth.

The evidence for this causal link is found first of all in a number of cross-country studies (King and Levine, 1993a and 1993b; Levine and Zervos, 1996). These papers find that the level of financial development, proxied by variables capturing size and importance of financial intermediaries, is a good predictor for future growth and capital accumulation. Importantly, these studies control for a number of other variables that determine growth (Levine, 1997). In addition to the cross-country evidence, studies at the industry- or firm-level (Jayaratne and Strahan, 1996, and Demirgücs-Kunt and Maksimovic, 1996) also confirm the importance of financial intermediaries for growth. Overall, the evidence in support of the notion that financial development improves growth prospects is fairly strong.

Since financial institutions reduce information and transaction costs, their crucial role in the growth process can also be shown theoretically. Via their key activities such as the mobilization of savings, the pooling and diversification of risk and the monitoring of investments, they facilitate the process of capital accumulation and technical progress (Levine, 1997). As these functions are organized differently under different financial systems, the question about relative merits of bank-based versus market-based finance follows naturally.

However, the studies about the finance–growth nexus do not provide an answer concerning the optimal design of the financial sector. Generally, these studies define financial services very broadly, including both bank-based and market-based intermediaries. A first reading of the evidence suggests that both stockmarkets and banks appear to have a positive impact on growth, but to sort out the relative contributions of the two poses a number of important conceptual challenges. First, and here I completely agree with the authors, theoretical considerations alone are of little help in ranking the relative usefulness of the competing models, especially since there is considerable overlap in the functions that they provide. Second, no good empirical proxies exist to quantitatively capture the rather subtle and complex contributions or differences in contributions of banks and stockmarkets to financial intermediation (Levine, 1997).

We can thus conclude with fairly high confidence that financial development, broadly-defined, supports the growth process. This includes both influences from the stockmarket and the banking system. However, we know a lot less about the relative contributions of the two intermediaries and differences in the channels of transmission. Thus we have neither a firm empirical nor theoretical base for ranking the contributions to growth from bank-based and market-based intermediation.

This picture is complicated by the fact that convergence in financial services is occurring. Brichs Serra, Buch and Nienaber (1997) find that many of the differences between banking in Germany and the United

States are due to the regulatory structures of the economy. As regulations and institutions are changing, further convergence is likely to occur. In continental Europe, for example, it can be expected that European Monetary Union will provide a powerful stimulus for the development of securities markets (Prati and Schinasy, 1997). While the size effect from a uniform currency will increase liquidity in bond- and stockmarkets, the full benefits of a unified market can only be obtained with the removal of legal, tax and regulatory barriers. These require institutional and legal changes and will facilitate the functioning of market-based intermediation and can be expected to lead to capital markets in Germany which have a lot more Anglo-American features than currently.

These observations should not imply that differences between bank-based and market-based intermediation will disappear. They only serve as a warning against making too much of the distinction between Rhenish and Anglo-American models of intermediation when contemplating the search for an optimal financial structure, especially since it remains hard to pin down empirically the relative merits of the two systems.

Macroeconomic policy and financial structure

Given that the financial structure in different countries shows large variations, it is logical to ask whether these structural dissimilarities are responsible for differing effects of macroeconomic policies. Studies like Bockelmann (1996) or Collignon (1998) show large differences among individual countries on such issues as development of financial markets, debt structure, debt instruments and payment structure. The studies also find that these dissimilarities appear to affect the ways in which policy is transmitted to the real economy. In both papers the tentative nature of the conclusions is stressed, mainly because it is not easy to control for factors besides variation in institutional design in such cross-country studies.

While a lot more work along these lines is desirable, I am disappointed by the treatment of this issue in the chapter at hand. First, I find that results from previous research are relied on and interpreted too heavily. Original empirical work with a clearly stated hypothesis in mind would have been more useful than the reinterpretation of statistical results which were obtained in previous research.

Second, I am also sceptical about the theoretical validity of the underlying approach. Essentially the differences between the German and Anglo-American systems are reduced to the fact that equity provides a hedge against inflation, while debt-contracts do not. As a consequence it is said that the Anglo-American system is better suited to a world where inflation is non-negligible, while a German-type system is 'favourable in prosperous macroeconomic constellations.'

Two observations make me wonder whether this stress on inflation is really warranted. First, the debate about bank-based versus market-based finance revolves mainly around fairly subtle differences in the way risk is handled, managers are monitored or resources are allocated. What all these factors have in common is that they are essentially real influences. To conclude that these differences are mainly manifested in a different reaction to nominal disturbances is surprising to me. Second, market-based intermediation also relies heavily on bond markets. In fact, the amount of new financing from bonds in the United States by far surpasses financing through new equity (Mischkin, 1992). Bonds are also debt contracts that obviously do not provide an inflation hedge.

My own opinion is that differences in the two systems are more likely found in the way in which changes in monetary policy are passed on to bank balance sheets, because of different approaches towards monitoring or pooling of risk. Bernanke, Gertler and Gilchrist (1996) have introduced the concept of a 'financial accelerator,' where small changes in interest rates have large effects on output via credit market conditions. If credit markets are organised differently under different prototypes of intermediation, it is possible that the financial accelerator has different magnitudes. As a consequence, the effects of monetary policy on real output will differ.

The bad-debt problem

The banking sector in Central East Europe is still in a very fragile state and one reason for this is the bad-debt problem hampering the banks. The analysis of the bad-debt problem is carried out in terms of the choice between a rehabilitation and a liberalisation strategy. Put simply, in the rehabilitation approach bad debts are kept on the books of the banks. These banks are sheltered from competition and can reduce the bad debt via quasi-rents. In the liberalisation approach, bad debts are collected by the government and tax-financed. The banking system is then opened up to competition.

The authors seem to reject a pure liberalisation approach because they fear that the 'stock problem' will cause insurmountable problems for such a strategy. Namely, the transfer of bad loans to the state would risk macroeconomic instability, since an orderly work-out via higher taxes or less spending is said to be infeasible.

However, their proposed solution, which is to leave the bad loans on the books of the banks and to 'assume growth' defines the problem away. If there is indeed growth, the bad-debt problem can be outgrown regardless of where it is held. The question thus is a more difficult one: under a given growth scenario, which strategy will lead to larger distortions and thus greater cost to the economy: a tax financed bail-out or a bail-out financed via 'quasi-rents' derived from constraining competition. Here I miss an explicit analysis of the two scenarios under the assumption of given growth. Especially the point that distortions are moved from one part of the economy to another, namely from the banking to the state sector, lends itself to a systematic evaluation.

Finally, it is not quite clear how this part of the chapter is linked to the discussion of the theoretical prototypes of bank-based vs market-based finance. If a 'flow solution' is adopted, heavy protection of the financial system is required according to the authors and the outcome resembles neither the German nor the Anglo-American model. The theoretical challenge then is to start from a 'stock solution' with liberalisation, and to show that this leads, as is also claimed by the authors, inevitably to an Anglo-American system.

References

Bernanke, B., Gertler M. and Gilchrist S. (1996) 'The Financial Accelerator and the Flight to Quality', *Review of Economics and Statistics,* pp. 1–15.

Bockelmann, H. (1996) 'Unterschiede in den nationalen Finanzstrukturen und ihre makroökonomische Bedeutung', in D. *Duwendag (ed.), Finanzmärkte, Finanzinnovationen und Geldpolitik, Schriften des Vereins für Socialpolitik* N.F. Bd. 242 (Berlin: Duncker und Humblot).

Brichs Sera, E., Buch C. and Nienaber T. (1997) 'The Role of Banks – Evidence from Germany and the US', Kiel Working Paper No. 802.

Collignon, S. (1998) 'Monetary Integration between Economies with Different Financial Structures', in S. Black and M. Moersch (eds), *Competition and Convergence in Financial Markets: The German and Anglo-American Models* (Elsevier Science).

Demirgücs-Kunt, A. and Maksimovic, V. (1996) 'Financial Constraints, Uses of Funds, and Firm Growth: An International Comparison', World Bank mimeo.

Jayaratne, J. and Strahan, P. (1996) 'The Finance–Growth Nexus: Evidence from Bank Branch Regulation', *Quarterly Journal of Economics,* pp. 639–70.

King, R. and Levine, R. (1993a) 'Finance and Growth: Schumpeter Might be Right', *Quarterly Journal of Economics,* pp. 717–37.

King, R. and Levine, R. (1993b) 'Finance, Entrepreneurship, and Growth: Theory and Evidence', *Journal of Monetary Economics,* pp. 513–42.

Levine, R. (1997) 'Financial Development and Economic Growth: Views and Agenda', *Journal of Economic Literature*, pp. 688–726.
Levine, R. and Zervos, S. (1996) 'Stock Markets, Banks and Economic Growth', World Bank Policy Research Working Paper, no. 1690.
Mishkin, F. (1992) *The Economics of Money, Banking, and Financial Markets*, 3rd edn (New York: Harper and Collins)
Prati, A. and Schinasi, G. (1997) 'Welchen Einfluss wird die EWU auf die europäischen Wertpapiermärkte haben?', *Finanzierung und Entwicklung*, September, pp. 43–6.

15
Social Banking and Affordable Housing in Germany: the Example of an Inclusive Bank Product

Udo Reifner and Juliane Pfau

Social responsibility of financial institutions

Banking for the public good

'Public goods cannot be provided by private enterprise'. This statement by a representative of one of the leading German banks emphasises the traditional borderline between state responsibility and market mechanisms, between the redistribution of wealth and its concentration in a profit-orientated market. It expresses rather well the present philosophy of private bank managers in Germany who may be active in sponsoring cultural events, but nevertheless remain quite remote from what in the Anglo-American context is understood as community reinvestment and social banking.

But as clear as this distinction between public and private has been drawn in the last decades, it has become increasingly questionable in the context of the very dramatic economic downturn following unification in Germany. In fact, pressure has been exercised to invest in the former East Germany, as when the German government asked private banks for the often referred to 'Bank Billion' of investment in the so-called Neue Bundesländer. In 1995 the German Bankers' Association recommended signing an agreement promising to offer minimum bank accounts to low-income families. The publicly-owned savings banks have improved their position in the retail banking market and have opposed the moves for their privatisation by a campaign underlining their public role and regional responsibility. Observers of the situation may conclude that the private banks are attempting to mobilise public powers to proceed with their campaign in Brussels since they are unable to show the superiority of privately-owned banks in the market.

The biggest challenge comes from the labour market where there is increasing concern for small-business start-ups as well as the rescue of small enterprise from overindebtedness. Here again the banks seem to be at the heart of the problem when they are reproached for discriminating against small businesses in their lending policies.

It is not wishful thinking that banks should become engaged in social affairs when the welfare state retires from social responsibility. It is far less the fear that modern banking will become an additional threat to the social coherence of society. Impersonal computerised banking shifts services away from ordinary people who need explanation, advice and even personal assistance. A generalised scoring system singles out small businesses which in former times have intuitively been granted credit on their 'personality', while now the computers need real securities to score them properly. Under the pressure of competitive cost-efficiency losses have been identified by the size of credit and have led to minimum amounts that exclude smaller entities.[1] Just to keep up with traditional standards of access, equal opportunities and care in banking, banks are forced to investigate whether the outcome of computerised lean banking in a global large-scale economy has effects which threaten even the consensus about the merits of the market economy.

The pressure on banks to rethink their public role only expresses the deeper and long-lasting relation between the activities of private banking and public policy. Banks are exclusively linked to the supply of a commodity, which is here submitted as the most 'public' good that exists in market society. Money is produced, secured and protected by the state. Banks are trustees of other economic actors in society who do produce the real wealth in goods and services, whereas banks only allocate and mediate this wealth. Banks therefore have always had to reflect on their public role when their clients, investors and other stakeholders asked them to do so.

The German, French and Italian languages all derive their distinction between private (privat, privé, privato) and public (öffentlich, publique, publico) from the legal system which again defines its difference by the legally acknowledged position of the state in society.[2] It presupposes a general consensus about the answer to the question that a specific relation is of 'publicam utilitatem' as the Roman lawyer Ulpian put it. In the common law context, instead, the word 'public' is not monopolised by the legal system but open to discussion and disrcetion. The dichotomy between private and public is therefore artificially set through nominal definitions. The English language use of 'public interest' takes us closer to the truth that public policy concerns are only aspects of individual interest and are inseparably linked to private elements. Privatisation does not mean that the public element is given up, and state activity does not exclude profit-making mechanisms.

Banks should therefore give up such simplistic formulas and rethink their public role in society. The following indications, developed elsewhere more deeply,[3] may suffice to illustrate why the public role of banks has to increase in the future:

- banks are not designed for private goals but for private profit. For what goals profit may be supplied lies solely in the definition power of the demand side which in the last resort is the consumer. If, as I have argued elsewhere,[4] the definition of consumer demand – that is, the goods and services for which consumers will be willing to pay for in the future – will gradually shift from a mere individual (choice) towards a more social (future expectations) and finally to a more collective (ecological, regional, political) definition of usefulness, this may imply a pressure to supply public goods in the private sector and the marketing of individual goods.
- in Germany more than 50 per cent of the banking market, especially in retail banking, is covered by successful publicly-chartered savings banks which, although private competitors on the market, claim that their only reason for existence is to serve public goals.
- the most recent banking crisis in the USA (the 'savings-and-loan crisis') and those in Scandinavia, Italy, France and recently in Japan have revealed that the banking sector cannot survive without public and especially state support. It is the very idea of market mechanisms that the state should not give this support without return. This insight will rule the future EU banking legislation as it has already largely influenced US banking law.
- banks which are unaware of the social impact of their behaviour, blindly ceding to market pressure of cost-efficiency and unidimensional client relations, may suddenly be confronted with an explosion of mistrust and hostility by their own clients.
- banks will increasingly be trapped by the contradiction between teaching their employees ethical behaviour, not to enrich themselves personally and to refrain from criminal actions, while on the other hand the bank's own philosophy is just profit maximisation with a simple reference to shareholder value, competition and cost-efficiency irrespective of its source and effects in society.

The answer to the challenge is indicated by the notion 'social banking'[5] or 'sustainable banking' which means that ordinary bank business is conducted in such a way that its social effects are monitored without renouncing profit. It serves as a pragmatic concept to respond to a variety of demands from politics, law and ethics but also from modern concepts of marketing, customer relations and corporate identity[6] as well as employee-motivation schemes.

Social banking cannot be discussed philosophically – its forms and manifestations reveal its inner structure only by practical experience. If ordinary and profitable banking activity has effects that in the context of sustainable community development are comprehensible, it is part of 'social banking' regardless of whether these ends were intended or not.

This was the result of a two-year research project of the Volksfürsorge Insurance Company that brought together the Institute for Financial Services with the experienced Hanover-based City Development Consulting (AGB). The principal contradictions apparent in the original design of the project faded away when both groups focused independently on the concrete possibilities of sustainable investment and distribution of financial services in a deprived area of Hamburg (St Georgy). Banking requirements and necessities of city development were like two overlapping circles thus marking the realm of further discussion and research. Social banking was revealed to be the effort to make this overlapping area bigger without giving up the polycentric approach.[7]

In the meantime, successful examples of development banking have been collected worldwide, especially in the areas of housing finance, consumer credit, minimum bank accounts, small-business lending, micro-lending and pension funds.[8] This benchmarking on best practice is the way social banking may progress in the field of housing finance which seems to be the core part of sustainable banking in the future.

The new role of banks in housing finance

Banks traditionally finance individual houses in the form of an investment. The function of 'living' in a house is left entirely to the care either of wealthy home-owners or to landlords who function as an intermediary between capital investment and use of the houses or flats. This is changing dramatically. Banks are increasingly confronted with individual home-ownership where, due to a lack of equity and income, the acquisition of real property is not investment but rather a means to be able to live in one's 'own' flat.[9] At least in Germany and in other countries on the continent, banks seem not to be prepared for the challenge of this new role although their contribution is crucial for the future of a just and coherent society and, at least in housing, there seems to be nobody else to take on this function in the future.

Extended home-ownership has the potential for solving various problems in modern developments of metropolitan areas. Owner-occupied houses are the environment in which low-income people may use their labour force productively if the labour market does not offer them other possibilities.[10] It gives incentives to save and to work if the market excludes people. The housing situation deeply affects the psychology of people and educates them for self-reliance and it is the place where the future generation is brought up. It serves as a stable and inflation-proof retirement investment[11] and improves the quality of life.[12] Housing is the basis of social coherence defining neighbourhoods that may serve as a basis for community activity and coherence, so desperately needed in a world that has left feudal structures of family and professional ties behind without offering adequate replacements.

Rented houses are gradually replaced by individual home-ownership which marks the path from feudal dependency on landlords towards individual responsibility for one's own living. Individual housing also serves as a local incubator. While large housing companies acting as intermediaries between banks and tenants concentrate construction as well as repair work and other services with suppliers that may come from outside, individual home-owners tend to favour the local economy which again creates new enterpreneurship and builds up a local business-exchange network.

This progress is also reflected in the attitudes of more than 75 per cent of the German population for whom, according to a survey, individual home-ownership is the favoured type of investment.[13]

But it is in fact less the advantage of individual home-ownership but the threat that the present structure of housing contains for a further degradation of housing conditions which brings banks directly into contact with housing requirements of middle and lower-income households. Higher prices in inner-city areas, a liberalised rent market, crime, violence and environmental pollution in the cities have increased the flux of people into the suburbs.[14] While the wealthier concentrate in new villages with high living standards, others either remain in those parts of the inner-cities that are most affected by economic deterioration with unemployment rates of up to 50 per cent, or move to ghost cities where they are kept in subsidised flats excluded from normal economic life. From time to time the impact of such policies becomes visible when riots break out.[15]

It is obvious that the traditional politics of subsidised housing co-operatives that create huge amounts of flats can no longer serve as a solution. After the breakdown of the Neue Heimat (New Home), the biggest trade-union-run housing company in Germany, it has become apparent that most of those not-for-profit companies will not survive in the long run by being artificially kept alive by a costly system of misallocated state subsidies. They are increasingly forced to sell part of their property to individual home-owners. Only manipulated balance sheets as well as preferential lending schemes from state-owned banks save these companioes from bankruptcy. In East Germany the bankruptcy of all housing companies could only be prevented by a generous takeover of all interest payments by the Federal Republic. In exchange, the government has made this help conditional on a yearly 10 per cent rate of property sales. The federal government itself, as well as Länder governments like Hamburg and Berlin, have already entered a fixed sum into their financial projections which is supposed to come from sales of their own flats.

With 42 per cent in the West and 26 per cent in the East, Germany has the lowest rate of individual home-ownership in the European Union[16] compared with France (54 per cent) as well as Belgium, England and Italy with close to 70 per cent and Spain even with 80 per cent.[17] In the USA 65 per cent of households own their homes.[18]

Although there seems to be a high potential for privately-financed activity in the Germany housing sector, the obstacles built into the system of housing supply are so importrant[19] that the present policy is not even able to cope with the deterioration in the housing situation of lower-income families, not to speak of taking advantage of the huge market lying ahead of them:

- the state, which heavily subsidises the housing market, is still focused on multi-family rented houses as far as low-income housing is concerned. Subsidies for individual housing is focused on investment home-owners from the upper-middle class. The subsidies to the rented flats go exclusively to intermediaries who live totally on subsidised income. These subsidies have additional adverse effects:
- as they subsidise rented flats up to 50 per cent of their value, they make private alternatives uncompetitive;
- they create a huge bureaucracy of housing administration that opposes any new privately-organised models; and
- flexible and unstable distribution mechanisms open the door for political corruption and a welfare mentality among recipients.

Vandalism and apathy increase the costs and render the whole system more and more ineffective.

- the housing construction market mirrors the dichotomy of wealthier individual home-ownership and state subsidised multi-family housing. House prices in Germany are three times as high as in the USA and about double those in the Netherlands and the UK.[20] Minimum standards as well as other bureaucratic prescriptions guarantee that individual houses and flats in attractive smaller multi-family units are too expensive, while rental houses are built in a way that by lieu of size as well as comfort they have no chance to be sold to individual home-owners.
- finally, the banks are not prepared to offer solutions in this area. The mortgage banks (Hypothekenbanken), the building-savings banks (Bausparkassen), the life insurance companies as well as the state-owned housing-finance banks (Wohnungsbaukreditanstalt) are all equipped and designed according to the state subsidies they can offer: subsidy (Eigenheimzulage)[21] or tax deduction for the mortgage banks in their services to the middle classes, savings premiums for the Bausparkassen, tax exemption for the insurance companies and rent subsidies, state guarantees and interest subsidies for the rental housing companies. The subsidies are not designed for housing but for institutions that pretend to guarantee a sufficient supply of housing. Why should banks change this system which offers the best opportunities of large-scale state-backed credit with high subsidies and reliable partners from the housing companies? The products, scoring systems and counselling mechanisms in the housing retail banking sector reflect the middle-class investment attitude in which credit is understood as a negative savings plan, while English and American banks have learned to take over much of the role of landlords who proivde not only capital but housing itself.

Discriminating products: investment credit for low-income residents?

The new target group: cash-flow lenders

The new target group in housing finance consists of families which traditionally were seen as typical tenants. This group is made up of lower-middle-class and low-income strata which have no additional income to build up significant wealth, either in the form of equity or in the form of liquid assets. Their income as employees is burdened with an obligatory contribution of 20 per cent for social security contributions which leaves no room for other forms of old-age investment[22] especially not in the form of equity in real estate like the liberal professions who are free to decide how they want to save for their old age.

These families are most involved in economic life between the ages of 25 and 45. At 25 they need a home for their families when their expenditures are at their highest and when their income is still quite low. They need more room for their increasing families, credit to bridge the gap between increased spending for the newly-formed household and reduced earnings, both due to children. They have to mobilise the future surplus income when the falling curve of expenditure cuts the rising curve of income after the age of 40.[23] This group is not necessarily 'low income', but in the eyes of the present system of individual housing finance they have 'too little assets'. They can be described as a group with insignificant savings whose total earnings between 25 and 45 equal their total expenditures for living in the time period. In lending terms we can address these households as 'cash flow' households distinct from 'investment households' because they have to pay their mortgages out of their cash flow which is thus totally absorbed and does not leave any surplus for investment and savings.

In an empirical survey conducted for the German Federal Ministry of Housing, we found such households dominating the files of bankrupt home-owners.[24] The research surveyed bank and customer behaviour at four different stages: the conclusion of the contract, first problems and their consequences for the financial construction including adaptation, the financial breakdown, and the seizure of property including forced sales and debt recovery at the end.

The analysis revealed that inadequate financing, odd banking behaviour and loss-maximising remedies played a major part in the failure of the home-owners with devastating consequences for the whole family and sometimes even neighbours and relatives:

- at the initial stage, when less equity could be provided, financial products dominated, designed for households with high savings potential. The necessary adaptation increased both the costs and risks for customers. Most of the clients had been burdened with significant amounts of credit savings plans which are the most inadequate form of cash-flow financing.
- as the first problems arose, this situation was mostly exploited for selling even more expensive and more dangerous products in line with the initial set of inadequate products.

- banks reacted to the foreseeable financial breakdown so rigorously that the home-owners had no chance to smooth the effects or to offer solutions that could moderate the losses.
- the foreclosure of property as well as debt-recovery mechanisms seemed to follow an intention to use a maximum of costly mechanisms without regard to their efficiency, and especially with no concern for the family's housing situation.

Although these findings seem to imply that banks offer the wrong products for the wrong families, the message of this research when evaluated on the basis of current knowledge of the German housing finance market is quite different. The dominant conservative-type of safe-and-sound housing finance is not accessible to households with cash-flow problems. This discrimination by the ordinary banking system opens the door for other banks which, due to their outdated systems of investment financing (especially the Bausparkassen), have no choice but to address clients who have to accept any financial package. As most of these most inadequate packages were sold in doorstep sales with high brokerage fees, clients did not even have rational choices or adequate information.

Therefore, it is no solution to ban inadequate forms of housing finance to households with cash-flow problems. Such a course would even aggravate the present discrimination in mortgage lending in Germany.[25] Only the opening and adaptation of the general housing finance market of mortgage banks as well as savings banks and commercial banks to cash-flow-problem households would ameliorate the situation for these potential home-owners who are currently pressed into obscure market segments of outdated forms of banking. The following descriptioin illustrates these inadequacies.

Problems of conventional mortgage loans for cash-flow-problem households

The market on housing credit is dominated by mortgage loans (61.9 per cent[26]) in which mortgage banks issuing debentures ('pfandbriefe') can offer the lowest interest rates. But their lending is limited to first mortgages and up to 60 per cent of the equity; which covers about two-thirds of all mortgage lending. The building societies (Bausparkassen) market share with their own savings-and-loan product is less than 4 per cent but including ordinary mortgage loans, totalling about 10 per cent. Life insurance companies with another 8 per cent cover the rest of the market.[27]

A typical mortgage loan as it is modelled in the Law on Mortgage Banks is a loan with fixed annuities,[28] a fixed interest rate for mostly between five and ten years,[29] and a right to prolong this loan at a rate offered by the bank. Also adjustable-rate loans are offered at lower market rates especially in low-interest periods, while fixed rates reflect the risk a bank occurs by guaranteeing low market rates when refinancing conditions seem to be sure to deteriorate during the coming lifetime of the credit.[30]

While in the beginning loans with fixed annuities (and rising levels of repayment in every instalment) were offered along with loans with falling instalments and fixed redemptioin rates, only those loans which have increasing repayment obligations starting mostly with 1 or 2 per cent repayment in the first years[31] are typical.

Equity requirements

The German system of home financing is built on the assumptioin that home-ownership should be preceded by savings, thus excluding cash-flow households in general. The 'golden rule' of housing finance still propagated assumes that one-tird of the purchase price or construction cost should be paid in cash out of actual savings, another third should stem from a mature savings-and-loan plan (implying another 40 per cent savings from 33 per cent equal 13.2 per cent of the total price), and the last third should be financed by a mortgage loan. As savings-and-loan plans require a high redemptioin rate of 7 per cent annually, this system requires that nearly half of the amount necessary to purchase a home is from one's own-assets, and for the rest assumes that a third of it will be paid back within 15 years while the rest may be paid back in 30 years. After 15 years the borrower should have built equity of more than three-thirds of the house.

If a borrower wants to go beyond these limits, he or she will face lending limits by law. Arts 11 and 12 of the Act on Mortgage Banks limits the amount of credit such banks can extend on a first mortgage to three-fifths of the property value.[32] The property value is assessed[33] by the asset-value method ('Schwertverfahren') and (less important for individual home-ownership) the gross rental method ('Ertragswertverfahren').[34]

Thus, mortgage banks are mostly excluded from offering a complete solution for cash-flow borrowers in housing. But, also, ordinary banks are restricted because the conservative methods of property-value assessment cover only 90 per cent of the real house price. In this undervaluation of real estate prices, cash-flow households are trapped in a vicious circle. Excluded from mortgage loans, the demand for affordable houses in the form of individual home-ownership is quite low, while on the other hand there is an oversupply of formerly rented flats which especially the state and the cities want to sell. While in construction costs these houses compete with normal investment houses, they fall into a difficult market situation. Therefore banks run a special risk of overvaluing such property which is not due to the concerned households' behaviour.

In practice, intermediaries and questionable bankers have filled the gap between credit needs and credit lines with daring constructions:

- in calculating imaginative sweat-equity, the bank assumes that a house-builder will extend the construction to a second flat by using his or her own labour. As the total value of the house is thus artificially increased an apparent 80 per cent financing will come out as a true 120 per cent equity financing
- some banks cover the difference between financing and required cost-coverage through (expensive) consumer instalment credit with high redemption rates
- insurance companies offer up to 100 per cent financing by selling endowment insurance as a savings plan which is immediately financed by a credit. Thus the insurance serves as the main security disguising the lack of security in real estate. As such insurance contracts cannot be terminated without bigger losses, and as the additional amount for financing the savings component makes the credit more expensive, the cash-flow household is burdened by additional costs and risk
- building societies who by law have to require a previous savings period simulate such savings by selling fully-financed savings plans in order to extend immediate credit (which again seems to be secured by future savings). Such contracts have caused enormous difficulties for low-income families who are burdened by the extremely high cost as well as the inflexibility of the system, and the high repayment obligations in the future.

In fact all approaches seem to be necessary to bridge the gap between the equity requirements of the traditional system and the situation of cash-flow households.

'Sweat-equity' is especially interesting for cash-flow households where a member of the household can provide professional skills useful in house construction work which investment households may not be able to provide. Very often the potential of do-it-yourself work lies with friends and relatives, but little effort has been invested by ordinary banks to offer serious, adequate and safe solutions for the incorporation of sweat-equity into the credit calculation.[35]

The same is true for the use of savings and retirement plans. The fact that the German tax law one-sidedly favours life insurance as the only tax-exempted means for retirement plans, in turn means that only investment households are able to (mis-)use this form for housing finance in a proper way which provides savings of up to 50 per cent of the interest paid through tax-exemptions. Savings are even higher and may result in a net subsidy if the money is invested into houses that are let to third parties at least for the initial 10 years after purchase. Cash-flow households have no chance to profit from this legislation and banks have not yet tried to offer collective forms of home-ownership which could make these advantages accessible for such households.

Credit-scoring

There are already significant disadvantages as far as the assessment of the value of the property that serves as security are concerned. Additional problems arise in the form of future expectations on the safety of the repayments. Cash-flow households can offer their own labour, a firm commitment to repayment, and a network of friends and family who can at least help to support their living conditions. The actual scoring system does not recognise any of these virtues.

At a purchase price (incidental expenses included) of €140,000, the minimum of owner's equity required is €42,000. The required loan amounts to €98,000. With an interest rate of 7 per cent p.a. and a redemption rate of 1 per cent the monthly instalment will come to €653.5. The minimum income of families for running expenditures is €600 for a single household and €900 for a married couple plus €175 for each child.[36] A three-person household would therefore need €1728 monthly in order to qualify for a loan of €98,000. Current expenses like, for example, insurance and small credits are not included in the income of €1728, so that in fact €2000 monthly income is necessary. An additional monthly salary in December as well as family allocations are not validated in the credit scoring because they are assumed to be unstable.

Young families, the most important potential cash-flow buyers of residential property in the future, are literally excluded from this market. If they intend to build a new home they are even faced with the problem of overlapping costs for the rent of their present home as well as the interest for the credit. As most banks oblige their customers to contract the whole credit, before needed, causing additional fees for the availability pay indemnities, the burden is higher than necessary.

Interest rates

Fixed-rate loans are typical for owner-occupied property. The fixed rate represent a convenient calculation for both lenders and borrowers. In low-interest-periods[37] the costs of loans are less problematic, but the opposite occurs in high-interest periods as was the case in the early 1980s and 1990s.[38]

Investment households who are able to take risks opt for variable-rate credit in high-interest-rate periods. They profit from the lower actual burden in order to switch to fixed-rate credit when the long-term interest rates come down. With a functioning market, banks should offer relatively cheaper long-term credit in high-interest periods. But statistical evidence shows that the margin between variable and fixed rates is significantly lower in high-interest-rate periods than in low-interest periods. This is because fixed-rate customers often have no choice, unlike variable-rate customers, so that competition cannot work in favour of them.

Cash-flow families have calculated their monthly instalments so narrowly that they cannot afford to take any risks of interest-rate rises which would increase their monthly payments. Therefore the chances offered by the money markets disadvantage cash-flow households. With far too expensive rate caps where the floating of the rate is limited to a span, some banks try to open the door to lower income strata to offer variable-rate credit. But the price is too high.

The recourse of cash-flow households to fully-financed savings-and-loan schemes confronts these clients with an inadequate interest rate which disguises the true burden of the loan through the combination of a costly financing of savings that yields very little. As the market is clearly split into a first mortgage of up to 60 per cent of the property value, a second mortgage with about 1 per cent p.a. higher costs for the additional 20 per cent up to 80 per cent and credit that may cost as much as 6 per cent more for the remainder, cash-flow households pay even more than investment households.

Monthly instalments

The most subsidised loans in Germany, the savings-and-loan mortgages, require an absurdly high redemption rate of 7 per cent on the initial capital. Due to the inflexible rate, the redemption rate rises every year. A loan for an average €150,000 flat would thus require a repayment of €1500 every month which is unaffordable for the cash-flow household which may have a maximum of €750 to spend for housing.

In ordinary mortgage loans the situation is not much better. A 1 per cent redemption rate doubles after ten years and rises to 3.57 per cent after 15 years if the same loans persists. The initial instalment is far too high and borrowers have to repay loans faster than disclosed by the initial 1 per cent rate.[39] Artificially high instalments at the beginning of the loan fall onto cash-flow households at a time in their life-cycle where they have general higher expenditures than income. High instalments make such households vulnerable to the slightest accident or loss of income with devastating effects for the whole financing.[40]

In some cases suspension of redemption is possible, but due to risk-aversive bank behaviour[41] amortisation has to begin not later than ten years after the contract was concluded.[42] Socially-conscious banking could easily offer significantly lower instalments if the bank would keep the average redemption rate at 1 per cent for the lifetime of the credit, which would lower the initial rate to far less than 1 per cent.

The other form of forced savings included in ordinary loans stems from the nominal basis of calculation. While house prices in metropolitan areas have increased by 42 per cent during the last 15 years,[44] the credit granted was calculated at the present value of the acquired good. The instalment equally ignored the potential of a steady general 3 per cent inflation rate thus putting the highest burden at the beginning of the credit. The French state tried out special 'Access-to-Credit' (PAP) loans where the inflation rate was calculated in such a way that borrowers could start with a reduced payment which increased every year by a certain fixed percentage based on the expected inflation rate.[45] The Italian banks achieved this goal by lending mortgages in ECUs. The inflexibility of this system, in which the risk of 'no inflation' had been left with the borrowers in both countries who had to pay the high increases even without inflation in their own country, caused enormous stress for the housing market. But if these risks could have been covered by insurance or through futures, the idea itself could help to open the mortgage market for cash-flow households.

High risks

Unlike the USA or Denmark, mortgage loans in Germany are normally offered for no more than ten years. Competition seems not to be strong enough to counteract the effect of Art. 609a of the Civil Code which gives consumers a right to rescind after ten years irrespective of the contents of the contract. Such a credit lifetime is too short for most cash-flow households. It burdens them with the risk of higher interest rates after 10 years, and even in times of depreciation of real estate prices there is the danger of not finding adequate credit at all.

The German system of 10-year contracts is extremely rigid and risky for cash-flow households. While these households are often under high pressure to move into other regions, to buy a smaller house when the children leave or, in case of unemployment or accidents, even to give up their home, the system of early repayment is quite disadvantageous for borrowers. Also, if borrowers have to repay their loans before maturity they[46] have to pay an indemnity which covers the losses a bank occurs from actual lower market rates as well as from the loss of profits from the old credit.[47]

Especially critical are the provisions in case of payment difficulties. A debtor who fails in financing a first home will never get a second chance. Serious also are the high indemnities with early cancellation due to default, the absence of instruments to bridge income losses and payment problems, and especially the rigid system of forced sale and seizure of property in which a loss of house value up to nearly 40 per cent of the market price is nearly guaranteed by an outdated auctioning system. A variety of associations representing overindebted former house owners[48] have specialised in defending such former home owners.

Building standards

The house prices and building standards in Germany reflect the focus of housing finance on investment households. Compared with neighbouring countries like Denmark and the Netherlands, expensive building materials and construction methods are favoured so that prices have soared steadily in the last decade. Only recently has research on more cost-efficient architecture and cheaper building standards been carried out at the initiative of local governments and now also supported by private banks. It has produced evidence that instead of average house prices of around €150,000, single family units of less than €100,000 could be provided if banks could finance the respective demand of cash-flow households.

Conclusions

The present system of housing finance in Germany is modelled after investment households. Inflexible, with enormous requirements for previously accumulated own-capital, front-loaded and with high repayment rates, it discriminates against cash-flow households who have just enough money to pay for the use of their homes without being able to 'invest' in them. While the tenant–landlord market exercises strong pressure on cash-flow households to enter individual home-ownership this demand is even exploited by intermediaries who misuse this situation for selling more expensive and riskier financial products.

This discrimination in the German mortgage market is neither necessary nor are the obstacles insurmountable. The English and American markets show creative forms of mortgage lending in which cash-flow households have better opportunities to live in their own property and enjoy the benefits of home-ownership. But as the following section will show, the state although publicly in favour of increased home-ownership for former tenants upholds a huge system of subsidies that gives the wrong incentives to banks who are rewarded for conservative behaviour.

The wrong incentives: state subsidies in the housing market

It is official German policy to support individual home-ownership. This policy is dictated by stagnation in the construction industry, high losses in the public-housing sector, and the near-bankruptcy of many of the not-for-profit housing companies. But this official policy contrasts with a huge amounts of ill-allocated subsidies in the German housing market. By far the greater part of these subsidies still go into rented housing either in the form of direct rent subsidies to tenants or in the form of subsidising landlords in low-income housing. Those subsidies which are designed for owner-occupied housing are modelled according to the requirement of traditional investment housing so that they cannot reach those who are the official target group.

State subsidies for rented housing

By far the greater part of the subsidies are to the rented housing market to reduce rents and make housing affordable for lower-income households.

Rent subsidies

The German federal government gives a total of €1.75 billion annually to individual tenants who are not able to pay their rents from their normal incomes. A tenant gets the right to 'Wohngeld' (housing subsidy) if a legally defined income ceiling, fixed according to the family size, is not reached – the amount of the subsidy up to a maximum rent is again fixed according to the situation (old, new, with or without bathroom) of the flat. If the burden of the monthly rent exceeds that part of the income which is supposed to be free for housing, the difference is paid by the state. While welfare recipients are not part of the system because they have their rent paid on top of their welfare cheque if a rent maximum is not reached, the 'wohngeld' is paid directly in cash to households living above the welfare limits.

In fact this system, which is different for East and West Germany, tries to keep up rents in areas where households with moderate income would not be able to pay the required amount. In theory, home-owners may claim the same benefits by calculating the interest due on the capital adding the running cost of the home with respect to their income. But as there are fixed upper income levels, with no support to people above these limits, and as the market for individual home-ownership is characterised by an average price of close to €150,000, cash-flow households have no chance to profit from this system.

Subsidies for public multi-family housing (Sozialer Wohnungsbau)

The so-called 'Sozialer Wohnungsbau' is a 70-year-old system of public housing in Germany in which the state heavily subsidises the construction as well as the rents in multi-family units that are reserved for people with lower incomes. In fact all these subsidies are channelled through special state-owned banks (wohnungsbaukreditanstalt) and reach not-for-profit housing companies who are either owned by the cities or trade unions or welfare organisations.

There are three forms of subsidies:

- direct subsidies for the construction of a home including the supply of land;[49]
- interest-rate subsidies in the form of access to subsidised loans including guarantees for the safety of the loans; and
- rent subsidies to the housing company to keep the rent low.

The benefits are directly paid to investors who have to provide 15 per cent of the purchase price as own-capital. The own-capital may be provided in cash or in own-labour.[50] A flat has to fulfil certain minimum standards[51] including its size, parking facilities and even special kitchen equipment. Flats have to be reserved for families who have a certificate testifying their neediness.[52] In addition, half of the flats have to be let to people on the housing list kept by the social welfare administration.[53]

The investor gets the right to a fixed-rate long-term credit whose effective rate is according to different schemes of the Länder subsidised down to about 1 or 2 per cent below the market rate. The most important subsidies which usually amount to more than 50 per cent of the total expenditure for interest and administration of the house come from rent subsidies. The investor has the right to a rent of up to €10.75 per square metre to cover his costs of interest payments, administration and repair of the house. As the effective rent for the tenants is actually limited to €4.45 per square metre, the investor gets the difference of €5.80 as a subsidy over 27 years.[54] If house prices are calculated at €1750 per square metre this would mean that the state pays slightly more than the cost, that is €1879 per square metre during this period in subsidies. In terms of the interest rate, total costs are subsidised with 3.98 per cent p.a. in interest subsidies, and if the subsidy on the loan is included the total subsidy may approach 5 per cent p.a. which may be the total cost of the investment.

The generosity of this scheme, still backed by loan guarantees, make these investments so unquestionably safe and profitable that private forms supplying housing finance for low-income families have little chance to compete.

But there are two important limitations: the above-cited scheme is limited to the amount the federal government allocates yearly for such purposes. Additional measures for households with slightly higher incomes are left totally to the discretion of the Länder. Due to the present state of state finance these subsidies limited to about €1 billion are on the one hand far from meeting the total demand but, where they are given, their amount is so generous that competing models look very bad in the eyes of banks and investors. Theoretically, interest subsidies can also be applied for by individual home-owners who would qualify for such flats. But as an own-capital of 30 per cent is required, cash-flow households do not normally qualify for this scheme. Besides, there is no legal right to this subsidy, so that some Länder have ended these programmes.[55]

In practice private investors do not use this scheme although the profit rate could easily be calculated at close to 30 per cent p.a. The obligations connected with the investment, as well as the long-term freezing of the invested capital, makes this form of investment unattractive so that publicly-supported organisations have taken over this role.

Tax deductions for rented houses

Costs arising from investments into rented flats and houses which are not owner-occupied can be deducted from taxable income. If high income levels taxed at a rate up to 53 per cent are combined with 'losses' from investments into rented flats, the net profit may amount to 10 per cent p.a. for the investor. As a linear depreciation of the value of the house may be higher than the rental income and is counted as a loss,[56] even if the house increases in value such investments receive enormous tax deductable.

But these tax-exemption schemes, which have led to closed real estate funds whose shares are sold especially to the liberal professions, have not led to a single low-income dwelling. They are solely used for luxury buildings which have a fair chance of being sold after the minimum period of 10 years at a reasonable price when losses are no longer allowed.

Subsidies for owner-occupied housing

Until the 1980s the subsidies for housing investment were totally dominated by the investment model. While investment into rented houses received and still receives most subsidies through the acknowledgement of fictive cost elements, owner-occupied homes equally had the right to claim fictitious depreciation of the property but at a fixed rate and limited to certain amounts and durations (seven years). This system favoured those who paid higher and more taxes, as against lower-income households. This has been changed in recent years to allow further and more just access to home-ownership.

Home-ownership subsidy ('Eigenheimzulage')

In the new scheme of a home-ownership subsidy every person that wants to build a new house or acquire an old home or flat (50 per cent of the new-home subsidy) gets a fixed year's cash contribution over eight years which amounts to €2500 per year and another €750 per year per child. This subsidy is only paid once in a lifetime and is accessible to nearly all but the highest income level (more than €120 000 per year per family) irrespective of their taxation.[57]

Thus a three-person family gets a subsidy of €26 000 per home. As this subsidy is not paid at the beginning but over the first eight years, it does not replace the needed equity. Besides, its limitation to eight years is dangerous for cash-flow households. As the problem of access to mortgage credit is not touched in this scheme, it has nearly no effect on the number of people from cash-flow households who acquire their own homes. It also ignores those households who have already tried in vain to acquire their own homes and who want to try again.

As this subsidy addresses only individual home-owners (with a small concession to co-ops), collective forms in which home-ownership may be achieved gradually through forms of shared home-ownership are neglected. The enormous subsidies to those families who would in any case be able to buy their own homes as investors is hard to understand under the present financial situation of the Germany government.

Publicly-assisted housing

Within the scope of owner-occupied property, some federal states of Germany have built up schemes to aid low-income families with children through subsidised loans.[58] The first year's amortisation is suspended, interest rates are low and the state provides for securities. The loans are also 'end-loaded'; no repayment of the principal in the beginning and high-interest subsidies keep the initial instalment low.[59] The limits of annual income are derived from the 'second Wohnungsbaugesetz'.[60]

These programmes are still rather small, and they only seem to work where additional state programmes like those in North Rhine Westfalia help with the construction of houses, with ensuring low prices and with the bureaucracy necessary to become a home-owner and bank borrower in Germany.

Conclusions

State subsidies for housing in Germany are designed in such a way that they all stabilise the given dichotomy between rented houses where living is the most important function for poorer people, and home-ownership whose function lies primarily in building up own-wealth through investments for the wealthier part of society. The upper parts of the cash-flow household sector who alone would be able to create a new form of individual cash-flow home-ownership with adequate forms of supply in homes and financing are spared in both systems.

The subsidisation of the rented-housing market amounts altogether to about €7.5 billion per annum in Germany. Although these subsidies are theoretically accessible for low-income home-owners, their share in these subsidies is insignificant. The reason lies in the fact that all subsidies are based on the philosophy that the poorest people should be helped first and most. With scarce budgets the state therefore excludes all cash-flow households who might be the first to be able to cross the border from tenantship to home-ownership. The macroeconomic effect is an over-subsidisation of the tenants market which again makes this market more profitable for investors than it really is. Its relatively high administration and repair cost and its incapacity to mobilise the cost-effective potential of cash-flow households has no chance to appear in a comparison between both markets.

As the home-ownership market is comprised of investment households, more expensive buildings promise bigger profits and give better opportunities for long-term investment. It is just these households which are subsidised by home-ownership subsidisation, especially by tax exemption and the new system of ownership subsidies. It neither addresses the problems of exclusion, nor gives incentives to develop new models of social banking. Instead it forms coalitions between banks, tenants and not-for-profit housing companies to seek maximum state subsidies.

Thus the prices of such houses and condominiums are kept high, financial products are designed for investment only, and the market remains closed for cash-flow households who need end-loaded, cheap and flexibly financed homes with little risk for their cash-flow, and with opt-out possibilities at reasonable prices with little or no own equity requirements. Only if such households start to enter the market at a significant rate will the necessary demand for such goods and services be exercised to create adequate housing finance, which in turn would be able to exercise additional capital in a market segment where poverty could gradually be combated by own forces. The strange effect of the German system is therefore that in the name of securing housing for low-income households and individual home-ownership, it drives market forces in a direction that aggravates the problems for these households.

Social banking instead needs a totally-targeted and just system of state subsidies which neither legally nor in its economic effect favours one form of housing over the other.

New approaches: shared home-ownership and a real estate tenants' fund

Individual home-ownership in Germany can only be furthered if, first, the higher-income strata of cash-flow households are targeted in order to create market demand that would stir the housing and housing-finance markets into a direction which would finally create models for privately-financed affordable housing for low-income households as has been experienced in the United States.[61]

To develop such ideas a two-year empirical project financed by the Ministry of Social Affairs of Mecklenburg-Vorpommern in the City of Rostock in East Germany, and the Institute for Financial Services together with a group of economics students have conducted research in collaboration with a group of tenants[62] that were willing to purchase their own homes.[63] The project monitored the demand side in so far as the financial potential of the future home-owners was surveyed. On the supply side, financial products and instruments as well as forms of acquiring and rehabilitating property at low cost to meet the demands of the tenant group were studied.

Targets for social banking: weakness and strength of cash-flow households

In the first stage the weaknesses and strengths of cash-flow households were evaluated in a form that would allow their use as development tools in future collective cash-flow prognoses by banks.[64] The group was comprised of 14 households forming an association of people looking for homes. Old and young people, families as well as single mothers and bachelors were part of the group. Some were in work, others were living on social welfare or pensions.

Their financial data revealed that only three of these households had a slight chance to acquire their own homes in the traditional way. While the older people had enough equity, they would not get a loan due to their shorter life expectation. Some equity of middle households was long-term-fixed and could only be mobilised by incurring high losses. Younger households with small children had too high expenditures and little income, but better expectations for the future. Families with children aged around 14 still needed much space but could foreseeably renounce some of it in a few years, while newly-married couples with a high cash flow were expected to enter that same situation soon. Only two families qualified for state subsidies in general.

Individually, the group had so many disadvantages for individual home-ownership that a financial counsellor would probably have persuaded most of them not to try to leave the rented-housing market. But their associative behaviour, their organisation into a special association of home-seekers, was taken as a unique financial asset which should be exploited for their own individual profit. The project therefore evaluated the collective financial situation.

The estimation of the future cash flow of every individual family for 10 years in advance, taking into account all kinds of individual changes in family composition and professions, and other prospects as well as inflation and the rise of rent payments, revealed that in total their cash flow was quite stable at a rather high level. Summed up, their accumulated assets at the beginning, irrespective of the possibilities of cashing in on them, amounted to about 10 per cent of the value of the houses including the costs of renovation and distribution to the different families.

Individually, none of these households had enough security to offer for a loan, but collectively a quite average risk-structure for the prospect of steady repayment could be produced. There was also quite a high potential of do-it-yourself capital ('sweat-equity') in the group, if the use of existing spare time as well as skills could be pooled.

Finally, the aggregate demand of all households amounted to more than €1.5 million. Used as a bargaining tool, this could be turned into a saving on housing costs of up to 30 per cent compared with a traditional system in which houses are acquired by an investor who than rehabilitates them and sells them by the use of intermediaries and costly procedures. In addition, by including existing tenants additional savings up to 15 per cent could be made of the price normally necessary to buy out such tenants from their legally-protected rent contracts.

As the model assumed that all households would be part of the home-ownership model, the accumulated subsidies for home-ownership could amount to a total subsidy of nearly 20 per cent in respect to the cost of the flats if they could be mobilised for all of them. In addition, accumulated bargaining power in hiring craftsmen and construction firms, and reduced administration costs through cost-efficient housing were calculated as additional income.

Finally, the advantages of a single credit contract for more than €1.5 million using interest swaps and other advanced financial instruments, as well as the economics of scale expressed in a more competitive interest rate as well as a form of credit that was more closely linked to the real credit needs in the cash-flow development of the community, led to a calculation that the cost for each household per flat could be reduced from about €1300 per month with individual home-ownership to about €800 per month in the present model.

Of course these findings were neither revolutionary nor new. They had been the basis for the development of co-operative housing in Germany at the turn of the nineteenth century. It could therefore be argued that the price of individual home-ownership and its apparent advantages over collective forms of home-ownership was just the difference calculated as a profit of the collective view. So a simple co-operative form could be the proper solution.

The research report contains extensive arguments why co-operatives are not the solution. It concludes that they provide for collectivised forms of living which individual home-owners do not want – they make it difficult to mobilise invested own-capital for other purposes, they are closed for profitable investments of outside capital, and their form of rented flats do not meet the psychological aspirations of the target group. High transaction costs and sharp differences from investment housing have made these models a dead end for collective forms of housing.

The approach tried not to presuppose that collective housing was good in itself. Its collective approach was limited to the assumption that aggregate demand organised solely in the field of financing could produce such enormous surpluses that its distribution to individuals would make organisational costs and the use of advice and help profitable. As such it was developed into a model of social banking and not into a model of 'social housing'.

The supply of equity: a closed-end real estate fund

The most important barrier to housing finance for cash-flow households lies in their lack of equity. As such problems in the economy are normally solved through participatory forms, we chose a closed-end real estate fund ('geschlossener Immobilienfonds') as a model to raise own-capital for a house.

The fund is the only 'owner' of the property, takes up the credit for all users of it, and is free to contract all kinds of flexible rights with residents as well as investors for whom participation rights gradually develop into property rights. The only weak part of a fund is its vulnerability in case of bankruptcy. It therefore has to be totally secured by the value of the property, supervised externally by trustworthy financial institutions, and seen as the guarantor for property-related links between residents and their flats or houses.

Raising own-capital through investors

Closed-end real estate funds[65] are quite common in Germany, and most banks use this form to develop commercial estates and offer profitable tax-exempt investment for smaller sums. In a mixture between a limited company (GmbH) and a company with personal responsibility (KG), the KG allows investors to place small amounts of money into a house to acquire shares, and to participate in the losses occurred by the forms of legal depreciation described above without personal liability for more than their share.

The investment can be liquidated if the property is sold after the minimum term of 10 years, with profits paid out according to the property value at the time of sale.

The problems of such funds which mostly depend on tax preferences lie in the fact that initial losses are welcomed by many investors, so that only the bankruptcy of such a fund in the future makes apparent that the project not only had legal but factual losses. Banks are therefore often quite reluctant to lend to such funds if they do not manage them themselves.

The advantage of such a fund for tenants is the supply of own-capital up to, for example, 30 per cent which together with existing own-capital comes close to the 60 per cent rate for the best mortgage deals in secured loans. Besides, additional tax deductions make savings on interest payments for this capital. The biggest advantage for investors and property owners stems from the fact that the increase in value of the investment is hoarded up in the value of the property itself, which does not burden the tenants' cash flow by regular interest payments while giving the opportunity to investors to pay taxes on the returns at a time of his or her own choosing (mostly at retirement age when income as well as taxation is low)

Traditionally, real estate funds are disliked by tenants who occupy the premises. As most investors receive losses during the first 10 years they all want to maximise their profits after this time. This is only possible either through increased rents or, better, through the sale of such houses with vacant possession. The liquidation of such funds normally have very high transaction costs because the two groups, tenant and owner-investor, are in opposition.

In the proposed model, the whole system tries to further early co-operation between both groups for their mutual benefit. Only modest tax advantages are admitted in the first five years in order to make the investments profitable and to remove the pressure for liquidation. From the very beginning the tenants are seen as the primary target group for acquiring the property, which helps to mobilise their co-operation by raising its market value, image and by lowering all kinds of costs which could affect this value. As the tenants have their own shares in the fund from the very beginning, they equally participate in the property's appreciation.

Finally, not-for-profit investors like cities, welfare administrations, beneficial institutions, and also potential sponsors for local developments, have the possibility to make a visible and at the same time limited contribution to housing development for a special target group, without having to have recourse to donations.

The tenants' shares

The shares of the fund are divided into shares for outside investors and for future home-owners. This second category of shares is earmarked and its amount fixed for the first 10 years. A transformation of home-owner shares into investor shares is not possible during this time and is limited afterwards.

Financially, the owners' shares have the same financial status as the others. They especially participate in the appreciation of the property, but they cannot be liquidated if not bought by either the fund itself or other residents. As these shares gradually give access to the right of achieving the total individual property, the contracts between the residents and the fund provide for stages which strengthen the property rights of the residents to their flats.

Tenants' shares can be achieved either through direct payments which in the initial phase are obligatory as far as liquid assets can be provided; or, later on, tenants may use all kinds of liquid assets to improve their rights to their flat. But they may also acquire shares through do-it-yourself contributions. The incentive to buy their own shares and to use other kinds of liquid assets lies in the fact that the rent is directly linked to the amount of own-capital a tenant possesses. In addition, the rent contains a part for administration and entertainment, which if replaced by own-work directly lowers the general level of rent payments.

As in tax law, for example in leasing, it is acknowledged that economic ownership may be seen as equal to legal ownership, in taxation the fund will declare tenants' shares as identical with financed ownership of owner-occupied houses in order to obtain the state subsidies for home-ownership. If a household faces a liquidity crisis the fund may help by buying back tenant shares. It may also offer rent schemes in which negative equity is allowed to mobilise future inflation and other profits to bridge actual liquidity problems of a household. There may also be a market between the different residents on tenants' shares which may result in the fact that one tenant will gradually own more flats.

As such shares are tradable it can be assumed that most tenants will see these investments as a valid form of retirement savings. If liquidity is provided by a credit line that secures internal investors against events where they would need their money back, much of the liquidity that low-income households usually store in fear of unexpected events may be mobilised. The tenants' shares serve as a form of private currency between residents in order to solve their liquidity problems. It guarantees adequate return, interest and security for neighbours who help other neighbours.

The present form also gives tenants the chance to move and sell their acquired part of the house to a successor, to the fund or to other residents. The form of a fund also makes mixed forms possible. A housing company may buy enough tenants' shares to place social welfare clients into the house using the state rent subsidies. If the fund is short of money there will even be a collective interest of residents to accept and integrate such neighbours if the subsidies and the official partner provides the necessary liquidity and equity.

Collective bargaining power

The fund will take up credit in a large amount offering the investment shares as equity. As the residents are highly motivated to keep up the value of the property, banks will not have to fear real depreciation of the property or vandalism. Instead, a motivated group of inhabitants that work for their own profit may serve as an incubator for city development which may make real estate prices rise.

The credit can be split into a credit line to cover changes in liquidity expected during the lifetime of the credit, and a larger fixed-rate credit with no redemption and little administration cost. In addition, the residents can offer mutual personal guarantees up to the value of their inhabited property as an additional incentive to finance and administer the project. The bank will also win new customers from among the residents. As a partner to residents in a low-income housing project, the bank may obtain additional advantages through, for example, a high visibility of its social commitment as well as direct publicity attached to the building project itself. The higher transaction cost for the administration of the fund can be paid out of the savings the construction can provide.

The fund may also make preferential contracts with construction firms including a duty for these firms to use do-it-yourself labour at a certain level from the residents. This could solve the problem of quality, supervision, equipment and pricing in sweat-equity lending, and further local economies where such skills in using the unskilled labour of future residents may best be allocated.

Opportunities for social banking

Banks would have many opportunities in learning how to finance cash-flow households in their housing demands. They could develop structures for such fund approaches through own consulting firms which could cover their initial research costs through public subsidies. Such structures should include:

- a marketing tool for the idea as well as the sale of the investment shares;
- a fund to buy and sell used home-ownership fund shares in order to create a secondary market where official development agencies may invest; and
- an educational programme to teach potential residents about the possibilities of such a fund.

This knowledge would also help to monitor the performance of other loan portfolios and give insights into how bad credits in residential property may be saved from bankruptcy. Having a reliable partner to discuss all problems with the representatives of each fund the bank could easily improve their marketing tools. The engagement of a bank in this form of financing could also be used to obtain savings which may be exclusively targeted in the form of 'development savings' linked to certain city areas.

The present example only gives ideas on how banks could be helpful in upgrading the social situation in metropolitan areas without relinquishing profits. At the same time their contribution is crucial for such developments because it will be the organisation of the financial side that is critical for the success of such undertakings. The bank's name is needed for trust and reputation, its credit facility is necessary to give adequate and cash-flow-adjusted credit to the residents at affordable rates, its knowledge in marketing financial products could help to raise own-capital, and its tax advisers and lawyers may settle the necessary disputes with the internal revenue services.

Notes

1. U. Reifner and J. Evers, *Credit and the New Entrepreneur*, Baden-Baden, 1998 (Report on 'Small Business Lending in Regional Development – Northern Approaches and Programs in Development Financing', mandated by OECD and IRED Nord (1995).
2. Referred to as the 'subjective' or 'subordination' theory in law to distinguish between private and administrative law.
3. For a broader discussion see U. Reifner, 'Social Banking – Ansätze und Erfahrungen über die integration sozialer Zielsetzungen in privatwirtschaftliche Finanzdienstleistungen', in L. Schuster (ed.), *Die gesellschaftliche Verantwortung der Banken* (Berlin: Erich Schmidt, 1997), p. 205 ff; U. Reifner, and J. Evers (eds), 'Social Responsibility of Banks: Towards Reporting on Social Effects', Baden-Baden, 1998 (Study on the Transferability of the US Community Reinvestment Act to the European Union, for DG XXIII of the EU-Commission, 1997, authors: Jan Evers, Udo Reifner, Benoît Granger, Malcolm Lynch, Leo Haidar); U. Reifner, J. Evers and D. Sievers, *Community Reinvestment – eine amerikanische Besonderheit für den deutschen Banken – und*

Sparkassenmarkt? Baden-Baden, 1998; U. Reifner, 'Moralische Dimensionen der Wirtschaft und Recht – Besprechungsaufsatz zu Etzioni (1988) u. (1993)', *Kritische Justiz*, Vol. III, (1996), 384; U. Reifner, 'Social Banking and New Poverty – Towards a New Approach in Law and Economics', in Reifner and Ford (eds), *Banking for People*, Vol. 1, *Social Banking and New Poverty* (Berlin and New York, 1992), p. 23 ff; U. Reifner, 'Principles of Justice in Financial Services', in E. Paasivirta and K. Rissanen, *Principles of Justice and The Law of the European Union – Proceedings of the Helsinki Seminar*, European Commission Brüssel, 1995, pp. 383–406; U. Reifner, 'Das Recht auf ein Girokonto', *Zeitschrift für Bankrecht* (1995), p. 244 ff; U. Reifner, 'Banken und Verbraucherpolitik – Perspektiven einer schwierigen Partnerschaft', *Zeitschrift für das gesamte Kreditwesen*, Vol. VII (1995), p. 314 ff.

4. U. Reifner, 'Banken und Verbraucherpolitik – Perspektiven einer schwierigen Partnerschaft', *Zeitschrift für das gesamte Kreditwesen*, Vol. **VII** (1995), p. 314 ff.
5. See U. Reifner, 'Social Banking – Ansätze und Erfahrungen über die Integration sozialer Zielsetzungen in privatwirtschaftliche Finanzdienstleistungen', in L. Schuster (ed.), *Die gesellschaftliche Verantwortung der Banken* (Berlin: Erich Schmidt, 1997) p. 205 ff; U. Reifner, 'Social Banking and New Poverty – Towards a New Approach in Law and Economics', in Reifner and Ford (eds), *Banking for People*, Vol. 1 *Social Banking and New Poverty* (Berlin and New York: de Gruyter, 1992), p. 23 ff.
6. Süchting, J. (1992), *Bankmanagement*, 3rd ed. (Stuttgart) p. 484.
7. It is interesting to note that the project transferred to another quarter of Hamburg where major banks participating in the endeavour for its practical application failed because the city of Hamburg repealed their support on political reasons. City development under private leadership in socially weak areas seems to be in conflict with existing bureaucracies that claim a monopoly on the social economy.
8. These examples are collected in Reifner and Ford (eds), *Banking for People*, i.e.: J. Shapiro, 'Shorebank Corporation: A Private Sector Banking Initiative to Renew Distressed Communities', Vol. 1 *Social Banking and New Poverty*, pp. 183–209; P. R. Rodrigues, G. J. Schep, and N. J. H. Huls, *Careful Lenders and Social Security – Trends in Unemployment, Consumer Credit and Debt in the Netherlands*, Vol. 2 *Overindebteness, Unemployment and Policy Responses – National Reports*, pp. 573–604; U. Reifner and B. Haane, 'Bank Safety – A General Introduction', in Institute for Financial Services (ed.), *Bank Safety and Soundness – The Bergamo Report* (Hamburg, 1993), p. 13 ff; U. Reifner and J. Evers, 'Small Business Financing', in Institut for Financial Services' (ed.), *Banque et Region – The Strasbourg Report* (Hamburg, 1996), p. 113 ff. (to be requested through iff@iff-hamburg.de)
9. In Germany a 'typical' mortgage loan for owner-occupied property is needed in the amount of €157 224 (in comparison, in Ireland €47 000 is required). German owners take out more credit relative to the value of their home-ownership; see European Mortgage Federation, *Owner-occupied Property in the European Union, Tax Exemption, Subsidies and Costs – Comparative Study*, Brüssel, January 1997, p. 274.
10. The unemployment rate in 1997 in East Germany was 19.2 per cent, and in West Germany 9.9 per cent. Altogether 11.7 per cent (4.5 millions) of all active persons are out of work, see Deutsche Bundesbank, Monatbericht, October 1997, p. 14.

11. H. Nietzer, 'Gutes Bausparklima lässt Wohneigentumsquote ansteigen', *Der Langfristige Kredit*, Vol. XXIV (1995), p. 24 ff.
12. K. Gibb and M. Munro, *Housing Finance in the UK* (London, 1991), p. 1.
13. 'Die eigene Immobilie bleibt Lebensziel', *Der Langfristige Kredit*, Vol. II (1997), p. 8.
14. Eduard Pestel Institut für Systemforschung e.V. Hannover, *Der Wohnungsmarkt in Hamburg – Perspektiven und Herausforderungen bis zum Jahr 2010, Deutsche Siedlungs- und Landesrentenbank*, ed. (Bonn/Hamburg November 1997) p. 8 ff.
15. The most impressive result can be observed in France where 20 years of cleaning up Paris and Lyon has created an uncontrollable situation in the suburbs. In spite of this example the German government unconsciously created a similar situation by asking higher rents form better-off residents in subsidised houses. With the popular argument of fighting against the misuse of subsidies, they chased those last families from these suburbs who still had access to an ordinary income, creating ghettos that will sooner or later explode. Meanwhile many cities have ceased to execute this policy but partly already too late.
16. Home ownership in high-income groups now exceeds 60 per cent. Among small-income households only 30 per cent maximum dispose of home-ownership, see 'Wealth is distributed unequally in Germany', *Handelsblatt*, 9.1.1997, p. 41.
17. H. Wielens, 'Eurowährung und Bausparen', *Der langfristige Kredit*, Vol. XIII (1996), p. 14.
18. S. Chan, 'Residential Mobility and Mortgages', NBER Working Paper Series (National Bureau of Economic Research, July 1995), p. 1.
19. As insolvencies in the building industry increase in 1994 there were 3971 bankrupties; in 1995, 5542; and in 1996, 7041), it is necessary to revitalize the building trade, see Statistisches Bundesamt, *Wirtschaft und Statistik*, August 1997, p. 422 (statistics part).
20. E. C. Mortage federation, *Comparative Study With Regard to Costs Related to the Purchase of Second-hand Property in the European Union*, Brüssels, 1993, p. 2.
21. §§ 9 ff. *Eigenheimzulagegesetz* (law on subsidies to create private house ownership).
22. In recent years the gap between gross earned income and net earnings has increased. In 1991 the net income came to 55.75 per cent of the gross income, in 1995 to only 51.7 per cent. Later on the differences rise, see Deutsche Bundesbank, *Monatsbericht*, July 1997, p. 27.
23. For this life-cycle approach see A. Masson, 'Cycle de vie et Accumulation Patrimoniale', in D. Kessler and A. Masson (eds), *Cycle de Vie et Générations* (Paris: Economica, 1985), p. 53 ff.
24. U. Reifner, *Risiko Baufinanzierung, rechtliche und wirtschaftliche Probleme privater Bauherren* (The Risk of Financing One's Home), 2nd edn (Kriftel: Luchterhand, 1977), p. 25 ff.
25. See Verbraucher-Zentrale Nordrhein-Westfalen e.V., *Baufinanzierung – Planungshilfen, Finanzierungsformen, Förderungsmöglichkeiten* (1996), p. 138 ff.
26. Verband Deutscher Hypothekenbanken, *Jahresbericht 1996*, p. 46.
27. *Ibid.*, p. 47.
28. Instalment credits with fixed amounts for redemption, also exist as well as credits with final maturity.

29. Art. 609a of the Civil Code gives each borrower the right to cancel any credit after 10 years without any right of indemnisation for a bank; most banks are reluctant to offer fixed interest rates for a longer time period which bind them unilaterally.
30. D. Bellinger, and Ralf, A. 'Markt für Wohnungsbaufinanzierungsmittel und Wohnungsbaufinanzierung', in Kühne-Büning, L. and Heuer, J. (eds), *Grundlagen der Wohnungs- und Immobilienwirtschaft* (Frankfurt am Main, 1994), p. 421 ff.
31. E. Murfeld (ed.), *Spezielle Betriebswirtschaftslehre der Grundstücks und Wohnungswirtschaft* (Hamburg, 1995), p. 471.
32. §§11 (Beleihungsgrenze) und 12 (Beleihungswert) *Hypothekenbankgesetz*.
33. See Beleihungswertrichtlinien ('Guidelines for the Assessed Value') of the Deutsche Genossenschafts-Hypothekenbank AG, from May 1995.
34. E. Murfeld, *op. cit.*, p. 472 f.
35. U. Reifner, *op. cit.*, (Fu. 24) p. 85.
36. Immobilienrichtlinien – Bonität – der Deutschen Genossenschafts-Hypothekenbank AG, July 1997. (Guidelines for credit-scoring in Mortgage Credits of DG-Bank.)
37. With an interest rate of 6.1 per cent p.a. (effectively 6.3 per cent with 100 per cent payout, 1 per cent down-payment and monthly payments) the time to maturity is 32 years.
38. In normal cases annuity loans are contracted.
39. With an interest rate of 9.1 per cent p.a. the time to maturity is 25 years.
40. S. Knoke, 'Konzepte der Wohnungsbaufinanzierung bei Inflation', Band 33 der Reihe *Materialien zum Siedlungs- und Wohnungswesen und zur Raumplanung*, des Instituts für Siedlungs- und Wohnungswesen (Münster, 1996) p. 34f.
41. S. Laternser, 'Konzept, Struktur und Bewertung von kollateralisierten Anleihen', dissertation (Liechtenstein, 1997) p. 58f.
42. § 20 *Hypothekenbankgesetz*.
43. The years of higher income (not allowing for the risks of unemployment) are mostly in later years when the spouse looking after children begins to take up thier duties again.
44. See Platow-Brief (3 September 1997) (a newsletter).
45. E. Auclair, 'Minimum Wages, Rate Ceilings and Social Solidarity against Poverty – Unemployment and Consumer Debts in France', in Reifner and Ford (eds), *Banking for People*, *op. cit.*, p. 441 ff.
46. § 21 *Hypothekenbnkgesetz*.
47. According to the *Annual Report 1996* of the Union of German Mortgage Banks ('Deutscher Hypothekenverband') p. 81, the Union underlines the incompatibility of early repayment and irredeemability of debentures.
48. Best known is the Association of Borrowers damaged by banks (Verein der Kreditgeschädigten) in Sulingen whose president wrote a quite successful book entitled *Alone against the Banks*.
49. Hamburgische Wohnungsbaukreditanstalt, 'Fördergrundsätze zum Wohnungsbauprogramm 1995 zzgl. Einlegeblatt für die Programmjahre', 1996/1997', Merkblatt 1, p. 1.
50. Hamburgische Wohnungsbaukreditanstalt, 'Kurzinformation über die Förderung von Miet- und Genossenschaftswohnungen in Mehrfamilienhäusern in Hamburg', 1995 and 1996, p. 1.

51. *Ibid.*, p. 9. The floor space of flats or houses is limited of 44 square metres per head, two persons 60 square metres, three persons 70, four persons 85, and five members of the family 90 square metres.
52. Hamburgische Wohnungsbaukreditanstalt, *Merkblatt*, vol. 1, p. 14. Their income is at the supplementary benefit level.
53. Hamburgische Wohnungsbaukreditanstalt, *Merkblatt*, vol. 1 – Einlegeblatt for 1996/1997, p. 2.
54. see Art. 25–25d 2nd Wohnungsbaugesetz (Law on Homeconstruction).
55. Some states, for example Schleswig-Holstein and Niedersachsen, have reinstated their advantages programmes because of empty coffers.
56. 'Anderung des Fördergebietgesetztes', Article 19 of Bundessteuerblattes 1995, part 1, p. 580.
57. § 10e and 34f EStG (Law on Income Tax Within the limits of § 10e EST/G (the former article), higher income resulted in higher subsidies.
58. For example, Hamburg, with interest-rebated loans of the Wohnungsbaukreditanstanstalt.
59. *Ibid.*
60. § 25 ff. of the II. Wohnungsbaugesetztes (Second Law on the Promotion of Home Construction).
61. See for example N. Richman (ed.), *Homes of Our Own: Reclaiming the Neighborhoods of Vernon-Central*, UCLA Graduate Department of Architecture and Urban Planning, Affordable Housing Proposal for Vernon Central, Los Angeles, University of California, Los Angeles, 1995; Philadelphia Federal Reserve Bank, Cascade, a newsletter about 'Consumer Credit and Community Reinvestment', no. 28 (1995), p. 5 ff; Federal Home Loan Bank of San Francisco, Affordable Housing Advisory Council, *Annual Report 1993*, p. 18ff.; Community Financial Institution, The Low Income Housing Fund, *Annual Report 1992–1993*, p. 2 f; Gale Cincotta, 'From Redlining to Reinvestment – The Need for Eternal Vigilance', in Institut for Financial Services (ed.), *Banque et Region – The Strasbourg Report* (Hamburg, 1996), p. 26 ff., Thomas Lenz, 'Home Ownership initiatives in The United States', in Institute for Financial Services (ed.), *Banque et Region*, p. 99 ff.; Gilda Haas, 'Community Banking and the Community Reinvestment Act in The US', in Institute for Financial Services (ed.), *Bank Safety and Soundness – The Bergamo Report* (1993), p. 135.

References

Anstiftung (1994) ('Gemeinnützige Forschungsgesellschaft zur Förderung zukunftssichernder sozialer, kultureller und ökonomisch-ökologischer Maßnahmen'): *Immobilienfonds für sozial ortientierte Anleger* (Munich).

Auclair, E. (1992) 'Minimum Wages, Rate Ceilings and Social Solidarity against Poverty – Unemployment and Consumer Debts in France', in U. Reifner and J. Ford (eds), *Banking for People*, p. 441 ff.

Bellinger, D. and Ralf, A. (1994) 'Markt für Wohnungsbaufinanzierungsmittel und Wohnungsbaufinanzierung', in L. Kühne-Büning and J. Heuer.

Breckner, I. and Kirchmair, A. (1995) *Innovative Handlungsansätze im Wohnbereich, Information über Projekte, Träger und Initiativen in Deutschland und Europa* (Dortmund).

Chan, S. (1995) *Residential Mobility and Mortgages*, NBER Working Paper Series (National Bureau of Economic Research, July).

Cincotta, G. (1996) 'From Redlining to Reinvestment – The Need for Eternal Vigilance', in: U. Reifner and B. Haune, p. 26 ff.

Community Financial Institution (1994) *The Low Income Housing Fund*, Annual Report 1992–1993.

Deutsche Bundesbank (1997) *Monatsbericht*, October.

Deutsche Genossenschafts-Hypothekenbank AG (1997) *Immobilienrichtlinien–Bonität*, Hamburg: July.

E.C. Federation of Mortgage Banks (1993) *Comparative Study with regard to costs related to the purchase of second-hand property in the European Union*, Brussels.

Eduard Pestel Institut für Systemforschung e.V. (1997) *Der Wohnungsmarkt in Hamburg – Perspektiven und Herausforderungen bis zum Jahr 2010*, Deutsche Siedlungs- und Landesrentenbank (ed) (Bonn/Hamburg November).

Evers, J. and Reifner, U. (1998) (eds) *Social Responsibility of Credit Institutions in the EU*, Schriften des Institut für Finanzdienstleistungen e.V., vol. 2 (Baden-Baden: Nomos) (National Reports in English, French and German).

Federal Home Loan Bank of San Francisco (1993) Affordable Housing Advisory Council, *Annual Report*.

Federal Reserve Bank of Philadelphia (1995) 'Cascade, a newsletter about consumer credit and Community Reinvestment', no. 28, p. 5 ff.

Gibb, K. and Munro, M. (1991) *Housing Finance in the UK* (London).

Haas, G. (1996) 'Community Banking and the Community Reinvestment Act in The U.S.', in U. Reifner, p. 135f.

Hamburgische Wohnungsbaukreditanstalt (1995f), *Kurzinformation über die Förderung von Miet- und Genossenschaftswohnungen in Mehrfamilienhäusern in Hamburg* (Hamburg, 1995 and 1996).

Hamburgische Wohnungsbaukreditanstalt (1995ff) *Fördergrundsätze zum Wohnungsbauprogramm zzgl. Einlegeblatt für die Programmjahre 1996/1997*, Merkblatt 1 (Hamburg).

Herrling, E. and Federspiel, W. (1985) *Wege zu Wohneigentum*, 4th edn (Munich).

Johnson, S. (1992) 'Mortgage Debt in the United Kingdom', in U. Reifner and J. Ford.s

Keich, R. (1994) *Der Traum von den eigenen vier Wänden*, 3rd edn (Neuwied: Luchterhand).

Kleiner, H. (1996) 'Die Zukunft gehört dem preiswerten Eigenheimbau', *Wirtschaft & Markt*, p. 49.

Knoke, S. (1996) 'Konzepte der Wohnungsbaufinanzierung bei Inflation', vol. 33, *Materialien zum Siedlungs- und Wohnungswesen und zur Raumplanung* (Institut für Siedlungs- und Wohnungswesen: Münster).

Kühne-Büning, L. and Heuer, J. (1994) (eds) *Grundlagen der Wohnungs- und Immobilienwirtschaft* (Frankfurt am Main), p. 421 ff.

Laternser, S. (1997) Konzept *Struktur und Bewertung von kollateralisierten Anleihen*, Dissertation (Liechtenstein).

Lenz, Th. (1996) 'Home Ownership Initiatives in The United States', in U. Reifner, p. 99 ff.

Masson, A. (1985) 'Cycle de vie et Accumulation Patrimoniale', in D. Kessler and A. Masson (eds), *Cycle de Vie et Générations* (Paris: Economica), p. 53 ff.

Ministerium für Bauen und Wohnen des Landes Nordrhein-Westfalens (1997) *'Preiswert Wohneigentum schaffen'*, Ratgeber No. 8 (Düsseldorf).

Mishkin, F. (1995) *Money, Banking, and Financial Markets*, 4th edn (New York: Harper Collins).

Murfeld, E. (1995) (ed), *Spezielle Betriebswirtschaftslehre der Grundstücks- und Wohnungswirtschaft* (Hamburg).
Nietzer, H. (1995) 'Gutes Bausparklima lässt Wohneigentumsquote ansteigen', *Der Langfristige Kredit*, vol. XXIV, p. 24 ff.
NN (1997) 'Die eigene Immobilie als Lebensziel' *Der langfristige Kredit*, vol. 2, p. 8.
NN (1997) 'Die Wirtschaft muss sich ihre Entlastung teuer erkaufen', *Handelsblatt*, 27 January.
NN (1997) 'Wohnungsmarkt entspannt sich', *Handelsblatt*, 29/30 August, p. 47.
Pietsch, M. (1997) 'Nach dem Baukastenprinzip', *Hamburger Abendblatt*, 30 August, p. 49.
Reifner, U. (1992) 'Social Banking and New Poverty – Towards a New Approach in Law and Economics', in U. Reifner and J. Ford, p. 23 ff.
Reifner, U. (1995) 'Banken und Verbraucherpolitik – Perspektiven einer schwierigen Partnerschaft', *Zeitschrift für das gesamte Kreditwesen*, vol. VII, 314 ff.
Reifner, U. (1995a) 'Das Recht auf ein Girokonto', *Zeitschrift für Bankrercht*, 244 ff.
Reifner, U. (1995b) 'Principles of Justice in Financial Services', in E. Paasivirta and K. Rissanen. *Principles of Justice and The Law of the European Union –* Proceedings of the Helsinki Seminar, European Commission Brussels, p. 383–406.
Reifner, U. (1996) (ed.) *Bank Safety and Soundness – The Bergamo Report*, Conference on Bank Safety and Responsibility towards the Consumer, Proceedings of the 3rd. International Conference on Financial Services in Bergamo, Italy (Hamburg: Institut für Finanzdienstleistungen).
Reifner, U. (1996a) 'Bank Safety – A General Introduction', in Reifner, U., pp. 13–44.
Reifner, U. (1996b), *Risiko Baufinanzierung – rechtliche und wirtschaftliche Probleme privater Bauherren*, 2nd (ed.) (Kriftel: Luchterhand).
Reifner, U. (1996c), 'Moralische Dimensionen der Wirtschaft und Recht – Review of: Etzioni, A. *The Moral Dimension* (1988) and *The Spirit of Community* (1993), *Kritische Justiz*, vol. 3, p. 384.
Reifner, U. (1997) Social Banking – 'Ansätze und Erfahrungen über die Integration sozialer Zielsetzungen in privatwirtschaftliche Finanzdienstleistungen', in L. Schuster, *Die gesellschaftliche Verantwortung der Banken* (Berlin: Erich Schmidt Verlag), p. 205 ff.
Reifner, U. and Haane, B. (1996) (eds) *Banque et Region – European Monetary Union and the Regional Responsibility of Financial Institutions towards the Consumer*, Proceedings of the Strasbourg Conference (Hamburg: Institut für Finanzdienstleistungen).
Reifner, U. et al. (1997) *Mieter kaufen gemeinsam ihr Haus: Das Modell der Zukunft, Wie Sie Wohneigentum auch bei geringem Einkommen finanzieren*, (Reinbek: Rowohlt).
Reifner, U. and Evers, J. (1998) *Credit and the New Entrepreneur*, Schriften des Instituts für Finanzdienstleistungen e.V.), vol. 3 (baden-Baden: Nomos).
Reifner, U. and Evers, J. and Sievers, D. (1998) *Community Reinvestment – eine amerikanische Besonderheit für den deutschen Banken- und Sparkassenmarkt?* Schriften des Instituts für Finanzdienstleistungen e.V., vol. 1 (Baden-Baden: Nomos).

Reifner, U. and Evers, J. (1996) *Small Business Financing,* in Reifner, U., p. 113 ff.

Reifner, U. and Ford, J. (eds), (1992) *Banking for People,* vol. 1 *Social Banking and New Poverty,* vol. 2 *Unemployment and Consumer Debts* (Berlin and New York: de Gruyter).

Richman, N. (1995) (ed.), *Homes of Our Own: Reclaiming the Neighborhoods of Vernon-Central,* UCLA Graduate Department of Architecture & Urban Planning Affordable Housing Proposal for Vernon Central, Los Angeles, University of California, Los Angeles).

Rodrigues, P., Schep, G. and Huls, N. (1992) 'Careful Lenders and Social Security–Trends in Unemployment, Consumer Credit and Debt in the Netherlands' in U. Reifner and J. Ford, pp. 573-604.

Shapiro, J. (1992) 'Shorebank Corporation: A Private Sector Banking Initiative to Renew Distressed Communities', in U. Reifner and J. Ford, pp. 183–209.

Sonnenschein, J. (1998) 'Der gespaltene Wohnungsmarkt und die Fehlbeleger als Nutznießber des Sozialstaates', in U. Immengau, Möschel, W. and D. Reuter (eds) (Baden-Baden; Nomos) p. 1064ff.

Statistisches Bundesamt (1997), *Wirtschaft und Statistik,* August, p. 422 (statistical part).

Süchting, J. and Paul, S. (1998) *Bankmanagement,* 3rd ed. (Stuttgart: Schaeffer/ Poeschel).

Verband Deutscher Hypothekenbanken (1996) *Jahresbericht* (Bonn).

Verbraucher-Zentrale Nordrhein-Westfalen e.V. (1996), *Baufinanzierung – Planung-shilfen, Finanzierungsformen, Förderungsmöglichkeiten* (Düsseldorf).

Wielens, H. (1996) 'Eurowährung und Bausparen', *Der langfristige Kredit,* vol. 8, p. 14.

16
The Role of Compliance in Germany's Banking Culture

*Leo Schuster**

Introduction

Every period of time has its favourite topics and even fashionable catchwords, the propagandists of which are primarily the media. This is also true for business, one of whose latest terms in banking is 'Compliance', which in Germany is connected especially to insider trading. The day before this theme was the subject of a Von Hügel Institute lecture, the renowned German newspaper *Frankfurter Allgemeine Zeitung* (9 March 1998) published the news item that an accusation of insider advantage alleged to have been taken by the president and the chief economic adviser of the Deutsche Bundesbank was false and disgraceful. One can detect here a political game of using the current popularity of compliance and insider advantage.

Compliance in the frame of 'societal-oriented banking'

If banks are conceived as market economy institutions with the stakeholder principle as their underlying philosophy, then there is an assumption of a special societal responsibility. The far-reaching involvement of banks in the economy and therefore also in society is due to their special functions, such as financial intermediation, deposit-money creation, agency of central bank policy, maintenance of the payment transaction system, and so on. These demands can and do normally lead to various conflicts of interest, which the single bank cannot always solve satisfactorily as far as economic, social, legal,

* I would like to thank the Revd Dr Frank McHugh, Von Hügel Institute, Cambridge, for his valuable help with this material.

ethical and other responsibilities are concerned. The solution to this dilemma necessitates a set of instruments, reaching from individual codes of conduct or codes of ethics to national state or international law and regulations, supervised by the banks' self-governance or by supervisory institutions of the state (Schuster, 1997, p. 6ff). The reasons why profit-driven companies increasingly believe in ethics, and therefore behave in a societally responsible manner, may be sumarised as follows (see Caccese, 1997, p. 9):

- consumer pressure,
- high employee productivity and customer service,
- competition (being ethical is a clever marketing strategy),
- changing social values (people first, profit second), and
- fear of monetary and reputation damage from ethical breaches.

Conflicts of interest can arise almost anywhere in daily banking business. Due to the booming investment-banking industry, however, with its different well-known but also new and risky kinds of securities and derivatives, insider trading and related problems have become a special issue. According to their different macroeconomic cultures and law systems individual countries, such as the United States, Japan or Switzerland have chosen particular mechanisms of defense. Those countries, however, which belong to the European Union had to convert specific EU regulations into national law. In the case of Germany, the new laws came into force in 1994 and 1995, relatively late compared with other EU countries, especially Britain.

The most important amendment to these new laws has been the introduction of compliance, which has also become, since then, a 'German' term. Compliance, which is the theme of this chapter is further understood as an important tool of 'ethical control' of insider trading and related problems and, as such, compliance has also become part of the ethical foundation of banking. In this chapter, the focus will be particularly on Germany, and much less on other countries, with the exception of the United States which in this field has set the standards for the rest of the world.

Compliance as a tool of the banks' risk policy

Definition of compliance

The term compliance has not yet found a univocal definition, but the lowest common denominator could be the following: dealing in accordance with the law as it stands. In the absence of a general applicable and agreed definition, it may be useful to begin with the following case study: Salomon Brothers' senior dealer in government securities used to be a regular participant in the securities auctions of the American Treasury. Every institutional dealer – such as this officer – is allowed to make own offers up to 35 per cent of the underwriting volume. At an auction in spring 1991 this man, however, succeeded in skimming off 50 per cent of the underwriting volume through imaginary offers which he made in the name of unsuspecting customers, thereby circumvented the 35 per cent limit. This was a deliberate violation of the American Treasury rules. He continued in this fashion to manipulate the market for quite a while until his scam was finally discovered. Because of this fraud, Salomon Brothers almost lost its license and only narrowly avoided an enforced liquidation (Haueisen. 1996, pp. 10–14).

What can we learn from this example? Compliance clearly has to have a double function: it should be, at once, a protection of customers' interests (namely shareholders, investors and issuers) and of employee and manager positions. In respect of the latter, compliance offices provide help and advice when it comes to the question of legality and legitimacy of employees' own securities transactions, whether there are or are not conflicts of interest involved (so-called pre-clearing). Compliance can thus become, in modern conditions, an effective tool of corporate self-governance and discipline, especially if it can lead to the exclusion of the misuse of insider information (Mailaender, 1997, p. 237ff).

Differentiation of compliance from other monitoring instruments

Control systems in banking have been restricted hitherto to the internal audit, which has been organized according to the guidelines of banking supervision authorities. Besides these, there are group internal mechanisms on an international scale. But all of those institutions are tuned to discover fraud which has already been perpetrated and not to avoid violations that will be committed in future. Auditing has always been retrospective and therefore repressive, and never especially preventive. The perception of the necessity to introduce self-control elements that act as safeguards for the future has led to the modern compliance concept. The reasons for the statement that fraud is the main disease of the twentieth century are manifold: the high complexity of banking products, which complicates their understanding, risk-evaluation and controlability; the special leverages in the financial world, both profit and risk-related; the globalization of the financial markets; and the increasing importance of the own-account business and higher risk inclination, not to say risk mania (Mailaender, 1997. p. 234 ff). This concept, however, necessitates a specific corporate culture of trust which is especially difficult to build up in investment banking areas where there are mainly young people who are paid according to their performance and who are therefore competing fiercely (Ettore, 1996, p. 14; Partnoy, 1997, pp. 250–2).

The role of compliance in the USA

Compliance in US banks was introduced some years before it came to Europe in general and to Germany in particular. The reason for this is that the United States has endured bad experiences very early with insider information. Caccese (1997, p. 10) reports on the bull-market situation of the 1920s that there was a group of insiders that accumulated great wealth using private knowledge in addition to public information, a misuse which continued over the following decades. The 1934 Securities and Exchange Act was therefore amplified through the Insider Trading and Securities Fraud Enforcement Act of 1988, in order to strengthen bank supervision because of insider trading and capital-market violations. The main proscriptions of this law relate to trading on material non-public information (insider trading) and divulging such information to others who may trade on it (tipping).

Already in the late 1960s a code of ethics for investment management and financial analysis experts had been adopted. The aim of this code was to enable ethical market participants to distinguish themselves from the market players who merely obey the law. The standard text in all codes concerning insider trading reads as follows:

> The investment professional shall not trade while in possession of, nor communicate, material non-public information that was obtained because of a special relationship or misappropriation.

The importance of this precaution is shown in an international survey that was carried out in 1996 (Caccese, 1997, p. 13ff) according to which the most cited ethical infraction was still either trading on or communicating insider information.

In addition to legal provisions, the US supervisory institutions claimed that internal policies and procedures designed to prevent the misuse of insider information should be developed. The details of a compliance organisation are therefore not only regulated in the federal or state securities laws, but also through special court judgements and

Securities and Exchange Commission statements concerning bank practices. The result of these were the Chinese walls, the review procedures and policy statements as well as the Compliance Departments. One important factor for the introduction of these procedures has been the enaction of the US Federal Sentencing Guidelines, which do not focus on the personal responsibility of managers only, but on the punishment of the organization as a whole for criminal behaviour, such as bribery and money laundering. Companies are therefore regarded as 'moral agents', that is, institutions having a corporate moral and societal responsibility (Wagner, 1999).

Banks that did not take precautions and were punished because of irregularities and scandals enhanced this process, such as Kidder Peabody & Co. or Drexel Burnham Lambert Inc. In contrast to these cases the fraud at the investment bank Salomon Brothers a few years later (see above) showed that a Compliance Department, even if it fails in an individual case, will be accepted by the banking supervision authorities and the law courts as a matter of duty of care. The US supervisory practice follows the US Sentencing Guidelines for Organizations and imposes lower sanctions in those cases.

It is typical of the US law that in a case of abuse and if the Compliance Department is insufficiently organized, not only the compliance officer but also the whole management can be sued and made liable for compensation. This is also part of the banks' internal compliance philosophy which is passed on to all employees. The highly detailed Codes of Conduct in the United States are a further response to more rigorous legal provisions. On the other hand, US banks have to invest considerable personnel resources, especially because US Compliance Departments are not only in charge of ensuring capital-market-orientated law, but also of implementing all other legal provisions. Citicorp, for example, has developed a substantial *Compliance Guide and Resources Directory* which has been introduced as follows:

> It is nearly impossible to know all the details of all the laws and regulations with which you must comply in the many different activities you will encounter.

This refers to 37 different laws and regulations which can be violated by the employees.

Compliance in some US banks comprises, besides the observance of the laws, the ethical principles which lie below and beyond those laws. In its compliance guide and resource directory, Citicorp dedicates eight pages to the *Ethical Policies* alone relating to employees, including mundane rules such as receiving gifts or copying personal company software. German banks, with single or multiple branches in the United States, have to adapt to American regulations including compliance with the *Code of Ethics and Conduct.* Employees are expected to comply with this code, and failure to observe its requirements may result in disciplinary action up to and including termination of employment. The Codes state that they represent a minimum standard which may be superseded by specific higher standards in accordance with business practices in particular firms or corporations (Dresdner Kleinwort Benson North America, *Code of Ethics and Conduct,* 1996).

Compliance in German banks

Legal foundations

The Second Financial Market Enhancement Law (Zweites Finanzmarktfoerderungsgesetz) of 1994, which was further developed in 1995 into the German Securities Dealings Law is a capital market law with the twin aims of protecting capital markets as well as individual investors (Bauer, 1986, p. 6ff). The basis of the German regulation is the Insider Rule (Insiderrichtlinie) the Transparency Rule (Transparenzrichtlinie) and parts of the Securities Servicing Rule (Wertpapierdienstleistungsrichtlinie) of the European Union.

Important parts of the Second Financial Market Enhancement Law are the amendment of the Stock Exchange Law (Börsengesetz) and the Securities Dealings Law (Wertpapierhandelsgesetz). What is new is the establishment of the Federal Securities Commission in Frankfurt, which is already called 'the Stock Exchange police'. Paragraph 33. 2 & 3 of the Securities Dealings Law is concerned with conflicts of interest between bank and customer and between different customers of a single bank. In order to exclude these conflicts of interest, internal control procedures have to be introduced. This paragraph (33) is the legal basis of compliance in Germany. The aim of this law is to make Germany more attractive for foreign investors and to increase the competitiveness of the country.

Although there had been general criticism of malpractice in Germany, the first German bank that introduced a compliance organization was the Deutsche Bank in 1992, which it did before the law was enforced and therefore still on a voluntary basis. Today every bank has to have a compliance officer, whose main task is information management, essentially, to register compliance-relevant information (insider information) which relates mainly to those capital measures or orders with impact on exchange rates. A standard assessment by experienced people in the banking world is that 3–5 per cent of all information is compliance-relevant.

Many banks, especially the bigger ones, have not only introduced a compliance officer but also a whole Compliance Department with supporting staff. There, decisions are made as to whether compliance-relevant information leads to an entry of a stock company into the 'Watch List' or 'Restricted List'. The watch list contains all securities for which compliance-relevant information has been obtained; the Compliance Department has to monitor these cases for any suggestion of insider transactions.

If a company is put on the restricted list this may carry consequences of a prohibition of trade, especially own-bank trade, employee trade and active customer advice. Additional to these restrictions, so-called 'chinese walls' (or 'internal banking secrecy') have to be built up so that confidential information can be kept inside these departments. In the context of compliance, two further expressions have become common currency:

- *the need-to-know principle*, which means the flow of information that has to be restricted to the necessary extent; and
- *wall crossing*, which is the passing-on of information beyond a zone of confidentiality, and which is only allowed if the calling-in of third parties is absolutely necessary and the keeping of confidentiality is secured (so-called permitted breaches).

The policy-mix of a compliance organisation contains, furthermore, the degree of compliance rules, the information, enlightenment and training of employees, giving advice to employees and managers, the permanent monitoring of the flow of information and the degree of business bans. Another very important function is the sanctioning of violations of the compliance rules and regulations. The Compliance Department also has the duty of storage and recording of relevant material.

Some examples of compliance in German banks

The ongoing globalization process of the capital markets has led to a considerable competitive disadvantage for German banks. The reasons for this have been manifold, but are especially due to a lack of insider rules and of central market control. The introduction of a compliance system has been one response to this development.

German banks understand compliance partly in the sense of the special Capital Market Law and partly, exceeding this, in terms of the wider American conception. The latter leads to the unification of the Compliance Department with the money laundering representative, according to paragraph 14 GwG (Money Laundering Law), and it is very likely that even more reponsibilities will be integrated, such as the environmental-protection representative and the tax-law consultant. In this context it has to be pointed out that in the event of new developments in the direction of so-called network organisations, new 'ethical gaps' will be discovered which, again, may lead to conflicts of interest. 'Networking' means the outsourcing of functions to other companies which then act as suppliers. These firms, of course, must themselves adhere to the compliance standards of the outsourcing company.

In this context it would be advisable to develop compliance procedures into an integrated management system to deal with potential conflicts of interest. Thus, it would become a preventive instrument for the whole bank which would help to monitor the complete range of conflicts of interest on different levels: between bank and customer, bank and employee, and between different customers and groups of customers. Anticipating theoretical developments, it would become an instrument of stakeholder reconciliation.

In order to manage conflicts of interest on the four levels mentioned above, several strategies could be adopted:

- avoidance of conflicts; that is, certain types of business or business with certain customers will not be carried out. This is the practice, for example, of the Royal Bank of Canada in cases where acceptable 'trade offs' cannot honourably be made, and the only permissible alternative is to withdraw from the 'conflict situation' (Royal Bank of Canada, 1989, p. 23)
- disclosure of conflicts of interest which, however, should not violate banking secrecy
- self-restraint; that is, customer interests are prevalent *vis-à-vis* the bank's own interests
- separation of banking functions, for example through Chinese walls.

Hypobank, a Bavarian regional bank, which merged with Vereinsbank in 1997 to form the second biggest German bank, has developed a variety of instructions and directives designed to inform and to commit its employees in respect of the following matters: compliance, use of advantages, second jobs and money laundering. The bank did not stick to the narrow German approach of compliance but broadened it out on the American model. As it is also a mortgage bank, it has included the real estate sector in compliance, because in this field, too, there can occur the misuse of information. The bank's internal trade union representatives were also involved so as to ensure that compliance has become part of every labour contract. As regards lines of authority, the Compliance Department has to report directly to the CEO!

Another example in the German banking sector is the Dresdner Bank, also a major player in the German banking sector. This bank has developed ten commandments, in addition to its insider rules, to be followed by its employees, the securities business codex, the rules concerning employees' own banking transactions, and the Compliance Handbook regulations (Dresdner Bank, 1997):

1. *Need-to-know principle.* Information of the Compliance Department in case of wall crossing. Confidential information may only be transmitted in those cases in which it belongs to the nature of the employees' task. Such information can be insider-relevant. Therefore the Compliance Department has to be informed immediately if confidential and price-sensitive information is given and in case such information is passed on to employees of other banking departments.
2. *No business* if employees involved dispose of confidential, price-sensitive information. If this information is available, the employees concerned should not buy, sell or recommend securities, foreign exchange, precious metals or derivatives.
3. *Priority of customer orders.* The interest of the bank's customers always comes first. If there are pending orders from customers or if the employee expects those orders, there should be no transaction initiated on the personal account of the employee or his own family members. This does not apply in the case where the employee's orders are of a small size and the liquidity of the value is high.
4. *No front-running, head-free principle.* If employees are preparing investment decisions, recommendations or research studies, they are not allowed to place their own orders. This restriction becomes ineffective when decisions are realized and customers have been able to place their deals. Employees should never affect their independence by personal account dealing in securities of which they are in charge.

5. *Keeping-time of 180 days for subscription of new issues by bank employees involved.* Insider information can easily be gained if bank employees manage a new issue. This aspect can lead to the prohibition to buy those securities. In any case, they are allowed only to subscribe at the beginning of the subscription period and within the maximum allotment money. Furthermore, employees are not allowed to place limit orders, but they have to keep the securities for at least six months after allotment.
6. *Values of which bank employees can dispose* in account of the bank or its customers should only be bought or sold through the stock exchange. If the bank's employees can dispose of securities, foreign exchange, precious metals or derivatives only stock exchange orders are allowed.
7. *Dresdner Bank own shares.* The bank welcomes the engagement in personal share-owning, though some relevant departments have to report to the Compliance Office before their deals are placed.
8. *Bank employees' orders in asset management, no same-day deals, no direct order.* Bank employees' own stock exchange business should create wealth according to the relevant internal rules. This is no longer ensured except in the case where short-term (within two weeks) profit-taking is realised. Same-day business is absolutely not allowed. This applies also to foreign currency and derivative deals. Orders have to be placed through a special employees' department.
9. *The advice of the bank.* In doubt, ask the Compliance Department. As the image of the bank and the employees' reputation can be questioned even if only in cases of suspicion, the Compliance Department should be involved if there is any doubt.
10. *Report of account authorization and securities deals/account with third banks.* All authorizations of accounts with Dresdner Bank have to be reported to the Compliance Department. This also applies to powers of attorney with third institutions.

The problem of compliance: structural and psychological aspects

A core problem of compliance relates to regulatory risks on the one hand, (confidentiality), and to the minimizing of profit risks (efficiency), on the other (Wagner, 1999, p. 348). The protection against loss of reputation because of insider dealings is often a constraint on the advantages of the universal banking system of the German type, which should exist in the cooperation of people of different departments as far as complex problem-solving for a customer is concerned. Commentators on the law (Assmann and Schneider, 1995, p. 489) therefore recommend that areas of confidentiality, that is separate departments, should be created in a universal bank as follows: own-bank securities trade; customer securities business; asset management-securities issues; loan department; research and analysis; and administration of share investments in other companies. The jurists even make concrete proposals as to how the departments have to be structured, that self-contained office spaces are appropriate, that the contacts between people of different areas of confidentiality are not too intimate, that computer-storage information does not exceed the limits of confidentiality, and that the salary system has to be adequately structured so that information-holders are not tempted to pass on their knowledge illegitimately.

This analysis of the functions and duties of compliance should have clarified that there are obvious impacts on ethics. There are two main questions which require fuller elucidation in this context: firstly, the breadth of the compliance concept itself, that is, its possible application in other sectors outside the securities departments (Wagner, 1999). Because Compliance Departments are new organizational units, at least in German banks, there is a tendency for compliance personnel to try to get as much power into their hands as possible. At this early stage this is a quite understandable reaction. It does, however, raise the question about who really takes the risk if compliance fails to give the right advice (this is the experience of this author who is the chairman of the Committee of Compliance Officers in Germany and where this question has been discussed very often).

Secondly, the depth of the compliance programme, that is the problem of the exclusive law-oriented approach versus the so-called integrity-oriented approach (Paine, 1994, p. 106ff). This latter aspect concerns the voluntary self-restraint which can be adopted for use in international banking, which, as it happens, very often lacks special regulations. A very good example of the integrity approach is Switzerland. This country has also introduced regulations for securities dealers (22 January 1997) but on a voluntary basis on the initiative of the Swiss Bankers Association (Schweizerische Bankiervereinignung, 1997). This Code of Ethics has to be applied by all Swiss banks that deal in securities and makes sure that there is intelligibility of the settlements, avoidance ('as far as possible') of conflicts of interest, equality of all customers, chronological execution of transactions, a ban of front-running and of the use and manipulation of prices.

Personally I am very much in favour of the integrity approach rather than any exclusive prescriptions by law. The reasons are that banking should remain a market-driven business with primarily economic reasons behind decisions. The actual tendencies, however, lead to standardised and predetermined banking policies which have been set by the law-makers, commentators and judges, and no longer by business administration personnel according to business rules and market opportunities.

Notwithstanding the different kinds of compliance, banks have to develop their own ethical code of conduct in which compliance has to be embedded as one important cornerstone, and where a sensible compromise between legal necessities and the integrity approach has to be found. American and British banks have tried to take account of this compromise already for some time. German banks, however, have been slow to develop such an instrument which, if judiciously formulated, would become a mirror of a bank's ethical values. Paine puts it in the *Harvard Business Review* as follows:

> Prompted by the prospect of leniency, many companies are rushing to implement compliance-based ethics programs. Designed by corporate counsel, the goal of these programs is to prevent, detect, and punish legal violations. But organizational ethics means more than avoiding illegal practice; and providing employees with a rule book will do little to address the problems underlying unlawful conduct. To foster a climate that encourages exemplary behavior, corporations need a comprehensive approach that goes beyond the often punitive legal compliance stance.

References

Assmann, H.-D. and Schneider, U. (eds) (1995) Wertpapierhandelsgesetz Kommentar (Cologne), 'Compliance, Die praktische Umsetzung des 2. Finanzmarktförderungsgesetzes in einer Universalbank', *Forum Wirtschaftsethik,* no. 3, pp. 6–10.

Bauer, A. M. (1996) 'Compliance, "Die praktische Umsetzung des 2. Finanzmarktfoerderungsgesetzes in einer Universalbank', *Forum Wirtschaftsethik,* no. 3, pp. 6–10.

Caccese, M. S. (1997) 'Ethics and the Financial Analyst', *Financial Analysts Journal,* Jan.-Feb., pp. 9–14.

Citicorp (Corporate Compliance Advisory and Coordination) (ed.) (1997) *Compliance Guide and Resource Directory,* March.

Dresdner Bank (Compliance/Finanzermittlungen)(ed.) (1997) 'Die zehn Compliance-Empfehlungen für Mitarbeiter in Vertraulichkeitsbereichen', internal paper, April.

Dresdner Kleinwort Benson North America (ed.) (1996) *Code of Ethics and Conduct.*

Ettore, B., (1996) 'Temptation of Big Money', *Management Review*, February, pp. 13–17.

Haueisen ,G. K. (1996) 'Das Compliance-System:, Eine kritische Analyse', *Forum Wirtschaftsethik,* nr. 3, pp. 10–14.

Mailaender, K. P. (1997) 'Die Selbstkontrolle und ihre Schutzwirkungen im Bankgeschäft', in D. Hummel, W. Buehler, L. Schuster (eds), *Banken in globalen und regionalen Umbruchsituationen.* (Stuttgart: Schäffer-Poeschel).

Royal Bank of Canada (1989) *Securities, Understanding the Rules; An Employee Guide,* June.

Paine, L. S. (1994) 'Managing for Organizational Integrity', *Harvard Business Review,* March-April, pp. 106–117.

Partnoy, F. (1997) *F.I.A.S.C.O.: Blood in the Water on Wall Street* (London: Profile Books).

Schuster, L. (ed.) (1997) *Die gesellschaftliche Verantwortung der Banken* (Berlin: Erich Schmidt Verlag).

Schuster, L. and Wagner, A. (1998) 'Ethik, Moral und Führung', in J. H. von Stein and P. Siebertz (eds), *Handbuch Banken und Personal (*Frankfurt: Fritz Knapp Verlag).

Schweizerische Bankiervereinigung (ed.) (1997) *Verhaltensregeln für Effektenhändler bei der Durchführung des Effektenhandelsgeschäftes: Richtlinien* (Basle).

Wagner, A. (1999) Unternehmensethik in Banken (Vienna: Orac Verlag).

Author Index

Note: **bold** numbers refer to tabular/illustrative material as well as to contributors' own papers.

Subject Index